DARTNELL'S
PUBLIC RELATIONS
HANDBOOK

DARTNELL is a publisher serving the world of business with books, manuals, newsletters and bulletins, and training materials for executives, managers, supervisors, salespeople, financial officials, personnel executives, and office employees. Dartnell also produces management and sales training videos and audiocassettes, publishes many useful business forms, and many of its materials and films are available in languages other than English. Dartnell, established in 1917, serves the world's business community. For details, catalogs, and product information, write to:

THE DARTNELL CORPORATION,
4660 N Ravenswood Ave,
Chicago, IL 60640-4595, U.S.A.
or phone (800) 621-5463, in U.S. and Canada.

This publication is designed to provide accurate and authoritative information in regard to the subject matter covered. It is sold with the understanding that the publisher is not engaged in rendering legal, accounting, or other professional service. If legal advice or other expert assistance is required, the services of a competent professional person should be sought.

From a Declaration of Principles jointly adopted by a Committee of the American Bar Association and a Committee of Publishers.

Dartnell's Public Relations Handbook

Robert L. Dilenschneider
Editor

Fourth Edition

FIRST EDITION — 1967
SECOND EDITION — 1979
THIRD EDITION — 1987
Second Printing, 1989
Third Printing, 1990
Fourth Printing, 1994
FOURTH EDITION — 1996

Other Dartnell Handbooks:
Advertising Manager's Handbook
Direct Mail and Mail Order Handbook
Marketing Manager's Handbook
Office Administration Handbook
Personnel Administration Handbook
Sales Manager's Handbook
Sales Promotion Handbook

CONTENTS

INTRODUCTION

Welcome to the fast-changing, deeply challenging, hugely stimulating new world of public relations.

Though P.R. has been practiced professionally for nearly a century, the field is truly new — for a variety of reasons. In just the last few years, P.R., at its best, has become vastly more sophisticated, strategic, and technological. The top professionals not only shape and communicate messages but also help set the strategies of the companies, agencies, and other institutions for which they work. They deal not only with the media but also with their company's or client's many constituencies: customers, employees, shareholders, communities, governments. They seek to convey messages not only from the company to the public but also from the public to the company. And in all this, they increasingly use not only phone, fax, and photocopy machines but also e-mail and the Internet, which enable them to target their messages to specific clusters of people based on their shared interests.

Let me thank Robert Dilenschneider, the creator and editor of this action-oriented book, for inviting me to write the introduction. Bob is at once a highly successful P.R. professional, a sought-after mentor to many other P.R. practitioners around the world, and a thoughtful and big-hearted person. I reckon that any project that Bob masterminds will draw a serious and influential audience and will provoke us to think. Besides, I'm happy and honored to share some thoughts with you — fellow communicators — particularly at this time of change and challenge.

You in public relations and we in journalism play different roles and have an arm's-length relationship, but we hold much in common. Both of us are in the information business — gathering, analyzing, and disseminating information. Both of us have stories we yearn to tell. Both of us often have to work under severe deadline pressure, with less-than-complete information, sometimes in the midst of crisis. Both of us are committed to the truth.

But, beyond that, there is no "one-size-fits-all," stereotypical P.R. person or journalist. Consider your own situation: You may be a nurse who has just inherited P.R. duties at a hospital, or an officer of a P.R. agency, or the head of P.R. at a Fortune 500 company or a smaller entrepreneurial firm. The journalist with whom you deal may be a reporter, writer, editor, or broadcaster; he or she may work for a magazine, newspaper, wire service, TV or radio station, or network. More importantly, both the P.R. person and the journalist may be professional, responsible, informed. and genuinely searching for the truth — or not.

So I would advise P.R. professionals to avoid the easy temptation of thinking of "the media" as a single, cohesive, and often adversarial force. Rather, I'd urge you to consider us as individual journalists working for quite distinct institutions, often with different missions.

The media are diverse. Put simply, *Fortune* is vastly different from the sensation-seeking 7 o'clock local TV news, and you're much more likely to get a fairer shake from the former than the latter.

That leads to my first message: Distinguish among the various elements that comprise the press.

We should not speak of "the media" or "the press" without recognizing their many disparate parts. When people condemn "the media" and I probe them a bit, it soon becomes clear that their objections overwhelmingly are directed at television, usually local television — which lives or dies by its short-term audience ratings and thrives on a diet of murder and mayhem, conflict and confrontation, scandal and sensationalism.

Too often I have encountered business chiefs who swear that they will never again respond to a request from the press for an interview because they have been badly burned once before. Again, when I peel the onion, I usually find that the business person had one bad experience with TV, often local TV.

Yes, there are countless excellent local TV news departments, and, yes, there are too many newspapers and magazines that also reach for the lowest common denominator. But we should recognize that the print press — while hardly guiltless — is quite different from television. And if the latter insults you or gets your story wrong, don't hold it against the quality media, which try very hard to be fair and to get the story right.

The responsibility of the P.R. person then is to persuade the chief that he should communicate forcefully and frequently, and to help shape his message. While that message should have a central core, which is often repeated and never wavers, it also should be tailored and separated to have the maximum impact among the various elements of the press. When dealing with TV, always provide the famous nine-second sound bite. When dealing with newspapers, always provide the obvious headline and first paragraph. When dealing with magazines, which have more space and longer lead times (a writer sometimes may invest a month or two reporting and writing a major story), always provide depth, detail, and nuance.

With that in mind, let me give you five rules for effective public relations:

One: Do speak with the press — and do so on a regular basis. Evasion or "no comment" just raises suspicion on the part of journalists. Also, your silence creates an information vacuum that your critics, competitors, and opponents will be only to happy to fill — with their own spin.

The business press is so pervasive now that it is hard to hide from it, even if you try. But it rarely makes sense to try. There are so many avenues to get your story across that if you find one of them blocked, you probably can break through on another.

When I started in journalism, there were no national newspapers; now there are three. There were no large circulation personal finance magazines; now there are three. There were no half-hour nightly TV news broadcasts; now there are three. There are also CNN, CNNfn, CNBC, 24-hour radio, and vastly expanded and improved coverage of business by local and regional newspapers. And I submit that my successors at Fortune have made that magazine better than ever in its 66-year history.

Readers and viewers want more depth and analysis in the reporting of business just at a time when the subject is becoming more complex, sometimes maddeningly so. We journalists can never know enough; we constantly have to educate ourselves — and re-educate ourselves — to the wrenching changes in the world around us. And I think the same applies to P.R. professionals.

Two: Be proactive, not just reactive. Be open, not closed. Seek out journalists to whom to tell your story. I have often been impressed when a P.R. person called me and said he would like to bring me together with his chief executive, perhaps for a no-agenda, getting-to-know-you lunch or just an informal meeting in my office or the CEO's. The chief executive would explain his organization's strategy, frankly discuss its problems ("there are four challenges that we face, and here's what we're doing about them"), give me his view of the industry and often provide information for useful stories. When some news broke in the company — good or bad — I felt I could get an explanation from the CEO, and I certainly would have a good line of communication with his P.R. person.

Three: In times of crisis, tell as much as you can as soon as you can — that is, as soon as you have confirmed the information sufficiently to release it. In that way, you get to control the flow of news. That's because you present the information in a way that, while being totally honest, is likely to be favorable to you. If you fail to do this, then erroneous speculation is bound to dribble out, bit by painful bit. What could have been a one-day story drags on and on.

Get all the facts. Make sure that your colleagues continue to provide you with all the facts as this dramatic incident proceeds. Respond quickly. Tell as much as you can as soon as you can. To repeat: A principal theorem of crisis management is to get the bad news out — as fast and fully as possible. If you don't, somebody else will.

Four: Don't quite kill all the lawyers, but also don't let them dictate what you do and say. Lawyers exist to keep your company or your client out of court. But that's cold comfort if you lose in the court of public opinion. A public relations disaster can be much worse than a law suit. The public relations department, not the legal department, should determine your communications policy and your relationship with the press.

Five: Your chief executive should be your primary spokesperson, not just in times of triumph but, even more important, in moments of trial and crisis. The CEO has to stand up, speak out, and take the heat. It's his or her responsibility to break any bad news, to explain why it occurred and what the company is doing to address the situation.

Don't forget the key word: Compassion — that is, compassion for anyone who may have been hurt by the downsizing, the plant closing, the unfortunate accident. In difficult times it helps tremendously to hear the CEO say, "We are sincerely sorry." That does not show that you are legally vulnerable, but that you are human.

James Burke of Johnson & Johnson famously did just that in the wake of the Tylenol case — when in 1982, seven people died after taking some of the pills that had been tampered with by an unknown killer. Burke sought out every form of print and broadcast media and forthrightly delivered his message — that J&J was withdrawing its most profitable product from the market until it was tamper-proof and the company, while blameless, was genuinely sorry for the victims and their families. Burke won the sympathy of the nation, and within one year Tylenol, with new, tamper-proof packaging, was back on the market and setting sales records.

Contrast his classy, effective performance with that of Exxon CEO Lawrence Rawls after the Exxon Valdez oil tanker in 1989 ran aground in Prince William Sound, Alaska, disgorging 11 million gallons of oil and generally fouling the environment. Rawls is a good and decent man, but he made the key mistake of playing it by the book, going down the organization chart and deputizing one of his staff to the crucial task of jetting to the site, getting the facts, and speaking to the nation. That mission, absent the CEO, failed.

When, 10 days later, Exxon made what purported to be an apology, it was hedged and muffled, dodged full responsibility and tried to minimize the gravity of the situation. Doubtless the lawyers had been at work — but their huffing and puffing only blew the house down. Rawls never regained his reputation; for years thereafter, Exxon was linked with environmental catastrophe, and the company ultimately had to pay fines of $5.3 billion to commercial fishing operations, natives, and businesses harmed by the spill.

One lesson is that P.R. professionals must have the courage to speak up, and speak bluntly, when they feel their boss is making a mistake. Surely there comes a time when a decision has to be made and all managers must join to support it (or else resign). But until that moment comes, you have an obligation to fearlessly prescribe what you believe. Your arguments will be more successful, of course, if you previously have established a bond of trust with your boss and with other key executives in your organization.

While the CEO should be your primary spokesman in times of crisis, the P.R. chief should have that role in more normal times. Thus, executives should know that when a query comes to them from the press, they should turn it over to you. If you've been doing your job, you'll know the reporter who has made the approach—or you'll know how to get a quick fix on what he or she wants. You can ask the reporter what is the thrust or direction of the story and how the executive whom he or she is calling can help.

Then you can fill in that executive, help him get his or her thoughts in order, and prepare an intelligent response. It's always wise to write out two or three points you wish to make — and make each of them at least twice in the course of speaking with the reporter.

Here are half a dozen other practices that you may find worthwhile when dealing with journalists (and for these I am indebted to Time Warner's former Editor-in-Chief, Jason McManus):

- Clarify what the story will be about. Before the interview, ask what the focus of the story will be. This will help keep the journalist more concentrated on the story and not on some hidden agenda.
- Ask the journalist if you can tape the interview. If the journalist tapes his interviews (as I do), he or she certainly cannot object to you doing the same; if he doesn't use a recorder, offer to send him a copy of your tape. The existence of a tape of the interview makes everyone more careful about getting the story straight.
- If the reporter takes notes, monitor what he writes down. That's a clue to what the journalist is listening for. If you say something important and the reporter doesn't write it in his or her notebook (or tap it out on his computer), call attention to the point and explain why it's significant.
- Don't say anything that you wouldn't want printed or broadcast—unless it's clearly off the record. Often I have heard sources complain that they spent a full hour with a journalist, but he then highlighted only a minor throwaway line. In fact, those throwaways can be terribly revealing—and don't casually toss them out unless you're prepared to read them or hear them in the media.
- If the reporter claims to have heard something negative from another source, ask the general nature of the source. You're entitled to say something like, "That's a new one on me. Where, in general, does that come from? I really find that hard to believe. Please double-check what's been said."
- Offer to be helpful after the interview. Before the reporter leaves, emphasize that you and other sources within the organization are available to clarify any questions. This may help the story to be accurate and will put you on high moral ground in case of any errors.

Remember that journalists live for, and sometimes lust after, the great story. Often you can help him or her find such a tale. Yes, there will be plenty of quarterly reports and annual statements that will occur as routinely as the seasons. But you can reach beyond those often predictable pronouncements to find the unusual, often instructive, even inspirational stories within your own organization. Let me wind up with three broad examples:

First, we live in an era when big institutions are under assault — big business, big government, big media — but the individual entrepreneur is folk hero. The creative idea person, the builder of a new line of business is king (or queen). Surely you have some of these often flaky, nerdy-but-visionary, and gutsy individuals tucked within in your organization. Tell me about them, and how they have managed to push their ideas through the bureaucracy.

Second, we read and hear so much about macroeconomic statistics and broad trends that we hunger for something up close and personal. Yes, tell me about your quarterly numbers and about your plans for expansion, but tell me how all that will affect my family, my job, my community, my future. Give me information that has relevance and urgency for me — now, and in the future.

Third, we are tired of hearing about problems that seem beyond repair. What we want are solutions, or if the problems are so intractable that they defy solutions, then give us first steps. As IBM Chairman Louis Gerstner says, "No prizes for predicting rain. Prizes only for building arks." In each of our companies, agencies, and other organizations there are men and women hammering out good ideas for building arks. It is our privilege and responsibility, fellow communicators, to tell the whole world about those magnificent carpenters and their provocative proposals.

— Marshall Loeb
Former Managing Editor of *Fortune* and *Money* magazines,
and author of *Marshall Loeb's Lifetime Financial Strategies*

ACKNOWLEDGMENTS

In 1987, when the third edition of *The Dartnell Handbook* was published, one of the trends reported that made that edition so important was the integration of public relations into the marketing mix.

Today, The Dilenschneider Group staff who contributed to this fourth edition are students of a whole new discipline of techniques unheard of nine years ago. There still are marketing and public relations but today the trends are Web sites, e-mail, downlinks, and CD-ROM, among others.

And so, it is with this acknowledgment of a whole new communications era that I recognize and publicly thank and congratulate the authors and editors of this edition.

In addition to those persons whose bylines appear with each chapter, recognition is due to another group of very special people without whose dedication and professionalism we couldn't have done the job.

Among this group were Mary Jane Genova for her marvelous overall editorial support; Jim Wieghart, for his wisdom and ability to counsel one and all; Wes Truesdell who had all the right answers about the financial community; Bob Stone for his savvy understanding of the past, present, and future of this business; and Vera Derr and Kathleen Ineman, who provided the necessary editorial support at Dartnell.

John Kasic, a member of The Dilenschneider Group's administrative staff, worked many long hours to convert all the disks and e-mail, chapter after chapter, to meet deadlines.

Once again, Joan Avagliano, my executive assistant, worked many extra hours, nights and over weekends as she has done several times before in these situations to be sure that all the pieces fit together.

—RLD
April 1996

Tom Jordan, a member of our staff whose byline appears on the chapter, "Staffing and Budgeting," unfortunately did not live to see his work in print. Shortly after completing his chapter for the handbook, Tom died. We shall miss him but will always remember his contribution.

Dartnell also wishes to thank the two content experts who reviewed the manuscript and provided insight and thoughtful suggestions and comments: Diane Dunne, president of DunneWrite Communications, Chicago, IL; and Richard Nelson, vice president of Public Affairs for the NutraSweet Kelco Company, located in the Chicago area.

ABOUT THE EDITOR

Robert L. Dilenschneider formed The Dilenschneider Group in October 1991. Prior to forming his own firm, Dilenschneider served as president and chief executive officer of Hill and Knowlton from 1986 to 1991. Dilenschneider started in public relations in 1967 in New York, shortly after receiving an M.A. in journalism from Ohio State University, and a B.A. from the University of Notre Dame.

His experience covers a variety of fields, ranging from major corporations and professional groups to trade associations and educational institutions, and includes dealing with regulatory agencies, labor unions, consumer groups, and minorities, among others.

Dilenschneider directed communications activities during the Chilean grape tampering crisis, the U.S. Steel/Marathon merger, the Kansas City Hyatt disaster, the Three-Mile Island accident, and the Bendix/Martin Marietta takeover, and participated in communicating the redeployment of assets in numerous companies, ranging from high-tech business to heavy industry. He has also personally counseled seven of *Fortune*'s "10 Toughest Bosses."

Dilenschneider serves as a director of several corporate boards. He is a member of the Board of Governors of the American Red Cross and a member of the advisory boards of The New York Hospital-Cornell Medical Center and the College of Business Administration at the University of Notre Dame. He is also a member of the board of trustees of the Institute for International Education.

Dilenschneider serves as a member of the Council of Foreign Relations, the U.S.–Japan Business Council, the Public Relations Society of America, the Economics Clubs of New York and Chicago, the International Public Relations Association, the Wisemen, and the Florida Council of 100. He received New York's "Big Apple" Award in recognition of his contributions to making that city great.

Dilenschneider is widely published, having authored the best selling *Power and Influence, A Briefing for Leaders*, and, most recently, *On Power*. He has lectured before scores of professional organizations and colleges, including the University of Notre Dame, Ohio State University, New York University, and The Harvard Business School.

PREFACE

This is the book I've been meaning to write for 30 years. For about that long, I have been observing public relations from a number of vantage points, and I have developed some strong opinions about this profession.

My first look at public relations came in the early 1960s. I journeyed to the Big Apple from Columbus, Ohio, and went to work as an account representative in a large public relations agency. The agency had a broad range of clients, everything from staid businesspeople to nonprofits operating on a shoestring.

The amazing thing was that we somehow managed to help them all. Even when Columbia University was being besieged by the counterculture we were able to break the back of the momentum. I felt like Merlin. This thing called "public relations," I decided, was a wonderful force in the universe. I decided that when I became a "brand name" in this profession I would launch a campaign that public relations be a mandatory course in college.

My next stop was Chicago. At the agency's Chicago office I was to be a "Chief." That led me to see public relations from another very different point of view.

When I was an "Indian" in Manhattan, I had often been a Monday-morning quarterback. I would speculate that we shouldn't have been so patient with Client X and that we should have given better service to Client Y. I wondered for days about why one of my colleagues had been asked to resign. He had been my hero.

In Chicago, the buck stopped with me. It was *moi* who had to make decisions about the ethics of taking a certain account, shaking loose a client who wasn't profitable, 'fessing up to a client that we dropped the ball, and, toughest of all, having to ask underachievers to resign.

From the point of view of Chicago, public relations looked like a business. That business seemed to have more than its share of uncertainties:

- Through no fault of ours, a client could receive bad press, any day, in any media. Sure, we could work to neutralize it but for some reason, clients think we control the media. The best we can do is stay wired in enough to pick up signals that a negative piece is in the works.

- A client may not renew with us after the contract is up. That hurts. We swallow our pride and try to find out why this happened. We even approach the client directly and see what's the matter. But there are no guarantees in the game — no matter how much dazzling publicity we've gotten for them.

Maybe the president's brother-in-law started his own public relations agency. Maybe the client just didn't like my tie.

- Top performers could go seek supposedly greener pastures. As a chief, you're thinking about loyalty. As an Indian, they're thinking about their right — actually, their duty — to seek out the sweetest deal. When they leave, that great team you've nurtured has to be rebuilt. Talent is a wild card in the agency business. Will this new team be able to dazzle the client like the former team?

This uncertainty humbled me. The business of running an agency took more effort, good judgment, and creativity than directly serving clients. When I left that position I didn't have such grandiose notions of what public relations could do. All I knew, I realized, is that if you have the right people on the right team and they're a good fit with clients, you could see terrific results.

My third perspective for viewing public relations was being the founder of a brand new agency in Manhattan: The Dilenschneider Group. Around 1990, I decided to make a reality of the fantasy I've long had about having my own shop. When I made a commitment to form The Dilenschneider Group, I was flying high.

To my surprise I haven't crashed. When you have your own business, you can reduce some of the uncertainties. If experience tells you not to take that chocolate account, you turn it down. If your gut says don't hire this well-known business writer with great references, you don't. If a client is draining your energy and resources, you can allow that account to slip away — and not answer to anyone. That frees you up to hit more home runs on other accounts.

From my five years at The Dilenschneider Group, I've learned how important environment is to your performance. If you're in a wrong fit — a corporate job versus an agency job, nonprofit versus profit, business versus politics, or employee versus owner — it's bound to show up in performance. I'm vigilant about bad fits. I try to pick them up before they're hired or before we take that account. Some wisdom I've picked up: Bad fits will never develop into good fits. If you somehow get involved with them, cut your loses and cut them loose.

Now that I've had these experiences I'm aware that there are few absolutes in public relations. A chief would describe the business very differently than would an account representative. And an owner's point of view would be very different than a vice president's who works in someone else's agency. What's "true" or "feels right" depends on your vantage point.

That's why I put such high value on individual experience. When I decided to do this book, I wanted it to be the varied perspectives of pros in their fields. How they operate in this profession will tell you a lot about what's going on right now in their specialty. It's a snapshot of, say, media relations or working with a public relations agency.

For instance, you may disagree with Mary Jane Genova that certain images such as Alice in Wonderland are clichés and shouldn't be used in speeches. But what that chapter on speechwriting allows you to do is look at what you're doing or what you plan to do with a broader perspective. I like to think of these chapters as the "Windows 95 of public relations." They enable you to do a lot of things you couldn't manage before.

You'll notice that a number of the contributors are associated with The Dilenschneider Group. When I wanted to contract pros for this project, I realized that some of the best people were those I've already worked with. I knew they would give you something to think about. So they're a major part of this collection.

How should you approach this book? If I were you I'd read it slowly. Take the time to reflect on a strategy or on an ethical ramification of a certain action. Compare what Dick Kosmicki and Fred Bona are saying about media relations with your own experience.

Keep a notebook nearby to jot down words and phrases. A lot of our business has to do with language. If you can pick up the language of what the expert is discussing you begin to tame that subject matter and make it yours. Think of yourself as a lion tamer. Your power over the lion is words.

More than a decade ago, I heard the story of how a Ph.D. from Harvard took a job in public relations at Chrysler when the company was on the verge of bankruptcy. That was the early 1980s. Things were very chaotic. This gentleman—and that's what he was—had never before worked in the auto industry. No one had the time to help him get up to speed on the industry. A skeleton crew was left in public relations and they were working 18-hour days managing the media and helping with trade shows.

But this Ph.D. was astute enough to pick up on the words—and not worry too much what they exactly meant. He assumed that if he got the language down he would somehow get a hang for what the words all meant. He did. Every day he would make sure that he added lots of new terms to his Chrysler vocabulary. They included: OEM, turbocharged, short lead and long lead, tag relief, changeover, wind tunnel, in-line sequencing, and just-in-time manufacturing. Soon, this gentleman got so skillful at using the language that he was even able to make a joke about "just-in-time speechwriting." That was when an executive called and asked when his speech will be ready. Incidentally, the executive loved the joke. As a result of focusing on the language, this man was able to navigate the waters in this strange territory.

So, learn the lingo. It empowers you.

Also, while you're reading be alert and try to determine what opinions in this book you may disagree with. Remember, much of public relations is point of view.

If you want to share your point of view with me or any of the experts you can reach us at:

The Dilenschneider Group
200 Park Ave.
New York, NY 10166
212-922-0900 (voice)
212-922-0971 (fax)

—RLD

PUBLIC RELATIONS: AN OVERVIEW

Public relations — or the art of influence — is probably as old as mankind. To survive, our ancestors had to persuade members of their group to adopt certain behaviors. Hunting had to be done this way and farming that way. The people who did the influencing had to be credible leaders.

As the art of influence, public relations delivers its message indirectly. That's why it's such a versatile tool — and often gets results when marketing tactics fail. Here are some examples of how public relations works:

- At the rotary, executives give speeches that show how federal taxes significantly reduce the amount of capital available for a business to expand.
- The executive director of a non-profit organization writes an opinion-editorial on child abuse for the *Chicago Tribune*.
- A lobbyist for the coal industry goes to Washington, D.C., and explains how many jobs will be lost if a certain energy regulation is passed; like Ross Perot, he brings along charts.
- A consumer-products company hosts a gigantic picnic; at it they serve their new soft drink.
- A meat company issues a brochure discussing the nutritional value of beef.
- An auto manufacturer invites security analysts to tour its new plant.
- A bank in the Midwest sponsors a little league team.
- After an explosion at its plant in Spain, the chief executive of an American company meets with the international media and explains the situation to the worldwide employees via e-mail.

All of this is what has been called the "soft sell." Unlike marketing, which is usually more direct and a "harder sell," public relations usually doesn't issue commands such as "Buy Brand X." It suggests. It positions points of view, products, and services in a favorable light. And it leaves the audience with a suggestion rather than a command: "Nothing wrong with an egg now and then for breakfast, is there?" "GE has certainly achieved a great deal." And "If only the whole world could be as wholesome as 'Toy Story.'"

Because public relations isn't usually a hard sell, isn't as intrusive as marketing, and is relatively cost-effective, it's a field that's growing in prestige and influence. Its tools are being used across the board, including in politics, government, big business and small business, non-profit organizations, trade associations, churches, schools, and individual self-promotional campaigns.

What public relations counselors do is analyze a client's situation and create a strategic plan. The tactics they recommend may include a higher or lower profile, more or less media relations, more or less print matter, visual support material, a recognition program for the sales force, more lobbying and third-party endorsements, special events such as an ethnic festival, and sponsorship of a literacy program.

One area that is growing rapidly and attracting attention is what could be called "marketing public relations," "marketing communications," or "multi-channel marketing." According the Thomas Harris in *The Marketer's Guide to Public Relations*, about one-fifth of each public relations dollar spent now goes towards multi-channel marketing.[1]

In this chapter you'll find out why. You'll also review the history of public relations and where public relations is today.

When public relations started out it was primarily to influence opinion, not pave the way for the sale of products or services as it often does now. According to Kathleen O'Neill in the *Public Relations Journal*, the Sophists of Ancient Greece were an early form of lobbyist. Skilled in logic and communications, they debated issues in public places in hopes of gathering votes for certain causes.[2]

Over the centuries, much of the art, such as the medieval cathedral, and the literature, such as Homer's *Iliad* and the Bible, were meant to influence. In that sense they could be considered to be a form of public relations. When the peasant went to town, for example, the first and biggest thing he saw from the road was a cathedral. He's going to be reminded of Christianity. That's a message he can't miss.

Change agents, such as Martin Luther who created Protestantism, had to know how to use public relations. When Luther nailed his protest to the door of a Catholic Church, he was applying a number of public relations principles including the use of drama or "theater in the streets." Thomas Jefferson, Jerry Rubin, and Ralph Nader were all change agents and all masters of influence.

Here in the New Land — America — public relations thrived. The United States is known as a country of promoters. That great promoter P.T. Barnum probably couldn't have been as successful in a country that was more reserved. Could Barnum have built his circus empire in France? The French would probably have perceived him as excessive and ignored his Greatest Show on Earth.

The first documented case of the use of public relations in the United States was in fundraising — that is, positioning a cause in just the right light to attract donations. It was 1641 and a group of clergy sailed from the colonies to England to raise money for Harvard College. As soon as they landed they realized they needed a brochure. Nowadays, of course, just about every institution of higher learning has a fully staffed public relations department.

The first high point in public relations in America was the time of the American Revolution. The leaders of the revolution had to be very skillful to persuade the colonists to go to war against their mother country. The Boston Tea Party, the slogan "No taxation without representation," the Declaration of Independence, and the Federalist papers were all brilliant tactics. Equally shrewd was how the leaders used the violence of what was called the "Boston Massacre" to generate sympathy for the cause and antipathy toward the British.

Much of the early public relations activities in America was media-related. Newspapers and later magazines and wire services were the cable television, FM radio, and Internet of their day. Those were the platforms for influencing opinion as well as creating interest in products and services. But because some of the press agents played fast and loose with the truth, the reputation of public relations took some blows.

Despite those occasional clouds over its reputation, public relations found its way into every aspect of American life. Political parties, government, non-profit organizations, and businesses all embraced its strategies and learned to use its tools resourcefully. Here are some examples.

• **Politics.** President Andrew Jackson hired Amos Kendall to do everything from handle the media to ghostwrite his speeches. FDR used the new technology of radio to bring his message of hope to the people. JFK knew the public relations value of everything from Caroline's photo to using a top-notch ghostwriter.

• **Government.** During World War I, President Woodrow Wilson drafted journalist George Creel to help shape opinion in support of the war and increase the sale of war bonds. Creel enlisted the aid of a man who was to become a public relations legend: Edward Bernays. During World War II, the Office of War Information (OWI) was also established to encourage patriotism and the sale of bonds. Now just about every government agency has an office of public affairs or public information.

• **Nonprofit.** In 1855, the American Medical Association passed a resolution that it would cooperate with the media. The medical profession was recognizing the media's growing power. With increased competition, reduced sources of funding and more demands for accountability, all nonprofits have had to become sophisticated in their public relations. No longer can any organization, no matter what's its mission, ignore the job of shaping public opinion.

• **Business.** During the 1850s, land developers and the railroads used public relations, especially media, to encourage people to come out to that great unknown — the Wild West — settle and make a life. In *Effective Public Relations*, Scott Cutlip, Allen Center, and Glen Broom attribute the success of the westward migration to public relations.[3]

It's difficult to name a corporation today that isn't concerned with how its public relations is going. The corporate world recognizes: Perception is often reality.

Just about every development in the United States, ranging from increased suffrage to technical breakthroughs, led to a greater need for public relations. That's because there was greater demand for information.

Next to the American Revolution. probably the most exciting era in public relations was that of the muckrakers. During the last part of the 1800s, America was fast becoming an urban, industrial country. The ambitious were leaving their farms and coming to cities to work in factories. There was as much economic and social turmoil then as there is now with globalization and rapid developments in technology.

Back in the muckraking era, steel, coal, petroleum, and meat-packing became big business and provided employment to millions of people. But business leaders were secretive and impersonal. They were also accused of exploiting labor, having unsafe working conditions, and not always being square shooters with consumers. At the time there were few labor laws, and consumers really had no one on their side.

In response, around 1900, journalists started exposing the abuses in big bigness. They included Mark Sullivan, who wrote exposes about newspapers; Upton Sinclair, who attacked the meat-packing industry; and Ida Tarbell, who took on the petroleum industry. Their forums were newspapers, magazines, wire services, and books. They knew how to get and keep the public's attention and sympathy. It could be said that many of the reforms in the workplace and in how business is conducted date back to the muckrakers.

As a result of the exposés, business began to recognize that it had to tell its side of the story. Business would probably have done that eventually, even without the muckrakers. Back in 1889, George Westinghouse sensed the need for Westinghouse to get its messages out to the media. He set up the first corporate public relations department.

So in the beginning of the 20th century, businesses began taking into account how they were perceived. Some of them, like Westinghouse, set up in-house public relations departments. Others sought counsel from the outside. The first public relations agency was formed in 1900 by George Michaelis, Herbert Small, and Thomas Marvin. In 1906, it was representing the railroads to prevent regulation.

As workers, voters, and consumers became more skilled in voicing their discontent, there grew an urgent need for public relations counsel. Since the press was the most important forum many public relations people at that time came from a journalism background. But public relations wasn't just an outgrowth of journalism. It became a profession in its own right.

For instance, there was beginning to be courses in public relations. In 1923, publicist Bernays started a public relations course at New York University, and publicist Rex Harlowe taught public relations courses at Stanford University at the end of the 1930s. Several years later, Harlowe established the *Public Relations Journal* and the American Council on Public Relations, which evolved into the Public

Relations Society of America (PRSA). In 1950 the PRSA adopted a code of ethics. Five years later, the Council on Public Relations was established. In 1964, the PRSA established an accreditation program.

As public relations became a profession, it began to have its giants. During the early part of the 20th century, two men stand out for their contributions to public relations.

One was Ivy Lee. In 1903, he left a journalism job for a better-paying job as a publicist for a political figure. In 1906, he represented management in the anthracite coal strike. At first management refused to talk with the press. Lee persuaded them to cooperate. He also issued a "Declaration of Principles," which stated that the press and the public are to be provided with accurate and timely information. This revolutionized relations among the press, business, and the public. The precedent was set for business to tell the whole story, including negative parts.

Bernays, one of the most influential leaders in public relations, wrote the then-famous *Crystallizing Public Opinion* in 1923. A sort of Bible for the profession, this book codified and explained what should be the principles, policies, and values of public relations. He also applied the principles of public relations to marketing. For example, he orchestrated a public relations campaign to position bacon and eggs as a good breakfast. He certainly succeeded. It's only current information about fat and cholesterol that has affected the popularity of this breakfast.

Over the years, public relations thrived. As Cutlip et al. point out, by the mid 1960s there were 100,000 practitioners of public relations.[5] The concept of "image" was becoming a powerful force. Columnists like Walter Winchell and the 1960 Kennedy-Nixon presidential debate brought home how critical the right image could be. Large public relations agencies, such as Carl Byoir and Hill and Knowlton, were established.

In addition many organizations had their own in-house staff. At the former Gulf Oil the head count in public relations was more than 100 in the late 1970s. At that time energy supply was a major issue and so were the industry's "windfall" profits. Gulf had staff in both Washington, D.C., and state capitals.

The vice president of public relations at the time, Bill Moffett, conducted a high-powered integrated campaign to tell the government and consumers the facts about the energy problem. Gulf surveyed the public to check if what they were doing was working. Today, Moffett's approach in governmental relations is now standard. Very few businesses don't have representatives in Washington, D.C., and in states where they do business.

In addition to governmental relations, a number of specialties in public relations are becoming increasingly valued in organizations.

That's happening for a number of reasons. In the early 1980s, businesses recognized that the marketplace had become global; there was no turning back. That changed all the rules. And American business was turned upside down. That had ripple effects on every other institution in America.

As a result a revolution occurred. It has been just as overwhelming as the first Industrial Revolution. Millions of white-collar workers lost their jobs. Chief executive officers, such as General Motors' Robert Stempel and IBM's John Akers, were forced out because they were perceived not to be moving fast enough in restructuring the corporation. Information about all this had to be communicated to the media, employees, communities, and investors. At the time, technology also had been changing the world of work. The personal computer made everyone virtually self-sufficient. That revolution is still going on. And, in response, a number of areas of public relations are becoming increasingly important.

  • **Governmental relations.** As stated previously, public relations is a tool lobbyists use to make their case. The vehicle for delivering their message could be one-on-one meetings, testimony, letters to government leaders, third-party materials sent to government and the media, interviews with the media, opinion-editorials and articles, sponsorship of activities and special events.

If power continues to flow to the states, there'll be a build-up of corporate staff in state capitals. (See Chapter 14 on government relations for more information.)

  • **Media relations.** A seasoned pro is worth his or her weight in gold. A $75,000 media representative can get millions of dollars of free publicity for an organization. In addition, that publicity would be more credible than advertising since it's coming from a third party.

Also the fragmentation of the media has made it more difficult to reach people. That's upped the demands put on media representatives. For instance, at one time if you put ads or articles in a few of the women's magazines such as *Family Circle*, you could be sure of reaching many women. No more. The women's market has fragmented into niches ranging from working mothers to weight watchers.

The emergence of cable television has also divided up the audience. Not too long ago, if a public relations representative placed an author on "Today" and a magazine-format television show, often that was all that was needed. Now, with the proliferation of channels, there's more work to be done promoting anything, including a book.

Zines or magazines oriented toward youth, including those on the Internet, are another option media representatives now have to explore. Both technology and youth or Generation X are reshaping what media are important. (See Chapter 4 on working with the media and Chapter 5 on the trade press for more information on media relations.)

• **Employee communications.** The old social contract—lifetime employment and a good pension—is dead. Now executives have to use other methods to keep employees motivated. In addition, as threats of layoffs are ever present, employees want to know how the company is doing.

The importance of employee communications is making the field very dynamic. All kinds of tools are being used: "Town meetings" with the corporate leadership, electronic mail, videos, hot-off-the-press newsletters, and investor-oriented materials.

What's being produced is more candid and audience-friendly than employee communications use to be. Remember the days of the monthly glossy employee newsletter that contained all upbeat news? Technology and crisis have made that approach an anachronism. A subsidiary of NYNEX introduced a no-frills newsletter called *The Competitor*. It keeps employees posted on what the competition is up to and what the company has to do to preserve its market share.

A lot of interviewing and measuring is going on in employee communications. Before and after employees read or see something from the company, there will be focus groups and surveys. The results are taken seriously. (See Chapter 9 on employee communications for more information.)

• **Investor relations.** Institutional investors, such as pension funds, have become or are trying to become influential in the company's affairs. They might press for the removal of a certain executive or the sale of an unprofitable division. And more often than not these days, their requests are granted. These institutional investors are the corporation's most important audience.

In addition to communicating with large investors, corporations must keep in close touch with other members of the financial community, ranging from security analysts to the financial media. That's because the financial community has quite a bit of control over stock price and how the company will be presented in the media. A negative article in *The Wall Street Journal* or *Forbes* can bring down the stock price.

Another key audience is the average shareholder. Shareholders are now paying attention. For this reason you might have to produce your annual report more cost effectively. They could balk if the report looks too expensive. Also, shareholders want financial information discussed so that they can understand it. And they won't tolerate lack of candor about negative developments at the company. (See Chapter 7 on financial communications for more information.)

• **Crisis communications.** Today there's probably no organization that hasn't weathered a crisis. In fact, crisis is so commonplace that many companies have plans in place for when there will be one. Many of these upheavals are the result of changes in the organization.

Executives are forced out, managers are laid off and the survivors are expected to do more with less. As the survivors try to cope, there seems to be an ongoing crisis.

As recently as the early 1980s, a crisis situation would sometimes be overlooked in an organization. As long as the media didn't get wind of it, it was assumed things could be officially ignored. Today, if the company is in denial, employees aren't. They've been known to leak information to the media now that the old social contract is dead. (See Chapter 10 on crisis communications for more information.)

• **Global communications.** A client based in Mexico wants a higher profile for his company in the United States and parts of Latin America. A client in New York wants to establish a brand identity for a soap in China. A subsidiary of a large American financial-services company wants to educate the intelligentsia about AIDS in India.

All of these types of assignments are now routine. That means public relations people must understand the international media, the customs of a country, and any problems the client has that could cause difficulties in other cultures.

The day will soon come when dealing with all clients means dealing with global issues. For example, a university in Boston could be in direct competition for students with a university in China. Every account will be approached from a global perspective. (See Chapter 6 on global communications for more information.)

• **Multi-channel marketing.** The new "marketing mix" puts to work—jointly—the tools of marketing and of public relations. This used to be called "integrated marketing." And the glue that holds the whole thing together is public relations. For example, those against pet abuse could use a public relations tool—sponsorship of free birth control for pets—to create an image for the organization. Or an organization can host special events such as Retooling Days for the unemployed.

But this approach, of course, is nothing new. Bernays, as you recall, promoted bacon and eggs and, years ago, Hallmark and Kraft sponsored high-quality television programs that were closely associated with them. Elsie the cow pushed diary products. The empire created by Mickey Mouse was built on an image—wholesomeness. Rheingold beer used the Miss Rheingold contest to increase interest in the beverage. Campbell Soup had the pudgy Campbell kids. The American Express green card at one time represented prestige. Joe's Friendly Pizza would sponsor the town's little league team. Estee Lauder would have Makeover Day at stores selling its products. There would be articles in magazines about the benefits of using liquid versus powdered detergent. (See Chapter 1 on new strategies for more information.)

What is new, though, is how widespread the use of these tools are. Why are more marketers increasingly turning to public relations to promote products and services? There are four reasons.

1. Need to reduce costs. Global competition put pricing pressure on American businesses. That meant costs had to be cut. Excess was out. One of the costs looked at was how much money was required to sell a Chevy or a recreational vehicle. Advertising, it was seen, was a very expensive activity.

Questions arose about what kind of results advertising was getting. The joke used to be: Yes, advertising works. At least half of it. We just don't know which half. That joke is no longer a source of amusement. There's now greater accountability in advertising. Marketing departments were motivated to search for less expensive ways to get results.

2. Fragmentation of the media. In the 1950s and 1960s companies could put an ad in *Woman's Day* and be sure it was reaching many women who were concerned about how their homes looked. Those days are gone. The mass market has been replaced with market niches. Even on the Internet there are niches or special interests. Now, to reach as many people as they did back then marketers have to use a variety of tools.

3. Clutter of commercial messages. It is difficult to think of a situation in which there are no promotional messages. They are coming at people in a variety of ways: Advertising, free-standing inserts, direct mail, telemarketing, radio, television, the Internet, in the rest room, on paper and plastic bags, on t-shirts, on mugs, on pens, inside shopping carts in the supermarket, free samples, cents-off coupons at the cash register for a competitors' product, and church bulletins.

The challenge is to break through this clutter and have your message noticed. Not an easy thing to do. As a result, there's a significant amount of experimentation with new approaches. That leaves the door wide open for the creative public relations person.

4. Increased competition. There seems to be an overcapacity or glut of just about everything in America, ranging from computers to legal counsel to hospital beds. Remember how at one time there was only one store with a certain concept? Only one Staples, which handled discount office supplies. Only one Kmart, which sold discount household supplies. Now a concept is quickly copied. The challenge is: How to get consumers to your company and not your competition's — without shooting yourself in the foot by using, for example, a price war.

In all these cases what public relations will do is to pave the way for the introduction, consumption, or repositioning of a product or a service. Public relations staff at Chrysler, for example, will talk to the media months before a new type of truck is actually put on the market. If the media runs articles on this new vehicle interest will build before the truck is for sale. Remember how much free publicity Microsoft's Windows 95 received? That was thanks to media relations, not advertising. The same was true for the joint venture between NBC and Microsoft established to operate 24-hour news. The announcement was actually handled as a media event.

But does all this hoopla actually wind up selling products and services?

Harris, in his 1991 book on the use of public relations in marketing, offers some amazing statistics. Harris points out:

- Ford Motor Company had orders for 146,000 Taurus and Sable automobiles before they were advertised. The orders were the result of public relations.
- Cuisinart's annual sales were once small. Then there was an article in *Gourmet* magazine about it. Within two years, sales were at 250,000—even though this product was priced at a premium.
- The movie *E.T.* increased Reese's Pieces candy sales by 65 percent.
- And a National Soup Month campaign by Campbell increased sales 36 percent.[4]

Probably one of the biggest success stories of applying public relations to marketing was the Chrysler miracle. During the early 1980s, Iacocca and his team brought the auto company back from the brink of bankruptcy. Iacocca was skilled in public relations. The K-car and then minivan, it was said, saved Chrysler. Iacocca won the public over to support these vehicles—even though there was a danger they'd be "orphaned" if the company folded—with iconoclastic approaches to public relations.

He broke through the clutter and had his messages noticed by being very conversational and candid. The Chrysler tone bordered on slang as opposed to the statesman-like tone in the rest of corporate America. Iacocca openly confessed the sins of the American auto industry and of Chrysler at a time when business still held its cards close to its vest. Also, Iacocca didn't try to whitewash being fired from Ford.

Everything in the public relations plan was integrated. All executives had to give a certain number of speeches. In every speech was a pitch for the cars and a preview of the coming minivan. When Chrysler executives hit the road to give their speeches, media interviews were set up for them.

Chrysler was continually in the news, print and electronic. The company was positioned as the feisty underdog who wanted one more chance to take on the big guys like General Motors and Toyota. Every newspaper, magazine, and TV and radio station was eager to run stories on Chrysler. Buying a Chrysler car was seen as downright patriotic.

Internally, all the things being said externally were reinforced with newsletters, videos, and "To Be the Best" program. Yes, there was advertising. But could Iacocca's TV ads have worked so well without the public relations campaign? That's doubtful.

According to Jack O'Dwyer, who produces the best-read newsletter in the field, there are about 350,000 public relations practitioners today. Just about every library, every mayor's office, every first lady, every church, every political campaign, every committee of this or of that, and every day care center has some type of public information function. The function has become ubiquitous.

Moreover, the language of public relations — positioning, image, perception — has become part of the culture. Seniors in college ponder how to position themselves for the job market. Women returning to the workforce after taking care of children say they have to update their image. Many qualify what they say with "that's at least the way I perceive it."

That means clients know more and therefore are often more trusting of what public relations can do for them. That trust, plus your strategy and imagination, can create magic for clients. The Chrysler miracle is not an aberration. What Iacocca and his team did any resourceful public relations person can also do. Those miracles can happen in a Mom-and-Pop deli, a global bank in New York, an organization for the homeless, a mainline church, or in the life of individuals who want to improve their image.

NOTES

1. Thomas Harris, *The Marketer's Guide to Public Relations* (New York: John Wiley & Sons, Inc., 1991), 9.

2. Kathleen O'Neill, *Public Relations Journal* 47 (11): 28-31 (November 1991).

3. Scott Cutlip, Allen Center and Glen Broom, *Effective Public Relations* (Englewood Cliffs, New Jersey: Prentice Hall 1995).

4. Harris, 3.

5. Cutlip, et al., 99.

DARTNELL'S
PUBLIC RELATIONS
HANDBOOK

Kathleen F. Connelly joined Robert L. Dilenschneider to create The Dilenschneider Group in October 1991. Prior to that, Connelly served as an executive vice president responsible for worldwide business development at Hill and Knowlton, and was a member of the board of directors, as well as director of the firm's global strategic planning group.

Connelly's areas of expertise include corporate change and restructuring initiatives, merger and acquisition communications; public offerings; corporate positioning programs; crisis counsel and communications; professional services marketing; business-to-business marketing; public affairs and issues planning.

Before joining Hill and Knowlton, Connelly served as an officer at Continental Bank of Chicago, where she worked in bond trading; and prior to that, public affairs, where she organized the bank's issues system and managed its public affairs programs. She also has worked as a legislative aide on consumer and environmental issues.

Connelly is an honors graduate of Newton College in Newton, Massachusetts, where she was class president and held the President's Scholarship. She received a master's degree in political science from the Eagleton Institute of Politics at Rutgers University under a Ford Foundation grant and has attended the Graduate School of Business at the University of Chicago.

Connelly serves as a director on several boards. She has lectured at The Harvard Business School, Carnegie-Mellon, Northwestern University Journalism and Business Schools, and the University of Notre Dame Business School.

I'd like to acknowledge the contribution that Joseph Marconi, an expert in marketing and branding, made to some of the ideas contained within this chapter.

— Kathleen F. Connelly

CHAPTER 1

NEW STRATEGIES
IN PUBLIC RELATIONS

*This is not the end. It is not even the beginning of the end. But it
is, perhaps, the end of the beginning.*
— Winston Churchill[1]

In many ways, the events of the last decade have created a sea
change in public relations, transforming its place in the work world
from a primarily executional focus to a strategic essential. Some of this
transformation has been evolutionary, naturally building on the work
that has gone before. In other cases, the sea change has been more a
matter of survival, of staying up with the curve, rather than staying
ahead of it.

The world, the world of clients and companies, and the world of
their clients' clients have all been changing. Downsizing has turned into
rightsizing and then, in some cases, evolved into capsizing. Budgets are
tighter. Doing more with less has migrated from the environmental
movement to corporate America. Many middle managers now handle
responsibilities previously split among two or three managers and lean
and mean remains the battle cry of the day. Demands have become
more urgent and time to execute has slipped accordingly. Accountability
is higher. And the clutter of messages keeps getting denser.

One of the additional outcomes of this period of blinding change
has been the need for all leaders to be prepared to respond effectively
and instantly — anytime, anywhere — in creative ways that cut through
the clutter and cacophony of contemporary life and reach the critical
audiences.

No one said it would be simple. The application of technology to
all aspects of communications has been extraordinary and a major
mover of public relations — from inputting and delivering messages
through multiple gateways to reliance on computers for everything from
graphics to research to word processing. The intersection of all these
events has placed a challenge on performance-driven public relations
professionals to develop strategies for corporate positioning, customer
responsiveness, crisis communications, leveraging cutting-edge technology, and delivering meaningful internal communications programs.

The development of the personal computer, the Intenet and the
World Wide Web has forever changed the way we think about outreach, time, and communications boundaries, not to mention traditional
mail versus e-mail, where all addresses end in the ubiquitous "dot,
com." With these advances has also come new ways of thinking about
what is now possible in terms of public influence, market segmentation, new customers, new products, new services and creative outreach.

No matter what the reasons, it's a new communications world out there, a world where a developing corporate problem now takes on a new urgency when it becomes unexpectedly discussed in online forums by anonymous people, and then flamed on the Intenet. Remember the impact of the Intel Chip problem! It demonstrates the power of electronic communications and the challenges of trying to masterfully communicate in cyberspace and maintain control of messages, with an audience you can't touch, see, understand, or depend on to be there tomorrow.

Clearly, the bar has been raised significantly for communicators and leaders, and along with it, levels of expectation on the public's part about what leaders can do to really deliver and perform. The enormity of the communications challenge becomes apparent when it becomes clear that all markets are segmented so finely that there is a micro-market for virtually everything. How can public relations practitioners strategically deal with all this complexity in ways that make a substantive difference for management and leadership? The answers are as varied as the opportunities and challenges and include all of the following techniques, some of which are new, and some of which are recycled and applied to current needs and technology developments.

• For example, there's "multi-channel marketing." Its track record is terrific for producing results inexpensively. Using multi-channel marketing, the public relations professional does more than just have a press conference to announce a new macadamia ice cream. In addition, there might be a global contest via e-mail to name the new flavor. The company could set up old-fashioned ice-cream parlors in the corridors of malls and sell scoops at cost; a percentage of those revenues would then be donated to help children with cancer.

• Some companies want to be closely associated with the "zines" on the Internet. In this way they're saying: We're with it.

• There are also the new partnerships. A company might form a strategic alliance with another company or a nonprofit organization to deliver a joint message. This summer, for example, a chicken company and a barbecue-sauce company would jointly offer a coupon for 50-cents off if consumers bought both products. Or a corporation might join with a nonprofit dedicated to environmentalism. The purpose would be to demonstrate that, like the nonprofit, the corporation is concerned with environmental issues. For the nonprofit, there would be the message that it is businesslike in its approach.

• A nonprofit may be planning to write a grant to get funding for a poll on how people perceive charities these days.

• A large restaurant might be considering introducing a Smart Diners Card. For every ten meals, patrons would get one free. In addition, Smart Diners would get to sit in a special section of the restaurant and receive a monthly newsletter with recipes.

As Thomas Harris points out in *The Marketer's Guide to Public Relations*, many in public relations are now thinking in this way. About one-fifth of every public-relations dollar is now spent on multi-channel marketing.[2] That's because clients are searching for more effective, more affordable ways to communicate their messages.

SOME KEY DEVELOPMENTS SHAPING PUBLIC RELATIONS

There are several developments that are helping create a new, continuous change environment for business, government, and nonprofits.

EXHIBIT 1.1 — TRENDS IMPACTING PUBLIC RELATIONS

1. Organizational re-engineering
2. New technology
3. Cable television
4. Talk shows
5. Infomercials
6. Tabloids
7. Competition
8. Polling and surveys
9. Special interests

1. Organizational re-engineering. Corporations, universities, government, and other nonprofit organizations are changing how they operate. The drivers behind this are cost reduction, providing value, and a need for improved performance. This consolidation is taking many forms:

- New England-based Fleet Bank acquires a number of other banks in the region.
- IBM acquires Lotus.
- AT&T decides to spin off some businesses and eliminate 40,000 jobs in three years.
- Like the Japanese, Chrysler is reducing the number of vendors it uses and is creating close working relationships with those it keeps.
- SNET, the "local phone company," in Connecticut offers long distance.
- Seton Hill College in Greensburg, Pennsylvania, introduces a graduate program.

Not only does this re-engineering represent an upheaval, it's an upheaval that is ongoing. After AT&T eliminates 40,000 jobs, that may not be the end of restructuring at the telecommunications company. Many of the audiences for public relations, including the executive tier, are striving to learn how to live in a world of work, which is no longer predictable. They're looking to public relations to deliver messages which will guide them.

2. New technology. The way people communicate is also different, thanks to technology. There are the Internet, e-mail, cellular, and voice mail. Even the fax is getting new features. If organizations aren't communicating in these high-tech ways, they're likely to be conspicuous by their absence. For example, if a soft-drink manufacturer whose target market is Generation X doesn't have a page on the Internet, young people will probably wonder why. Organizations that want a 21st-century image will make sure they're involved with all new technologies. And their public relations will have to reflect this.

3. Cable television is no longer gee-whiz. Its ratings and audiences match those of the networks, and it has created a new mindset among viewers. Audiences now expect there will be programs to suit their individual interests whether those interests be wildlife in Africa or historical figures. Public relations has to take into consideration the existence, quality, and techniques of all the various channels, and their impact on the business world.

4. Talk shows. America has again become a populist nation, with the average person having the chance to voice opinions on issues.

Obviously this changes audiences' expectations. They anticipate interacting with those on the program. They also expect a "show." That means it's more difficult to get and hold their interest. What kind of effect does that have, for example, on the kinds of speeches clients give? Is the old "monologue" approach dead? Should the speech be shorter and discussion longer? On television, should the chief executive officer of the company sound statesmanlike or imitate the communications patterns of talk-show hosts? To be credible, is it now necessary for executives to bare their souls the way talk-show guests do?

5. Infomercials. This new hybrid of promotion and information has blurred the line between entertainment and news. Viewers enjoy them. Most channels report there's a waiting list for available infomercial time. This medium can't be ignored when considering what's appropriate for clients. Maybe a well-placed infomercial could be more effective than an equal amount spent on conventional print and electronic advertising. Moreover, the existence of this form influences how public relations practitioners create all their promotional materials.

6. Tabloids. Both television magazine shows and print magazines have taken a sharp turn toward the tabloid. As with changes in all the other media, this affects the audience's thought patterns. Many now think in headlines: Princess Di fights back. The Queen is a cold fish. The Jacksons split.

Should clients also be communicating in sound bites and headlines? Should a newsletter be mostly headlines? Also important here is the sense of drama that headlines convey. Shouldn't public relations representatives be helping clients tell audiences what's so exciting about that new printer or the revised graduate program in business?

7. Competition. The amount and intensity of competition are reshaping how organizations as well as individuals promote themselves. The gloves are off. Controversy, in-your-face approaches, and attack ads have become common. In telecommunications, that which were once clients become competitors. Public relations professionals must understand these developments and devise appropriate positioning for their clients. Where does that client stand in regard to that new competitor?

Suppose there is a new approach to weight management. Its promotional approach is in-your-face public relations. How should clients who are also in weight management respond?

Clients don't have to respond in kind. Clients can circumvent a lot of negativism and bad taste by introducing a positive approach that gets attention. Just one way of doing this is through social activism. The weight-control client can offer free services to the unemployed in Akron, Ohio, or welfare mothers on the south side of Chicago.

8. Polling and surveys. As is obvious in politics, the results of polls and surveys are treated seriously. Campaign strategies can change overnight as the result of one poll. In advising clients, this type of research must be considered. Also public relations practitioners have to learn to become skillful in creating research strategies. A poorly designed poll or one which never should have been brought into existence can do more to hurt than help clients. Virtually every news report and feature story carries a reference to a poll or survey that purports to offer the inside scoop on what's really going on. In fact, research such as this itself frequently becomes the news.

Polling and surveying have become ubiquitous because Americans are interested in answers to: What are people thinking? How will they vote? What do they want? Who do they like? What are the negatives a person, company, product, or profession need to erase to have a more appropriate image?

For example, there are daily conversations about how a political figure should change his image or how a once-famous star needs to be repositioned.

9. Special interest publications. General interest magazines are having a rough time, but special interest publications, such as those devoted to computers or cats, are flourishing.

For promotional purposes, the mass market can be considered dead in the United States. In his article "Marketing in an Age of Diversity," in the *Harvard Business Review*, Regis McKenna says, "Gone is the convenient fiction of a single, homogeneous market."[3] In *Making Niche Marketing Work*, Robert Linneman and John Stanton, Jr., point out, "There are no more mass markets."[4] Proof of the death of the mass market has been the decline of department stores and the success of niche players, such as stores devoted to just socks or sportswear.

Therefore, in public relations the strategy must be targeted. This requires more research about what constitutes each market. It also requires more research about what are the most effective vehicles to use in each segment. If one segment is young, working women, it might be worthwhile to buy air time during drive time. The company may have to focus on several segments, such as working mothers, stay-at-home mothers, foster mothers, grandmothers, child-care personnel, and pediatricians. What's the best ways to reach these groups?

THE NEW "IMPROVED" STRATEGIES OF PUBLIC RELATIONS

EXHIBIT 1.2 — THE NEW "IMPROVED" STRATEGIES OF PUBLIC RELATIONS

- Target
- The Information Superhighway
- The Club
- Polls and Surveys
- Interest Groups
- The "Green" Road
- Cause Marketing
- The Institute
- Brand-Naming Events
- Cross Marketing and Joint Promotions
- Events and Series Sponsorships

How can public relations practitioners harness the power of these trends and make them work for them? Here are a number of recommendations.

Target.

Focus, slice and dice messages, mediums and tactics is the name of the most important game in public relations today. Market segmentation and fragmentation, grassroots political activism, and the emergence of special interests have made marketing to the masses ineffective. The homogenous audience that used to watch "Hallmark Hall of Fame" or "Ed Sullivan" on television is gone. In its place are audiences interested in specific niches, such as up-to-the-minute business news, the weather, old movies, the arts, and home improvement.

Narrow-focusing and market/message segmenting applies to all areas and levels of public relations, not just marketing. For example, corporations looking for support of special board actions or internal policies cannot assume that because an individual falls within one category of involvement, such as a shareowner, that all shareowners care about the same thing or act the same. Just like carefully focusing on a consumer's buying behavior, companies need to take the individuality of members of their audience into account as they prepare messages and materials.

On the marketing side, focusing is truer than ever. For example, the client, a financial-services company, might need to reach baby-boomers who have already purchased a mutual fund; small business owners without disability insurance; unemployed executives who formerly earned $200,000; and mothers out of the work force for five years. How do public relations representatives find out who those people are and what vehicles to use to reach them?

The p.r. staff can consult a direct-marketing firm that handles segments such as these. The firm will provide lists of names. As for the vehicles to reach them, each segment might be handled differently. That's the beauty of targeting; different strategies can be applied to different niches.

Baby boomers would be contacted through direct mail; they would receive a free newsletter that carries retirement-oriented articles. In addition representatives of the client could be booked on talk shows that baby boomers watch. An op-ed can be placed in local papers regarding the financial problems of baby boomers.

The small business owners could be reached through e-mail, an ad in *Inc.*, and free lectures in the community. There can also be a joint promotion with an office-supply store.

Unemployed executives could be contacted through a partnership with area churches and outplacement facilities. There's also the Internet.

Mothers wanting to return to work can be reached through an ad in the food section of the newspaper; a club created to support women trying to get back into the work world; and a joint promotion with the local supermarkets.

As public relations professionals continue to get more deeply involved on a strategic level in marketing efforts, practitioners might want to learn more about marketing concepts. They can teach themselves by getting some marketing textbooks from the library or a university book store. There is also a large selection of books on marketing in super bookstores. Most institutions of higher learning offer courses on marketing. Professional organizations such as the Direct Marketing Association also offer brief seminars and workshops.

The Information Superhighway.
High-tech gets attention in the marketplace. The lack of it also gets noticed. Virtually every ad, announcement, or offer now provides an e-mail address alongside the telephone and fax numbers. When public relations staff use vehicles such as wired magazines, electronic bulletin boards and e-mail for disseminating announcements and press releases and have interactive hotlines and crisis-information lines, they are telling their audiences two things: The client company is up on high-tech and it is making itself accessible.

Effectively and completely briefing key technology analysts, such as the Gartner Group, is critical to the long-term perception of the technology-driven company. Building in "virtual" customer-service features wherever possible, along with helping companies figure out who the new technology writers and media are with whom to build a relationship are both critical aspects of new public relations strategy, which also incorporates historical best practices, but with a new twist. Public relations representatives must ask themselves these questions: How do we make urgent information available to customers, associates, shareholders or the board of directors? How are we communicating with employees during a threatened takeover? Are we keeping the community up-to-date about how our business is doing?

Technology, though, is not a substitute for knowledge and experience. Gee-whiz electronics won't bridge the gap where there are few appropriate public relations strategies.

The Club.

Can the company create a membership in an exclusive club? Conferring VIP or membership status is not new in itself. That marketing device has been used for many years. Many baby boomers remember being members of the Mickey Mouse Club.

What is new is the growing awareness that club membership for audiences of all types increases power — both for the members and for the sponsor.

There is, for example, the recognition that there is strength in numbers. A senator is more apt to notice a letter from the Association of Direct Mail Specialists than from an individual who works in direct mail. Could the mothers in MADD have accomplished all they did if each had worked separately?

Also, a sense of belonging can make members feel important. In *The Leader in You*, Stuart Levine and Michael Crom assert that the need to feel important is basic to mankind. Clients who tap into this need will be more successful than those who ignore it.[5]

In addition, membership in a club, such as frequent fliers clubs, can increase customer loyalty. Many children's products and services have clubs for those who purchase a doll or miniature race car. Celebrities take their fan clubs very seriously.

Membership in a group can also give status. Sales-oriented organizations have their 100-percent clubs for sales reps making quota. The real estate firm has a million-dollar club for those who have sold that much property. They often put this information on their sales cards.

Club members are excellent ambassadors of goodwill. They're usually enthusiastic about telling the organization's story in all kinds of settings, ranging from the halls of Congress to the six o'clock news to a luncheon at the Rotary. They write letters to the editor. They appear on talk shows. All for free. Public relations representatives establishing a Speakers' Bureau ought to create some of that club spirit. To do that, some bureaus have regular meetings.

There are an infinite number of ways to use clubs in public relations work. All new purchasers of the company's printer could be welcomed into the club. They would receive monthly newsletters and special offers. There could be a special 800-number for them.

Interested third parties can also be welcomed into an association. If the client is a paper manufacturer he might want fast food restaurants to join in the fight against proposed legislation. A chocolate manufacturer forms an association with convenience store owners to educate the public and legislators about the need for fat in the diet.

Clients' employees who maintain healthy lifestyles can become members of a company health club. They get to use community gym facilities at a discount. They log hours for workouts; at so many hours they get a free gift or a day off. Their names and photos are displayed in the company building.

Polls and Surveys.

Using polls and surveys is at the same time both one of the oldest and one of the freshest strategies to undertake in the new segmented, populist environment. It is no longer just the province of marketers, but applicable to most audience needs. The public has expressed a keen interest in what others think and in registering their own opinion. To be heard, people are even willing to call 900-numbers and pick up the tab for expressing their point of view. Also, in terms of the organization, citing research enhances credibility. In addition, the research itself can be the subject of a press conference.

How can public relations people make the best use of the popularity of research? They'll need two things. One, they need to understand what the focus of the client's message is. Two, they need to interview research organizations to find out what they can offer at what price. The best way to find out about firms is through word of mouth. Call colleagues for names of good firms.

To enhance credibility corporations might want to underwrite research done by a third party. If the client is a food company he may have a department of nutrition at a university or an institute conduct the research.

To spread the cost and enhance credibility, organizations jointly sponsor or fund research. All the electric utilities in the Southwest might jointly conduct research on usage patterns among those over 65 years of age.

In addition to polls and surveys, there are focus groups. They've become pervasive. That's primarily because this qualitative type of research is open-ended and yields all sorts of unexpected information. Focus groups with employees conducted before an executive presentation, for example, have totally reshaped how the executive planned to approach a topic.

Focus groups can be done on a shoestring budget. Many of those in nonprofit organizations conduct the focus groups themselves. Colleagues in the business sector or their agencies can brief them on how to hold a focus group.

Participants are usually happy to participate in focus groups. They are flattered someone wants their opinion. A hospital in northern New Jersey wanted former patients to express opinions about post-op care. Providing them with a free lunch was enough to make them feel appreciated.

Interest Groups.

Organizations and individuals have found interest groups an important source of influence through the ages. They help spread the word about points of view, products and services. The most common ways to communicate with interest groups are through newsletters, 800-numbers, and 900-number telephone reports.

- A conservative radio commentator, for instance, offers a paid-subscription newsletter, a line of signature merchandise, and an invitation to communicate directly on CompuServe. As a result the commentator has a mailing list of people who share a point of view and are willing to engage in advocacy work to "preach the gospel."
- A popular author provides a free newsletter that promotes his opinions, books, tapes, speeches, and seminars. The mailing list is a gold mine.
- To attract like-minded people, organizations and individuals have sponsored medical-information lines, laugh lines, sports lines, and prayer lines. Sometimes revenues come from these lines. But the more important purpose is to have access to people and a forum for delivering a message.

What kind of interest groups can clients form? That depends on what messages they want to deliver. Would charging for the material sent out enhance their worth? The most commonly used strategy is to produce a free newsletter.

The "Green" Road.

Although this strategy has been developing for over two decades, encouraged by Rachel Carson's critical book, it continues to gain momentum across the United States. Concern about the environment has become a mainstream activity. Thinking green is now as American as apple pie. What clients want to do is to tap into this momentum.

Clients can sponsor awards for environmental accomplishments, conduct essay, photography or video contests, publish environmental newsletters, offer 800-environmental hotlines, have a computer "home page," and host an environmental forum.

If appropriate, routine communications coming from clients should include the environmental implications of a decision. For example, if the plant is making a new product, what steps were taken to protect the environment? How much money was invested in determining those environmental impacts? If the organization has been proactive on environmental matters that should be made known too.

Corporate Cause Marketing.

The Body Shop, McDonald's, VISA, and Ben & Jerry's have done well by doing good. They all used what's called "cause marketing." That means that in some way they share their profits on behalf of a good cause.

Clients may also want to associate their organization, product, or service with a worthy cause such as the environment, literacy, children's diseases, historic sites, or community outreach. They can do this by donating money, putting aside a percentage of profits for the cause, donating executive time, acting as a spokesperson for the cause, providing their facilities or equipment free of charge and hosting a conference.

Remember when Chrysler was associated with the restoration of the Statue of Liberty? That turned out to be a very successful venture for the auto company. But there's always a risk things could have turned out otherwise. For example, the client is donating money to an environmental cause that uses sensationalistic techniques like blocking roads so that loggers can't transport their products. That tactic, which is being frowned on by many Americans, could reflect badly on the client's organization.

Before clients adopt a cause, there are many questions to ask about the cause's mission, strategies, budget, and other supporters. The client company, for instance, could look foolish if the organization was found to waste money.

However, nothing is forever. Clients can decide to engage in cause marketing for a short period of time. There's no requirement that clients stay with a cause.

The Institute.

Another strategic option is for clients to create or support a foundation, institute, or center that champions research which could benefit them. This allows a company, such as the former General Foods, to become identified with important issues like world hunger.

Most of these institutes are "think tanks." Their research must be credible.

Brand-Naming Events.

An increasing popular positioning strategy is for clients to adopt a power phrase or brand-name for what they're doing. "Operation Desert Storm" and "Operative Desert Shield" are a lot more memorable than "the war in the Middle East." We all remember the New Deal, the New Frontier, and the Contract with America.

A power phrase or brand-name is the first step in promoting a promotion. Well-done promotions often take on a life of their own and the promotion becomes as much an entity as the product or service itself. Remember Woodstock? Companies that put on a "Real Texas Barbecue" for 10,000 or the "World According to Pasta" for 50,000 usually get a lot of attention. The wholesomeness of the events can also enhance their image.

Clients might have sponsored exciting promotions but never bothered to name them. The result was that those promotions probably didn't get maximum coverage by the media. A catchy name can increase coverage exponentially.

Cross Marketing and Joint Promotions.

Charities, hospitals, trade associations, and sports teams offer VISA cards bearing their names and logos; users of those cards know that a portion of the balance will go to that cause. Fast foods restaurants sell or give away merchandise from a hot movie or a sports figure. The restaurant across from the theater advertises what's playing at the theater and gives 15 percent discounts to theater patrons; the theater advertises the restaurant.

This in itself is nothing new. Small businesses have been doing this for decades. For example, if you bring in at least 10 pounds of winter clothing to be cleaned, you can get a free flower from the florist next door. And years ago, local cleaners gave away bookcovers with their name on it and the name of the local sports team; the sports team let it be known that its uniforms were maintained by the local cleaners. In the field, for example, there was a big ad about this arrangement.

The difference now is that cross marketing and joint promotions are big business. They increase the level of exposure and reduce the promotional cost for each participant. In summer there will be joint promotions for 60-cents off branded hot dogs and branded buns or $60 dollars off a weekend in a Manhattan hotel and a dinner in a certain restaurant.

This strategy isn't used enough by organizations that perceive they're in competition with one another. Often, they have different strengths they can jointly promote. For example, in the local paper, in a joint ad focusing on art, one local college can highlight its film program and another can stress its music program.

Who can clients join forces with?

Can the local law firm join with the local college in offering a writing course to make prose simpler and clearer? There could be excellent local media pick up on that. Can a large computer company offer X-dollars off a rock-star's concert tickets? The possibilities are infinite.

Events and Series Sponsorships.

Whether it be a golf tournament, a rock-star's concert, or Shakespeare in the Park, organizations get tremendous visibility and goodwill from sponsoring events. Often the organization's name is on the stage, on the program, on the tickets, in newspaper ads, and on all sorts of paraphernalia, such as T-shirts and mugs.

Sometimes, but not always, this requires money. For example, a soft drink company invested about $10 million to sponsor a rock star's concert. But a nonprofit organization can join with other nonprofits or with a business to sponsor a walk for health. Because the nonprofit event is a public service, much of the promotion will be done free by the media.

There is a risk, however. The star whose concert is being sponsored may get in trouble with the law. Or a hospital is sponsoring a marathon and a study is released saying marathons are hazardous to health. However, the rewards usually outweigh the potential risks. The image enhancement can be tremendous.

SUMMARY

These are just a handful of new strategies as well as some recycled strategies with a new twist. The best way public relations persons can come up with their own new strategies is to be willing to think "out of the box." To get new ideas, public relations representatives wheel a cart around a supermarket and study the positioning and packaging; analyze how a big name in running shoes, soft drinks, cars, or snacks is repositioning its image; be critical of how local nonprofits are missing chances to promote themselves; think about what suggestions they might make to a cereal manufacturer to revive a dying brand; and volunteer to help their alma mater with an upcoming public-relations project.

For those willing to think in different ways and take on some risk, public relations has evolved into a fast-paced, satisfying profession. The stage has been set. The strategies are clear. The tools are available to make a major difference for the organization. And perhaps the best motivator of all was one offered by Will Rogers who once said, "Even if you're on the right track, you'll get run over if you just sit there."[6]

FOOTNOTES

1. Winston Churchill, Speech, November 10, 1942

2. Thomas Harris, *The Marketer's Guide to Public Relations* (New York: John Wiley & Sons, Inc. 1991), 9.

3. Regis McKenna, "Marketing in an Age of Diversity," *Harvard Business Review* (September-October 1988), 88.

4. Robert Linneman and John Stanton, Jr., *Making Niche Marketing Work* (New York: McGraw-Hill, 1991), 1.

5. Stuart Levine and Michael Crom, *The Leader in You* (New York: Simon & Schuster, 1993), 45-56.

6. Will Rogers

This chapter on Staffing and Budgeting was prepared by Thomas R. Jordan, who died on January 20, 1996, and serves in memory of his contributions to the field of public relations. We hope that many will gain from his wisdom and insight.

Thomas R. Jordan was a principal of The Dilenschneider Group in New York and was head of the firm's energy/utility practice. Prior to joining The Dilenschneider Group, he was a senior vice president in the corporate counseling division of Hill and Knowlton. He was formerly managing director of The Jordan Group, a public policy and strategy development firm he founded. His energy/utility background covered a wide range of issues, including nuclear power; the relationships between electric power and economic development; environmental and human health issues associated with electric power production and use; improving energy efficiencies on both the supply and demand sides; and research and development as an element in utility strategic planning. Jordan was a graduate of the United States Coast Guard Academy, held a degree in electrical engineering, and had done graduate work in journalism.

CHAPTER 2

STAFFING AND BUDGETING

All too often public relations practitioners on both the agency and client side of the table tend to forget that public relations is, in the final analysis, a *business* for the agency and a *business function* for the client. For the agency that means it must make a profit. For the client it means that the public relations department must be a "value added" component for the company, and not merely a cost... a cost seen by many executives as an unnecessary one at that.

But times are changing for business and governments and not-for-profit organizations, such as hospitals, universities, charities, and civic service and cultural organizations.

As a competent public relations practitioner, you need to be aware of the implications of those changes for the P.R. function within your company or organization. So let us examine those changes and implications briefly before we get into the specifics of staffing and budgeting.

TWO "THRESHOLD" WORDS

There are two "threshold" words that practitioners of effective communications today must keep in mind.

The first is *Competition*, and the second is *Technology*. Competition, which is being driven largely by the inexorable world-wide move toward global markets, means that your public relations function must, in turn, become more effective in two ways. One, your messages themselves must be more effective if they are to be heard — and listened to — above a rising, worldwide cacophony of diverse voices, all competing to be heard.

But the cacophony can also be thought of as good news for P.R. practitioners because it implies a more important role for your communications. That applies whether you are supporting a product, providing consumer information, responding to government officials or the news media, or raising funds for worthy charitable, civic, or cultural causes. Put another way, competition will make good communications count... and it will penalize poor communications.

Two — and this in some ways is the bad news — is that your messages or information must be delivered in more cost-effective ways. That is, you will be expected — no, required — to deliver more P.R. bang for the buck.

The second of the two threshold words for you to keep in mind is *technology*, which can be both a bane and a blessing. A bane because it helps give rise to the din of so many voices, a blessing because it is opening up all kinds of exciting new communications channels to you.

So, with *competition* and *technology* forming a collective and

changing background, or what might be called "a framework for speculation," let's consider in some detail the staffing and budgeting of your
public relations function or department.

STAFFING THE PUBLIC RELATIONS FUNCTION

To staff the public relations function properly, you must consider
three important questions:

1. Where should you locate the public relations department on
   your organizational chart?
2. What communications tasks and responsibilities do you plan to
   assign to the department?
3. How many qualified people do you need to meet and carry out
   those responsibilities and assignments?

On the Organization Chart.

Let's begin with the first question. The growing competition that
virtually all companies and organizations are facing today strongly
suggests that communications, broadly defined, is or should be a management function. It must be treated the same way that finance, law,
manufacturing, and marketing are treated — as management functions.
If you accept that premise, then it follows that the P.R. people who are
charged with communications responsibilities must have reasonable
access to top management. hat, in turn, means the P.R. function must
be located near the top of your organizational chart and must report
directly to top management.

You need to put it there for several reasons. First, competent public relations professionals can and should provide input to management's deliberations and policy-making decisions. They should act like
the company's (or organization's) eyes and ears, and monitor and evaluate the opinions and views of key audiences toward the company. You
must be knowledgeable and up to date on what key audiences or
"publics" know (or think they know) about your organization, if you
expect to communicate effectively with them.

One of the more effective approaches to keeping on top of public
opinion — and using changes in opinion as an input to the formulation
of public relations policies and programs — is that employed by the
investor-owned electric utilities in the United States. Moreover, they
have been doing it effectively for more than four decades at the national, state, and local levels.

Nationally, the Edison Electric Institute, the utilities' trade association, has an opinion-monitoring mechanism that is virtually continuous, geographically discriminate, and produces information in real
time and in short order.

Locally and at the state level, individual utilities do much the
same thing. Western Resources, the parent company of Kansas Gas and
Electric Company, and The Kansas Power and Light Company, pro-

vides an outstanding example in this respect. Western Resources Executive Vice President Carl M. Koupal points out that public-opinion monitoring is used not only to keep track of the public's views of the company, but also as an adjunct to the competitive marketing of its electricity, gas and energy-related services.

"You must understand," Koupal says, "that we are literally a market- and customer service-driven company. Because our customers are in large measure also our public, it is critically important that we know not only what they know and think about us at any given time, but also that we be able to identify early on any economic, social, or political developments that may influence or change their opinions about us, and by extension, our products and services.

"That continually incoming information — we call it customer research — is shared at all levels of the company — from the CEO down through our middle management and marketing people, and when necessary, down to the interface with customers and the public — our line crews and meter readers."

A second reason for putting P.R. near the top of the organizational chart is that proximity to top management should help you understand better management's goals and policies, and to develop and implement more effective P.R. programs in support of those goals and objectives.

The close-proximity-to-top-management principle also applies to the agency/client relationship. More than 35 years of P.R. practice has made it abundantly clear that in order for an agency to be effective, it must have access to the client's top management because that's where the decisions are made. And the agency, like the internal P.R. staff, needs to understand firsthand where management is coming from, and where it wants to go, if it is to help the company or organization get there with effective communications.

Third, much of your work will be in areas of direct concern to top management — shareholder and investor relations, employee communications, news media contact and relations, corporate publications, community relations, fund-raising in the case of not-for-profits, and possibly government relations.[1] Clearly, having a direct reporting relationship with top management will facilitate your work in these areas.

Finally, being near the top of the management hierarchy should help you to lower what might be called your organization's "response time" to take advantage of communications opportunities or to respond to challenges and crises.

And response time has another dimension: If it is rapid, it is a potential competitive advantage because it allows you, like the great Confederate General Nathan Bedford Forrest, "to git thar fustest with the mostest," thereby increasing your chances of winning ... or at least, prevailing. Conversely, a slow response time can be an enormous and sometimes decisive competitive disadvantage, perhaps enough to knock you out of the game. In a quickly changing competitive arena, a slow response time could mean that by the time you address the problem or issue, it has changed, or even has ceased to exist!

It is not surprising, therefore, that the unwieldy bureaucracy — where the slow response was invented — is yielding everywhere to the leaner, rapid-response, market-driven organization.

By placing the P.R. function near the top of your organizational chart, you will be following the accumulated wisdom and experience of many organizations, large and small, profit and not-for-profit, private-sector and government, for most of the last 50 years.

Some examples of these kinds of organizations include: Ford Motor Company; Bristol-Myers Squibb; Western Resources; Pacific Gas and Electric Company; Procter & Gamble; The American Red Cross; and The Nature Conservancy. In government, from the White House to the state house to city hall, the ubiquitous communications people are always at the top, which is to say, at their chief's side.

Your actual reporting relationship to top management will, of course, vary with the size and nature of your company or organization. Ideally, you should report directly to and work with the chief executive officer, and in very small companies and organizations, that should be the arrangement. Alternatively — and this is frequently the case in medium-size firms — the senior P.R. person will report to the chief operating officer or the executive vice president.

Staffing.

This brings us to the second staffing question: What communications tasks and responsibilities do you plan to assign to your new or reorganized public relations department?

To answer that, you should begin by identifying or classifying the functions or services that the department will be expected to perform. Current public relations practice suggests that they include at least the following:

1. *Counseling*. You should be prepared to offer management advice and counsel on problems and issues that affect — or are likely to affect — your company or organization. This advice and counsel should be an input to corporate policy- and decision-making. Your recommendations may cover everything from the best way to communicate a specific piece of information, to changing company policies, to publishing or producing printed and/or visual materials that will support the company's or organization's goals.

   Consider the value of wise P.R. counsel in the following example, which took place in one variation or another in many corporate boardrooms across the country during the past three decades.

   Today's pervasive and effective environmental movement

began in the mid-1960s as a thrust toward preserving and restoring much of our country's "natural beauty." This nascent effort gathered strength and political impetus from *The White House Conference on Natural Beauty* in 1964. It was very clear to any astute observer that this movement was becoming a "motherhood" issue, that is, one that would be difficult to confront head-on or to ignore.

Furthermore, it assumed a legitimacy derived directly from people's everyday experiences and observations. After all, we *had* polluted many of our rivers and lakes. We *had* scarred the land and failed to restore left it. We *had* fouled the air in many of our cities and towns.

The perceived public and political wisdom of the time was that the environment had to be cleaned up and the country was wealthy enough to pay for it. Few people gave much thought to the *costs* of cleaning up. Those costs, we discovered over time and often too late, were astronomical and in many cases unaffordable. Informed and intelligent public relations and public affairs people began counseling their managements to focus the public dialogue on a benefits-to-cost approach; that is, to try to determine whether the putative environmental and social *benefits* of a proposed law or regulation were greater than its economic costs. This was an alternative to direct opposition to environmental laws and regulations. Moreover — and this is important — it implied a message to the public and government that said, in effect, as business people are *not* against clean air, clean water, and restored lands; what they want is to achieve the cleanups in an economically sound way. Put another way, it shifted the debate from *ends* to *means*, and means are usually more open to negotiation and compromise than are ends.

2. *Communications Services.* These cover a wide range of activities that collectively amount to your company's "voice," and they are those that most people frequently associate with P.R. Communications services typically include such activities/projects/programs as drafting and putting out news releases and announcements; editing and producing organizational publications — annual and quarterly reports; employee communications, including magazines and videos; speech writing and speaker placement; preparation and dissemination of testimony for legislative or regulatory hearings (if the department also has a government affairs responsibility); community relations, and, of course, contacting and dealing with the news media.

3. *Issues Analysis.* As the words imply, this is the process of monitoring and analyzing public issues that will or could affect your organization. In some respects it is the other side of the coin of communication services. It involves gathering information from

sources outside your company or organization and analyzing it for management, rather than disseminating management's information or views to external audiences. In your role as an issues analyst, you can expect to work frequently with your organization's legal counsel and government affairs people. Your continuing purpose here may well be to bring a broader view or interpretation to the analysis of an issue than would a lawyer, whose focus is largely (sometimes exclusively) a legal one; or the government-affairs specialist who thinks principally in legislative and political terms.

Put another way, you may be expected to bring a longer-term *strategic* perspective to an issue versus a near-term tactical one.

Consider the following real-world example. A senior public relations counselor had occasion to work recently on a product-liability issue with his client's lawyers and government affairs people. A federal regulatory agency banned one of the client's products, except for certain uses, but stopped short of saying it was not safe. The client pulled the product from the market, although a gathering body of credible independent the scientific research pointed toward its safety, ceased manufacturing it, and had no plans to re-enter that business. The lawyer's primary focus was to limit the company's financial liability for those products already in use. The government-relations folk concentrated on getting the regulatory ban lifted through congressional action.

While the P.R. counselor shared those concerns, he felt the client might get hanged on its own petard: the company could be seen as pushing hard to lift a ban on a product it was no longer making and selling, and would not resume making and selling even if the ban were lifted. "Why," a disinterested observer might then ask, "do you care about the ban?"

The answer was that the client *had* to care for several important reasons. First, a continuing government ban cast a shadow of questionable or uncertain safety about its products already in use, and the client wanted to assure the public that they were safe. That safety was confirmed repeatedly by a growing body of scientific evidence. Second, the client believed that the ban was an undeserved black mark on its as a responsible maker and seller of ethical products. Third, the ban had the effect of increasing the company's exposure in product liability suits, whether or not it has been justified. Finally, the ban posed a cloud of uncertainty over the publicly held company in the financial community. Security analysts frequently asked whether the ban carried a significant price tag, and how that might affect earnings. For these reasons we recommended that the client try to get the ban lifted, but to do so discreetly and by working with other companies that were also adversely affected by the ban. The company has taken that approach, but as of this writing the issue has not been resolved.

4. *Special Projects, Programs.* You can and should expect from your public relations department a certain creative-cum-proactive ability that results in special P.R. projects and activities. In addition to creating or maintaining visibility or goodwill for your company or organization, these special projects are intended to exploit special opportunities or to address specific situations, problems and challenges. Examples: company-sponsored seminars and conferences on timely issues; fund-raising events; cause-related philanthropy; other activities that will elicit favorable public attitudes toward your organization but that are overtly non-commercial in nature. Examples would include: the *Annual Energy Efficiency Forum* in Washington, sponsored by Johnson Controls; and the ongoing series of conferences for utility executives sponsored by the Public Utilities Reports, a trade publishing house. Both of these are planned and carried by outside agencies.

How Many People.

Finally, the third and very important question that brings us to the heart of this chapter: How many qualified people do you need to carry out your communications responsibilities and assignments?

Inasmuch as companies and organizations vary so widely in size and purpose, it is neither possible nor desirable to take a "one size fits all" approach to setting up and staffing your P.R. department. On the other hand, it is clearly beyond the scope of this handbook to anticipate every organizational contingency or nuance that might affect the structure of your department.

Therefore, we have elected to focus on the small and medium-sized companies or organizations that plan to establish a P.R. department from scratch or want to modify an existing one to meet the organization's changing communications needs in an increasingly competitive world. We can safely assume that large companies and organizations have already addressed this problem:

Small Firms: The P.R. Options.

The size and organization of a small company P.R. department will depend on (a) the size and resources of the company itself, and (b) on the tasks assigned to it. P.R. departments in very small organizations can range from a one-person operation to those employing five or six people.

Moreover, the senior P.R. person may have public relations as his or her sole responsibility or he or she might be a senior executive whose primary responsibility is in another management area and who supervises public relations as a collateral responsibility.

Also, it is quite common among small firms or organizations to "outsource" some of their P.R. capabilities by retaining public relations agencies for services and/or counsel.

The advantages of outsourcing are several. First of all, the agency can usually bring a wider range of contacts and resources into play than can the small company or organization, and this can mean a better work product.

Second, the client does not have to devote what may be relatively large resources — principally staff time — to a one-time, one-of-a-kind project. The client does not have to divert these resources away from his or her main concern — the company's business or in the case of a non-profit organization, its principal mission.

The principal alleged disadvantage — and this may not be true in most cases — is that using an agency generally costs more than managing the project internally. While the initial cost outlay may be greater using an agency, doing so might be quite cost-competitive in the long run. Because if all client costs — such as allocated overheads and opportunity costs (the dollar value of what the staff would otherwise be doing, if it were not engaged in the project) — are taken into account, the cost gap narrows, may disappear, or even become a benefit.

What should the organizational chart of the P.R. department of a small firm or organization look like? Since there is no single answer, you should structure the department in a way that best suits your company's communications requirements and resources.

Exhibit 2.1 illustrates the set-up for a one-person department. Inasmuch as you do not need an organization table for one person, other than to show to whom he or she reports, this figure focuses on the functions or tasks that one person can reasonably be expected to perform.

EXHIBIT 2.1 — ORGANIZATION CHART: THE ONE-PERSON DEPARTMENT

PUBLIC RELATIONS DIRECTOR
Media Contact and Relations
Employee Communications
Community Relations
Product Publicity
Marketing Communications
Company Publications
Company Support for Charities, Civic and Cultural Organizations

Let's look now at several of your options in structuring and staffing a P.R. department of, say, five to six people — again for a small company or organization.

Keeping our four classifications of activities in mind — counseling, communications services, issues analysis, and special projects — how would a five-to six-person P.R. department look? Exhibits 2.2 and 2.3 offer two possibilities. Exhibit 2.2 assumes that the government-affairs function is domiciled in the P.R. department; Exhibit 2.3 assumes that it is staffed separately, either by a company official or an outside agency. Exhibit 2.4 shows what a typical five- to six-person department might look like for a modest not-for-profit organization, such as a local charity or hospital.

Medium-Size Firms: More Options.

For the medium-size company or organization, the typical public relations department will have between 12-25 people.

The ratio of professionals to support staff becomes an increasingly important efficiency parameter as the staff grows larger. During the past decade, this ratio has increased in many organizations; that is, there has been a trend toward employing fewer support staff for each professional. It can be explained, at least in part, by the ever-growing applications of computer and telecommunications technologies in public relations practice. The growth of word processing, computer-generated messages and mailing lists, faxes, e-mail, voice-mail, cellular telephones, and beepers has replaced in some measure the secretaries, stenographers, mailing-list compilers, and messengers of P.R.'s earlier days.

The staffing of a medium-size P.R. department, like that for the small organization, begins with deciding what role(s) you want the department to play. The medium-sized department will do all the things and more that the smaller organization does, and it will do them in greater depth and detail.

For example, the medium-sized P.R. department may be part of a publicly owned company, the shares of which are traded on one of the stock exchanges. That means it will have a responsibility to communicate with shareholders, the financial and investment community, the Securities and Exchange Commission, and the business/financial press. The smaller P.R. department, which probably is part of a privately held company, does not have any of these investor or financial relations responsibilities.

Exhibit 2.5 illustrates the organization of a typical medium-size public relations department that has government affairs as an integral part of its responsibilities.

Exhibit 2.6 illustrates a medium-size P.R. department in an organization in which government affairs is a separate but integrated function. Note that the two functions are brought together at a senior management level.

Finally, Exhibit 2.7 shows the organizational set-up for a medium-size not-for-profit entity — in this case, a hospital — in which the emphasis is on "Development" (a euphemism for fund-raising), and on public and community relations.

THE ROLE OF THE P.R. AGENCY

No discussion that addresses staffing the public relations function would be complete without talking about the roles the department might assign to a public relations agency.

All qualified full-service agencies are staffed and equipped to offer clients all of the four classifications of services previously mentioned, and to do it in any combination or mix that best suits the client's needs and resources.

That said, it needs to be added that most clients use agencies more for three of those services — counseling, issues analysis, and special projects or programs.

Counseling is premier service of many P.R. firms. You could turn to an agency to provide you with an independent — that is, disinterested, third-party, but informed — view of what your firm should or could do in a difficult problem or situation. The benefits can be twofold. First, the agency may be able to provide fresh insights or a new approach to the problem. For example, the chief executive officer of a major utility company was counseled not to make himself available to the news media while a rate case was being considered by the state regulatory commission, and was being covered by the news media. If he took a position or made a statement, it would be much more difficult to modify it, or back off from it, than if it were made by a spokesperson lower in the management echelon. The recommendation, which he accepted, was to let the senior P.R. person, who was well known to the media, do the talking.

Second, the agency may confirm or challenge your proposed course of action or response. You can use it as a testing ground for proposed policies or actions before "going public" with them. Either way, you and your organization benefit.

Much the same can be said for the qualified agency in "issue analysis." Most agencies have on staff senior people who have experience in analyzing public issues similar to the ones your organization faces. You can tap into that "experience base" on an as-needed basis conveniently and probably much less expensively than you can by adding comparably experienced people to your own staff.

Finally, you can use agencies cost-effectively as a temporary, as-needed extension of your staff for special projects and programs. For example, a small or a medium-size firm will, in all probability, not have on staff a project coordinator who is experienced in setting up and

EXHIBIT 2.2 — ORGANIZATION CHART:
SMALL COMPANY INTEGRATED PUBLIC RELATIONS/GOVERNMENT RELATIONS DEPARTMENT

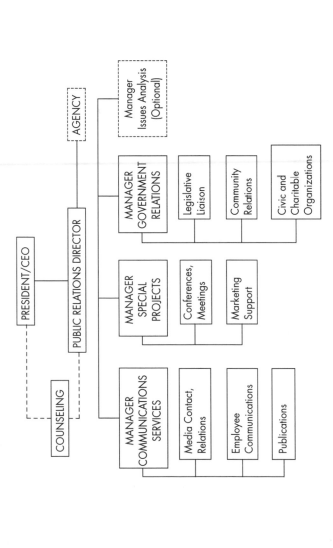

EXHIBIT 2.3 — ORGANIZATION CHART:
SMALL COMPANY PUBLIC RELATIONS DEPARTMENT (SEPARATE GOVERNMENT AFFAIR FUNCTION)

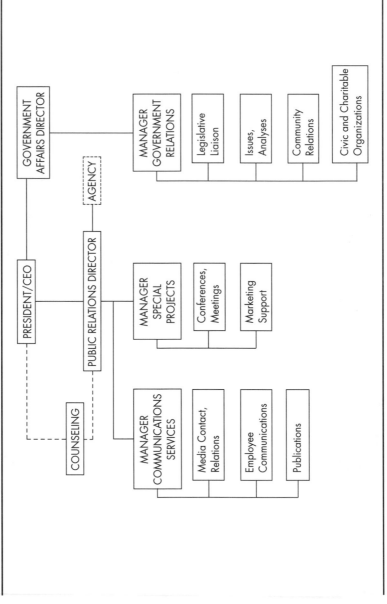

EXHIBIT 2.4 — ORGANIZATION CHART: MODEST-SIZE NOT-FOR-PROFIT ORGANIZATION

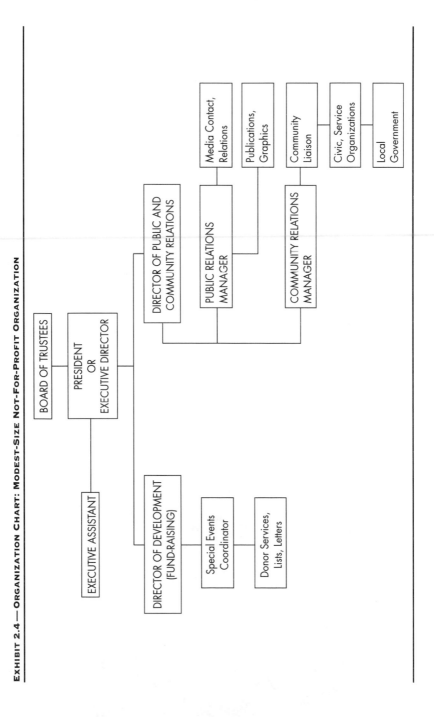

EXHIBIT 2.5 — ORGANIZATION CHART: MEDIUM-SIZE COMPANY INTEGRATED CORPORATE COMMUNICATIONS/GOVERNMENT AFFAIRS

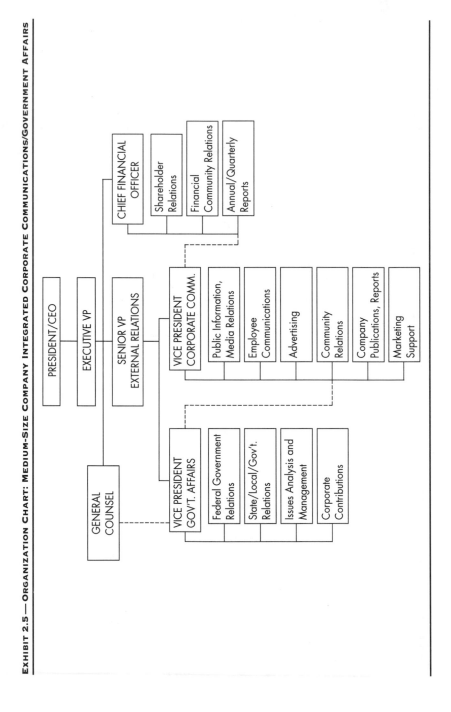

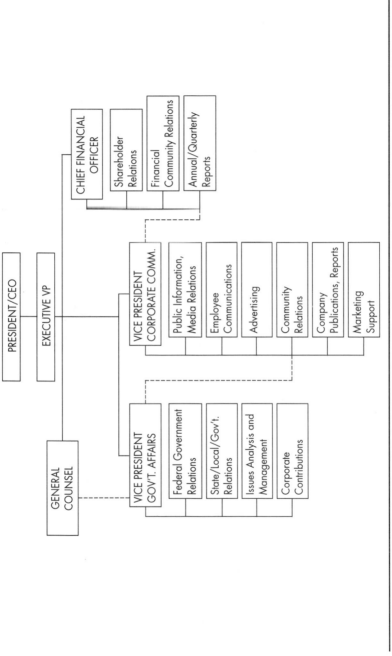

EXHIBIT 2.6 — ORGANIZATION CHART: MEDIUM-SIZE COMPANY SEPARATE CORPORATE COMMUNICATIONS AND GOVERNMENT AFFAIRS

PRESIDENT/CEO

EXECUTIVE VP

GENERAL COUNSEL

CHIEF FINANCIAL OFFICER

Shareholder Relations

Financial Community Relations

Annual/Quarterly Reports

VICE PRESIDENT CORPORATE COMM.

Public Information, Media Relations

Employee Communications

Advertising

Community Relations

Company Publications, Reports

Marketing Support

VICE PRESIDENT GOV'T. AFFAIRS

Federal Government Relations

State/Local/Gov't. Relations

Issues Analysis and Management

Corporate Contributions

EXHIBIT 2.7 — ORGANIZATION CHART: MODEST-SIZE NOT-FOR-PROFIT HOSPITAL

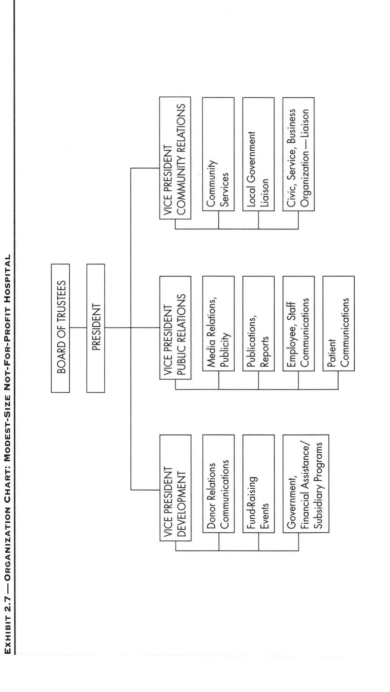

BOARD OF TRUSTEES

PRESIDENT

VICE PRESIDENT DEVELOPMENT
- Donor Relations Communications
- Fund-Raising Events
- Government, Financial Assistance/ Subsidiary Programs

VICE PRESIDENT PUBLIC RELATIONS
- Media Relations, Publicity
- Publications, Reports
- Employee, Staff Communications
- Patient Communications

VICE PRESIDENT COMMUNITY RELATIONS
- Community Services
- Local Government Liaison
- Civic, Service, Business Organization — Liaison

running company-sponsored meetings or conferences. It will almost always be more effective to "farm out" special activities and projects like these than to try to handle them in-house. Moreover, if the agency's project coordinator is experienced and well qualified, you probably will get a better end-product.

The questions, then, which the small or medium-size P.R. department head should ask when considering an agency are these:

- Does the agency bring to the table some special capability or qualification which I need but do not now have on staff?
- Are my needs for counsel, issue analysis, or special projects one-time needs or are they likely to be continuing?
- Are my company's problems or issues important enough to justify the costs of seeking an independent analysis or view of them?
- Will it be more cost effective to retain an agency, or can we do the job internally and still get the same quality of results?

Your answers to these questions will help you to decide whether or not you should go outside for help.

Several of the charts that accompany this chapter will show a dotted-line relationship with an outside agency. The purpose is to show where the agency fits into the scheme of things. Its inclusion should not be taken as an implicit recommendation to retain an outside P.R. firm.

So much for staffing the public relations function or department. Let's turn now to the second and equally important subject of this chapter: Budgeting.

BUDGETING THE PUBLIC RELATIONS FUNCTION

Most companies and organizations are very reluctant to talk about, much less reveal, their public relations budgets. Consequently, there are few articles written about budgets and even fewer publicized budget figures. However, a review of the somewhat sparse literature does reveal that many companies and not-for-profits use one of five approaches to establishing the amounts they plan to spend on public relations during a given year. These approaches are:

- *Last year, more or less.* This is probably the simplest approach of all. Management takes the dollars budgeted last year, then adds or subtracts some incremental amount. That increment may be purely arbitrary, but it is more likely to be some function of the projected increase (or decrease) in the coming year's business.
- *A percentage of sales or revenues.* The P.R. budget is set at some percentage — usually less than 1 percent — of the past year's revenues or forecast revenues for the coming year.
- *"Management says."* This is simple also, and arbitrary. Management sets the budget amount, and the P.R. department

lives within it. This approach is rapidly becoming passé because it lacks both foresight and flexibility. One sees it used in small companies and organizations that generally have little, if any, P.R. experience.

- *Zero-based budgeting.* This fourth method is task- or project-oriented. The P.R. staff identifies all the projects and activities to be implemented during the year, assigns individual costs to them, then totals those costs, plus a contingency amount, to arrive at a departmental budget.
- *Future-based budgeting.* Future-based budgeting[2] is the most complex approach and it involves seven steps or procedures:
  1. Determine what and where management wants the organization to be in 5 and/or 10 or more years;
  2. Identify the strengths as well as the weaknesses of the organization;
  3. Identify possible environmental constraints on actions and projects; and societal constraints, such as attitudes, opinions, and behavior of the organization's key publics;
  4. Specify those actions that are necessary to overcome weaknesses and to take advantage of opportunities;
  5. Use a cost/benefit analysis to assign priorities to prospective projects, programs, and activities;
  6. Select the high-priority items, prepare specific tactical plans for the current year and outline plans for future years; and
  7. Prepare departmental budgets based on the estimated costs of the high-priority programs and activities.

The first three approaches to setting up a P.R. budget are the most common, perhaps because they are easy. But because they are backward-looking and, in the third case, arbitrary, they cannot take into account the organization's future or projected needs. It can also be argued that they do not allow or help the organization to grow. The third method — management fiat — is the embodiment of "P.R. as a *cost*" thinking, with no value assigned to its potential contribution.

Indeed, future-based budgeting was developed to help correct that misconception. The process of identifying worthwhile P.R. projects and assigning a dollar figure to each of them implies a benefit for the company or organization. More often than not, these P.R. benefits are intangible so estimating that value in dollars is difficult, but you have to try in order to justify them with a benefit-to-cost rationale that is acceptable to management.

Preparing a realistic public relations budget involves making two estimates for your department's activities. You must estimate:

1. *The cost of your staff's time* in planning and implementing the activity or project. This estimate will be a function of the compensation of each staff member involved. You will have to

determine an hourly rate for each, which can be calculated by dividing the staffer's annual compensation plus an overhead factor, divided by a realistic number of working hours in a year, usually between 1700 and 1800.[3]

2. *The related expenses*—These include out-of-pocket disbursements, production costs, etc.—that can be associated with the project or activity. Out-of-pocket expenses include such items as postage, telephone and faxes, travel, delivery and messenger services, and similar items. Production costs include printing, graphics, photography, and art.

You can apply the billing rate(s) and related costs to your P.R. operations, regardless of the size of the department. Exhibit 2.8 is a hypothetical budget calculation sheet for a small (5 to 6 people) department. It shows the billing rates for three professionals; the staff time costs for four typical public relations activities; and the related expense categories. It is intended as a model you can adapt to establish your own budget.

Note that is not set up for a specific period—a month, quarter, or year. While you will have to prepare a yearly budget for planning purposes, you can also use this format for actual monthly or quarterly expenses. Then, using these real (not estimated) costs, you can adjust your projected figures for the balance of the year.

To track staff time devoted to specific P.R. projects and activities, you can borrow a leaf from agency practice: have your staff complete and turn in time sheets on a regular periodic basis. Properly designed timesheets can tell not only how much total staff time is being used, but also how time is being spent.

Exhibit 2.9 is a typical timesheet used by a medium-size agency; it has been modified for a comparably sized P.R. staff of a company or organization.

You can and should use your budgeting and tracking procedures to run your P.R. department on a more businesslike basis. By comparing the projected versus actual staff times and costs of individual employees for your department's projects, you can begin to gauge their respective capabilities, productivity, and talents.

This, in turn, will help you allocate assignments to the staff for improved efficiencies and cost-effectiveness. It will help you decide who can handle responsibility and who cannot. It can provide guidelines for who should be promoted and given raises or bonuses. It can be immensely helpful in measuring and tracking your department's performance.

Finally, it will enable you to gauge—beyond merely guessing—the value-added contribution your public relations department makes to your company's or organization's overall performance and mission.

Your management colleagues, then, will have to begin thinking of public relations as a value-added service and not merely as a cost.

EXHIBIT 2.8—TYPICAL BUDGET CALCULATIONS FOR SEVEN-PERSON PR DEPARTMENT

| STAFFING COSTS | | | | ACTIVITIES–PROJECTS–PROGRAMS | | | | |
Name/Position	Annual Compensation	Time OH Factor	Hourly Rate	Media Relations/Contacts, Placement	Special Projects/Conferences, Meetings	Writing Speeches, Articles, Publications	Counseling/Planning	Total Staff Cost Per Individual
Joe White Director	$75,000	$150,000	$110					
Sally Black Exec. Asst.	$25,000	50,000	$35					
Fred Green Professional	$45,000	90,000	$65					
Earl Gray Professional	$45,000	90,000	$65					
Pamela Blau Senior Professional	$55,000	$110,000	$80					
2 Secretaries @$18,000	$36,000	72,000	$50					
	Annual Staff Cost by Activity							

*Hourly rates computed at 1400 hours/year rounded to nearest $5/hour

EXHIBIT 2.9—XYZ COMPANY PUBLIC RELATIONS DEPARTMENT TIME SHEET

Name: _____
Employee No.: _____
Week of: _____

PR ACTIVITIES

	Media Relations Contacts, Placement	Special Projects, Meetings, Conferences	Writing— Speeches, Articles, Publications	Counseling/ Planning	Miscellaneous (Specify)	Daily Hours
Sunday						
Monday						
Tuesday						
Wednesday						
Thursday						
Friday						
Saturday						
Total Weekly Hours/Activity						

Notes: 1. Record time to nearest half-hour
2. Specify "Miscellaneous" time by Activity, Program, or Project
3. Use charge codes where appropriate

NOTES

1. Government relations is frequently a separate function in many companies and organizations, but the need for a close working relationship between public relations and government relations is obvious. Public relations must, through good communications, develop, build, and maintain public, constituent, and media support for your company's legislative or regulatory objectives in Washington, the state house, and in city hall.

2. The author is indebted to Professor David McNabb for his lucid explanation of future-based budgeting. See McNabb, David. "Future-Based Budgeting," *Public Relations Journal* (October 1982): 24.

3. A distinction needs to be made here. Working hours can be used by the client as a basis for calculating an internal "billing rate." An agency, however, must compute its rates on an assumed number of hours; i.e., hours actually spent on a client's business. Billable hours typically run 1,400-1,500 a year.

A. Joseph Dodson joined The Dilenschneider Group in August 1994 as an associate, and was named a principal in December 1995.

Dodson's responsibilities include the development and support of strategic public relations programs for a broad range of clients in industries including telecommunications, information and financial services, chemicals and pharmaceuticals.

He previously worked as general assignment reporter for The Brazosport Facts, a daily newspaper on the upper Texas coast, and The Advocate, a southwest Houston news weekly. Most recently at The Brazosport Facts, his coverage included concentrations in petrochemical manufacturing, utilities, and health and environmental issues.

Mr. Dodson is an honors graduate of The George Washington University, where he majored in American Literature.

CHAPTER 3

MEASURING PROBLEMS AND RESULTS IN PUBLIC RELATIONS

Intel never knew what hit it.

In the winter of 1994, Intel customers identified an obscure flaw in the company's heavily promoted Pentium chip, affecting a fraction of the company's users and only a small portion of the computations most of those customers might be expected to perform. The company, perhaps seeing the flaw as a molehill that could quickly swell into a mountainous problem, downplayed its severity and required customers to present proof that they were among the minority of users whose calculations demanded the accuracy of the flawless product before granting replacement chips.

Intel committed one of the most high-profile public relations gaffes of the year in part because the company's senior people felt that the relatively minor nature of the flaw could be used to measure the depth of the company's public relations problem. Instead of reassuring users about the product, Intel's response cast doubt on the company's commitment to its customers and its willingness to stand behind its products.

Ultimately, Intel was forced to recall its Pentium chips at a potential cost of $475 million.

Intel's problem was far from unique. Instinct and guesswork frequently guide decisions in public relations, despite a growing recognition of the value of solid research. Research can be expensive and time consuming, and the speed of communications and the pressures of competition often require immediate decisions.

But time and competition notwithstanding, few businesses can afford to risk their health on a scattershot approach to P.R. At best, forging ahead with a poor understanding of the problem risks precious resources on a misdirected campaign. At worst, there is a real risk of aggravating the problem through misunderstanding. It pays to conduct a little research and think things through.

As frequently as corporations and public relations counselors fail to measure the problem, there is often an even greater reluctance to attempt to measure results. A 1988 survey of public relations and corporate communications executives by Ketchum Communications found that fully 41 percent of all public relations executives believe measuring the impact of public relations in precise terms is, "next to impossible." In a telling comment, Walter Lindenmann, Ketchum's senior vice president and director of research, found it encouraging that the percentage of skeptics wasn't higher. Even today, measuring results is undertaken as an afterthought much more often than it is built into the goals of public relations programs.

Often, the root of this reluctance can probably be traced to the intangible nature of the product. No one has ever produced a box of P.R., something that can be measured, weighed, packaged, and shelved. The tools of the trade are words and ideas, and the products are understanding and persuasion. At the most basic level, results in public relations are measured not with copy inches in a newspaper or share of mind captured in a survey, but through the behavior of people. In order to measure true results in public relations, you have to link that behavior to the elements of your program, which is much more easily said than done.

RESEARCH OBJECTIVES

That reluctance is unfortunate, because there have never been so many tools, techniques, and research professionals available to the field. Technology and a growing appreciation for the value of research in public relations are driving rapid changes in the way the industry measures problems and results. Moreover, there is a well-established core of market research professionals that can and should be called upon for counseling and leg work in projects that require a large sample of the population, very specific research targets, or in situations such as a focus group, where the researcher must be extremely careful not to influence the results with his or her own biases in the presentation of questions and in their analysis.

That said, the objectives of public relations research are relatively straightforward—typically either to assist in the planning of a public relations campaign or to evaluate its results. Specifically, this can involve:

- **Establishing a baseline of information about how an issue, company, or product is perceived,** either as a foundation for a campaign or as a fixed point from which to measure results through subsequent research. In many ways, this is a fundamental step in any campaign or even a new relationship with a client or employer, and should inform and enhance virtually every step undertaken on their behalf. This basic research should involve:
  1. Defining a company's most important public constituencies;
  2. Discovering the "hot-button" issues a product or event is likely to run up against; and
  3. Giving an accurate scope and importance to potential or actual public relations problems.
- **Measuring a change in a previously established set of data to chart the effects of public relations activity.** Such changes might be measured through an increase in media coverage of a company or product, greater understanding about an

issue, acceptance of a company's point of view, or simply greater success in meeting an institution's objectives, such as sales growth for a corporation, increased donations for a non-profit organization, or the election of a political candidate.

• **Shedding light on the trends, attitudes, or events behind a known situation.** For example, a *Fortune* 100 company recently was featured in a front-page piece in *The Wall Street Journal* alleging that the company targeted malnourished addicts of crack cocaine as a market for an athletic nutritional supplement packaged as a vanilla shake. The initial basis for the story was traced to *The Source*, a magazine covering rap music and culture, which included the product in a list of "36 things that blew up because of crack."

There is a school of thought that teaches that anything worthwhile in business can and should be measured and broken down into exhaustive statistics. However, dense statistical analyses, charts, and formulas generally fail to shed light on the big picture: how a public thinks and feels about an issue, product, or event. Statistics can describe behavior — the loyalty of 13- to 18-year-old boys to a brand of soft drink, for example — but they fall short when it comes to explaining the thoughts and feelings that motivate behavior. Nor can they capture the give and take of ideas that characterize effective public relations.

A better approach to the problem might be defined as "organized listening," in the words of Boston P.R. consultant Kitty Ward. Instead of statistics, research should be conducted to discover the issues and themes that are important to an audience, the language it uses, and how public relations impacts its understanding and acceptance of a client's point of view.

THE TOOLS OF THE TRADE

The essential research tools of public relations — media and database searches, surveys, and focus groups, among others — are relatively simple. However, research should be planned with the same care as the publicity program itself, and often requires the same measure of creativity. Care must be taken that:

• **Research is focused on the proper audience.** A broad survey that is representative of the general public probably won't help a corporation looking for help recruiting minority employees;

• **The research tool captures information relevant to the problem at hand.** Simply put, the research should have clearly stated goals that either address a program's objectives or evaluate its results; and

• **The results of a research project do not exaggerate or understate the importance of a public relations problem**

or a program's results. If most of a company's recent media coverage is focused on labor problems in east Texas, for instance, it's easy to tell the client that their image has been tarnished by the dispute. But if this coverage was entirely confined to local newspapers, the client should probably be more concerned about a lack of coverage in the larger business publications that could affect its performance in the marketplace and on Wall Street.

Whatever the objectives of a research project, there are a variety of strategies, techniques, and commercial services that can help you get the data you need. What follows is an overview of some of the most commonly used tools and their most effective applications.

Media Searches/Data Retrieval

Media searches and reviews of other types of public data are among the most fundamental research tools available to public relations, and can be among the most important. A distinct industry has grown up in the past decade to create, service, and provide computer access to databases of news clippings, investment research, SEC filings, and other information. Accessing this type of information now is as simple as typing a few keywords into a database to scan for news clippings or files that contain references to your search targets. All that is needed is a computer and modem, although for heavy use a high-speed dedicated connection to the service can be more cost-effective and efficient.

The database of information available about a company becomes its public history, and that history is updated with each news story, press release, quarterly earnings report, and trading day on the stock market. Such news coverage and other materials are often the fastest way to measure the public's prior exposure to a company, but it should not be confused with public opinion itself. Database searches measure a dialogue consisting of press coverage, stock market analyses, and the company's own news releases. But journalists, analysts, and corporations undeniably do lead public opinion.

The scope and content of the database information provides a valuable thumbnail sketch of what the public has been told about a given subject. The content tells us what has been previously written; what hasn't been written (which can be more important); and whether the tone of coverage has been positive, negative, or neutral. The scope of coverage is a measure of how many readers would have seen the coverage, and whether they are of a general audience or belong to some more narrow group. Frequently, numbers alone are deceiving. While *The New York Times* has far more readers than *Chemical Week*, a story exposing technical problems with a new manufacturing process would probably be more detailed and carry more weight in the latter, which is read by scientists, senior executives, and investors in the chemical industry. Readers of the *Times* might or might not find the story interesting, but their ability to act on the information is much more limited.

Furthermore, as the public record of a company or institution, the database is used for background information by journalists and many others. Hence, knowing and managing its content has become an important function of public relations.

With the results of your media and data search in hand, it's a good idea to do a simple analysis of the material. Organize the stories according to subject and date of publication, and develop a few hunches on how your key audiences would have read and interpreted them. Is the information correct? Does it include the facts about a company that would appeal to investors, customers, or other audiences important to the client? How has the company responded to past crisis situations, and how were they portrayed in the media? Has the company been forthcoming with information, or has it been tight-lipped? Is the company's image one that clearly and correctly evokes its strategy and core businesses?

The answers to each of these questions and others will be crucial as you build your public relations plans and measure their results.

Once you have familiarized yourself with the contents in the database, give some thought to how you will keep up to date as the database changes. Monitor new stories, analyst reports, etc., as they are written, both to ensure that they are correct and for early warning of problems that could crop up in the future.

Some of the premium commercial sources of media and data retrieval include:

Lexis-Nexis: This is probably the granddaddy of them all. Every practitioner of public relations should be familiar with the contents of Lexis-Nexis, and if they don't know how to use it, they should make friends with someone who does. Lexis-Nexis was created in 1974, and now contains 166 libraries of various types of information. Among others, these include legal case compilations; corporate annual reports; full text of stories carried in more than 2,300 sources, including major newspapers, magazines, trade publications, and news wire services; and abstracts of articles from about 1,000 additional publications.

When using this and other services, be aware of the costs, which are generally structured to charge both for time spent online with the network and for each story retrieved. In most cases, the best initial approach is to start with a broad search that hits the major newspapers, business, and trade publications covering your subject of interest, and then follow up with a more targeted search based on your initial findings. Also, keep in mind that if you are looking for up-to-the-minute clippings, Lexis-Nexis may not be the best source. While first-tier publications are generally current, there is often a delay for less prominent sources, ranging from a few days to roughly a month.

DataTimes: Like Lexis-Nexis, DataTimes specializes in databases of stories in major news, business/financial and trade publications. As of mid 1995, DataTimes carries stories from 1,400 publications, with some overlap of Lexis-Nexis. In addition, DataTimes carries The Dun & Bradstreet Corporation's *Dun's Market Reports* on 7.2 million businesses in the United States and Canada and profiles on 10 million executives; Dow Jones stock market information; and a number of other data sources.

Dow Jones News/Retrieval: Dow Jones News/Retrieval offers access to the Dow Jones Clipping Service, carrying 1,200 publications; real-time stock quotes; up-to-date financial information on publicly traded companies; *Dun's Market Reports*; and a number of other services oriented toward users with an interest in business and financial information.

Bloomberg Business News: Bloomberg was founded in 1990 by journalist Mike Bloomberg as an online resource for investors. Since then, his operations have grown to include not only online services, but also radio and television broadcast news. As a research tool, Bloomberg's online services offers one of the broadest sources of information available about publicly traded companies. Information available through Bloomberg includes:

- Daily and historical share price, price-to-earnings rations, trading volume, significant block trades, and other timely market information about stocks, bonds, and other investments;
- Lists of investment analyst coverage and major investors by company and by industry;
- Full text of news releases by company and industry, as well as relevant press coverage by Bloomberg reporters. In addition, the service carries notices of published reports by securities firms, announcements of SEC mandated filings, and notification by company insiders of plans to buy or sell shares; and
- Technical charts and tables, used primarily by analysts to evaluate companies' performance and market potential.

In short, access to Bloomberg offers the public relations officer nearly exactly the information used by securities analysts and major investors to evaluate public companies. Moreover, once you're on the system, you have access to Bloomberg's full range of information. The service can be expensive, including the cost of a terminal and a dedicated line to access the network. But if the investment community is important to a company's business plan, Bloomberg can offer tremendous value.

First Call: First Call is a subscriber service targeted toward investors and investment analysts. The service is perhaps best used as a research tool by monitoring up-to-date news and investment analysis about a particular company or industry. First Call's top level of services includes a dedicated computer terminal and access to full-text of analyst reports on public companies, among other information. In addition, subscribers have the right to file company news releases on the system, where they reach members of the investment community throughout the world.

First Call, Lexis-Nexis, DataTimes, Dow Jones News/Retrieval, Bloomberg, and others offer the advantage of being able to access and sort large volumes of information quickly. Each offers a particular range of benefits, and what might be ideal for one company or agency could have relatively little to offer another. Furthermore, all of them are expensive. For peak levels of service, including a dedicated computer terminal and extensive, frequent database searches, a company can easily spend more than $20,000 per month. Before committing your company to a dedicated connection to any of these or other online services, consider whether your needs justify the costs. If you work with a highly visible corporation or a P.R. agency serving clients requiring real-time access to media coverage, the more expensive service probably makes sense. However, for many smaller companies and agencies, it could be that a less-expensive dial-up connection, offering much limited connection time, would serve your needs as well or better at a much lower cost.

Surveys

Although databases are a highly efficient resource for information on what has been previously published and written about a company, for the most accurate view of public opinion it is best to go directly to the source. A well-designed and executed survey can cast light in areas that are forever out of reach of the public database. After all, the objectives of P.R. are not to influence the press but to inform and persuade a public. The better you understand their ideas and opinions, the better you can design your program and measure your results.

Surveys can be used wherever there is a need to explain the motivations and attitudes driving a public's behavior, to anticipate likely reaction to an announcement, or to establish a baseline of information in order to measure the effects of a program of public relations.

The elements of a survey are the sample and the questionnaire. A sample is simply the audience targeted to be interviewed through the survey. Often the sample is designed to be representative of general population. This can be accomplished either by targeting a sample large enough that the results will reflect the overall population — a technique known as probability sampling — or by structuring the sample to contain specific demographic groups in equal proportion to their presence in the general public — which is known as quota sampling.

Alternately, your survey could be designed to reach a more targeted sample, such a group of investors with similar portfolios, or a specific demographic group. The objectives of your program will help you target an appropriate sample.

Likewise, the design of the questionnaire will be guided by the goals of the survey, but there are a few universal rules to keep in mind. Above all, keep your biases out of the process. The worst surveys are those designed not to confirm or uncover an audience's opinions but to prove a surveyor's own point of view—either to impress management or for use as a publicity tool. The former wastes resources and can lead to a misdirected campaign. The latter can and will damage your credibility and that of the industry.

In addition, be sure to review the questionnaire to ensure that neutral language is used, and that questions are worded such that they can be understood by every audience represented in the sample. Keep the questions and the questionnaire as short as possible. An over-long survey will annoy and bore the respondent. Either factor will impact the reliability of your results.

Finally, the last question of almost any survey should be designed to give respondents a chance to express their thoughts in their own words. The question can be as simple as, "Is there anything you would like to add to your answers?" Frequently, this kind of open-ended question gives respondents a chance to expand on answers they feel strongly about and touch on subjects and currents of opinion that the questionnaire misses entirely.

A wide variety of survey types exists for use in public relations, each with its own strengths and weaknesses. Used creatively, elements of several of the survey techniques that follow can be incorporated into the same research tool. Some of the most widely used survey techniques include:

Profile Surveys: Profile surveys are designed to create a mirror image of public opinion on a given issue at a given point in time. The questionnaire is typically composed of multiple choice and short-answer questions that measure a public's knowledge (or lack of knowledge) of the facts and their attitudes about what they understand to be true. A profile survey might be used if a company or organization is beginning a pubic relations campaign for the first time or contemplating action that could significantly change its public image.

Used correctly, profile surveys can build a detailed picture of public opinion and depth of feeling about a particular issue. A follow-up survey, after a period of activity, can indicate changes in public opinion and can be used as a measure of results, although care must be taken to account for other possible causes of the shift in opinion.

A typical questionnaire for a profile survey would begin by asking the respondent whether they have ever heard of the issue, company, etc., in question. A follow-up question might test that knowledge by asking the respondent to describe the issue or product in their own words. A series of questions would typically follow, asking the respondent to discuss their own involvement in the issue or to rate their positive or negative feelings. Again, both sorts of question can be structured for an open-ended or multiple-choice response. Depending on the objectives of the study, the survey might also include questions allowing the participant to suggest a solution to an issue in his or her own words, and measure their intensity of feeling about that solution on a scale of five to minus five. (See Exhibit 3.1 for an example of a profile survey.)

Soft Soundings: Frequently in public relations, the pressure for immediate action or the cost of reaching a large sample or the population will rule against profile surveys or other types of long-term research projects. In these cases, the best alternative may be to take a "soft sounding" of opinion leaders on the subject. Soft soundings can be the simplest and fastest route to an informed view of prevailing attitudes on a given topic.

Soft soundings measure the consensus among authorities and opinion leaders — stock market analysts, activists, academicians, industry leaders, and others — through fairly brief personal interviews. Typically, the sample will be limited to 15 to 20 individuals, of which perhaps 10 to 15 will agree to participate. If time pressure demands it, the entire process can be completed in about two to five days.

For example, a pharmaceutical company recently designed a soft soundings survey to measure its reputation for research and development. The company historically had avoided discussing projects in its development pipeline, and the survey would be used to justify continuing or changing that policy. The sample consisted primarily of stock market analysts and pharmaceutical journalists, about 30 in all.

The questionnaire consisted of questions that asked participants to compare five pharmaceutical companies' records in drug development, communications of their R&D programs, and, finally, about respondents' primary sources of information on the subject. The questions were open ended, designed to encourage each participant to expand on his or her answers at length. In this case, the client's identity was shielded by asking for a comparison among competing companies. This prevented answers from being influenced by a desire to shield management's feelings or to protect relationships with the company. Most importantly, the identities of the participants were kept confidential to allow them to discuss their views as frankly as possible.

Of the five companies included in the questionnaire, there was a nearly unanimous opinion that the client was the least effective in explaining its drugs development programs. More importantly, those same groups assumed that the company had little to talk about in its research pipeline, and consequently believed that its long-term performance would be lukewarm at best, despite a recent string of successes in bringing new drugs to market. Finally, the soft soundings survey proved to be a rich source of communications strategies that had been used successfully by the client's competitors to publicize their own drug development efforts. (See Exhibit 3.2 for an example of a soft soundings survey.)

Gap Surveys: A gap study overcomes some of the limitations of a traditional profile survey by focusing on the perceived "gap" between a company's current performance and the best possible performance they could be expected to achieve. Gap studies get beyond a focus on the current state of public opinion by asking respondents to offer suggestions about what and how much should be done to improve a situation, and can therefore be very useful planning aids.

Let's say the electrical utility Local Power & Lighting is interested in measuring and working to improve its reputation for environmental responsibility around its hometown. LL&P might design its gap study around the following questions:

1. How would you rate Local Power & Lighting on protecting the area's air and water quality (on a scale of 5 to –5)?
2. Explain why you give LL&P that rating.
3. How good do you think the company could get at protecting local resources (on the same scale of 5 to –5)?
4. What would LL&P have to do to achieve that level of performance?

The gap between current and ideal performance is established by the first three questions, with Question 2 stating what the perceived obstacle to that performance is. Question 4 offers a set of suggestions that the respondent believes to be both reasonable and possible.

Panel Surveys: Simply stated, a panel survey consists of a panel of participants who are sent a series of surveys over time in order to measure changes in their responses. The questions might be designed to establish a baseline and then to measure changes in public opinion after a public relations campaign or other activity. As such, they are one way of measuring results in public relations. Panel surveys might also be designed to test a panel's reaction to a variety of possible solutions to a given problem for use as a planning tool. Be aware, however, that eventually a panel's responses will begin to diverge from those of the general public because of the education it has received during the survey process.

A variation on the panel survey is known as a Delphi study.[3] The Delphi consists of a panel of authorities and representative individuals that participates in a series of perhaps three or four questionnaires. The first questionnaire is designed to be largely open ended, with broad questions that allow the panel to identify a problem or situation in their own words and suggest scenarios that might be used to correct the problem.

Ongoing questionnaires test the panel's reaction to solutions derived from its initial set of responses, and are sent only to those panelists who completed the preceding questionnaire. Delphi studies allow for direct input from a target audience, and provide a basis from which to predict reactions from various audience groups to a variety of potential scenarios. Moreover, the education panelists receive as result of the survey mimics that which the general public might receive as steps are taken to address the situation.

At times, the most challenging part of the project will be the task of identifying and reaching your sample. There are a number of ways to go about this, and for broad survey projects it may be worthwhile to bring in the assistance of a market research firm that maintains mailing lists of various demographic groups and residential areas and can assist in completing interviews.

For smaller projects, you might find that the target sample has characteristics such as a certain income range that will allow members to be identified by ZIP code. An issue-oriented sample can be targeted according to membership in various interest or activist groups. If the survey is designed to reach a broad segment of the population, it might be most efficient to post interviewers in areas where they can expect to encounter a similar cross section of the community, such as outside grocery stores or shopping malls.

Likewise, once you have targeted your sample, the survey can be conducted either by phone, through the mail, with personal interviews, or by personally dropping off surveys to be completed and returned through the mail. The least expensive of these are phone interviews or mailed questionnaires. However both have somewhat higher refusal rates as well.

Focus Groups

Focus groups are often considered the province of marketing, although they can be very useful to public relations as well. A focus group consists of a carefully targeted panel of participants who are questioned extensively on their thoughts and feelings toward a particular product, service, or issue, as well as supporting marketing and communications components. Typically, the focus group is conducted in a specially designed room that allows a team to observe and record the participants through a two-way mirror. Because of the extreme sensitivity of this type of data, the questions are typically administered by a professional with special training in leading the group.

Focus groups can be used to test a market's reaction to a new product, service, advertising or marketing campaign, or perhaps to accumulate customer input into the redesign of a product or service. In short, they are a method of pretesting products or sales materials before they go before the public on a broad scale. Focus group data can be a major component in the decision about how and even whether to proceed with a product introduction or sales campaign. Public relations executives look for much of the same information as their marketing counterparts: Who was most pleased or put off by the product? What supporting messages were most effective? What characteristics of the product were most important? These questions will be fundamental to designing a communications program to support the launch.

The focus group could also identify problems that were not anticipated by the product's marketers or designers. For instance, a company that manufactures cellular phones might assume that consumers will accept a 5 percent rate of disconnected calls. A strong negative reaction from focus group participants who had tested the phone will tell them otherwise. Further, it tells the public relations executive that consistent performance should be a key message included in the communications program.

A Word about the Internet

Few subjects since perhaps television have captured the imagination of the public relations industry like the Internet. The Internet is the global network of computers, founded in the 1960s by the U.S. National Science Foundation, which now has millions of linked computers and individual computer users. For most of its existence, the Internet was used primarily to send data between academicians, the military, and government. But within the past five years, the Internet has begun to attract millions of members of the general public, and most observers believe it will become widely commercialized within the foreseeable future.

With its relatively low cost and global reach, the Internet puts a publishing facility the likes of which Gutenberg never dreamt of into the hands of anyone with a personal computer and modem. Without exaggeration, the Internet holds the potential to dramatically change the practice of public relations. Those who ignore it do so at their peril.

Despite the seemingly endless flow of media coverage underway about the Internet, relatively little of its potential has been tapped so far. But given the pace of technology, it is in your best interest to get acquainted with the Internet and to familiarize yourself with the possibilities. The day is probably not be far off when most journalists will expect to receive press information, photos, and other materials electronically, all of which is possible today.

For P.R. researchers, the Net represents an audience of more than 30 million individuals who are already only a few key strokes away. Many of the research techniques we have discussed can be adapted to the Internet, and there many things that can be done on the Internet that can be done nowhere else. Two resources you will find important include:

The World Wide Web: For a variety of reasons, the World Wide Web is coming to define the Internet in many people's minds, and it is far and away the Internet's fastest-growing application. The Web is the first area of the Internet to combine all of its best elements. Graphics on the Web are frequently photographically sharp. So-called "hypertext markup language" (HTML) allows designers to build links into their pages that will move a user from one Web location to others on computers anywhere around the globe in seconds, without requiring the user to know a technical address.

Moreover, the technical savvy required to create Web pages is quickly falling, since most advanced word processors are incorporating the so-called HTML format that makes the construction of a Web page possible. In the very near future, the construction of a Web page will be barely more complicated than creating any other word-processed document. Web browsers — the software used to read material on the World Wide Web and to move from Web site to site on the Internet — are already extremely simple to use.

Because of the Web's ease of use and graphical capabilities, many corporations are using it to create a kind of online library of their marketing materials, and dozens of major newspapers and magazines have gone online with daily editions of their publications. Both can be useful sources of intelligence and information, but many organizations will find benefits in creating their own sites. The best Web sites attract new and repeat visitors by offering online services, entertainment, or other incentives, and that is also where some of the Web's best value as a research tool comes into play.

Most sites offering online services allow or require visitors to complete a user profile — detailing their occupation, title, computer equipment, personal, or professional interests, etc. Such surveys offer a fairly detailed demographic portrait of audiences with a strong interest in the company. Moreover, most sites contain an area where users can leave questions and comments about the Web site and the company itself, giving the general public an avenue of direct contact with the company that never before existed. In fact, an area offering users direct links to a company e-mail address can sometimes provide early-warning for developing issues.

News Groups: News groups are online forums of individuals with common interests in an endless variety of topics. The level of discussion will vary from very advanced social and scientific discussions, to sincerely motivated activist groups, to a wide field of groups focused on all things prurient — sex, conspiracy theories, patent medicine, you name it.

New groups offer some of the most valuable insights available on the Internet for the public relations researcher. It is almost a given that, whatever your topic, someone is discussing it on the Internet, and news groups can be an unparalleled source of street-level discussion. Some of the best information can be had simply by "lurking," that is, reading messages posted on relevant topics, without responding or influencing the dialogue.

If you have reason to believe that your company or product has become the focus of prolonged discussion in a news group, you are well advised to get the facts and consider a response. The Internet can be compared to an inexpensive ham radio, with the ability to broadcast to a global audience, and there is very little accountability for misinformation published online. Rumors or even outright lies can persist in cyberspace indefinitely. There are several commercial services that can assist you in navigating the Internet to find references to a particular topic, allowing you to determine if a problem exists.

Depending on the group, you might also try posting a surveys online, although this should be done with care. If such a posting violates the standards of the group, you can expected to be "spammed" with angry messages in protest for posting an off-topic message or for taking advantage of the group for advertising and marketing purposes. Worse, you could damage the reputation of your company or client in the process if the survey or posting is carelessly designed. Be aware of the potential consequences, but don't be afraid to experiment.

CONCLUSION

Researching problems and results in public relations can be expensive and to do it properly often takes time. But given what is at stake, forsaking that investment is often false economy. Moreover, much of the most effective research you will perform will be relatively simple and easily accomplished. A simple database search on a particular issue can speak volumes about how a similar set of circumstances might be covered by the media. By targeting a narrow group of opinion leaders, a soft-sounding of market analysts' thoughts on biotech companies could tell you more than an exhaustive survey of individual investors.

Likewise, a valid measurement of results in public relations can sometimes be deceptively simple. If the objectives of the program include reaching a certain target audience via the media, counting press clippings is a valid way to measure success. If the program calls for raising funds for a non-profit institution, standing-room-only attendance at a fund-raising banquet is certainly a measure of success. In an ideal world, participants might later be contacted to learn more about their attitudes toward the organization, its goals, and its methods. But when time and resources are in short supply, simple steps like database searches and soft soundings can be the difference between success and a misdirected campaign.

EXHIBIT 3.1 — PROFILE SURVEY

A typical profile survey is designed to measure a public's general understanding of a subject, and can contain a variety of different types of questions. This survey was developed to learn how public relations agencies and corporate communications departments are incorporating the Internet into their communications strategies.

1. What type of organization do you work for?

   ❑ PR practioner or group
   ❑ Gov't PR, PIO, or communications dept.
   ❑ Non-profit PR or communications dept.
   ❑ Corporate PR or communications dept.
   ❑ Other:

2. On a 0 to 5 scale indicate how important the following uses for the Internet are to your organization. 0 is Do not use this way, 1 is Not important at all, 5 is Very important.

   ____ Internal use
   ____ Corporate external communications
   ____ Investor relations
   ____ Marketing
   ____ Technical support
   ____ PR and/or advertising
   ____ E-mail
   ____ Other:

3. If you use the Internet for internal purposes, what do you use it for? Rate as above 0 to 5.

   ____ Corporate communications
   ____ Technical support
   ____ Employee newsletter/memos, etc.
   ____ Internal e-mail
   ____ Research
   ____ Other:

4. If your organization has an Internet domain or Web site, for how long?

   ❑ No site, no plans
   ❑ Plans, no site
   ❑ Site under construction
   ❑ Under 6 months
   ❑ Over 6 months but under 1 year
   ❑ 1 to 3 years
   ❑ Over 3 years

5. Do you recommend clients have online sites?

   ❑ Only if client asks
   ❑ Never
   ❑ Seldom
   ❑ Usually
   ❑ Routinely

Continued on next page

6. What criteria do you use to decide whether to put a client online?

_____

_____

7. How often do you recommend updating sites?
   - ❑ Daily
   - ❑ Weekly
   - ❑ Monthly
   - ❑ Every 6 months
   - ❑ Less than that

8. Rate the following for importance to attracting hits to sites. 1 is Not at all, 5 is Extremely important.

   ____ Flashy graphics
   ____ Modest graphics
   ____ Audio
   ____ Video
   ____ Cohesiveness with print media
   ____ Creative hooks to attract multiple hits
   ____ Links to other sites

9. What do you think makes sites work, what hooks do you recommend, if any?

_____

_____

10. What do you think works least on sites? Any total bombs? Why?

_____

_____

11. What URLs do you think are the most effective from a P.R. standpoint?

_____

_____

12. How much do you expect to spend on training and equipment for Internet use?
   - ❑ 0–$1,000
   - ❑ $1,001 to $5,000
   - ❑ $5,001 to $10,000
   - ❑ $10,001 to $25,000
   - ❑ $25,001 to $50,000
   - ❑ $50,001 to $100,000
   - ❑ Over $100,000

EXHIBIT 3.2 — SOFT SOUNDING SURVEY

This soft sounding questionnaire was developed for a pharmaceutical company concerned that its research and development initiatives were under-recognized among stock market analysts, journalists, and other key audiences. The survey results were used to justify a stepped-up effort to communicate the company's R&D programs, and yielded several specific tactics toward accomplishing that goal.

R&D COMMUNICATIONS SURVEY

1. How do you currently get information about research and development of new drugs and Investigational New Drug filings with the FDA?

2. How much importance is placed on new INDs as an indication of a company's potential for growth and new products?

3. In your perception, how would you rate the following companies in terms of leadership in R&D, clinical investigations and drugs in early stages of development?

   Eli Lilly

   Merck

   Pfizer

   Schering-Plough

   SmithKline Beecham

4. Which of the following companies are most effective in keeping you abreast of drugs in early stages of development? How do they communicate news about R&D?

   Eli-Lilly

   Merck

   Pfizer

   Schering–Plough

   Smith–Kline Beecham

5. What risk, if any, is there of creating unrealistic performance expectations in publicizing information on pharmaceutical research and development programs?

6. Is the press a reliable source of information on developments in pharmaceutical R&D?

7. How do you evaluate areas of research either prior to a company's filing for an IND, or in cases when an IND would not be filed by the company (such as in a partnership with a smaller firm)?

Richard J. Kosmicki is a principal of The Dilenschneider Group. Mr. Kosmicki has established strong relationships with the nation's business and financial press—both print and electronic. For some 30 years, he has been exceptionally effective developing and placing straight news, feature stories, product news, opinion-editorials, and corporate profiles. In addition, he has arranged numerous interviews for top management with leading newspapers, magazines, and network and cable television. His media contacts range from The Wall Street Journal, The New York Times, Forbes, and Fortune, to CBS and CNN. Mr. Kosmicki has directed public and press relations for some of the world's best-known corporations, including Goodyear Tire, Singer, Paramount Communications, Loews Corporation, and Allied Signal. He served as chairman of the board of the Asthma and Allergy Foundation of America from 1976 to 1980 and was a member of the board of directors of the Institute for Applied Economics from 1979 to 1982. He has been associated with the Multiple Sclerosis Society and is a member of the New York Press Club. Mr. Kosmicki has lectured on communications at New York University, the universities of Connecticut and Bridgeport, and the New School for Research. A former award-winning newspaper reporter, Mr. Kosmicki holds a degree from the University of Notre Dame and did graduate work at Columbia University.

Frederick E. Bona, an independent communications consultant to the Dilenschneider Group, has spent 35 years providing counsel in media relations. Thirty-three of those years were at W.R. Grace & Co. For the last seven of those years, he was corporate vice president, corporate communications. His responsibilities included media relations, public affairs, advertising, information services, internal communications, and publications. After he left W.R. Grace, Mr. Bona became a principal of The Dilenschneider Group, where he provides both domestic and international media counseling, as well as counseling on communications strategy, management issues, and mergers and acquisitions. Mr. Bona also led the media relations activities of President Reagan's Private Sector Survey on Cost Control (also known as the "Grace Commission"). He is a member of the Board of Governors of the Overseas Press Club. Mr. Bona received his B.S. degree in marketing from Fairleigh Dickinson University and attended The Dartmouth Institute.

CHAPTER 4

MEDIA RELATIONS:
HOW TO RELATE TO THE PRESS

As a practitioner of media relations, you serve three masters. One is your company, non-profit organization or, if you work in an agency, your client. The second is the print and electronic media. The third is the various publics who receive their information from the media. You are responsible to all three — yet you have little or no authority to influence or make final decisions. So, it takes great skill and experience to accommodate these three masters. In fact, if you're a smart communicator you'll treat the media, print and electronic, as well as you treat your employer, client, and the audiences the media serves.

If you doubt the importance of media relations consider what happened to Exxon's image after the Exxon Valdez oil spill in Alaska or how Union Carbide's reputation evaporated after the catastrophic gas leak in Bophal, India. Both cases are classic examples of incompetent media relations. When crises such as these occur, managements may dictate media relations policy, instead of allowing media relations professionals to implement what they've been trained to do.

One of the primary functions of public relations is to get fair — or, even better yet, favorable — coverage from the media. So, how do you do that?

Well, it calls for many talents. The most important of them is a nose for news: An understanding of how the media work and an in-depth knowledge of your organization's or client's business or mission.

As for a nose for the news, you have to be able to position or pitch a story in such as way that the media will be interested. You can't just say Company X is re-engineering. Many companies are re-engineering. You have to analyze the material and think up an "angle." What makes Company X's re-engineering newsworthy? Why would the media want to do an article on it? Will the media's readers or viewers be interested in this story? Why?

In addition, media often consider it an unforgivable sin if you don't know how they operate, what their needs are, their deadlines, and so on. In fact, each reporter or producer you approach will probably have a unique personality, expectations, likes, and dislikes which you must be aware of. Finding that out is part of your homework.

Also, the media expect you to have down cold all the facts about your organization as well as the topic you're pitching. One of the chief criticisms reporters have about public relations representatives is that we don't have sufficient knowledge of our subject. Whether it be a new manufacturing process or the expenditures of a local charity, you must have all of that information with you and be able to discuss it in a way

laypeople can understand. Remember that after you explain the manufacturing process or balance sheet to the media, they then have to
explain it to their audiences.

But even if you do all this homework, you still might not receive
coverage unless you take the initiative. You can't wait for the media to
contact you. Barring crises, this will seldom happen. Once you have
what you judge is a story media might be interested in, you must think
how and where you're going to place it.

When making that decision, you have to take into consideration
where your organization wants the story to appear and where you know
is most appropriate. The two may be different. That calls for persuasion skills. You have to take the role of an internal consultant to your
organization, explaining why getting your executive director on "Larry
King Live" is better than pitching the story as an exclusive to a national
newspaper. "Exclusive" means guaranteeing the medium that you're
giving the story to them first.

One thing more you have to know about the media. And that's
that they're fierce competitors. They want access to a story before their
competitors. An unseasoned media representative for a university sent
out letters to ten national media explaining the university's new "MBA-
like" program customized for engineers. One responded immediately
and asked the media rep if she had contacted anyone else in the media.
She went through the list. The reporter said he only wanted exclusives.
Those in the media can make a name for themselves by breaking a
story before anyone else.

Another fact of life in media is that print journalists, especially
those who work for trade publications, are somewhat more knowledgeable than are television reporters. That's primarily because those in
print have more day-to-day contact with companies. What's more, television usually allows an interviewee no more than a few sentences or
sound bites to get a message across. The print media, on the other
hand, allow you to expand and explain more to communicate your
message. That's because the medium of paper isn't as condensed as an
electronic medium. Print media journalists also tend to cover "beats,"
specializing in an area or concentrating on a topic, whereas journalists
in the electronic media are almost always generalists.

Just who exactly are the media? Today the media primarily consist of big businesses that are multimedia conglomerates. They include
Time-Warner, The New York Times Company, Dow Jones &
Company, and Gannett. These organizations typically own newspapers,
television stations, radio stations, and magazines; operate news syndi-
cates; and, in some cases, own outdoor advertising companies. For
example, print media may own daily and weekly newspapers, Sunday
supplements, consumer magazines, trade publications, wire services,
and newsletters.

The print media, due to its very nature, has somewhat more permanency than the electronic media. For instance, print media, such as *Newsweek* or *Time*, are passed along to other readers, left in lobbies, reception areas. and doctor and dentist offices, are available in libraries and online, and have a shelf life longer than the immediate impressions made by the electronic media.

Deadlines are the times when a publication must complete its research, writing, and editing, and begin to be laid out and printed. In the electronic media, such as the evening news, the deadline might be so many minutes before the news airs. The particular deadlines vary with the medium. In the media business, deadlines are taken very seriously. When dealing with the media make sure you know exactly each deadline.

Failure to meet deadlines will get you on the "drop dead" list of many reporters. And it doesn't matter how prestigious, powerful, or well-thought-of your organization is. The situation becomes even more of a disaster if you've promised a reporter that you would deliver information by a mutually-agreed-upon time. If you don't keep up your part of the agreement, you have probably made the reporter look bad before the editor. And no self-respecting representative of the media wants to be chewed out by a superior.

Several years ago Dick Kosmicki arranged an interview for the chief executive officer (CEO) of a *Fortune* 500 company with an influential business magazine. The CEO told the reporter he could not respond to a question right then because he had to check if his information was accurate. A week passed, and the CEO hadn't produced an answer. The reporter had even explained that if he didn't get the information immediately, he'd be forced to find another source for the information.

One month later, the story appeared. It contained inaccurate information from an investment banker, which was detrimental to the company. The correct information could have and should have been supplied by the CEO. Ironically, the CEO asked Kosmicki to draft a strong letter for him to the editor chastising the publication for not giving the CEO enough time to respond and for publishing material critical of the company. Kosmicki talked him out of it because the letter would have added insult to injury.

Here's one more story about a missed deadline. Dick Kosmicki called a Dow Jones reporter with a client's sales and earnings results. The reporter had two questions for the chief financial officer (CFO). Kosmicki called the CFO and explained how important it was for him to contact the reporter immediately. By the time the CFO finally did contact the reporter — nearly a half-hour later — the story had already been filed. A Wall Street analyst had supplied answers to the reporter's questions. They were slightly inaccurate and negative and hurt the client.

NEWSPAPERS

The number of daily and weekly newspapers has been dwindling in recent years as more people get their news electronically, especially through online news and television news shows. With CNN's around-the-clock news, it's no longer necessary to wait "until the newspaper comes out" to find out about a tragedy, war, or athletic outcome.

However, newspapers are still the most widely read of all the print media. There are 1,548 U.S. daily papers—635 morning, 935 evening, including "all-day." Also there are 886 Sunday papers.[1] The four largest newspapers in the United States, each with more than one-million daily circulation, are *The Wall Street Journal, USA Today, The New York Times*, and *The Los Angeles Times*.

Weekly newspapers are primarily local in nature and rarely cover international, national, or other news outside their readers' city, county, or state.

But whether daily or weekly, all newspapers contain three types of information:

- News, which is the backbone of a newspaper. The material is supposed to be presented in an unbiased manner. However, that is not always the case.
- Advertising, which is a major income source for newspapers. The information in the ads is presented exactly as the advertiser wants it—as long as the graphics and copy don't break any laws.
- And the opinion pages. These contain the points of view of the newspaper's editors, syndicated columnists, experts, leaders, and readers. They can express themselves through an opinion-editorial (op-ed) or a letter to the editor. Many public-relations representatives attempt to have their organization's or client's op-eds published in newspapers, national and local. Sometimes a well-done op-ed in a local paper can have more influence than one published in an important national one.

In addition to general-interest daily and weekly newspapers, there are a host of special-interest newspapers such as those addressed to women, the military, religious groups, Afro-Americans, Greek-Americans, and Hispanics.

Where To Go

If you need to find out more about national newspapers, including names, addresses, telephone numbers, the names and fax numbers of reporters, and editors, there are a number of excellent sources. They include:

Editor & Publisher Year Book
Editor & Publisher
11 West 19th Street
New York, NY 10011

Working Press Of The Nation Newspaper Directory
National Register Publishing
121 Chanlon Road
New Providence, NJ 07974

Burrelle's Media Directory
(available in Directory format or CD-ROM format)
Burrelle's Information Services
75 East Northfield Road
Livingston, NJ 07039

Bacon's Newspaper Directory
Bacon's Information Inc.
332 S. Michigan Avenue
Chicago, IL 60604

News Media Yellow Book
Leadership Directories, Inc.
104 Fifth Avenue
New York, NY 10011

For regional information:
New York Publicity Outlets
P.O. Box 1197
New Milford, CT 06776

SUNDAY SUPPLEMENTS

One of the sections that makes your Sunday newspaper so fat is the Sunday supplement. They are popular and widely read. An article or interview in them about your organization or client could have a great deal of influence.

Some supplements are produced locally by the newspaper. They include the *Denver Post Magazine, Boston Globe Magazine*, and *We Alaskans*. Others, such as *Parade* or *USA Weekend*, are produced nationally and are inserted in the local Sunday newspapers.

These publications contain feature-oriented stories that tend to cover "hot topics." A number of years ago a freelance writer was able to get an article on sex in nursing homes accepted by a national Sunday supplement. The subject was hot. Another example ... a *Fortune* 500 CEO headed a Presidential Commission on ways to eliminate waste in government by putting government on a business basis. This hot topic was covered in a Sunday supplement as well. Do you have any stories that are hot enough to get into a Sunday supplement? Deadlines for supplements are far in advance of the publication date.

CONSUMER MAGAZINES AND TRADE PUBLICATIONS

Consumer magazines tend to have a large readership. For example, *Time* has 4.3 million and *Newsweek* has 3.1 million.[2] In addition to these general news magazines, there are a broad variety of consumer magazines that specialize in a niche audience. For business readers there are *Forbes, Fortune,* and *BusinessWeek.* For sport enthusiasts there are *Field and Stream, Golf Digest,* and *Sports Illustrated.* There are also trade magazines (see Chapter 5, "Trading in on Trade Publications") such as *Ad Age* or *Laundry News.* Altogether, the consumer and trade magazines in the United States and Canada total more than 10,400.[3]

How do you work with these magazines? You must study each one you want to approach. *BusinessWeek,* for example, has a different tone than *Forbes.* The profile for *BusinessWeek* is: "Written for management level personnel interested in staying up-to-date on the news and trends that have an impact on the economy. Highlights include updates on management trends, marketing, Wall Street dealings, finances, transportation, new products, research, and the national/international market."[4] *Forbes,* on the other hand, has a similar profile but with different nuances: "Edited for management in U.S. companies, professional and private investors involved in the stock and securities markets. Provides a continuous review of market trends, analyses of trading developments, and corporate profiles and comparisons. Regularly features a business section, a corporate guide, and high-tech reviews."[5] These profiles are important to public relations people working with these publications. Find out their editorial requirements and deadlines. What stories did they carry during the past year? Would your story be a rehash of what has already been published? Do they use color photos? Creativity is good but don't ask them to do something that deviates too much from their usual modus operandi. And you must keep monitoring the magazine. In this competitive era, magazines are frequently changing to attract more readers. By becoming familiar with the contents of a publication, you won't be embarrassed by pitching a story that isn't a good fit.

WIRE SERVICES

If you want to get your story out to the world immediately, go to the wire services. Most wire services operate around the clock. Their reach is global. When you give a wire-service reporter news, if it's important, it'll be on the wire within minutes. Wire-service reporters do not have the luxury of analyzing and sitting on a story. They must "move" it as soon as possible in order to beat the competition. Keep that in mind when you deal with wire services. Their deadline is usually a matter of minutes.

Wire services provide "spot" — breaking news — or "of-the-moment" news stories, feature stories, and background information to other news organizations. In the United States, the most powerful wire services include The Associated Press, Reuters News Agency, Dow Jones News Service, and Bloomberg Business News. Overseas, the wire services with influence include Agence France Presse in France and Jiji Press in Japan.

When a story is run on a national wire service the distribution and impact can be enormous. Competition is fierce between the wire services. If a wire service gets a story out even a few seconds before a competitor, there is reason for great celebration. However, a wire service would rather be right than first — and found to be wrong.

How do wire-service reporters operate? Well, they report and file stories from all parts of the globe. Today they funnel information via video display terminals which years ago was distributed on ticker tape machines. Wire service stories are then used by news organizations as-is or reworked or reformatted for the particular use of the news organization.

As we pointed out earlier, the wire services often run on tight deadlines. Make sure you have all of your information before you contact them. Also inform your executives or clients about the need to move quickly. If a wire service contacts you, impress on everyone the need to be quick in retrieving information and providing a spokesperson.

NEWSLETTERS

Newsletters have become very popular. They deal with everything from investment advice to news about speechwriting. Because they don't usually carry advertising, their subscription cost is higher than newspapers and magazines. They come both in the mail and online.

How could a newsletter help your organization or client? Frequently they have interviews with leaders in a field, carry articles and op-eds written by people like your boss or client, and often publish information from media releases. For example, the "Speechwriter's Newsletter," which goes to many speechwriters and a number of executive-search firms, prints excerpts from media releases, carries articles and op-eds by speechwriters, and contains useful information about the field of speechwriting. If a speechwriter were interested in writing a guest column, the writer could call the editor and see if there's any interest in the topic. In this particular case, calling would be acceptable. For other newsletters, the editors might want to be contacted only through the mail. There's also "CPA Managing Partner Report," a newsletter for managing partners in public accounting firms, providing problem-solving tactics and management methods that can help the firm maintain stability and enhance profitability for short-term as well as long-range goals. It also accepts by-lined articles and will accept faxed proposals. Many industries and professional disciplines have a newsletter that covers their businesses. These newsletters include such titles as "Chemical Business," "Connoisseurs' Guide to California Wine," "Infectious Disease Practice," and "Funeral Service Insider Newsletter."

The time to get acquainted with the media is before you need them. Make sure you know all the newsletters in your field and study them.

Your sources of information about consumer magazines, trade publications, wire services, and newsletters are Bacon's Information, Inc., National Register Publishing, and New York Publicity Outlets (addresses appear earlier in this chapter).

ELECTRONIC MEDIA

The electronic media are quite different from print media. One of the first people to learn that was Richard M. Nixon. In his television debate with John F. Kennedy, Nixon didn't understand television and projected a poor image, visually and verbally. Kennedy, on the other hand, knew how to make love to the camera. He won that election.

Radio

In addition to television — network, cable, and public — the electronic media include radio. All are very powerful.

When television was first invented and grew in popularity, radio began to decline. However, radio has had a strong comeback. It is a good medium in which to place someone from your organization or a client. Unfortunately, many public-relations representatives overlook radio and just think of television. Also, because radio has frequent newscasts, your media releases could have a better chance of being used.

Right now there are some 5,770 AM and FM radio stations in the United States. The most popular formats are Talk, News, and Country. The reach of radio stations could be large. A 50,000-watt station in large cities is often picked up in other cities and throughout a whole region. Audience ratings for particular stations or shows play an important role in determining the most influential electronic media.

When you consider putting someone on a talk show, make sure you understand the style, strengths and weaknesses of the interviewer. Is this a program or personality that you want to become involved with? Another consideration: When does the program air? If it's 5:30 a.m., this might be a weak placement for your organization. Not all air time is created equal. Usually, the best slot is during commuter drive time, morning and evening.

As with print media, it pays to monitor radio stations and develop a relationship with producers and assignment editors. Supply them with background information on your topic. If they are, for instance, doing a week of shows on child abuse and using your executive director as an expert, offer them names of other experts who might make good guests. You can find out more about radio stations through Bacon's Information Inc., National Register Publishing, and New York Publicity Outlets.

Television

Television is clearly the medium with the greatest impact. More people obtain their information and news from television than any other medium. There are nearly 1,500 television stations in the United States and 700 cable systems. The three networks — ABC, CBS, and NBC, as well as Fox — produce national programming for local stations. You can choose to place someone on either a national or local program. Sometimes having your client on a popular local show can have more influence than national exposure. So don't overlook local programming. Various stations, and even particular shows, can have higher ratings than others. For example, appearing on WNBC-TV, the local New York NBC station, can be more influential than appearing on a low-rated network program, and certainly "Larry King Live" on CNN has a very wide audience and may reach the right segment of the public for you. On the other hand, programs with the highest ratings are the most difficult to place guests on. You must also consider what audience you want to reach. The viewers of "Meet the Press" are quite different from viewers of Oprah Winfrey, so you should determine which audience matches your message.

Cable is another option. One of the most influential cable systems is Cable News Network (CNN). It has become the network of record for breaking news, such as the Gulf War and the terrorist bombing in Oklahoma City.

The best way to develop a lasting relationship with television producers is to have a good story, a spokesperson who comes across well on television, and be willing to provide names of other guests who would enhance the show.

For instance, you want your client, the head of an entrepreneurial training center, to appear on a talk show. It may be useful to provide names and telephone numbers of others who could add value to that show. He or she could be an entrepreneur who succeeded, one who failed, and an outplacement director who often advises laid-off managers to consider starting a business. This kind of "packaging" is often called a "wraparound" story.

For more information about television stations, consult *Bacon's Information*, *National Register*, and *New York Publicity Outlets*.

HITTING HOME RUNS

To be successful with the media and get your organization or client the kind and amount of exposure they want, you must observe basic guidelines. You can hit home runs with the media, print and electronic, if you do the following:

- Be straightforward. Avoid industry jargon and pitch your story in plain English to the media. Let them decide if your story is newsworthy rather than oversell its merits. Overselling alienates media. And once you have made someone in the media a skeptic it might take a while for that reporter or producer to take you seriously again.
- Prepare a short agenda or, let's say, three messages or points you want to get across to the reporter or producer. Stay with these three points during the interview. The media is very busy. They'll be annoyed if you're not prepared and run off on tangents during the interview. If they want to hear about side issues, they'll ask you. Stay focused. And never go into an interview or send a client to an interview unprepared.
- Be low-key. You may have worked for Carr's Widget Inc. for 30 years, but don't approach the media as if they haven't the foggiest notion about what a widget is and its role in the national economy. For all you know, that particular reporter might have done ten stories on widgets. On the other hand, be prepared to brief the media on your subject. Have easy-to-digest background information for them as well as spokespeople who know how to simplify a complex subject or issue.
- If necessary, train your spokespeople. They may need help presenting themselves and the information they want communicated to the media. You can find good trainers by contacting colleagues in other organizations. Many of them are listed in O'Dwyer's *Directory of Corporate Communications*, 271 Madison Avenue, New York, NY 10016. Also, you can check the Yellow Pages under such categories as "Public Speaking." Ask for references and check them out. Find out how long the training takes and what it'll cost. Incidentally, there's no correlation between many training sessions or a high price and quality. The best in the business do their work quickly at a reasonable rate.
- Don't react. Some in the media are hostile, arrogant, or opinionated. However, it's not your job to cure them of these personality flaws. In fact, some reporters use such traits as a way to shake up public-relations representatives and have them drop their guard. If the media gives you a hard time, be aware of your tone of voice and body language. The best way to handle this is to stay calm.
- Review the reporter's or producer's work for the past year or so. Ask colleagues about them. This is to be done *before* you even approach the media. Find out how they usually treat their subjects. Are they strident? Do they have certain targets for their prejudices and anger? It's up to you to protect organiza-

tions and clients from highly-biased reporters. Those interviews could do more harm than good.

- Don't offer off-the-record information even if you "feel" or have heard that the reporter is trustworthy. Some reporters simply don't honor "off-the-record" agreements. Others will use your off-the-record comments by attributing them to unnamed industry sources.

- Approach the reporter or producer with a positive attitude, even if there are negatives in your story. If you're negative or on the defensive or even downright scared, don't let it show. The media will have you for lunch. Emphasize the positive parts of the story and be honest about the negative. Explain what plans the organization has for turning the negatives around.

- Hold a mock interview with every person who'll be meeting with the media. Ask questions they don't anticipate. And put it on videotape so they can watch their body language.

- Don't bluff. If you or your client do not know the answer, admit it and let the media know when you will have an answer. And before you release any information, have it checked by your lawyers, accountants, scientists, and so on.

- Be helpful. The media may need the names of consultants who can discuss global advertising. Or the media only has an hour to find and interview a senior executive who started out in the mail room. Perhaps they need to be briefed about a human resources issue or some method of environmental control. These are great opportunities to build a relationship with the media by serving them in ways that have nothing to do with your organization or client. If you prove dependable, they'll come to you often. And when you need something from them, the odds are they'll remember you favorably.

PITCHING TO THE MEDIA

There are a number of ways to present your story to the media. One is through the media release. A press, media, or news release is information prepared and positioned for the media. It ought to be written in the style of the media it is approaching, whether that be *Details* magazine or *The New York Times*. Every day the media receives cart loads of media releases. You have to make your release attract the attention of the person opening the envelope or taking it off the fax.

You can "break through the clutter" by analyzing your story and finding what in it would be most interesting to the media. That information should be used in the headline and the first sentence. Don't, however, overstate the importance of the product or discovery. That'll alienate you very quickly from the media. They hate overstatement, especially without credible documentation.

Here are other guidelines for releases:

- Ask yourself: Why would the media be interested in this story? If it's not of interest, don't send the release. There are organizations which send out releases about everything and the media no longer takes them seriously.
- Err on the side of being brief rather than verbose. The media are usually very busy.
- To find out what style's acceptable to most media, consult *The Associated Press Stylebook*, published by The Associated Press, 50 Rockefeller Plaza, New York, NY 10020.
- Always double-space your material. That gives room for editing.
- Always include a contact person's name, address, and telephone number. Make sure that person will be available for questions.
- Use only one side of paper. This also helps with the editing process.
- Indicate with "(more)" at the bottom of each page to be sure the editor knows additional information follows.
- Use a number sign "#" at the end of the press release to tell the editor the release ends there.
- If your release is only of interest to four mediums then just send it out to those four. Sending releases to inappropriate media earns you a bad reputation.

PRIVATE WIRE SERVICES

For regional, national, and international news releases, there are private wire services. That is, you pay for the wire service to distribute your release to hundreds of news media simultaneously. Because you're paying for this, you can issue it just about any way you want — as long as the material is in good taste and doesn't break any laws.

Two of the major private wire services are:

PR Newswire
810 Seventh Avenue
New York, NY 10019
800-832-5522
http://www.prnewswire.com

Business Wire
1185 Avenue of the Americas
New York, NY
212-575-8822

INTERVIEWS

Media interviews can take place in person, on the phone, in the air, at lunch, or in writing. Once you agree to an interview, the media is more or less in control. If you need some ground rules, set them *before* the interview begins. Also understand, there's no guarantee that a long interview will result in a long article about the company. Or that the article will be favorable.

At an oil company a business magazine interviewed the chief executive officer for a few hours, asking him tough questions. The CEO was furious with his media department when, months later, the article was published, and he was mentioned in only a few lines. Although what was said about him wasn't a disaster, it wasn't a plus. You must advise your spokespeople that the media offers no guarantee.

Every interview involves risk. Spokespeople can lower that risk by learning how to deal with the media. For example, a trainer inside or outside the organization can teach them how to reframe questions, turn a negative into a positive and build up their product or service without saying anything negative about the competition. They can point out the need to be enthusiastic, how to back up their statements with facts or examples, when to use everyday language to demonstrate a point, and, above all, to assure they are accurate, which can be increased by extensive preparation.

With electronic media, the stakes are always high. One reason is that more people tend to view television than read print material. Also, the electronic media is known for "selective editing." Maybe you've given them a one-hour interview, but they may only televise a 12-second part or 20-second piece of that interview. Sometimes those are considered "sound bites." And since they're taken out of context you could be portrayed as saying something you didn't mean. Prepare spokespeople to be aware of how damaging material could be used in a sound bite.

THE TELEPHONE PITCH

Calling the media can be a mixed bag. Some appreciate a phone call so that you can determine their interest before you fax the material to them. Others may cut you short.

Some public-relations representatives are under constant pressure to produce results. Unfortunately, they employ tactics that do more harm than good. Reporters for two influential newspapers showed us their "drop dead" list. That list contained the names of public relations people who have become pests by calling and calling, even to the reporters' homes.

Before you call, make sure the media are not working against a deadline. If their deadline for putting together a show is 9:00 a.m., you should steer clear of calling that morning. To demonstrate your concern for their time, it's always wise to ask them immediately, "Are you on deadline?"

You should pitch your story succinctly and not be long-winded. If the media aren't interested, it's probably more effective to approach other media than to "try to talk them into it."

If the media are interested in your story, you can ask them if they would prefer background material by fax, mail or messenger. Or right then and there they might want to set a time for an interview.

NEWS CONFERENCE

Breaking news should be released at a news conference. However, be sure the news justifies a conference. News conferences tend to be overdon — and inviting the media to what is a poor excuse for news will alienate them. You may one day hold a legitimate news conference and no media will show.

A news conference should consist of a 15- to 30-minute presentation of the news by your expert. He or she may be your executive director or chief financial officer. This should be followed by a 15- to 30-minute question-and-answer period.

The success of a news conference — that is, how many reporters cover it — often depends on where you hold it. Your headquarters may be in rural eastern Connecticut. The smart thing to do would be to hold the news conference in a centrally-located site in Manhattan. If you're an hour's drive from Washington, D.C., you should probably hold your conference at the National Press Club, which is in the center of D.C. Many media have their offices in that building.

The best way to invite media is to send a "media alert," that is, a few paragraphs which act as teasers about the news which will be announced. Send it 72 hours before the actual conference. If your teaser is good, there may be stories speculating about the news on television and in newspapers before the conference is held. Of course, if you are announcing a major development, 72 hours will need to be shortened to keep a lid on the news. You can also invite the media without a teaser or simply to say you are making an announcement about "a major development."

NEWS BRIEFING

When you don't have hard news to announce, the news briefing can serve a useful purpose. Reporters don't expect news. But they realize they'll be given background information and have an opportunity to question people in your organization.

For example, if the new CEO is turning around the company, he or she might want to brief the media before the earnings report is announced at a news conference next month. This briefing would give the media a good handle on what positive changes are being made in the company. For your organization, that could eventually yield lots of solid articles. Or your chief economist could cover the outlook for your industry, your environmental officer could provide insight into your company-wide environmental audit, and you could provide the media with an update on a special event planned for your community.

EDITORIAL BOARD MEETING

In the strictest sense of the term, an editorial board meeting is a get-together for your top person or people or your spokesperson and the editors and editorial writers of a publication. When a certain chief financial officer was developing a high profile for turning around companies, a well-known business magazine's top staff met with him. This helped them prepare articles about him, his company, and his turnaround techniques.

More broadly, an editorial board meeting could be applied to just about any group meeting between personnel from the publication and representatives of your organization. Before you agree to have one, ask who from the media will be there. This information can help your CEO prepare better for the meeting. One way to arrange this type of meeting is to contact the editorial page editor or his or her assistant. You will need to convince the editor why this meeting would be of interest to him or her and specifically what your representative will be prepared to discuss.

MEDIA TOURS

A media tour consists of your top person or spokespeople who are visiting several cities to hold news briefings, news conferences or interviews with as many representatives of the media as possible. To get media to come, it's wise to localize your story. For example, you would choose to go to cities where you had large operations. Plus you would think up a strong local angle.

To allow for proper scheduling of radio, television, and newspaper interviews, you would plan the details of the tour about eight weeks in advance.

VIDEO NEWS RELEASE

A video release is the visual version of a media release. Providing the media with a video release can make it easier for local stations to cover a special or newsworthy event. Usually 60 seconds long, it provides video footage of a new process, product, or event from a location that a local TV station would not have the time or budget to cover. It is presented just as if it were news on television.

For example, the New York branch of a Chicago-based hospital may have a new treatment for manic-depression. The public-relations people in Chicago would make a video release of that treatment and distribute it to the Chicago media. Distribution can also be national via satellite or mail.

B-ROLL

In essence, B-roll is a videotape cassette that usually contains diverse footage of your organization's buildings, activities, products, and services. You send the B-roll to television stations where you have operations. The media like to have that on hand in the event of a crisis. They would snip some of the B-roll to play when they cover the story.

One of the most interesting uses of B-roll that Fred Bona came across was by Pepsi-Cola when syringes were supposedly found in some soft-drink containers. Pepsi-Cola issued B-roll footage of their bottling process. That clearly showed that it would be impossible for syringes to have accidently fallen into a bottle of Pepsi. That B-roll convinced many viewers that if there had been syringes, they probably had been "planted" after the bottles had been filled at the processing plant with safe, quality-control measures.

FACT SHEETS, BACKGROUNDERS, AND WHITE PAPERS

Fact sheets contain information that could be useful to the media in creating their story. For example, a fact sheet on one of your residences for the homeless would tell where it is and how many of them are around the city, state, and nation. You would also include information about the building, how many men, women, and children it houses, if there's a waiting list, what services it offers, where its funding comes from, the credentials of the staff, if it uses volunteers, and where donations can be sent. It may be useful to list what happens there on a typical day.

Backgrounders are easy-to-read documents which contain comprehensive information about a subject in language laypeople can understand. For example, an energy company may issue backgrounders on what they do to protect the environment.

White papers are more formal. They're used to state the organization's position on a serious matter. That issue is usually controversial. Organizations try to get their white papers to all members of the media who cover a certain public policy, product, or service.

PHOTOGRAPHS

Giving photographs to the media is very useful if the photo makes a complex story simpler to understand. Always include a caption or cutline with the photo. That makes for easy identification.

The standard acceptable format is still an 8"x10" black and white glossy photo. But there is increased use of color which has varying requirements, from color photographs to slides. The highest professional quality still comes from 4"x5" color transparencies.

CYBERSPACE

The age of cyberspace — or communication between computer users — is providing the latest tools for dealing with the media. Many news organizations are using the Internet for research. Over the Internet, they pose queries and get quotes for stories.

Media lists, distribution lists, clipping services, databases, press release distribution, background web pages, and many other possibilities are available to public-relations representatives who want to use cyberspace. There's a new newsletter *Interactive Public Relations: Marketing Communications and PR in the Age of Cyberspace*. It's available from Lawrence Ragan Communications, Inc., 212 West Superior Street, Chicago, IL 60610, 312-335-0037.

SOMETHING TO THINK ABOUT

Media relations is probably the only public relations discipline that can make or break a public relations or marketing plan, bring a company to its knees — and destroy your career. Good media relations must be built over time, but bad media relations can strike like lightning and take years to repair. In short, your role is one of the most important in the organization. You are the gatekeeper for good and bad media coverage.

Unfortunately there is no formula that guarantees success. We've presented guidelines which can help. However, media relations, we are convinced, is an art form. Some of you will do better than others. Those who do better succeed because they recognize that you serve three masters: Your organization or client, the media, and the public. Those who serve only one, such as their organization or client, usually wind up on the media's "drop dead" list. Serving all three masters equally well may be the most formidable challenge in public relations.

NOTES

1. *Editor & Publisher International Year Book* (1995).

2. *Bacon's Magazine Directory* (1995).

3. *Bacon's Magazine Directory* (1995).

4. *Bacon's Magazine Directory* (1995).

5. *Bacon's Magazine Directory* (1995).

Joel Pomerantz has been a public relations professional, specializing in media placement, for nearly 35 years. Currently a principal at The Dilenschneider Group in New York City, he has also held executive positions with the Gavin Anderson Company, Doremus & Company, and Creamer Dickson Basford. In the course of his agency career, Mr. Pomerantz has written for — and placed countless dozens of articles in — trade magazines, covering everything from accounting to agriculture, and from moving vans to moving pictures. Prior to his agency affiliations, he served a long stint as public relations director of one of the nation's best-known resort hotels. Mr. Pomerantz began his career as a working newsman at The Newark Evening News.

Chapter 5

TRADING IN ON TRADE PUBLICATIONS

Making The Most Of A Valuable Publicity Outlet

It's been conservatively estimated that more than 6,000 trade and professional publications, reporting on the broadest imaginable spectrum of businesses, professions, and industries, are now distributed in the United States and Canada. They range from *Automotive News* to *Zoo Life*, *Turkey World* to *The Taxi Times*.

That 6,000-plus estimate was made by an editor of a leading trade magazine directory who acknowledges that even her own directory probably misses a certain number of relatively obscure publications.

Start a new industry, however marginal and esoteric, and it's a safe bet that a trade magazine will materialize almost overnight to cover it. The vast majority of commercial, ad-supported magazines published in this country happen to be trade magazines. They dwarf the consumer magazine sector.

There are about 2,500 consumer magazines now published in the United States — most of them so-called "specialist magazines." This latter category includes many well-known titles, such as *Flying Magazine*, *Better Homes & Gardens*, *Antiques Magazine*, *Stereo World*, *Car and Driver*, and *Golf Digest*, which are targeted at a very specific consumer audience and are read for information and/or entertainment unrelated to one's business or professional pursuits. There are also uncounted numbers of magazines, neither consumer nor trade, published by religious and fraternal groups, educational institutions, labor unions, special interest groups, and so on. (In this survey of the field, the term "trade magazine" is used to cover the full range of specialized business, industry, and professional journals.)

Trade publications are, overwhelmingly, magazines. They are largely monthlies with a considerably smaller number of weeklies and dailies. A small number are produced in newspaper and newsletter format. The newsletters, often weeklies featuring "insider" industry information and gossip, tend to focus on breaking news and often have considerable influence in their respective industries.

Trade magazine publishing is a very fluid enterprise. New publications surface and existing ones vanish all the time. Nearly all trade magazines are distributed by subscription although some of the better-known, more influential examples of the genre — *Advertising Age*, *Women's Wear Daily*, *Daily News Record*, *Variety*, *Folio*, *Publisher's Weekly*, and *Hollywood Reporter* — are occasionally sold at larger newsstands in major metropolitan centers such as New York, Chicago, Washington, and Los Angeles.

Trade magazine publishing is big business with some of the giant players, such as Cahners Publishing, putting out close to 70 different titles covering such diverse fields as publishing, computers, dairy products, graphic arts, show business, broadcasting, hotels, and packaging. Other heavy-hitter publishers with a broad spectrum of titles include Chilton, Penton, Fairchild, Faulkner & Gray, and Miller-Freeman.

Most trade magazines are national in scope, but there are a fair number of regional publications, often sponsored by a local or state trade association or professional society. The Illinois Bankers Association, for example, publishes the *Illinois Banker*; the Pharmaceutical Society of The State of New York publishes the *New York State Pharmacist*; and the Nebraska Motor Carriers Association publishes *Nebraska Trucker*.

In today's global economy, the public relations practitioner must also be aware of the surprisingly large number of trade magazines published outside of the United States and Canada in Europe, Asia, and Latin America.

EQUAL TOP CONSUMER MAGAZINES FOR QUALITY

Trade publications run the gamut from rather rudimentary efforts to glossy, slickly produced, ad-heavy products that rival the best of the consumer publications for design, graphics, and editorial content. Key trade and professional publications can be extremely influential. They are considered by many to be in the same league with top-rung consumer and business press outlets — especially in certain sectors such as health care (*New England Journal of Medicine*), energy (*Oil Daily*), advertising (*Advertising Age*), entertainment (*Variety, Billboard*), banking (*American Banker*), or computers (*Computerworld, Information Week*).

A favorable story in the trade press can sometimes have more impact, and a greater payoff, for a client than one appearing in the general business or consumer press. Talk to toilers in the nation's huge apparel industry — especially women's fashions — and they will probably tell you they care more about what appears in a publication such as *Women's Wear Daily* (*WWD*) than they do about the formidable *New York Times*. The power and prestige of *WWD* in the "rag trade" is legendary despite its comparatively small circulation.

The same is true in the book publishing field where a "money review" in *Library Journal*, which strongly influences the book purchases of librarians around the country, is probably more sought after than one appearing in a leading consumer outlet.

Though trade magazines lack the gargantuan circulation numbers of some consumer magazines, their public relations value stems, basically, from their highly-targeted readership. Typically, they enable you to reach decision makers on a managerial level in a particular trade or profession, or retailers, or wholesalers, or almost any kind of defined business/professional audience.

They also offer an indirect route to the mainstream press. Beat reporters covering specific business sectors for the major business media routinely mine these publications for story ideas and leads. Trade publication editors are generally better informed and more *au courant* about the industries they cover than other journalists. As a result, they are frequently called upon for commentary and opinion on important breaking news stories involving their respective bailiwicks.

And, not incidentally, stock and bond analysts and investment managers — all of whom can move markets — are regular subscribers to trade magazines. Anyone with a publicly traded company as a client can benefit from servicing these publications with corporate news.

HOW TO USE THE TRADE MEDIA

A case in point: Terex Corporation (NYSE), a billion-dollar industrial company that manufactures heavy-duty capital equipment including cranes, acquired a French-owned crane company in May 1995. The acquired company was merged with Terex's own crane unit to form a new global company, Terex Cranes, which became the second-largest crane manufacturer in North America and a leader in Europe. The investment community promptly began speculating about the implications of the acquisition.

At this early stage, little that the major business press might view as material could be added to the information found in the press release announcing the acquisition. But Terex's public relations consultant quickly developed credible, positive stories for a highly respected European crane trade magazine and a leading U.S. trade magazine.

Each reported positively, and in some detail, on the new company's plans, strategies, expectations, and projections based on interviews with the new CEO. Both articles were immediately reprinted and sent to the complete Terex Corporation mailing list of analysts, investment managers, institutional buyers, and so on.

Reprints are, in fact, an extremely important by-product of trade magazine placements. They can be distributed to many audiences besides the investment community, including existing and potential customers, employees, government officials, and suppliers.

By and large, trade publications represent an easier placement for the public relations professional than do the established major media. They rarely adopt an adversarial posture vis-a-vis business organizations. Simply put, they are much more receptive to public relations pitches and material than other media. That is not to say they have an open-door policy for anything you may pitch to them.

Trade magazine standards of professionalism very frequently equal the best of the general press. It is a serious mistake to treat the trade press as an also-ran or a stepchild. The vast majority are written and edited by skilled professionals who take considerable pride in their work. Those writers and editors must be approached with the same degree of respect and regard as the rest of the media. You should culti-vate them no differently than you would "romance" members of the consumer and business press.

In addition to direct story placement and company news detailed in press releases, trade magazines are open to by-lined articles by senior executives on topics of industry-wide interest which, in many instances, you will find yourself "ghosting" as well as "pitching."

Trade magazine writers and editors will also call on executives of your client company as a source of commentary and opinion when reporting on major industry trends and developments. The trick here is to make their availability and area of expertise known to trade media via a telephone call (about breaking news), letter, business card, Rolodex card, or any other reminder device.

THE CASE HISTORY IS BASIC

The staple trade magazine feature is some variation of what has come to be known as the "case history." It is a success story involving your client and an important customer or customers. Its purpose is to demonstrate a particular product or service's application and strong points. But any unique aspect of a client's operations can be the raw material for a good trade magazine feature including stories focusing on interesting personalities within the organization from the CEO on down.

A skilled public relations professional will maintain strong con-tacts — if not in person, at least by telephone — with client company executives who can provide ideas and information for case histories and related stories. These include plant managers, quality control man-agers, sales and marketing people, and others out in the field meeting customers on a regular basis.

You'll need their help, too, in getting the cooperation of the cus-tomer involved in any case history you propose. It's also productive to attend, when practical, company sales meetings, new product introduc-tions, and industry trade shows. Your presence will help you build up a valuable bank of potential case histories and related trade stories.

The essential truth about trade publications is that they exist because the companies comprising the industry they cover exist. And it is to their advantage to ensure that those companies continue to exist — even prosper. It is also true that most trade publications have small staffs and, consequently, must rely more heavily than non-trade media on public relations professionals as news sources.

The real world being what it is, editorial decisions on some trade magazines are undoubtedly influenced by advertising. That does not mean non-advertisers are unwelcome or excluded — news is news. But it does mean that advertisers have an edge when it comes to editorial decisions and space allocation — which is not altogether surprising.

Granted, all of the top-drawer trade publications proclaim and jealously guard their editorial independence. Nonetheless, their *raison d'etre* remains the companies and professions they cover and, consequently, their relationship to those companies and professions is strongly symbiotic, providing a reasonably hospitable climate for public relations activity.

TRADE MAGAZINES SOMETIMES SOLE OUTLET

The trade media's value to the public relations professional is too often underestimated. For certain clients in certain businesses and industries, they may be the only media outlets available on a consistent and reliable basis — particularly for smaller companies. The mainstream media tend to have minimal interest in companies that are not publicly owned; do not have easily recognizable names; or operate in marginal business sectors. Trade magazines are an invaluable medium for companies that market business-to-business products (or services), which normally are of lesser interest to the general press or consumer publications. When you are a supplier, for example, to an OEM (original equipment manufacturer), the trade press may be your most important publicity medium. In most instances, you will be talking directly to existing, or potential, customers.

Johnston Industries, Inc., a medium-size, publicly traded textile company with annual revenues of $300 million, offers a good example of how this works. Johnston makes textiles primarily for the industrial and home furnishings markets. The lion's share of volume is derived from textile converters and furniture manufacturers. The company sells no consumer products, and there has been relatively little movement in its share price in the past two years. Nonetheless, Johnston has been one of the most innovative companies in a very mature industry and a trailblazer introducing new technology.

Although it has not easy to get the mainstream business media to focus on the company, the textile trade press has enthusiastically embraced Johnston for its growth, innovations, and creative marketing in a rapidly changing textile marketplace. Typically, one of the industry's most influential trade books, *Textile World*, first named the company "Textile Model Mill Of The Year" (June 1994) in a 24-page cover story devoted exclusively to Johnston; and, the following year, named Gerald B. Andrews, Johnston's dynamic CEO, "Textile Leader Of The Year" with another multi-page cover spread. The impact of those two lengthy reports within the textile community can not be overstated.

Trade magazines rate the highest priority for the introduction of new products or services in the business-to-business arena since you can pinpoint trade publications covering the key industries in which a client company wishes to market the new product.

To illustrate: In 1994, Dun & Bradstreet Information Services began rolling out a new environmental product that provided valuable information about the environmental status of any commercial location in the United States with respect to potential liabilities and clean-up costs, existing regulatory citations, and so on. The unique environmental due diligence product was designed specifically for lawyers, bankers, accountants, commercial and investment bankers, real estate professionals, insurers, trustees, corporate managers, and anyone else directly involved in commercial real estate transactions.

TRADE OUTLETS ONLY

An intensive publicity effort aimed almost exclusively at trade journals covering those professions netted reports in over 35 trade outlets including *American Banker*, *CFO Magazine*, *Trusts & Estates*, *Insurance Advocate*, *The Journal of Accountancy*, *Business Insurance*, *Real Estate Finance Today*, *ABA Banking Journal*, *Secondary Marketing Executive*, *Real Estate New York*, *Problem Asset Reporter*, *Best's Review*, *Insurance & Technology*, *Bank Letter*, *Mortgage News*, *Indiana Banker*, *National Real Estate Investor*, *National Underwriter*, *Seller-Servicer Update*, *Banker & Tradesman*, *Law Technology Product News*, *Secondary Marketing Executive*, to list only a few. Every reader here was a potential buyer meaning zero "waste circulation."

Trade magazines are equally indispensable as a publicity outlet when a so-called "quick hit" is essential — meaning your impatient client wants to see some "ink" about the company somewhere and the major business media are indifferent.

In the major general or business press, you are, literally, competing for a finite amount of editorial space against the entire business universe. In the trade press, you are only going against other companies in your industry for the available space. More to the point, trade magazines will, characteristically, be more receptive to your material than the general media. Those differences are crucial.

As with the universe of consumer newspapers and magazines, there is a hierarchy — of importance and influence — among trade publications. Knowing the pecking order will enable you to select a target publication for a specific story that will have maximum value to your client.

It's always advantageous to learn which trade publications the senior managers of your client company read and make sure those outlets receive priority in determining the publications to target.

Circulation is also a useful, but not infallible, clue to which publications in a given industry are prime targets. But published numbers can be misleading. Because trade media are often controlled circulation publications distributed gratis to selected readers, circulation figures do not necessarily reflect actual readership.

Frequency of publication is another helpful indicator. The publication that appears daily, or weekly, has a leg up because it can report on breaking industry news in a timely fashion whereas the monthlies lag behind on spot news, tending to favor analysis, executive profiles, and trend pieces.

THE EXCLUSIVITY QUESTION

The question of exclusivity on a particular feature story has to be addressed since trade magazines, like any other business, are competitive. If you can spin off markedly different variants on a basic story idea, fine. If not, set up an order of preference and pitch your story on an exclusive basis. That implies you won't pitch the story, if accepted, anywhere else. The editor of a trade publication who is receptive to your proposal will probably inquire directly about exclusivity, anyway.

On the other hand, when distributing a press release about breaking news relating to your client — new products, new contracts, new technology, personnel announcements, earnings, acquisitions, divestitures, etc. — the usual procedure is to service every publication on the trade list across-the-board irrespective of its standing. Since most of these publications are probably monthlies, regular postal service will suffice unless you happen to know that a particular publication's deadline is rapidly approaching.

But for standard news releases about a client company going to dailies and weeklies, it's imperative that you to develop a fax list — or employ a messenger service — to make sure you don't miss their deadlines.

Trade magazines usually prefer some kind of graphics to accompany a piece. They are also inclined to be more cost-conscious than the free-spending general consumer publications. If you can provide quality art (photos, charts, logos, etc.) for any story idea you pitch, you will enjoy a distinct advantage.

If you are going to use the trade media as a publicity outlet, you must also have access to reliable directories that provide essential information — editors, editorial requirements, circulation, address, telephone number, fax number, etc. — about those publications.

WHICH DIRECTORY???

There are three principal sources for these lists: *Bacon's Magazine Directory* (which also carries newsletter and Canadian listings), published by Bacon's Information, Inc., in Chicago; *Burrelle's Media Directory Magazines and Newsletters*, published by Burrelle's Information Services in Livingston, New Jersey (which includes listings from Canada and Mexico); and *Working Press of the Nation Magazines and International Publications Directory*, published by the National Register Publications of New Providence, New Jersey.

None are, strictly speaking, trade magazine media directories since they all contain listings for consumer magazines and, in two instances, newsletters. *Bacon's* also publishes an *International Media Directory* covering Western Europe with information about some 24,000 publications of all types of which an estimated 80 percent are trade publications. *IMG, Inc.* of Nashua, New Hampshire, is another publisher of off-shore directories, including separate *International*

Media Guide volumes for trade media in Europe, Latin America, and a single volume covering Asia-Pacific, Africa, and the Middle East.

Bacon's is slightly more expensive than the other two directories. Though differences with *Burrelle's* are minimal, *Bacon's* may be the more detailed, providing, in addition to editors' names and a description of editorial content, useful information about whether or not the publication uses color photos, carries personnel announcements, accepts by-lined contributions, and so on. None of the three, however, are totally inclusive. There are always some marginal publications you won't locate in any directory.

In addition to print volumes, both *Bacon's* and *Burrelle's* distribute their directories in electronic formats on computer disks and CD-ROMs. The *Burrelle's* media directories can also be accessed through the Internet. *Working Press of the Nation*, although less comprehensive than either *Bacon's* or *Burrelle's*, has one strong point. With each listing, you will find a fairly detailed profile of the publication's typical readers. But *Burrelle's* and *Bacon's* listings also include some information about readership.

OTHER SOURCES

There are additional secondary sources for trade magazine listings, such as industry handbooks and directories published by national trade associations. These volumes frequently list trade media.

Another supplier, if you're planning an across-the-board mailing, are bulk mailing houses such as Media Distribution Services — the largest in the business. They offer updated, complete trade mailing lists for any business, profession, or industry you may specify as long as they also do the mailing for you — for a fee. The mailing house will, in most instances, supply a print-out with the names of the publications serviced, circulation, editor's name and phone number, but not the address. To the media placement specialist, directories also afford a convenient way to tap another extremely useful information compendium: annual media calendars. Along with most daily newspapers and some consumer magazines, the majority of trade magazines publish special sections and special issues throughout the year devoted to specific topics. They normally run in the same weekly or monthly issue every year and can cover anything from buyers' guides to product roundups, major trade shows to special industry reports.

Editors of these special issues or sections routinely solicit editorial material from company sources. Obviously, it's very advantageous to know when particular issues will appear so that you can plan timely and appropriate pitches or submissions. Your best guide here — especially for trade magazines — is Bacon's annual *Media Calendar Directory*. The listings in this volume are comprehensive and up-to-date. If you wish to avoid the cost of a directory, many trade magazines distribute free-standing editorial calendars to potential advertisers, which can usually be obtained upon request.

KNOW YOUR TRADE MEDIA

A familiar complaint voiced by media professionals about public relations practitioners is that many make inappropriate, irrelevant story proposals because they are unfamiliar with the editorial contents of a particular publication. In short, they do not read the media they pitch to. This wastes both the editor's time and the publicist's time and may raise doubts about the latter's professionalism.

This is no less the case pitching to trade publications. Reading, or at least skimming, as many of these publications as you can get your hands on, should be a given for any savvy professional involved in trade media relations. In addition to generating ideas for client stories, it's a valuable exercise that will enable you to keep abreast of industry trends.

Of course, subscribing to more than a handful of publications can turn out to be a costly proposition. Certainly, the key magazines covering a particular industry in which you have clients should come into your office on a regular basis. To familiarize yourself with the others, some larger local libraries may be helpful.

In New York, the Brooklyn Public Library Business Library located at 280 Cadman Plaza West in the Brooklyn Heights section of that borough (718-722-3333) keeps an extensive collection of trade magazines that can be consulted on a daily basis including Saturdays. The new Science Industry and Business Library (part of The New York Public Library), recently opened at East 34th Street and Madison Avenue in Manhattan, also carries a notably large selection of major trade publications.

Another option is to contact the advertising department of a particular trade magazine and request a media kit with a sample issue. If the ad people feel you can influence the outlay of advertising dollars, they will probably send you what you need.

However useful and valuable trade publications can be as an integral component of an overall public relations strategy, some clients — a small minority, to be sure — remain unimpressed and wish to have as little as possible to do with them. The rationale most often given is a disinclination to release any company information of potential value to competitors who read these publications.

That is a narrow, shortsighted attitude. No company is in the business of conveying to *any* media genuine "trade secrets" or authentic competitive data about its operations that is unavailable elsewhere. News and information issued directly, or culled from interviews, generally represent only what the company wishes to say and nothing more. Any journalist is, needless to add, free to consult other sources. But, on balance, trade magazines still offer an ideal forum for getting your story told in a medium that, as noted above, has standing, credibility, and is generally very supportive.

The bottom line: The value and importance of trade magazines are indisputable — a critical tool in the public relations professional's arsenal. When your company acquires a new client, act quickly to familiarize yourself with the trade media covering the client's industry. They should be read, studied, cultivated, and utilized for maximum benefit to your client.

EXHIBIT 5.1 — A PUBLIC RELATIONS DECALOGUE — PLUS 15!
25 COMMANDMENTS TO MEMORIZE AND LIVE BY

1. Thou shalt not intentionally lie to, or in any way mislead, the news media. Truth is the best damage control.

2. Thou shalt not release any information that has not been authorized by your client. But this does not mean stonewalling the media. Remember, when you trot out a rote "no comment" or "it's company policy not to comment on," etc., you often confirm suspicions and only spur a reporter to dig more deeply. At minimum, supply some context and explain your inability to be more responsive.

3. Thou shalt not say, or write, anything to a reporter about a client — on or off the record — you would not want to see in print.

4. Thou shalt not work for a client — or promote an idea, product, or activity — that you find morally or ideologically objectionable. Because of the guilt, conflict, and unease you feel, you will probably do a lousy job of it, anyway.

5. Thou shalt not issue "no news" press releases merely to give your client the impression of activity. That turns off the media and undermines your efforts when you actually have something newsworthy to disseminate.

6. Thou shalt always return a phone call from the media — and as promptly as possible.

7. Thou shalt not "cross" a reporter or editor no matter how shabbily, rudely, arrogantly, or unfairly you have been treated in the past. Remember, they ALWAYS have the last word. (Thin skins don't last too long in the public relations business.) By the same token, do not hesitate to correct demonstrable errors in reportage.

8. Thou shalt not telephone a reporter or editor on a daily or weekly publication at, or near, deadline time unless the call concerns a major breaking story. (Make it your business to find out about deadlines.)

9. Thou shalt not ask a reporter or editor for story approval before publication. If you're lucky and it's offered, fine. Then, make the most of it.

10. Thou shalt not make a pitch to any publication or broadcast outlet until you have read the publication or watched the particular show and understand its "style," its editorial needs, and its target audience.

11. Thou shalt not ask for a list of questions in advance of a client interview. An inquiry about the range of topics to be covered is, however, perfectly legitimate.

Continued on next page

12. Thou shalt be inoffensively persistent — but never insistent — when pitching a story. It's possible to be gracious, subtle, inventive, even amusing, when going back to the media repeatedly, but be careful about wearing out your welcome.

13. Thou shalt not inflate pitch letters with obvious information a reporter or editor already knows through covering a particular beat. That not only wastes valuable time and space, it's condescending to the reporter.

14. Thou shalt not request an advance copy of a story scheduled for publication unless a reporter or editor has previously volunteered to provide it. (If you're under pressure from a client to get an "advance," a publication's advertising or promotion department can sometimes be helpful, but don't get the editorial side involved.)

15. Thou shalt be creative in the literal sense of the word. The tried and true often work, but don't be a afraid to think a new thought, try a new approach, explore uncharted territory.

16. Thou shalt not promise exclusive access to your client if that is not your intention.

17. Thou shalt not issue press releases that deliberately — and usually, transparently — attempt to bury negative news. Reporters are not dumb and some have long memories.

18. Thou shalt make a thorough review of your media lists at least quarterly and up-date them accordingly. (In addition to mid-year directory supplements, media tips sheets such as *The Bulldog Reporter*, Jack O'Dwyer's *Newsletter*, *Contacts*, and *TJFR Business News Reporter* are invaluable for this exercise.)

19. Thou shalt not promise anything to a client that you may not be able to deliver.

20. Thou shalt not address a reporter or editor — on the telephone or in a written communication — by a first name unless you actually know him, or her, from ongoing telephone contacts or in-person meetings.

21. Thou shalt try to be present at all pre-arranged client media interviews — including those on the telephone — to make introductions, listen, and learn. Volunteer information only when requested; or when you are privy to some relevant facts the client may not know; or to bridge a lull or impasse in the conversation. If you wish to record the interview, ask the reporter's permission first.

22. Thou shalt not book a client on a TV or radio show without providing pre-interview training and briefing — especially if the client is new at the game.

23. Thou shalt not denigrate the efforts of a competitor. That's unseemly, unprofessional, and unnecessary. Inferior work will self-destruct sooner or later.

24. Thou shalt double-space all releases; print releases on only one side of a sheet of paper; get the news into the release's headline (a busy reporter/editor may not get any further); include a home phone number on the contact line if the release is issued late in the day or on a Friday; and make sure the client contacts listed at the top of the release actually will be available if called.

25. Thou shalt read, read, read all the media you can get your hands on. Being well, and broadly, informed is the real name of this game.

Kathleen F. Connelly joined Robert L. Dilenschneider to create The Dilenschneider Group in October 1991. Prior to that, Connelly served as an executive vice president responsible for worldwide business development at Hill and Knowlton, was a member of the board of directors, as well as director of the firm's global strategic planning group.

Connelly's areas of expertise include corporate change and restructuring initiatives; merger and acquisition communications; public offerings; corporate positioning programs; crisis counsel and communications; professional services marketing; business-to-business marketing; public affairs and issues planning.

Before joining Hill and Knowlton, Connelly served as an officer at Continental Bank of Chicago, where she worked in bond trading and before that, public affairs, where she organized the bank's issues system and managed its public affairs programs. She also has worked as a legislative aide on consumer and environmental issues.

Connelly is an honors graduate of Newton College in Newton, Massachusetts, where she was class president and held the President's Scholarship. She received a masters degree in political science from the Eagleton Institute of Politics at Rutgers University under a Ford Foundation grant and has attended the Graduate School of Business at the University of Chicago.

Connelly serves as a director on several boards and has served twice as a national committee member for selection of White House Fellows.

Additionally, she has has lectured at a number of leading business schools.

James Fitzpatrick, a principal with The Dilenschneider Group, was instrumental in the development of a number of concepts that appear in this chapter.

CHAPTER 6

GLOBAL PUBLIC RELATIONS

Look closely at most industries and you will see that global competition and cooperation have become a stubborn detail of everyday business life and no longer just a rallying cry at industry conventions. U.S. insurance companies process their claims in Ireland. Computer companies have their software written in India. Delegations from state governments roam the world to compete for foreign investment. Global hotel chains like Nikko, Meridien, Sofitel, and Swissotel are prominent in major U.S. business centers. U.S. manufacturers beg state agencies to deregulate electricity in order to get costs in line with foreign competition.

SHRINKING WORLD — EXPANDING AUDIENCES

That the world is shrinking has been a cliche for most of the 20th century, but the shrink rate has accelerated dramatically in recent years. There were 24,000 "transnational" corporations in the world's 14 richest countries in the mid-1990s according to the United Nations, up from a mere 7,000 in 1969.

The world is being shrunk by a potent mixture of communications technology and economic reform. Satellite technology allows the instantaneous sharing of news and information across the globe. The wholesale adoption of free market ideologies around the world has vastly expanded the market for information. For example, more than 30,000 satellite dishes were installed in a recent year in Albania, which had long kept its borders closed to foreign information. The world has fewer and fewer informational dead zones. Only Antarctica and parts of Greenland are unable to receive live news broadcasts from CNN, now transmitting through 13 satellites. The country of Namibia in southwest Africa has the highest pay-TV penetration in the world. Forty-three countries in Europe, Africa, and the Middle East receive pay television from a single Dutch-based company, NetHold.

Communications and information technology are eliminating the diseconomies of distance that have always kept suppliers and their markets close to each other. Fashions can be shown in Milan, copied and faxed to New York, sent out for bid to Taiwan and Malaysia, bids received in New York, and purchase orders issued and confirmed for production quantities ... all within 24 hours ... and the knockoff can be on store shelves across North America before the original.

The same thing can happen with reputation, image and information. A distorted version can make it on the record and to your audience's mind before the true version. Computerized news databases can then cause distorted images to multiply until, in the communications version of Gresham's law, bad news drives out good.

If left unprotected in the international arena, reputation and image can be as vulnerable as a fashion design. The challenge to you as a public relations practitioner can be enormous, requiring you to be able to mediate instantly between events and audiences that can be worlds apart. You may have to practice on an intercontinental scale the strategic art of "information dominance" — a term from the Gulf War of 1991, known on the coalition side as Operation Desert Storm.

"Desert Storm introduced information dominance as a reckoning force, rivaling weapons and tactics in importance," wrote one commentator. Satellite and other communications systems delivered critical information to coalition forces, gave them "an unprecedented view of the battlefield" and allowed them "to see, hear, and talk while the enemy fought blindly." In the rest of this chapter, we will survey some of the terrain of the international public relations battlefield.

EXPORTERS AND GLOBALISTS — WHAT'S THE DIFFERENCE?

"We were behaving like all Europeans, like exporters, which meant we were not really in the country." So said the CEO of IKEA, the Swedish-based global furniture retailer-manufacturer, in summing up IKEA's early failure to adapt to the U.S. market and its inability to turn a profit with its first seven U.S. stores. After making the necessary adaptations, IKEA became quite successful in the United States.

When the Boeing 737 lost out in the U.S. market to the DC9, Boeing modified the plane to adapt to third-world markets, where airport conditions and pilot practices required quicker take-offs and shorter landings. The 737 went on to become one of the most successful commercial jets in history.

These two examples are meant to illustrate that global companies like IKEA and Boeing succeed by looking at markets differently from an exporter. Global companies also look at production and raw material sourcing differently.

The prototype of the Mazda MX-5 Miata sports car was created in the United Kingdom. An assembly process was designed using advanced electronic components invented in New Jersey and fabricated in Japan. The actual assembly lines for the Miata were in Michigan and Mexico. The original design of the car was accomplished in California, which was the principal target market.

By definition, a global firm is one with a worldwide dispersion of competence, authority, resources, and fixed capital investment along with the ability to integrate, focus, and adapt these dispersed competitive advantages to fit the needs of local markets. At the other end of a spectrum of possibilities, an exporter merely exports its product or know-how to a market that is willing to buy it. In between, there is the international firm that sets up foreign subsidiaries to leverage its home market expertise.

Bausch & Lomb is a company that went from one end of the spectrum to the other in the course of a single decade. In the early 1980s, "foreign subsidiaries used to be treated as sales adjuncts to the U.S. divisions," according to a B&L executive quoted in *Fortune*. Production and marketing policies all came from the company's Rochester, New York, headquarters. Of the 25 new sunglasses introduced in a typical year, only one was developed especially for a foreign market.

A decade later, more than half of new sunglasses models were being developed for particular foreign markets. Plants had been built specifically to meet the unique product requirements of different national markets. Distinctive sales and marketing programs were tailored precisely to individual markets. Local managers were encouraged to make their own decisions.

One distinction between the two approaches is that, in the first case, influence and authority emanate outward from the home market, whereas in the truly global firm, there are so many centers of influence and authority that there is really no single "home" market.

It has been said of Citicorp, for example, that "its consumer business transfers marketing innovations from East to West and back again." Its Citigold service for the wealthy was developed for upper-class consumers in Asia, where it became a great success before being imported to Europe and North America.

"A SINGLE TUNE FOR ALL THE WORLD?"

Those were the words used by Ted Levitt, a Harvard Business School professor, in his groundbreaking 1983 article, "The Globalization of Markets," in the *Harvard Business Review*. Levitt argued that consumers worldwide wanted similar products and that the successful firm of the future would standardize products, manufacturing, promotion and pricing across national borders.

Globalizing a brand in Levitt's sense, so that it can be sold with "a single tune for all the world," is an enormous challenge. Business magazines are full of stories of expensive failures. One success story comes from Colgate-Palmolive with its Total antibacterial toothpaste.

After test-marketing Total in the Philippines, Australia, Colombia, Greece, Portugal and the United Kingdom, Colgate synthesized the input from these diverse markets into a unified marketing image. "Today," says *Brandweek*, "Total is a $150 million brand worldwide, selling in 75 countries, with virtually identical packaging, positioning and advertising irrespective of the cultural nuances, societal demarcations and entrenched local business practices that have so daunted marketers up to now."

Total is a stunning success story, and it is a product that was created from scratch for a global market. More common is the attempt to create demand in new markets for a product that has been successful elsewhere. Kellogg's campaign to promote Kellogg's Corn Flakes to the hundreds of millions of consumers in the former Soviet bloc is an example. With slogans like "The world is having breakfast with us," and using TV commercials and "taste testings" in grocery stores, Kellogg is trying to wean Eastern Europe from the traditional breakfast of cold sausage and heavy bread.

Levitt's "single tune" is usually not enough. Coca-Cola sang "I want to buy the world a Coke ... " throughout the world, but its success in Japan, where it has 70 percent of the soft drink market, is due much more to its route sales force, its franchised vending machines, and its rapid introduction of special products for the Japanese market.

And a global marketer can deliberately reject the "single tune" approach in order to get a strategic advantage in a significant part of the world. In the worldwide wars between the two global colas, Coke is far ahead globally with bottling plants in 197 different countries, leveraging its brand with what *Fortune* has called "Coca-Cola's commandment of soft drink marketing — a cola is the ultimate global brand, transferable from Tulsa to Tibet to Timbuktu." Looking for a chink in its competitor's armor, Pepsi introduced a brand designed to exclude part of the world. Pepsi Max, a no-sugar cola designed specifically for non-American consumers, was introduced in Europe in 1993 and subsequently rolled out in the Far East and Latin America.

The global brand is much more an ideal, the end point on a continuum of possibility, than it is a widespread reality in any sort of pure form. So also is the global firm. Very few of the 37,000 transnational companies identified by the United Nations are truly global, but many transnationals owe some of their competitive strength to having achieved success in the two areas of competence that define the global firm:

- Having the geographical competence to source inputs more advantageously than purely local or national competitors.
- Having the competence to integrate, focus, and adapt these diverse resources to fit the needs of different local markets in ways that local or national competitors cannot.

A "BORDERLESS WORLD"?

Operating and marketing across national borders can place a special demand on the public relations practitioner to soften or mute the national identity of the company, even to add different national identities for different markets. This is an extraordinarily difficult assignment. There are very few models for a global identity. Even the Roman Catholic Church, established around the world for centuries, has an identity and image that radiates out from the Vatican. Organizations like the United Nations, the World Bank, the International Monetary Fund, and the Red Cross perhaps come close to having global identities. The president of Toyota recently suggested that the local

Japanese operations in the Japanese corporation of the future would be no more important or "central" than the many other operations of a worldwide network. We can envisage this happening easier than we can envisage Toyota shaking its national identity. The vice chairman of Booz, Allen & Hamilton recently said that large transnational corporations cannot lose their national identity because they will always be perceived as having a home base.

The chairman of SmithKline Beecham puts the challenge differently. "You don't have to lose your American identity or your Japanese identity in order to gain another one. It's not a zero-sum game. You add national identities because you have enormous obligations in other countries that you cannot avoid or evade, and should not."

Nomura, the largest securities firm in the world, offers an example of a global firm trying to differentiate its national identities. For Asian markets outside of Japan, Nomura wanted to establish an Asian identity rather than a Japanese one. It moved its Asian offices out of Tokyo to Hong Kong and Singapore and began running television advertisements stressing its Asian identity. The campaign met with skepticism from rival investment bankers from other countries who said that Nomura would remain "incorrigibly Japanese."

Establishing multiple national identities will always be a demanding challenge for public relations professionals.

STANDARDIZE OR CUSTOMIZE?

The issue of national identity is part of the larger issue of standardization versus customization, which is the central issue of global public relations. The issue can be stated as the question: Are our markets so different as to require different public relations approaches for each one or can we standardize our approach for all markets and reap some scale advantages from uniform branding, positioning, and buying?

In the real world, individual circumstances will dictate the answer to this question. Two cosmetics brands may take opposite approaches. For example, Procter & Gamble launched Max Factor International with exactly the same colors and identical advertising around the world. Maybelline Inc., however, customizes its mix for each country on the grounds that different markets demand different features. Women in Asia do not want products with fragrance added while South American women prefer richer color tones.

Another example comes from the banking industry, where two global banking giants are taking opposite approaches to establishing a consumer banking network around the world. Citicorp is using the same brand everywhere. HSBC Holdings, the U.K.-based bank, operates its global consumer businesses through subsidiaries with individual branding and positioning programs.

In favor of standardization, it can be argued that consistency of messages, images and point of view is needed to gain the economic advantages of a global offering. When Gillette introduced the SensorExcell razor in 19 countries simultaneously, it engaged one public relations firm to take the lead to ensure integrated, coordinated communications.

Yet, extremes of standardization are probably more characteristic of a simple exporter or of a mainly domestic company with foreign subsidiaries than of a truly global firm. Though Gillette used one lead firm for the SensorExcell, 10 different local firms worked with the lead firm to tailor the marketing support materials. The lead firm developed the core messages and prototype materials and served as the central coordinator and resource point. The local firms adapted these messages and materials to fit local languages, customs, media channels and types of retail outlets.

The mix of standardized and customized elements in this integrated program was described as follows by a Gillette executive speaking to the *Public Relations Journal*: "While the strategy and messages are global, the public relations has to be local. That's why we left to local discretion the nature of the message delivery. In some markets, our representatives held one-on-one conferences with the media; in other areas, a press event was the main vehicle for announcing the new product."

ADAPTING ON THE FRINGES

Yet, no single rule of thumb exists for achieving the right balance between standardization and customization. Often it can pay to stick to your guns, even when your standard way of doing things seems at first glance to be inappropriate to the local culture. When TGI Friday's Inc. expanded into England, the restaurant company was faced with the prospect of having to relax its requirement that customers be greeted and served with a very American kind of outgoing sociability. Waiters in Britain, the company was told, were much too reserved for all that and just would not be comfortable or convincing singing "Happy Birthday" to customers. TGI Friday's solution was to keep their American-grown standard, which was at the core of their service offering, and to change their screening procedures for job applicants by replacing the traditional job interview with theaterlike onstage auditions designed to pick out the candidates who could comfortably project the desired warm cheerful friendliness.

A standardized approach worked for TGI Friday's but it required special adaptation for marketplace differences. The ability to adapt on the fringes while retaining the core service offering is often the key to success in global marketing. IKEA almost foundered in the U.S. market before it was able to make the necessary adaptations. In the process, it had to revise its most basic tenet, which was, in the words of *The Economist*, "that it could sell the same product in the same way in Houston as it could in Helsingborg."

Products were redesigned and manufacturing locations added for the U.S. market. When research showed that American shoppers would not tolerate the lengthy checkout lines customary in IKEA's European outlets, the company made changes in store layout and installed additional cash registers to speed throughput by 20 percent. The image or identity itself required changes. Advertising and promotional materials had been stressing not only clean Scandinavian design but also the blue and yellow Swedish national colors. For the U.S. market, IKEA's identity had to evolve into "a new alloy," according to the head of North American operations. "It's still blue and yellow, but mixing in the stars and stripes."

In building a standard global image for its pens, Parker Pen used a promotional program featuring letters from satisfied customers. The core materials were developed in London and then the letters were revised and edited by local agencies in continental Europe, the United States, Australia, the Far East, Argentina, Mexico, and South Africa to fit the cultures of the different markets.

There are times when standardization has to be reduced to the bare minimum. "In Japan, Mr. Donut changed everything about its product/service, except for the logo," in the words of Kenichi Ohmae.

VARIABLE POSITIONING

When everything but Mr. Donut's logo can change, it shows the degree to which brand or company image and positioning can vary from one national market to another. Often this results not from a grand plan, but from a series of pragmatic adjustments to the value structures and the demands of different markets.

In the United Kingdom, the name Heinz is associated most often with beans; in the United States, Heinz more often means ketchup. The Ramada Inns and Radisson Hotels are positioned at the higher end of the scale in Europe but midscale in the United States. Fran Wilson Creative Cosmetics is positioned as a budget brand in the United States, but much more upscale in Europe.

LEARNING THE HARD WAY

Adjusting to the market is not always painless. Many a public relations practitioner has labored fruitlessly to develop promotional and informational materials and programs to persuade a target market that it didn't really need what it was asking for.

When Diebold, the Ohio-based manufacturer of automated teller machines (ATMs), entered the European market, it learned that some European countries require that signals from the keyboard of the ATM to the computer be encrypted. This was a totally unnecessary step in the opinion of the company's engineers. Diebold subsequently lost 18 months in some markets trying to persuade buyers that they didn't really need this feature, which they were asking for. "That's called learning the hard way," said the Diebold CEO, looking back on the experience.

Bausch & Lomb had a similar experience in Japan with contact lenses, where the company faced what seemed to be irrational demands from the market. Japanese ophthalmologists were demanding a nearly perfect contact lens surface — one that far exceeded clinical requirements elsewhere. Unable to persuade the market to change its requirements, Bausch & Lomb developed a new process and built a new plant to meet the Japanese specifications and eventually captured 11 percent of the market.

WORKING WITH RISK FACTORS

A standardized image, positioning, branding, or public relations program may need to be modified in response to special risks posed by particular national markets.

Many countries, for example, place limits on the amounts of money that can be taken out of the country, which effectively forces foreign companies to reinvest their revenues or their profits in the country in order to build its economy. A comprehensive public relations program in such a country might well incorporate ongoing efforts to publicize your company's contribution and long-term commitment to the country's economy. Speaking of one such economically significant third-world country, an experienced executive of a global firm said, "You don't go in there with a three- or five-year plan. You better have a fifty-year plan."

In extreme circumstances, the risk could be one of expropriation or nationalization of assets. More commonly today, the risk is simply one of excessive bureaucratic delays or other difficulties in obtaining the required licenses to do business. Regardless, it is a worthwhile communications objective in most parts of the world to demonstrate an ongoing commitment to the economic welfare and prosperity of the country in which you are doing business. For example, when Marks and Spencer, the British retailer, opened an office in Shanghai to study the possibility of putting stores on mainland China, it released the information that it already was buying more than $150 million in merchandise a year from the country. On the same day, the British Overseas Development Commission announced an aid grant of $4 million for projects to improve Shanghai's municipal water supply.

In all parts of the world, there is always the risk of a sudden imposition of restrictive tariffs, import quotas, and hard currency quarantines. For example, according to an account in *The Economist*, Brazil suddenly and without consultation with its Mercosur trading partners announced quotas in mid-1995 that would cut car imports in half, imperiling the investments in inventory and production capacity of Argentinean car makers dependent on the Brazilian market. Reacting to the outrage that this unilateral move provoked, Brazil agreed to suspend the quotas while the two countries talked.

Finally, there are special risks that are unique to particular countries at particular times in their histories. These are risks for which no experience in your home country could quite prepare you. Punitive damage awards by juries in the United States would fall in this category. Among the more memorable awards of recent years was the $11 billion in damages against Texaco awarded to Pennzoil by a jury in Texas for interfering with a merger agreement between Pennzoil and Getty Oil. No less memorable if on a smaller scale was the $2.7 million award against McDonald's granted by an New Mexico jury to a woman who, while opening a cup of hot coffee that she had placed between her legs while sitting in a car, spilled it and burned herself. Overseas companies setting up operations in the United States would have to count the U.S. legal doctrine of punitive damages as a special hazard of the country.

CRISES

With the dramatic advances in communications technology and the freeing up of information markets around the world, the need for prompt and decisive action in dealing with public relations crises has risen accordingly. Bad news travels much faster and farther now than it did even a decade ago. There was no CNN to break the news and provide continuous coverage of the worst industrial accident in history at Bhopal, India, in 1984. There were no fax machines or e-mail connections between the Danbury, Connecticut, headquarters of Union Carbide and the accident site where thousands died.

A company that operates globally will find that a local disaster or crisis can put its reputation at risk around the world. Crisis management then has to take account of markets far removed from the crisis site and prepare materials to keep operations around the world informed and prepared to respond to inquiries from local media.

Perrier dealt very effectively with the contamination crisis in the United States in 1990, recalling 72 million bottles while keeping the public and media in this country informed. The Perrier brand retained consumer confidence in the United States, but local media coverage in parts of Europe damaged consumer confidence there.

Disasters that occur on foreign ground can heighten sensitivities between countries and may call for extra measures to demonstrate total corporate concern and an unbounded urgent commitment to minimize suffering and damage and to restore order. A company's response sends a message to all countries and markets around the world with regard to the esteem in which it holds its foreign markets. The failure of the CEO of Union Carbide to show up in India at the time of the Bhopal catastrophe had great symbolic significance for the entire world. The international implications of Bhopal made the no-show there a greater public relations blunder than the failure of the CEO of Exxon to show up after the Valdez ran aground off Alaska.

It takes a high level of in-country sophistication to be able to manage the public relations side of a crisis. If you do not work regularly in the country of crisis, you should not attempt to go it alone. Local counsel should be retained — not to formulate policy but to advise on local conditions and to work under direction on implementation.

An important aspect of international public relations management is the monitoring of national risks and the preparation of policies and plans for dealing with them. Depending on your degree of exposure in the country, these plans may need to be quite detailed with names, phone numbers, and fax numbers of local journalists, governmental administrators, and key politicians, procedures for approving communications, designation of spokespersons, and so forth.

KNOW YOUR AUDIENCE

Knowing your risks is ultimately a matter of knowing your markets and your audiences. For that, you have to get up close and look carefully. From afar, different markets can look beguilingly similar.

The channels of public relations influence differ enormously from one country to another, even between market segments within a country. An integrated public relations program to support your company's product, service, objective, or image in a particular region of the world needs to reflect an understanding of who needs to be influenced, in what order, and what communications vehicles and channels are most effective. In some regions of the world, it would be impolitic to approach the public through a media campaign without first securing the support of the right government ministry. In other regions, it would be pointless to approach the ministry without having first developed a threshold level of popular demand. In some countries, there are newspapers in every hamlet and crossroads village; in others, newspapers have no influence outside of the principal urban areas.

Every market, nation, and culture has its own totems and taboos to which the global communicator cannot afford to be oblivious if he or she wishes to have influence in the chosen market. If you don't know the market intimately, you need to work with someone who does — and not just a long-time emigrant who still keeps up with the language. You need someone who is immersed in the day-to-day bustle of the marketplace.

THE BUZZ OF THE MARKET

At one level, there is the endless daily flow of scandal, notoriety, and celebrity that becomes the subject of much of the everyday conversation of people in the culture. Most of this is fleeting and totally obscure to outsiders. Take, for example, the counterfeit lemonade scheme that made the papers in the United Kingdom in 1995. A gang of criminals manufactured and sold millions of pounds sterling of counterfeit Coca-Cola and Schweppes lemonade. One gang member, fearing violence to his family, chose imprisonment rather than obey a court order to talk.

If you were in the beverage industry and had significant foreign operations in England, you would not want to be represented there by a media or public relations person who could stay oblivious to the lemonade scandal through the summer of 1995. When you are trying to persuade people that your organization or cause has their best interests at heart and that your product or service is up to the minute and exactly what they need today, you don't want to be ignorant of the local buzz in your particular market or industry. You certainly do not want to project a public relations presence that looks out of touch and clueless.

If you were in the wines and spirits business on the European continent in the fall of 1995, you would want to have local public relations counsel savvy enough to pick up on newspaper stories that Sweden had decided to import 5,000 metric tons of cheap red wine from Spain to fuel environmentally friendly buses after the price of ethanol rose by 30 percent.

There are organizations and causes that achieve such extraordinary celebrity in their home countries for a period of time that every communicator working in the culture needs to be aware of them. In picking a partner to handle public relations for you in the United States, you wouldn't want someone who didn't know of the organization Mothers Against Drunk Driving (MADD). Similarly, in relying on someone to be your public relations voice in Russia, you don't want someone who doesn't know of the Soldiers' Mothers Committee, which achieved national prominence in the Chechen war when women traveled to the war zone to collect their sons and bring them home and which now works to help young men find legal ways to beat the military draft.

LANGUAGE

There are more permanent characteristics within each culture that communicators must be able to deal with. The most important, of course, is language. It is a mistake to assume that English is always suitable just because it is the world language of business. Even in the face-to-face industrial marketing of highly specialized products and even when most of the customer's people can speak some English, it is far better to have sales aids, such as videotapes and brochures, produced in the language that the customer speaks every day. This calls for more than enlisting the local high school teacher of the language to do a translation. The pieces should sound and look at home and up to the minute in the customer's culture.

Language is more than words. An article in *Brandweek* recounts the example of a U.S. ad for a laundry detergent that was translated into Arabic and the ad sent to an Arab agency for placement in local media. The words had been translated but the order of the three panels in the ad remained the same. When read from right to left as is the custom in Arabic, the ad started out with clean, freshly laundered clothes in the first panel, continued with detergent being added to a washing machine in the second panel, and finished with a pile of soiled clothes in the third.

Some experts advise thinking globally from the beginning. This means that the piece is written with several languages in mind, perhaps by bilingual writers. Obvious translation difficulties are avoided. Plays on words, for example, are extremely difficult to translate and many idioms and folk sayings do not convey the same message when translated literally into another language.

A number of major global firms, such as American Express, IBM, and UPS, routinely produce their employee newsletters, annual reports, and sales brochures in a variety of languages.

Whatever the case, issues of language should be thought through carefully: If you send out a press release translated into Japanese just to impress your Japanese distributor, you better have a speaker of Japanese available to handle phone calls from Japanese journalists.

THOUGHT CONTROL AND INFORMATION QUARANTINES

Cultures also differ greatly in the degree to which they impose controls on the free flow of information. In the 1970s and 1980s, photocopying machines were outlawed in many countries of the former Soviet bloc. Even today, in the wake of the collapse of command economies all over the world, there are governments that try to retain tight controls over the channels of communication.

The Vietnamese government recently announced its intent to control all Internet communications in and out of the country in order to stem unwanted foreign influences. An executive of the Vietnam Data Communication Company was quoted in the *Financial Times* as saying, "The Internet must be controlled, not only for technical and security reasons but from the cultural aspect." He cited foreign pornography as one concern. The other: "Abroad there are some organisations that don't like our state. From abroad, they can send information."

MARKETS HAVE LONG MEMORIES

Cultural biases that the public relations communicator has to deal with often go back far in the collective memory of the culture. Markets have long memories. For example, the roots of France's successful current trade relationships with Africa have been traced back to the colonial era. In the words of *The Economist*: "The British colonial-era norm was to keep Africa at bay with gin-and-tonics sipped in a white English club, while the French were more inclined to go out to hear Zairumba music at African clubs."

The public relations practitioner needs to know how the target market remembers his or her company or industry. Deservedly or not, the company's reputation may need rebuilding through a carefully orchestrated communications campaign. Many companies that fail in early attempts to penetrate foreign markets find that the battle for credibility gets harder each time because of the accumulating burden of earlier failures. Even when earlier attempts enjoyed great success, changed political circumstances may have effectively rewritten the record in the minds of those in power today.

Consider the South Korean chaebol who have been very actively funding investments in Vietnam since the United States normalized relations with that country. Many of them launched their international successes with military supply contracts and enormous construction projects for U.S. military installations during the Vietnam war some 30 years ago and now regard Vietnam as their own back yard. Memory associations in the market might understandably be complex and ambivalent.

In another example, the old-line Hong Kong investment banking firm of Jardine Fleming has used its history and contacts to great advantage in many Asian markets, but its links to the colonial era may work to its disadvantage in China. According to an account in *The Economist*, "one of Jardine Fleming's parents, Jardine Matheson, has an awkward relationship with the Chinese government which some trace back to the Opium wars in the 19th century."

As a final example of market memory, the 19th-century legacy of the British East India Company is said to be still alive in India. In the words of *Business Week*, it "has bred a suspicion of foreigners that applies to companies, ideas, even tourists."

KNOWING THE MEDIA

Knowing the market means knowing the media. Despite the so-called globalization of popular culture and instantaneous presentation of news around the globe through satellite transmission, most media is still very much a thing of its own country. The reach of the media varies from country to country, the style and expectations vary, the accessibility varies.

Advertising legislation and regulation differs. Even within the European Community, big differences exist from one country to another on "what can be aired when, through what media, with what message, at what cost, with what disclaimers," in the words of the *International Journal of Advertising*.

On all important matters, you should engage local counsel to help you implement local promotion, publicity and information programs. What follows is just a very small sampling of media diversity around the world.

- Dealing with newspapers in Egypt is so unpredictable that experts say that the best chance for publicity is through special events.
- In many Latin America countries, because newspapers and

magazines don't reach mass audiences, products are promoted through community relations and sponsorship activities, including pop star tours.

- Because of their smaller size, it is harder to get business news placed in general circulation newspapers in France than it is in the United States. English language papers like the *Financial Times*, the *International Herald Tribune*, and the European edition of *The Wall Street Journal* are distributed, but coverage in these papers does not reach a general audience of domestic business people. For promoting business news in France, events, salons, and business fairs are very popular.

- In Eastern Europe, the excellent reach of television, with 80 percent of the population watching it daily, has to be balanced against limitations in some countries on the availability of programming and the amount of advertising that is allowed. In Poland, for example, advertising at one point was limited to 10 minutes per day. The situation, however, is changing rapidly. All of Central and Eastern Europe has undertaken a revision of press, media, and information laws.

- Newspaper readership varies greatly across Central and Eastern Europe, with high rates of readership in Hungary and the Czech Republic and much lower rates in Poland. As you would expect, press readership is much higher in urban than in rural areas and greater among the more educated segment of the population. Western publishers and broadcasts are making investments and acquiring media properties in the former Soviet-style command economies.

- The media mix is changing rapidly in Western Europe too, with television programming and channels continually being added. Cable is also growing, with some cities receiving channels in as many as seven different languages.

- Television advertising in China is rapidly growing in importance and now represents more than one-third of the country's advertising expenditures. At one point in the 1980s some stations carried more advertising than regular programming. China Central Television barters advertising space for programming from foreign producers. As television increases in importance, China's 14,000 newspapers will undoubtedly lose some share of influence.

Some useful guides to international media are *Bacon's International Media Directory*; *International Media Guide*; and *Ulrich's International Periodical Directory*.

FREEDOM OF THE MEDIA

Media standards vary greatly from one country to another. Editorial independence, for example, is treasured in the United States and is protected by Article One of the Constitution. Different societies, however, have different notions about the importance of independence or even whether it is desirable.

Some cultures place a greater value on editorial cooperation than on independence. The media is often expected to support a national agenda on political and economic matters. For example, many observers are struck by the extent to which Japanese journalists closely align themselves with the government and collaborate with large industrial organizations.

In another example, Singapore recently placed restrictions on the circulation of *The Economist* for failing to cooperate completely with government demands that the magazine publish its rebuttal statements in full without editorial deletions. Previously Singapore had restricted the circulations of *Time*, the *Asian Wall Street Journal*, *Asiaweek*, and the *Far Eastern Economic Review*.

In some countries, it is customary for the organization seeking media coverage to share or subsidize the cost. Only a few years have elapsed since the president of Mexico announced that the government would no longer pay the expenses of reporters on the government beat, but picking up a reporter's travel and meal expenses is still a tradition in many parts of the world.

Where there has been a long tradition of governmental propaganda of the agitprop type coupled with total state control of public communications, the public may be suspicious of media advertising. This is true in the former Soviet Union and some of Eastern Europe. Though attitudes may change over time as restrictions loosen, some experts still recommend avoiding the kind of direct product promotion that is taken for granted in consumer-oriented free-market economies. Infomercials and advertorials are recommended instead.

For similar reasons, audience or consumer research can be a ticklish subject in countries where all audience research was done by state propaganda agencies and kept highly secret. An historical parallel to this touchiness can be found in the pre-revolutionary American colonies where the public was dead set against the idea of the British crown taking a census of the population.

CULTURAL FAULT LINES

The job of the global communicator includes being sensitive to the fault lines in the cultures of his markets. Many of these fault lines reflect ancient splits between peoples based on ethnic, language, tribal, and religious differences. Often, these differences are exacerbated by economic disparities and political agendas. They can spawn passions great enough to mobilize whole populations to prolonged violence. They can be dormant for generations, erupt in bloodshed, and then become dormant again.

Dormant or healing now are the 20th century splits between East and West Germany, North and South Vietnam, North and South Korea, and black and white South Africa. Old fissures still undermine society in Canada, Spain, Ireland, and Turkey; new divides are opening up in many of the independent republics of the former Soviet Union; issues of religious fundamentalism continue to fracture societies in the Middle East and North Africa; while civilization itself has nearly been extinguished for a time in Rwanda and Bosnia.

KNOWING THE TRADE CHANNELS

Though vital, transparent, and all important to those dependent on them, specific trade channels can be as obscure and treacherous to outsiders as the backwater tributaries of large rivers. Many multi-million dollar marketing initiatives have foundered on a misreading of the importance of apparently trivial differences between superficially similar distribution channels. The complexity increases exponentially across global markets, and local help is absolutely essential.

The retailing infrastructure differs enormously from country to country; a so-called global brand can find itself sold door-to-door in one country and in department stores in another. Automobile retailing in Japan has traditionally meant dealer salesmen armed with product literature calling on customers in their homes instead of the U.S. practice of customers going out to shop around at dealer showrooms.

Direct mail marketing is nowhere developed to the extent that it is in the United States. Some countries do not allow mail to be addressed to Occupant. Retail catalog companies in Europe will not exchange, rent, or sell their lists. Magazine subscription files that direct mail marketers rely on in the United States are not nearly so useful in Europe, particularly in the United Kingdom where most magazines are bought at the newsstand.

The databases and information services that a trade channel takes for granted in one country may not be available in another. When Golub & Co., a Chicago real estate development firm, entered the Eastern European market, it found that there were no databases with the information that was essential for decision making in its industry — square footage of office space, occupancy rates, zoning codes, and so forth. Golub created its own databases before getting involved in large office projects in Moscow, St. Petersburg, and Warsaw.

Companies operating in global markets often have to find creative solutions to unusual distribution problems. Here are a few examples.

- In Australia, facing restrictions on the number of retail branches that it could open, Citicorp formed a partnership with a chain of drugstores and trained store clerks to accept bank deposits.
- Wanting a presence in Singapore but believing that there were too few buyers and sellers to support a separate auction house, Sotheby's, the international art auctioneer, set up a local view-

ing room with a televised link to its auction room in Hong Kong.

- The Islamic republic of Iran has turned two Persian Gulf islands into trade zones, complete with shopping malls, restaurants, and hotels, to circumvent constitutional prohibitions on foreign ownership of business assets and restrictions on currency export. Iranian importers use the islands of Kish and Qeshm as a bridge to the West.

GUIDELINES FOR SURVIVAL

This brief review of the terrain of the international public relations battlefield concludes with a list of guidelines for survival. The guidelines more or less summarize the material of the chapter. They are meant to be helpful for both the novice and the experienced practitioner who find themselves facing a professional challenge with international dimensions.

For the novice, the guidelines are meant to stimulate thinking and provide a starting point for organizing his efforts. For the experienced practitioner, the guidelines are meant to serve as a checklist for recalling, gathering, and applying the lessons of his or her own experience.

Guideline One.

Think through the standardization versus customization issue. Look at the trade-offs. Most solutions involve a compromise. Standardization is for overall efficiency; customization is for local effectiveness. Standardization provides leverage; customization provides precision. Some products, services, organizations and causes lend themselves to standardized programs more than others. Where does yours fit?

Guideline Two.

Get local help for local implementation. No matter how detailed the central plan, execution and implementation are always local events. Remember that things change. "Local" means on-the-spot and up-to-the-minute.

Guideline Three.

Remember that a lot more than language changes as you cross national borders. Look for differences in media channels, editorial practices, retail infrastructure, distribution channels, trade practices, government regulations, commercial specifications, and so forth.

Guideline Four.

Check into the intangibles of the target market and how they could affect your program. Consider the memory of the market, the buzz of the marketplace, the customs of the country, and the taboos of the culture. Look for the right balance between tradition and fashion.

Guideline Five.
Be realistic about scope and scale. As you cross cultural and national borders, the complexity of the communications challenge increases exponentially. Evaluate your ability to achieve information dominance in the necessary channels.

Guideline Six.
Be smart about unusual risks. Each market, nation, and culture has its own. Make a risk list. Critique your ability and readiness to react. Develop risk avoidance and minimization plans. Weigh risks against rewards.

REFERENCES

"A Singapore saga," *The Economist*, August 7, 1993.

"Border crossings: brands unify image to counter cult of culture (companies strive to develop global brand products)," *Brandweek*, October 31, 1994.

"Dangerous liaisons," *The Economist*, July 23, 1994.

"Drinks racketeer jailed," *Financial Times*, September 19, 1995.

"Free for all, but keep your veil on," *The Economist*, September 10, 1994.

"Furnishing the world," *The Economist*, November 19, 1994.

"Hammering Asia," *The Economist*, September 17, 1994.

"Inside the empire of Exxon the unloved," *The Economist*, March 5, 1994.

"Marks and Spencer dips toe into China," *Financial Times*, October 12, 1995.

"Red wine to fuel Swedish buses," *Financial Times*, September 20, 1995.

"Shanghai to get UK aid," *Financial Times*, October 12, 1995.

"The discreet charm of the multicultural multinational," *The Economist*, July 30, 1994.

"The Americas drift towards free trade," *The Economist*, July 8, 1995.

"Where the action is," *The Economist*, November 12, 1994.

Anderson, Stephen. "Successfully working with international journalists," *Communication World*, September 1994.

Atkinson, Lisa. "China TV guide," *The China Business Review*, September-October 1994.

Birch, John. "New factors in crisis planning and response," *Public Relations Quarterly*, Spring 1994.

Brookman, Faye. "Global concerns for the cosmetics industry," *Soap Perfumery & Cosmetics*, June 1993.

Caporimo, James. "Worldwide advertising has benefits, but one size doesn't always fit all," *Brandweek*, July 17, 1995.

Dempsey, Gerry. "Global communication comes into its own," *Communication World*, December 1992.

Dibb, Sally, et al. "Pan-European advertising: think Europe — act local," *International Journal of Advertising*, Spring 1994.

Doolin, Wallace. "Taking your business on the road abroad," Manager's Journal, *The Wall Street Journal*, July 25, 1994.

Evans, David. "Innocence abroad (pitfalls of marketing overseas)," *Marketing Computers*, May 1995.

Freeland, Chrystia. "Anger mounts over military draft," *Financial Times*, September 19, 1995.

Gapper, John. "Big is beautiful once again (global banks)," *Financial Times*, October 6, 1995.

Grant, Jeremy. "Vietnamese move to bring the Internet under control may backfire," *Financial Times*, September 19, 1995.

Gray, Frank. "Cracking a lucrative market," *Financial Times*, September 26, 1995.

Hamm, Steve. "Sound the gong," *PC Week*, July 24, 1995.

Hammonds, Keith H. "Ted Levitt is back in the trenches," *Business Week*, April 9, 1990.

Hannemann, Timothy. "Defense diversification," *Harvard International Review*, Summer 1994.

Hauss, Deborah. "Global communications come of age," *Public Relations Journal*, August 1993.

Hibbert, Ray E. "Global public relations in a post-communist world," *Public Relations Review*, Summer 1992.

—————. "Public relations and mass communication in Eastern Europe," *Public Relations Review*, Summer 1992.

Howard, Elizabeth. "Going global: what it really means to communicators," *Communication World*, April 1995.

Jacob, Rahul. "Citicorp, capturing the global consumer," *Fortune*, December 13, 1993.

—————. "Corporate performance [Bausch & Lomb]," *Fortune*, May 4, 1992.

Josephs, Ray and Juanita W. "Public relations in France," *Public Relations Journal*, July 1993.

—————. "Public relations the U.K. way," *Public Relations Journal*, April 1994.

Miller, Cyndee. "Not quite global: marketers 'discover' the world but still have much to learn," *Marketing News*, July 3, 1995.

Moshavi, Sharon. "Get the 'Foreign Devils,'" *Business Week*, October 23, 1995.

Nakamoto, Michiyo. "Forced out by yen," *Financial Times*, September 25, 1995.

Norton, Rob. "Strategies for the new export boom," *Fortune*, August 22, 1994.

Ohmae, Kenichi. *The Borderless World: Power and Strategy in the Interlinked Economy* (1990).

Sellers, Patricia. "Pepsi opens a second front," *Fortune*, August 8, 1994.

Sharlach, Jeffrey R. "A new era in Latin America: free markets force changes in five key nations," *Public Relations Journal*, September 1993.

Sharpe, Melvin L. "The impact of social and cultural conditioning on global public relations," *Public Relations Review*, Summer 1992.

Snoddy, Raymond. "Broadcasters dish up a revolution," *Financial Times*, October 6, 1995.

————. "TV takes a worldwide view," *Financial Times*, October 6, 1995.

Spiers, Paul. "Public Relations in Egypt and the Middle East," *Communication World*, February 1992.

Tagliabue, John. "Coca-Cola reaches into impoverished Albania," *The New York Times*, May 20, 1994.

Treaster, Joseph B. "Kellogg seeks to reset Latvia's breakfast table," *The New York Times*, May 19, 1994.

Tylee, John. "Global Parker idea allows local slants," *Campaign*, December 6, 1991.

Walker, Richard. "Chaebol eye Vietnamese market," *Financial Times*, September 19, 1995.

Wiesendanger, Betsy. "Competition changing Mexican media," *Public Relations Journal*, June-July 1994.

Yelpaala, Kojo. "Strategy and planning in global product distribution," *Law and Policy in International Business*, Spring 1994.

Joseph A. Kopec is a principal with The Dilenschneider Group in Chicago. He's advised Fortune 100 (NYSE) companies on many of the largest restructuring communications in recent years. He has created, written, and advised on financial communications issues related to mergers, acquisitions, and divestitures.

From 1982 to 1991 he was a senior vice president and managing director with Hill and Knowlton where he advised corporations on all aspects of communications. Prior to joining Hill and Knowlton, he was director of communications for the Hay Group, a division of Saatchi & Saatchi. He directed public information for the Attorney General of Ohio and was part of Senator John Glenn's election campaign.

Art Gormley, a principal in The Dilenschneider Group, joined DGI from Hill and Knowlton in April of 1992. Gormley, who had been a senior vice president and a unit manager in H&K's financial relations division since 1989, counseled and oversaw a number of that division's largest and most active accounts.

Prior to Hill and Knowlton, Gormley was a senior vice president and a member of the management committee of Doremus Public Relations, an agency specializing in corporate and financial communications.

Gormley has an extensive financial background. He is a certified public accountant and was a senior member of the financial staff of Weeden & Company, the securities house, in the mid-1970s. He began his career with Arthur Andersen & Company, the international public accounting firm.

CHAPTER 7

INVESTOR RELATIONS

Investor relations that work are based on the simple principle that no individual or institution should invest in the securities of a company unless he or she is fully informed about the current business and its future prospects.

As A.R. Roalman said in the Foreword to *Investor Relations Handbook* (Roalman, AMACOM 1974):

> This book is based on the premise that an individual is not likely to invest his money — whether it's a thousand dollars, ten thousand dollars, a hundred dollars, or a million dollars — in a corporation's stocks, bonds, commercial paper, or other financial pledges unless he believes strongly that he understands fully what is likely to happen to that corporation in the future. This book reflects the belief that more investors' willingness to invest in a corporation is influenced by their trust in its management.

Trust isn't built overnight. It is a result of long-term actions by the corporation to provide factual financial information in proper perspective. It is the result of well-grounded, honorable investor relations activities.

Unfortunately, investor relations is ill-defined and poorly understood by many managers. Just what is it?

Investor relations is, in fact, a science. There are many laws that specify what must be done and what must not be done. It is also an art. Many unstructured situations with investor relations develop in the course of a corporate year. Only extensive experience, a strong commitment to the most honorable relationships with investors, and a management style predicated on the belief that a corporate entity must act in its long-term interests (rather than short-term ones) can develop the best programs.

Much has changed since Roalman edited this formative book for the National Investor Relations Institute more than 20 years ago. Yet much remains the same. Today much emphasis is placed on shareholder value, "marketing" companies in the domestic and international stock markets, and targeting institutional investors using sophisticated electronic, computer-driven models that massage vast quantities of data to find just the right money managers or analysts to invest in a company. And yet, the fundamentals of investor relations require honorable relationships, trust, and a commitment of management to communicate in times of adverse results as well as in balmy days when stock markets rise and stocks are doing well.

In the following pages, we present two different aspects of effective investor relations. The section on Investor Relations for Newly Public Companies describes how a company goes public. Many corporations are going through restructurings that include spinoffs, carve-outs, and public offerings. This section will appeal to executives who are contemplating taking their company public or who have never been responsible for investor relations and now face the prospect of being a senior executive in a company that must report significant and material information on a regular basis.

The second section, Creating an Investor Relations Program, deals with an entire year in the life of a publicly traded company. Though it too discusses "going public for a new company," this section reviews all those activities that a company undertakes on a recurring basis. These include 10K and 10Q forms, proxy solicitation, the annual meeting, and annual report. A discussion of "disclosure" and the concept of "material information" is kept brief. The chapter then shifts to discretionary investor relations activities, such as various other relationships, meetings, publications, and investor relations R&D.

INVESTOR RELATIONS FOR NEWLY PUBLIC COMPANIES

Investor relations activities make an essential contribution to a public company's ability to compete effectively for the attention of the investment community. While the IR function itself does not create a company's underlying value, it brings the company's fundamental attributes to the attention of the financial marketplace.

On one side of the equation is operating management, with the responsibility for operational results and prospects that constitute the "productive" aspect of enhancing shareholder value. On the "explanatory" side is IR, whose job it is to create and maintain the relationships with investors and other key audiences that will ensure a receptive and well-informed market for a company's stock.

It is important to note the fundamental difference between investor relations in the going public process and the practice of IR once the company has gone public. IR during an initial public offering (IPO) is a function that has a beginning and an end, starting with the pre-registration planning stage and ending with the closing of the offering. Investor relations activities directly related to this process can be viewed as project-oriented.

Once the company has completed its offering, investor relations takes on a larger role within the framework of the strategic plans of the company. It is ongoing and future-focused. While the immediate benefit may be more difficult to measure than during the going public process, it will continue to evolve as the company grows both in size and recognition.

Through written descriptions, timelines, charts, and other information, this guide presents a framework for investor relations' value-added contribution to the going public process and to the company's first years of operation in the public sector. The practice of investor relations in a newly public company is distinctly different from IR in a corporation that has an established presence in the securities markets.

This section seeks to address the policies and practice of IR from the unique perspective of the company planning an IPO. Why? Because you've only got one chance to make a first impression.

Pre-Registration Activities

Once the seminal questions of "Can We Go Public?" and "Should We Go Public?" are answered affirmatively, the real work begins.

Descriptions of the process of going public (Exhibit 7.1) often concentrate almost exclusively on the so-called registration stage, which begins roughly at the time the Board of Directors authorizes proceeding with the IPO (and the underwriters are brought in) and ends with the Closing (i.c. cash-in-hand).

EXHIBIT 7.1 — THE PROCESS/PRE-REGISTRATION

PRE-REGISTRATION	REGISTRATION	PUBLIC COMPANY
⟶		

This focus is well deserved, for the registration period requires an intense amount of work, carefully choreographed by the Securities and Exchange Commission (SEC), and performed by a troupe of underwriters, lawyers and accountants. However, the importance of investor relations-oriented activities in the pre-registration period cannot be ignored or underestimated. Though often only vaguely described in most available materials about going public, or given mere passing mention in outlines provided by underwriters or legal counsel (e.g. "Discuss communications strategy"), pre-registration IR activities provide a crucial foundation for the marketing of the stock during and after the IPO.

The performance of an IPO is related to a number of factors including the amount of capital to be raised; the price; the percentage of the company being offered; market conditions; and the quality of underwriting. How smoothly the registration process flows is a function of how quickly the SEC processes the application papers, how well prepared the company is as a result of the pre-registration planning effort, and the degree of intra-team coordination and cooperation. The SEC is an external variable; the degree of teamwork is an internal variable that can be greatly enhanced by careful pre-registration planning.

Pre-registration investor relations activities must be established and conducted within the legal constraints of the registration process, and coordinated with the marketing agenda of the underwriters, once this group is brought on board.

Because there are no "investors," per se, for the company to "relate" to as yet, the activities to be considered before a company launches into the registration period often are described as "financial" or "public" relations. While public relations activities necessarily are complementary, IR in an IPO is to be distinguished from any pre-existing advertising or public relations programs the company has operative as a private entity. In those cases where a company has active public relations programs or product/corporate advertising, such programs may serve as a foundation on which to build a pre-registration IR program. But it is still necessary to evaluate them in light of the audiences they reach and, more importantly, review and adjust them to ensure they fall within the legal boundaries of the IPO process.

The Goals of Pre-Registration Investor Relations

In general, there are two goals of pre-registration investor relations:

- To inform the financial community and general public about the company and its business; and
- To establish a (so-called) "normal" pattern of communications activities.

Companies are well advised to commence activities towards achieving these goals at least a year prior to launching into the registration process. Once that process begins, the SEC imposes a moratorium on any activities that can be construed as an offering to sell the stock (outside of its carefully prescribed procedures) or as an effort to "condition the market."

The investor relations activities during the pre-registration period are one part of a broader effort known as pre-registration "house cleaning," which may include:

- Reorganizing the corporate organizational structure so as to be more suitable (understandable; describable; secure against insider transactions); reorganizing the capital structure;
- Developing and/or revising Articles of Incorporation and by-laws (to remove archaic or unnecessary provisions, or accommodate anti-take over considerations);
- Rethinking and reworking financial reporting methods and controls;
- Bringing on new management;
- Adopting or revising employee benefit plans, evaluating tax issues and cleaning up pending litigation.

The IR review involves examining existing public relations and advertising programs and, in absence of these, creating such programs, within the development and implementation context of an overall "communications strategy."

This strategy will be followed throughout the registration period until the time when SEC restrictions on the marketing activities of an IPO are lifted. It will address the assignment of responsibilities within the company for investor relations tasks such as writing and disseminating press releases and writing speeches for the "Road Show" presentations. It may propose a more sophisticated approach to how and what materials will be prepared for the Road Show, such as a video presentation or use of color graphics in the prospectus. It also should include the company's strategy for investor relations once the company has gone public, including staffing the function and developing an investor relations program.

It is equally important in the early planning stages of going public for the company to educate itself about the IPO scene. Establishing personal contact with principals of other companies that recently have gone public as well as developing an increased sensitivity to public information on initial public offerings in the press is to be encouraged. Venture and INC magazines have monthly columns reviewing recent public offerings; the national business press regularly publishes overviews of activity in the IPO market as well as individual vignettes. Experience is, and remains, the best teacher, and there is value in learning as much as possible from the experiences of others.

Related to this are a significant number of "research-oriented" tasks that can be started. Foremost is investigation of the underwriting services, which can be provided by the company's current investment bankers as well as by other firms that may have capabilities more appropriate for the circumstances. Experienced legal counsel is crucial, too. There are also decisions to be made that require careful research such as whether the company should list its securities on one of the exchanges or trade over the counter through the NASDAQ system. The company may find that this decision is made "by default" (if the company does not meet the criteria for listing established by the New York and American Stock Exchanges) but if there is a choice, the advantages and disadvantages, with particular regard for the effect on the marketability of the stock, must be weighed.

Formulating a plan for pre-registration investor relations requires two distinct activities. First, a comprehensive review should be made of the statutory prohibitions that will restrict and define activities during the registration period (and a discussion scheduled with legal counsel specifically on this topic). Second, a thorough, objective, introspective evaluation of the company and its strengths should be made from the investor's point of view. From this evaluation will emerge an initial orientation to the company which then can be molded into what will become the company's "story" to present to investors.

Overview of Activities

General guidelines in the form of lists of the types of communications activities that are — and aren't — permissible during an initial public offering always run the risk of being incomplete or misapplied to the individual circumstances of each company (see Exhibit 7.2). The advice of legal counsel is recommended before, and at the time, the pre-registration IR plan is designed.

Developing a Communications Strategy

At the same time the company is "educating" itself as to the impact of the '33 Act on its communications activities (both current and planned), it also needs to perform the self-analysis mentioned as the second part of pre-registration IPO planning.

The purpose of this effort is to develop an orientation: how will the company present itself to potential investors? And who are the investors to which this "story" will appeal?

Each company's investor relations (see Exhibit 7.3) plan for the registration process will evolve from an analysis of these factors:

- Current Programs of advertising or public relations — how much recognition preexists among potential investors? Is there a planned program for product advertising or has it been off-and-on?

- Ambitions, or long range plans, missions, goals — what are they? Is the company seeking vertical or horizontal expansion? Is it looking for future growth and recognition across the country or overseas? How is corporate strategy articulated? Is there a corporate mission statement?

- Nature of the Offering — the envisioned "deal," including how much capital is to be raised; number of shares and pricing configuration possibilities; whether the underwriters will agree to a "firm commitment" offering (where they will buy the entire issue and take responsibility for reselling it). The circumstances of the offering — is this a start-up company with no track record or public awareness, or a spin-off of a larger corporation; a private company in operation for some time seeking a new source of capital or a "reverse LBO"?

- Peer/Competitive Activity — both in the industry and in the new-issues market — what other companies are competing for investor attention and dollars? How are they publicizing the effort? Who will the industry "peers" be once the company has gone public and what are their investor relations activities?

- Market Factors — is the market tight or good for IPOs? Is it volatile and likely to shift by the time the Registration Statement is filed? What are the market factors affecting peer industry stocks? Who is buying IPOs and why?

- Company and Business — size, history of operations, diverse

EXHIBIT 7.2 — OVERVIEW OF PERMISSIBLE/IMPERMISSIBLE ACTIVITIES DURING AN INITIAL PUBLIC OFFERING

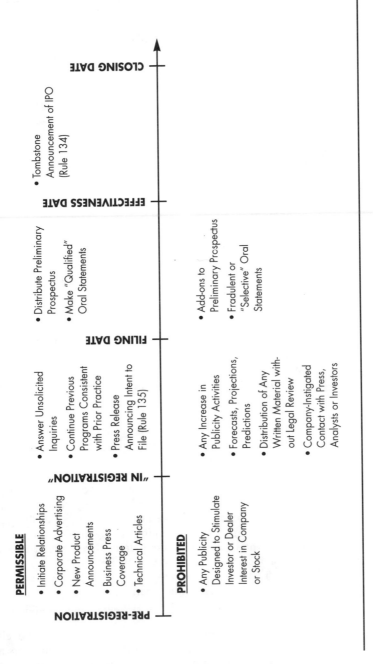

PRE-REGISTRATION

PERMISSIBLE

- Initiate Relationships
- Corporate Advertising
- New Product Announcements
- Business Press Coverage
- Technical Articles

PROHIBITED

- Any Publicity Designed to Stimulate Investor or Dealer Interest in Company or Stock

"IN REGISTRATION"

- Answer Unsolicited Inquiries
- Continue Previous Programs Consistent with Prior Practice
- Press Release Announcing Intent to File (Rule 135)

- Any Increase in Publicity Activities
- Forecasts, Projections, Predictions
- Distribution of Any Written Material without Legal Review
- Company-Instigated Contact with Press, Analysts or Investors

FILING DATE

- Distribute Preliminary Prospectus
- Make "Qualified" Oral Statements

- Add-ons to Preliminary Prospectus
- Fradulent or "Selective" Oral Statements

EFFECTIVENESS DATE

- Tombstone Announcement of IPO (Rule 134)

CLOSING DATE

EXHIBIT 7.3 — COMMUNICATIONS STRATEGY

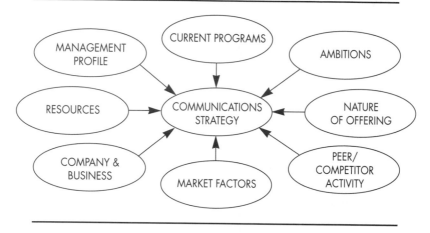

or single-industry, nature of products, distributors, customers, markets, geography and complexity of business. Is the technology established or new? Is the company in the consumer, or industrial products sector, or in the service industry? Is it located in, near or far from a major financial center? What are its growth rates, both historical and projected?

- Resources — internal and external; financial and management; how much is the company willing to spend and what are the "benefits" of each cost component? Will the company hire from within or go outside to find investor relations help? Who currently handles investment banking and legal activities?
- Management Profile — fresh or experienced; corporate culture and organizational structure; management credentials and confidence. Who's running the store?

Registration Activities

The boundary between the "pre-registration" and the "in registration" periods is very blurred. "In registration" is roughly defined as that period of time when all attention is turned toward the filing of the registration statement with the SEC, obtaining the agency's green-light go-ahead (otherwise known as having the plan declared effective) and closing the initial public offering (sealed with a check).

But is there any cut-and-dried rule as to when, exactly, the company ceases to be in a "pre-registration period," and is officially "in registration" and at once subject to the disclosure requirements and prohibitions of the '33 Act?

The answer is no. Any of a number of activities can effectively place a company in registration: a meeting of the Board of Directors at which the plans for the IPO activities are discussed and authorized;

issuance of an "intent to file" press release; the first "all hands" organizational meeting of the registration team members; the final selection of a managing underwriter. All these actions are symbolic of the commitment a company has made to proceed with the offering.

The best advice we can offer here is this: A company is in registration when its lawyers say it is.

What next? Exhibit 7.4 shows the process.

EXHIBIT 7.4 — THE PROCESS/REGISTRATION

PRE-REGISTRATION   **REGISTRATION**   **PUBLIC COMPANY**

⟶

The Registration Statement

The predominant preoccupation of the company and its registration team (described a few pages forward) is creation of the "Registration Statement," the formidable document that discloses information about the company in an orderly and legally prescribed fashion.

It includes information concerning risk factors, use of proceeds, dividends, capitalization, dilution, consolidated financial data, an "MD&A" section (management discussion and analysis of financial · condition and operating results), descriptions of the business of the company, management profiles, eligibility of shares for future sales, underwriting, legal opinions, expert opinions ... and, of course, financial statements and exhibits.

Once this document has been filed with the SEC for review and approval, it may be distributed as a "preliminary prospectus," or "Red Herring" (one and the same, the latter making reference to the required red-ink notification that it has not yet been declared effective). Only when the SEC approves the offering can the actual selling begin. The document, stripped of its warning, is printed in bulk and becomes "The Prospectus."

Due Diligence

Another equally significant activity that takes place during the registration period is the due diligence investigation. This is the practice whereby the company and its management undergo intense scrutiny of business activities and plans. This effort is directed toward proving that various claims are defensible; verifying the accuracy and completeness of disclosures made in the prospectus and building a possible defense to future litigation that might be instigated. An IPO, after all, inherently presents greater risk to the investor, and due diligence purports to reduce or eliminate the risk of misrepresentation which

EXHIBIT 7.5 — OVERVIEW OF THE REGISTRATION PROCESS

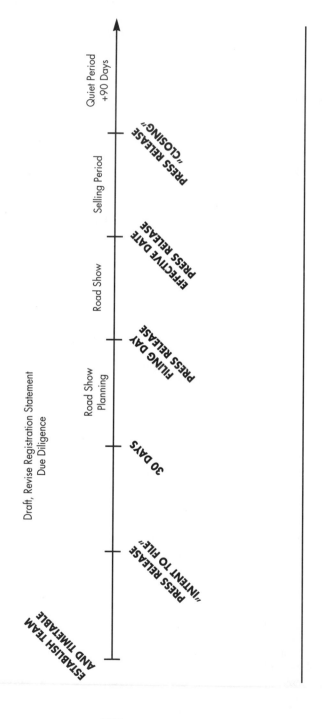

may advertently or inadvertently occur. Also considering the absence of other sources of information about a company, and since it is the company itself producing the registration statement, due diligence serves to validate the legitimacy of the company's practices and plans.

Due diligence activities typically include an investigation of the industry the company is in, a legal audit, and a comprehensive inspection of the company itself, including a thorough review of management, the company's business, and financials. This procedure encompasses a review of the charter, by-laws, and Board minutes for the past five years (or more) and of audited and unaudited financial statements over the same time period. The company's products, and relationships with customers, suppliers, banks, creditors, and trade associations are examined. Interviews with key company officials, on-site inspection of products, plant and equipment, and consultation with technical experts are also part of the process. Finally, each material fact contained in the Registration Statement is examined and verified.

Additional Documents

And this is still not the end of it. There are over a dozen additional documents that must be prepared to accompany the Registration Statement or supplement the process of going public. These include:

Agreement Among Underwriters — details the distribution of compensation and responsibilities among syndicate members and authorizes managing underwriter to sign underwriting agreement with issuer;

Underwriting Agreement — describes terms of offering, offering price and underwriting compensation for underwriters;

Underwriter's Questionnaire — document circulated among prospective syndicate members to verify names and addresses, relationships with issuers, etc.;

Underwriter's Memorandum — sales document about the offering prepared by underwriters for syndicate members;

Blue Sky Memorandum (or Survey) — indicates states in which dealers may offer securities for sale and offering conditions, circulated to syndicate members;

Powers of Attorney For Underwriters and Directors;

Letter of Intent — non-binding agreement between company and managing underwriter describing general terms of offering, and compensation for underwriter;

Officers' and Directors' Questionnaire — circulated to directors, officers and 10% shareholders to gather information to be disclosed in Registration Statement;

Comfort Letter — document prepared by auditors to "comfort" underwriters as part of due diligence including assurances specified in underwriting agreement that auditor's work has been independent and that the Registration Statement is in compliance with the '33 Act; Exchange/NASDAQ Listing Applications;

Board Resolutions — on a variety of registration-related matters;

Transmittal Letters — to accompany Registration Statement when it is filed with SEC and Exchange listing applications;

Press Releases — as permitted, to announce intent to file, filing, SEC declaration of effectiveness and closing (described in following pages);

Tombstone Advertisement — standard form of advertising the offering indicating where the prospectus may be obtained. Traditionally paid for and placed in media by underwriters, though placement may be arranged in additional newspapers or magazines at company's request (and expense);

Opinions of Counsel — letters prepared by legal counsel for company and legal counsel for underwriter delivered to underwriter at closing. They confirm authorization of underwriting agreement; that the stock issue conforms to descriptions and shares have been duly authorized, issued and paid for; that the Registration Statement is effective and that the company now is in existence as a public company.

The Road Show

The Road Show takes place during the ironically named "Waiting Period," the time period between the filing of the registration documents and the SEC's declaration of effectiveness. It tends to be a hectic period.

Organized by the underwriters, the Road Show is the linchpin of the marketing effort for the new issue. It offers an excellent opportunity for company management to establish relationships with future investors and investment advisors — above and far beyond a handshake-level.

The Road Show team, typically the CEO, the CFO, and the company's investor relations professional, escorted by members from the underwriting group, travels on a tight schedule to key financial centers around the country (and possibly abroad) to breakfast, lunch, and dinner engagements where the company's "story" is presented. The goal is to build relationships; to "show and tell" the new issue and the company behind it, and to allow management a chance to demonstrate a dimension of talent and credibility beyond the prospectus in an effort to support the placement effort. Often it is the company's first opportunity to face a purely investment-oriented audience. It is always the first opportunity to test-market the company's "story" as presented in the prospectus and as represented by management. The shaping of this "story" is a key area of investor relations responsibility. Sizing up the audience and understanding their expectations before the Road Show team leaves company headquarters is essential to creating a meaningful presentation. The IR professional shoulders the overall responsibility for developing the theme and "message" of the presentation.

EXHIBIT 7.6 — TIMETABLE/OVERVIEW OF SPECIFIC INVESTOR RELATIONS ACTIVITIES

PRINCIPAL ACTIVITIES	SPECIFIC ACTIVITIES	FUTURE-FOCUSED IR ACTIVITIES
1. Days 1–30		
Press Release: "Intent to File"	Media List for Distribution; Track Responses and Update	Contact Newspapers About Listing Stock
General Plan for Road Show	List if Necessary	Prices
	Must be Circulated & Revised as Required	Schedule Release Date for First Earnings Date
		Plan First Quarterly Report to Shareholders
2. Day 30 to Effective Date		
Press Release "Filing"	Continue Ongoing "Communications Plan"	Shareholder Welcome Letter or Materials;
	Materials for Road Show: Fact Sheet, Video, Slides	Shareholder Survey
	Assist with Draft/Revision of Registration Statement	Investigate Moody's, S&P, Value Line Listings
	Road Show: Complete Invitation List, Room Reservations, Menus, & Presentation	IR Plan for Market Makers Formulate Disclosure Policy
3. Filing Date — Effective Date		
Issue "Filing" Release	Track Response	Compile Analyst List
Road Show Preparation	Mail Invitations; Rehearse Presentation; Drill on Q&A; Determine Placement	Work on IR Plan
Tombstone Preparation Road Show	Attend Road Show; Help Prepare Underwriter Selling	
Press Release: "Effective Date"	Memorandum; Follow-up to Road Show	
4. Effective Date to Closing		
Issue "Effective" Release	Track Responses	Begin Planning Internal Aspects or IR Program;
Release Tombstone		Meetings Schedule; Planned Publications;
Mail Final Prospects to Media		Annual Report; Meeting
Press Release "Closing"		
5. Closing		
Issue "Closing" Release	Track Response	

Just as IPOs vary by factors such as type, size and distribution, so do Road Shows. If the offering is small, and handled by a regional underwriter with predominately local contacts, the Road Show may not take place any further down the road than the local country club dining room. On the other hand, it may be a whirlwind adventure, and run up a tab of $25,000 or more (the estimated cost of keeping eight people on the road for a week in the United States).

The elements of a successful Road Show, if "success" can be measured (in terms, perhaps, of post-effective demand for the offering), include a well-articulated presentation and demonstrated competence at fielding questions. Potential investors not only will be assessing the attractiveness of the company as described in the prospectus, but also will be taking measure of the management team and judging how well management has mastered the business and financial details of the company.

Supplemental tools include slides, video presentations, or product displays and handouts, all of which have been pre-screened by legal counsel (and possibly the SEC). The executives must be well rehearsed and the schedule intelligently coordinated. Practice makes perfect: as with a Broadway play, out-of-town "tryouts" should be considered before making presentations in major financial centers.

While the underwriters play a key role in setting up the show, it is management who is "on the line" here. Overall responsibility for reserving meeting rooms, coordinating schedules and itineraries, designing the invitations and choosing menus usually fall to the underwriters, though participation of the company's own investor relations professional or outside IR counsel can be invaluable.

In addition, the Road Show not only should be viewed as an opportunity for investors to get a look at and feel for the company, but for management to "kick the tires" of the financial community to get a sense of what investors think. An essential and fruitful IR role is keeping track of who attended and who-asked-what for subsequent follow-up and further development of the new relationships.

A Registration Timetable

As an IPO candidate, the company can anticipate receiving (or should demand) a personalized timetable from the underwriter, legal counsel, or both.

Because there are infinite variations on how long this process may take, the sample timetable that follows has been broken into:

1. The first 30 days, or "launching" activities;
2. The time period beyond that through to the filing of the Registration Statement with the SEC (at this point, the remainder of the schedule depends primarily upon receipt of SEC comments);
3. From the filing date through to the effective date;

4. From the effective date through to the closing; and

5. Closing of the offering.

Tasks with an inherent investor relations responsibility are italicized. These include preparation and dissemination of several press releases ("Intent to File," "Filed," "Declared Effective," and "Closing" releases), placement of the "tombstone," and production of the "Road Show."

Beyond these, the individual charged with responsibility for IR can and should be involved with other tasks in the registration process, notably assisting with the effort of writing the registration statement and helping arrange the due diligence proceedings. Active participation of the company's investor relations person in the drafting sessions both for the Registration Statement and Due Diligence meetings is ideal "hands-on" training towards building a foundation of knowledge about how the company has positioned itself for going public, and the underlying reasons why.

And, there are optional activities of a marketing nature which the company may undertake to supplement the selling effort. These include preparation of a "Fact Sheet" or a video presentation, or other supplemental marketing materials that will add value to the effort.

Finally, perhaps the most important, yet often ignored and certainly undocumented, responsibility of the IR professional during the registration process is "thinking ahead." Attention of company executives during this time is intensely focused on working towards a successful closing. It is not "spare time" work. The activities on the company's timetable present a procedural means to this end. But the IR effort also must look beyond to the important events that will occur in rapid order once the company goes public: the Annual Report, the Annual Meeting, and launching the IR program.

EXHIBIT 7.7 — TIMETABLE

CODE: **A TEAM**=ALL   **LC-UW**=LEGAL COUNSEL FOR UNDERWRITERS
       CO=COMPANY   **LC-CO**=LEGAL COUNSEL FOR COMPANY
       AUD=AUDITORS   **RS**=REGISTRATION STATEMENT
       UW=UNDERWRITERS

Procedures in italics are functions of particular note for investor relations

RESPONSIBILITY FOR SPECIFIC PROCEDURES

1. DAYS 1-30

COMPANY
- Board of Directors Approves Offering; Authorizes Issuance of Additional Stock
- Preparation of RS for SEC Filing
- Retention of Counsel & Negotiation of UW Agreement

COMPANY
- Meetings, Discussion & Negotiations with Possible Underwriters; Determine Choice of Underwriter

A TEAM
- Meeting to Discuss Preparation & Filing; Responsibilities, Time Table; Structure of Offering & Underwriting Arrangements

CO, UW
- General Terms of Offering Established

CO, LC-CO
- Work on 1st Draft RS: Textual Information/Description of Business

AUD
- Financial Statements, Schedules, Performas

CO, UW
- *Press Release: "Intent to File"*
- *Press Release Disseminated*
- Letter of Intent Signed/Delivered

UW
- Syndicate List Developed

LC-UW
- Underwriting Agreement
- Agreement Among Underwriters
- UW Questionnaires
- Draft Cold Comfort Letter
- Blue Sky Survey

A TEAM
- Due Diligence Commences; Review Board Minutes, Reports to Shareholders, Strategic Plan, Corporate Records & Contracts

LC-CO
- Questionnaire to Directors, Officers, Principals & Selling Shareholders

A TEAM
- Circulate First Draft RS
- Circulate Draft Financials & Cold Comfort Letter

CO, UW
- *Road Show Plans Developed*

2. DAY 30 TO FILING DATE

COMPANY
- Appoint Transfer Agent & Registrar
- Arrange for Stock Certificates
- Select Financial Printer

CO, LC	• Reserve Quote Symbol
A TEAM	• Meet to Review Comments on First Draft; Update Schedule; Discuss Financial Statements and Proposed Cold Comfort Letter
LC-CO	• Prepare Power of Attorney for RS & Custody Agreements • Resolutions for Board Meeting
COMPANY **LC-CO**	• Send First Draft RS and Underwriting Agreement to Printer for First Proof
A TEAM	• Circulate Printed Proof • Circulate Draft UW Agreement
LC-CO, **LC-UW**	• Officers & Directors Questionnaires Returned and Reviewed
A TEAM	• Meet to Revise First Proof RS; Return to Printer
CO, UW	• *Prepare Press Release Announcing Filing*
COMPANY	• Prepare Check for SEC Filing Fee
LC-CO	• Directors & Officers Signature Page
LC-UW	• Accountants Opinion & Consent for RS
COMPANY	• Prepare Check for Exchange Filing Fee & Blue Sky Filing Fees
LC-UW	• Prepare Transmittal Letter to SEC
LC-CO	• Prepare Transmittal Letter to Exchange/NASD
LC-UW, CO	• Complete Blue Sky Applications • Prepare Preliminary Blue Sky Memorandum

3. FILING DAY TO EFFECTIVE DATE

LC-UW	• RS Filed with SEC
LC-CO	• RS Filed with Exchange • Deliver Listing Application to Exchange
COMPANY	• *Issue Filing Press Release*
LC-CO	• Deliver Blue Sky Release • Start Steps for Qualification in Designated States with Checks for Filing Fees
CO, LC-CO	• Give Okay to Printer to Commence Printing Documents in Quantity
UW	• Invitations to Syndicate Members Sent with: Preliminary Prospectus ("Red Herring"), Questionnaire, Power of Attorney, Proof of UW Documents, Preliminary Blue Sky Memorandum
A TEAM	• Circulate Tombstone Format

Continued on next page

LC-CO	• Receive Clearance; Exchange, Blue Sky Clearances
CO, UW	• *"Road Show" Activities*
CO, LC-UW	• SEC Comments Received
A TEAM	• Meet to respond to SEC Comments • Discuss Current Price & Spread Ideas
LC-CO	• Distribute Draft of Closing Documents
A TEAM	• Meet to Revise and Amend RS in Response to SEC Comments
LC-UW	• File Amended RS with SEC
LC-CO	• Clear Timing for Effectiveness
CO, LC-CO, UW	• *Prepare "Effective Date" Press Release*
UW	• Determine Printing Quantities for Final Prospectus & Mailing/Labeling Instructions
LC-UW	• Deliver Request for Acceleration to SEC
CO, UW	• Determine Public Offering Price and Underwriters Discount
CO	• Board or Pricing Committee Approves Final Prospectus, Purchase Agreement
LC-CO	• Deliver Final Instructions to Printer

4. EFFECTIVE DATE TO CLOSING

UW, CO	• Agreement Among Underwriters Signed
AUD	• Cold Comfort Letter Delivered
UW, CO	• Underwriting Agreement Signed
LC-UW	• Pricing Amendment Filed with SEC
SEC	• Registration Declared Effective
CO	• Notify Underwriter
UW	• Send Telegrams to Dealers • Underwriting Allotments Set
UW, CO	• Prospectus Printed for General Distribution • *Issue "Effective" Release Tombstone Ad Placed*
UW	• Public Offering Commences
LC-UW	• Final Prospectus Filed with SEC
CO	• Final Prospectus to Media
LC-CO	• Final Prospectus to Exchange and Blue Sky Authorities

UW	• Names & Denominations of Common Stock Required for Closing Relayed to Company
CO	• Banknote Company Notified
UW	• Company Advised of Election with Respect to Over-Allotment Option
A TEAM	• Preliminary Closing; Revised Closing Memorandum
CO	• *Prepare Press Release Announcing Closing*

5. CLOSING DAY

UW	• Option of Counsel, Officers' Certificate & Cold Comfort Letter Distributed to Syndicate
LC-CO	• Closing Memorandum Distributed
CO	• Issue "Closing" Release

CREATING AN INVESTOR RELATIONS PROGRAM

This section is a basic overview of all of the legal and communications issues a company faces as a new public entity.

Introduction

We begin with a review of those activities that a newly public company will undertake on a recurring basis. These include filing of 10K and 10Q forms, proxy solicitation, the Annual Meeting and Annual Report. A discussion of "disclosure" and the concept of "material information" also is included.

The discussion then shifts to describe discretionary IR activities — "everything else." These fall into topical categories of "Relationships," "Meetings," "Publications," and "IR R&D."

It should be evident from even a cursory review of various IR programs that there is a wide range of choice in how a company implements its specific investor relations goals. These goals, and the manner in which a company proposes to achieve them, should be documented in an IR Plan that is appropriate to its needs, resources and ambitions. The IR plan should address three distinct topics: the overall objectives of the program (in context of the company's strategic plan); the investor relations function (its definition and policies, including disclosure); and a review of proposed activities to be implemented.

A company should develop and document an IR Plan even if it determines that in its first year or so of operation it cannot go beyond fulfillment of the basic (i.e. legally mandatory) requirements.

Regardless of the ultimate scope of the plan that is designed and implemented, all individual tasks and the sum of these activities taken as a whole should strive to meet the goals of "The Four Cs of Investor Relations":

1. Compliance with legal and ethical requirements and standards;
2. Credibility as fostered by a pro-active approach to delivering bad news as well as good; positioning the company appropriately; valuing quality of information over quantity;
3. Consistency and an ongoing, future-focused IR effort; developing a mechanism to deal effectively with adverse surprises; avoiding over or underkill; providing for equitable dissemination of information; and always remembering that in IR, "Inconsistency Breeds Contempt";
4. Commitment of senior management as demonstrated by a willingness to support and participate in the IR program; commitment by the company to the shareholders and the general investment community; and commitment to the principles and practice of investor relations.

Communication is, after all, the primary purpose of an investor relations program; effective communication in IR is a two-way street. Communications efforts towards creating understanding and awareness of the company within the investment community should at the same time promote an appreciation of the external expectations and views of the company.

BASIC OBLIGATIONS OF A NEWLY PUBLIC COMPANY

Periodic Reports: 10Qs and 10Ks, 8Ks, Earnings Releases

Interim or quarterly reports — the 10Qs — contain unaudited quarterly financial data and information about specific reportable events that may have occurred during the three months covered by the report. They must be filed with the SEC no later than 45 days after the end of each of the first three quarters of the fiscal year. The 10K, a more comprehensive document containing a description of the company's businesses, property and financial condition, is filed annually within 90 days after the end of the fiscal year.

Compilation of the material contained in the 10Qs and 10K is generally and primarily the responsibility of the accounting/finance and legal departments of a company. However, investor relations can and should anticipate some degree of involvement with the process of preparing these documents.

As a public disclosure document, the 10K or 10Q is of interest to the general financial community. A regular mailing to the company's list of analysts and portfolio managers therefore is recommended. The reports also should be available on an as-requested basis; the Annual Report must contain a statement advertising the availability of the 10K.

The 8K is an SEC document required "under special circumstances." The list of such circumstances is finite, and includes:
- Changes in control;
- Acquisition or disposition of a significant asset;
- A bankruptcy or receivership filing;
- Changing independent accounting firms;
- Certain resignations of directors;
- Other specific occurrences.

The company may in fact file an 8K at its own option even if the "event" about which it chooses to report is not on the list. The information in the 8K, which is due within 15 days of the occurrence of the event, is usually of no "surprise" to the public. Typically, it will have been announced in a press release issued and distributed prior to the 8K filing.

Quarterly Earnings should be scheduled for "release" as soon as the accuracy of the figures has been checked to the satisfaction of management. A yearly schedule (subject to change only under extenuating circumstances) can be set up once it is determined how soon all the figures will be in and verified after the close of a quarter. This is ordinarily well in advance of the last required day to file the 10Q or 10K. A schedule of these Release Dates may be distributed internally only, or sent to the company's analyst and financial media lists so that these parties are aware of the date when earnings will be released (and a host of inquiries about the release date each quarter can be avoided).

Outside of the filing of the 10Qs and 10K, there is no Securities Act line-item statutory obligation to release earnings. The requirement to do so comes from the Exchanges and NASDAQ. Quarterly earnings results are unquestionably "material" in nature, and as such have the potential of influencing investment decisions of individuals and institutions. And because of the confidential nature of earnings prior to release, they present a potential hazard as "insider information" so long as they are unreleased. From the time the company collects its quarter-end figures from its internal sources, through to the public announcement, the company should consider itself in a "Quiet Period," and subject to the same types of prohibitions on discussing or characterizing earnings with any outside party as in the Registration period.

Because earnings are released on an ongoing and regular basis, it is possible and advisable to set up an internal schedule to follow each quarter starting with the day "preliminary" figures are available. The schedule can detail the review and discussion process between accounting/finance staff and IR in preparation for writing the release and answering questions once the release is out. This dialogue will help the company spokesperson fully understand what is behind the numbers when he or she discusses the results with the financial community and helps characterize the reasons for changes in revenues or earnings. The actual news release itself then would be drafted and circulated for approvals within the company and among legal counsel and accounting advisors.

The mechanics of issuing the release, and a method for tracking responses to it (both print and verbal), also would be part of this planning process. Timing is, of course, key. Companies take different approaches, some preferring to release after the market's close to avoid turmoil in trading; others release early in the morning so that the market will have a full day to register its response. Friday afternoon or weekend releases may send a signal to the investment community that the company has something to hide.

The earnings release is written in a spare, factual style. Once the company establishes the form of its earnings release, it can utilize it as an outline for subsequent releases, with the numbers and explanatory discussion updated each time. A financial summary page is often attached and recommended as a regular practice. Circulation of the earnings release includes not only the wire services and media (local, trade, and financial), but also analysts and portfolio managers, market makers and underwriters (including syndicate members). As earnings are considered "material" news, an evenly timed and wide distribution effort should be standard policy.

Proxy Rules and Solicitation

The proxy system and implementation of the proxy collection process, is an example of an area where investor relations has shared, or "cross-over," responsibilities with another corporate function, the Corporate Secretarial/Legal Department.

The proxy process (Exhibit 7.10) is regulated by "rules" from three sources: the Securities Act of 1934, state law, and the by-laws of the individual company.

EXHIBIT 7.8 — THE PROCESS/A PUBLIC COMPANY

PRE-REGISTRATION	REGISTRATION	PUBLIC COMPANY
————————	————————	————————▶

EXHIBIT 7.9 — A YEAR IN THE LIFE

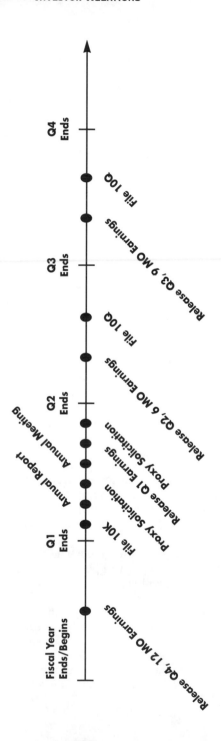

EXHIBIT 7.10 — PROXY SOLICITATION OVERVIEW:
FLOW OF PROXIES VIA DEPOSITORIES

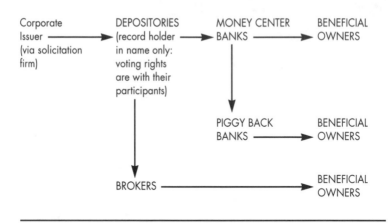

There are basically two parts to proxy solicitation: distribution of the proxy materials, and then "solicitation," or recall of the proxy cards.

The '34 Act requires companies soliciting proxies to provide a written description of the matters being submitted to voting (the "proxy statement") as well as some form on which to vote (the "proxy card"). Proxy materials are subject to review by the SEC before being released to shareholders. These same rules also require that an annual report be distributed to shareholders prior to or along with the proxy statement and card.

Complexities of the proxy process have evolved in part due to growth in the institutional sector and growth in this sector's active participation in the proxy process; an increase in non-routine shareholder proposals; takeover activities; and the difficulty of merely identifying who owns the stock. Ironically, the investor relations "goal" of diversifying the shareholder base often results in greater difficulty in identifying those shareholders. A wide geographical dispersion of shareholders means that relatively fewer will be able to attend the Annual Meeting in person, and more will utilize the proxy as a means of participation. This is an extremely simplified description of the proxy process, which comes complete with a vocabulary and nomenclature all its own: "CEDE," "KRAY," "IECA," "Transfer Sheets," "NOBOs," "OBOs," and "COBOs" being a small sample. A comprehensive review of the proxy rule requirements and tactics used to collect proxies easily could double the page count of this guide. But the subject is one of increasing importance and growing concern to management and shareholders alike, and a fundamental understanding of it is necessary for the IR professional.

Even when voting issues are of a routine nature (i.e., uncontested re-election of directors, ratification of auditors, etc.) the administrative processes of distributing, collecting and tallying proxies can be enormous. And if voting matters are other-than-routine (i.e., contested election of directors, controversial management or shareholder proposals, or any of the elements that constitute a so-called "proxy battle") all aspects of proxy solicitation become critical.

There are several important investor relations perspectives to the proxy process. Timing issues are involved in coordinating the Annual Report with the distribution of the proxies and the Annual Meeting; the proxy statement itself is a "shareholder publication," a disclosure document of interest to other segments of financial audiences as well as the shareholders. Finally, individual shareholders often use the opportunity presented by arrival of the proxy card to voice their opinion on proxy matters or other corporate policies. A personal response is in order, preferably from the investor relations officer, or through a letter drafted by investor relations for the signature of the CEO so as to be consistent with other statements on these issues.

Systems that have evolved towards expediting trading, simplifying record keeping, and protecting owner identity have at the same time made the seemingly straightforward objective of identifying the company's shareholders a complex process. Increasingly, large percentages of a company's shareholder population hold their stock in "Street Name" (i.e., shares registered in the name of a bank nominee account, or held in the name of a bank or broker). Further complicating the identification of shareholders is the evolution of the depository system whereby banks and brokers arrange for shares to be held at one of the principal depositories. These entities, though not the actual share owner, may seemingly "own" tens or hundreds of thousands of a company's shares since ownership is recorded in the name of the custodian.

This is all much easier to explain graphically. In the following chart (Exhibit 7.11), it is assumed that four million, or 80 percent of the company's five million shares outstanding, are held by institutions and investors in Street Name through various banks and brokerage firms. Most of these shares are held by institutions that are required to report their ownership positions on Form 13(F) to the SEC on a quarterly basis. A million shares are held by small custody accounts at banks and retail brokerage firms.

EXHIBIT 7.11 — DIVISION OF SHARES OUTSTANDING AMONG
SHAREHOLDER GROUPS

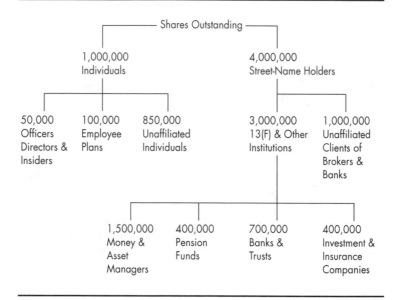

Few companies opt to solicit their proxies without professional assistance. There are compelling reasons for involving investor relations in the initial investigation and selection of an outside proxy solicitor. Establishing a long-term relationship is highly desirable in order to build on the strength of previous years of experience, and apply the information gained to related areas and services.

A key "cross-over" between proxy solicitation and investor relations is in the area of shareholder identification. As proxy solicitation involves finding investment advisors and the beneficial owners of the stock, shareholder identification involves determining who has voting authority for those shares (not always one and the same) since an investment advisor or a custodian bank may have full or partial voting authority. It is inevitable that in the course of this process, large positions will be "uncovered." Having identified its shareholders in this way, the company is in a position to make sure that it communicates directly and consistently to its shareholders. Knowing the composition of the shareholder base also enables the company to determine if any sizeable stakes are being accumulated, and to identify any potentially unfriendly shareholders. Moreover, this shareholder identification process will reveal the "mix" of ownership among individuals and institutions which is important information that will enable the company to determine if there is an optimal balance in its shareholder profile.

Knowledge of a company's shareholders and their voting track record can greatly affect the success or failure of proxy campaigns.

The services known as "shareholder identification" or "stock surveillance" are options many companies request of their outside IR counsel or proxy solicitor on an ongoing basis, and should be considered for inclusion in the investor relations program, either for the present or the future. Exhibit 7.12 details a sample planning schedule for a typical year.

Disclosure, a Quick Review

The following are two distinct approaches to disclosure: a "minimalist" policy (Company A) and a "detailed" policy excerpt (Company B).

Disclosure Policy, Company A: Securities Analysts and the Press cannot be given any information about the Company which is not publicly available.

Disclosure Policy Excerpt, Company B: The Investor Relations Department is responsible for the coordination, review and control of the release of public information ... Only the President, Vice President – Finance and Manager of Investor Relations are authorized to speak before securities analysts, brokers, financial writers, institutional investors, etc., or to hold interviews with the financial press. All employees are directed to refer inquiries by any of these groups to the investor relations manager ...

It is a priority for the newly public company to determine what its policy on disclosure will be, and then to develop a means to implement it.

First, a company's management must have an understanding of the legal obligations implicit in disclosure. Financial and strategic information which the company may have considered confidential when the company operated in the private sector, such as quarterly earnings, major loan agreements, significant new products or discoveries, labor disputes or management changes, take on a new dimension once the company goes public. Such information has the potential of affecting decisions investors may make about purchasing or selling the company's securities. It is therefore material. And the company has an obligation to make accurate and timely disclosure of certain material information.

Disclosure is currently a hot topic, in part due to differences of opinion (expressed in legal proceedings) between investors and companies as to what exactly constitutes "timely." The courts have ruled that if a legitimate business reason exists, a company may be justified in withholding information of a material nature for a short period. However, the company cannot misrepresent, deny, lie, or present incomplete disclosure of information while it prepares for full disclosure.

EXHIBIT 7.12 — AN INSIDER'S VIEW: PROXY SOLICITATION/ANNUAL MEETING/ANNUAL REPORT SAMPLE PLANNING SCHEDULE

By way of illustrating the necessary integration of the internal demands of the proxy process with the production of the Annual Report and the Annual Meeting, the following schedule provides an "insider's view" of the activities involved. It assumes a December 31 fiscal year end and a mid-April Annual Meeting date.

PROXY	ANNUAL MEETING	ANNUAL REPORT
OCTOBER		
Memo to Internal Depts. Detailing Information Needs for Proxy Statement		Memo Establishing Internal Team and Responsibilities
Find Out About any Proposed or New Benefit Plans		Review Potential Outside Vendors and Solicit Bids
		Research Current Annual Report Trends and Design Styles
NOVEMBER		
Review and Develop Proxy Card Format	Reserve Room (Including Day-Before for Rehearsal)	Circulate Planning Memo with Target Dates and Responsibilities
Set Up Mailing PLan and Tabulation System	Research Dates of Peer/Other Local Corporate Annual Meetings	Discuss Financial Information Needs with Finance/ Accounting
Deadline for Shareholder Proposals — Formulate Action Plan for Proposals Received	Research "Hot" Shareholder Issues	Discuss SEC Requirements with Legal Counsel
Prepare Board Resolutions		Develop Theme, Begin Rough Design, Begin Copy Outline
Develop Directors' and Officers' Questionnaires for Proxy Information		Plan Illustration and Photography
Select Inspectors of Election and Proxy Committee		Finalize Contract with Printer: Major Format, Delivery Dates, and Number of Copies

PROXY	**ANNUAL MEETING**	**ANNUAL REPORT**
Board Meeting		Work on Drafting Narrative and Format for Financials
Draft Proxy Statement and Related Matters		
Review Solicitation Process		
Contact Internal Staff and Audit Committee of Board to Prepare Resolution Appointment of Outside Auditors		

DECEMBER

Send Proxy Out to Bid for Financial Printing	Set Up Schedule to Attend Selected Other Annual Meetings	Design and Copy Revision
Board Meeting		Photography and Illustration Arranged, Completed
Review Accepted Shareholder Proxy Proposals		Release Photography to Printer
File Rejected Proposals with SEC		Continue Refinement of Narrative Copy
Notify Rejected Proposal Proponents Personally		Approve Comprehensive Layout
Mail Directors' and Officers' Questionnaires		
End of Fiscal Year		

JANUARY

Award Printing Contracts		Final Draft of Copy Approved
Board Meeting: Confirm Annual Meeting Date and Record Date		Send Narrative Copy to Typesetter
Notify Exchange and Transfer Agent of Annual Meeting and Record Dates		Narrative Readings: Circulate, Revise, Return to Printer
		Send Financial Copy to Typesetter

Continued on next page

PROXY	ANNUAL MEETING	ANNUAL REPORT

FEBRUARY

Prepare Statements of Opposition to Proxy Proposals and Submit to Proponents		Add Year-End Figures to Financial Section and Release to Printer (Only)
Mail Proxy Drafts to Board for Review		Receive Mechanicals: Review, Correct
Submit Resolutions on Inspectors of Elections, Proxy Committee, and Board Final Proxy Materials to Board		Release Mechanicals to Printer
Revise Proxy as Necessary		1st Blueprints Available, Corrected, Returned
Submit Proxy Material and Fee to SEC for Review		2nd Blueprints, Repeat Process
Board Meeting	Circulate Q&A Memo	Final Okay on Plates: On Press/Off Press
Release Proxy Matrials for Printing	Review Company and Industry Shareholder Issues	Printing, Binding and Delivery Complete
Record Date		
Update Shareholder Mailing List as of Record Date		

MARCH

Send Out Proxy Materials: Distribute Proxy to Insiders and Financial Community	Draft Script	Mail to Shareholders and Financial Community
Mail Proxy to SEC	Arrange for Security, Food/ Refreshments, Physical Set Up, Microphones, Ushers/ Receptionists, Coat Room, First Aid, Lobby Signs	
File Proxy—Exchange	Prepare Orders of Business, Script Revisions	
File Proxy—Underwriters	Arrange for Stockholders to Make Motions	
Obtain Affidavits of Mailing	Prepare Take-Away Literature	

PROXY	**ANNUAL MEETING**	**ANNUAL REPORT**
Prepare Ballots for Annual Meeting	Arrange for Video Taping or Photography, Banners, Parking Attendance Register, Alternate Site and Transport, Telephone Lines	
Obtain List of Shareholders as of Record Date	Set Up Rehearsal and Q&A Review Meeting	
Start Proxy Counts on Daily Basis	Draft of Script, Slides to Senior Management for Review	
Confirm Certification of Proxy Tabulation Procedure	Q&A Rehearsal Session	
Prepare Proxy and Inspector Forms for Signature at Annual Meeting		
Memo of Final Meeting Arrangements: Number of Shares Represented, Certificate Forms for Votes on Election of Directors		

APRIL

Prepare Folders for Proxy and Inspectors	Attend Other Annual Meetings	
Review of Proxy Returns	Issue Invitations and Internal Reminders	
Forward Comments on Proxy Cards for Response	Final Rehearsal	
Arrange for Outside Fee Payments	Annual Meeting	
Board Meeting		

The line item requirements of the Securities Act of 1934 (which require filing of the 10Qs, 10Ks and 8Ks) are but one source of guidance to a company in determining whether it has an obligation to immediately disclose information. The Exchanges and NASD specify disclosure requirements to which the company must conform (or risk being "delisted"). Prior public statements from the company which have become inconsistent with current circumstance present another instance where a duty to disclose arises. Disclosure must be made when rumors and leaks that can be traced to the company or a third party responsible to the company are discovered. If the company is actively engaged in the buying or selling of its own stock, it must disclose. And, if a corporate decision has been made to disclose in the absence of any immediate disclosure obligation, disclosure must be complete and accurate, and the information disclosed consistently described to all audiences.

Due to the inherent nature of their work, analysts and the press have an interest in information about a company that might affect an investor's decision to buy its stock. Management must strike an appropriate balance between providing a flow of candid information and providing no one party with material information that has not been disclosed publicly.

The company that seeks to maintain a competitive position in the marketplace may be caught in an awkward position if it is planning a major strategic move, such as an acquisition or divestiture, which it believes should be kept confidential from competitors. The company also may feel it needs more time to prepare for disclosure so that internal operations are not disrupted by the announcement. Disclosure timing for non-routine material information (quarterly earnings are always considered "routine") is often a judgment call, but there are some clear signals a company must heed which would indicate necessity for immediate disclosure.

One such signal is unusual market activity, which may result from speculation by investors in response to rumors, true or false, circulating in the marketplace. If the company knows of no reason for the activity, it usually issues a statement to this effect. If the activity is in response to a rumor which is false, it can be denied. Many companies take the position that they will not respond to market rumors at all. If the activity is attributable to leaks of information, however, an immediate release is called for.

Increased risk of violation of insider trading prohibitions is also an important consideration in formulating a disclosure policy. Insider trading occurs when the decision to buy or sell stock is based on information that has not been released to the public. Anyone in possession of information of a material nature may be considered an insider. This includes directors, officers and employees of the company as well as outside counsel, accountants, investment bankers, financial printers, investor relations counselors, and even husbands, wives, families and friends of employees. The prohibition on trading a company's securities based on information of a material, non-public nature is found in Rule 10(B)-5 of the '34 Act. A "10(B)-5 Letter," drafted by the company's legal counsel with assistance from investor relations, is recommended to be circulated on an annual basis among company management and employees determined to be privy to such information. Companies also should take positive action to protect sensitive information by establishing tight internal controls and evaluating the security of documents and computer systems.

A disclosure philosophy, once determined, should lead logically to a disclosure policy. The policy, in turn, will form the foundation for disclosure procedures to be followed by the company. A sound procedure includes an established communications network; specific delineation of who is authorized to speak on behalf of the company to its financial audiences; the manner in which the company will deal with reports of rumors and the method by which information will be disclosed (almost always, via release to the wire services and financial press). It also may state the company's stance on issuing forecasts and projections, and a variety of other matters concerning the company's association with analysts, such as furnishing requested information, correcting inaccuracies in analyst reports or responding to out-of-line estimates of projected earnings.

Common pitfalls of disclosure can be avoided by having a mechanism for reviewing disclosure decisions which assures a sound balance between the interests of the investment community and the company. Authority to make disclosure decisions should be centralized, to avoid premature or inadvertent announcements or statements that subsequently may have to be corrected. An understanding of disclosure requirements calls for an up-to-date grasp of what constitutes materiality and how timeliness has been interpreted in the courts and by the Exchanges. Finally, the company's commitment to the practice of investor relations which endorses the other three C's of investor relations — compliance, credibility and consistency — should provide clear direction for determining the company's disclosure philosophy, policy and procedures.

Discretionary Investor Relations Activities

Relationships, or The Many Relations of Investor Relations

Investor relations, by its very nature, is an outreach business. It seeks to go beyond mere obligatory reporting of information to a proactive approach towards marketing the company's securities.

The results of investor relations programs may be evaluated in many ways, as indicated later in this overview. For example, communications efforts to reach shareholder publics can be tallied up (i.e., "This year, we issued four press releases; held seven meetings and answered 22 questions from brokers ..."). Or, more substantively, the program may be considered against some pre-established goal, such as increased coverage of the firm by analysts or growth in the number of value-oriented investors in the company's shareholder base.

What is equally important, and far more difficult to measure, is the depth of development of relationships with individuals and groups within the company's target audience segments, or "publics."

Establishing and maintaining these relationships is accomplished via internally generated publications and written materials, exposure of the company through the media, ongoing telephone communication and meetings that present opportunities to communicate face-to-face. Media coverage of the company can serve to spark the interest of new groups, and help maintain visibility and recognition of the company.

"Targeting" an IR program is a standard battle cry of investor relations professionals. However, targeting is only part — the middle part — of an investor relations campaign. It must be preceded by segmentation of the company's audiences — shareholders and communications conduits to shareholders — and followed with careful selection of the medium and intelligent structuring of the "message" so as to most effectively reach those chosen "targets."

The "investment community" consists of a number of potentially important components. The most common manner in which a company "segments" its shareholder base is by determining its actual and ideal individual/institutional breakdown. The overall focus of the IR program should reflect an effort to satisfy proportionately the information needs of each of these groups if the company is satisfied with the breakdown, or to shift the percentages in a desired direction if not.

Within these broad breakdowns there are additional audience segments which must be examined. The segments within the "Institutions" category include Portfolio Managers, Investment Advisors and Counselors, Pension Funds, Banks and Trusts, Investment Companies, Insurance Companies, Brokerage Firm Analysts ("sell-side analysts"), Institutional Brokers and Analysts at Institutional Investment Firms ("buy-side analysts").

Institutions also can be classified by size of holdings in the company; overall magnitude of funds the institution has under management; investment philosophy; and the nature of the decision-making process (who makes the decision, what factors weigh heaviest and influential sources of information within and outside the company).

"Individuals" may be high net worth investors, local or regional concentrations of shareholders, employees and management or investment clubs. Each may have unique investment criteria and information needs. The individual, or retail, segment also includes registered representatives, or brokers, who are influential in individual investment decisions.

The key to successful "targeting" then, is successful segmentation, and a thorough understanding of the interrelationships among, and influences upon, actual and potential shareholder groups. This is put into action by structuring messages that position the company's favorable attributes in ways that appropriately and productively meet the information needs of each target group.

"Targeting" is also a far easier task if the company develops an approach that acknowledges current shareholders to be a "natural," accessible and preconditioned market for the stock. The next step is to identify and examine the potential shareholder market for the company.

Decision makers in the investment community receive information about a company from a variety of sources. The company may itself seek out and directly provide information to current shareholders and potential investors. However, the IR function also can reach investors via intermediaries who serve as independent conduits and interpreters of information from the company.

The classic depiction of how information flows through these "influencers" is pyramid-shaped, with information directed to the sell-side research analysts at the top. They provide information and analytical opinions to buy-side analysts, institutional salespeople and registered representatives, who in turn filter it down through to the institutional decision makers and individual investors.

For the newly public company, this "classic" presentation requires some adjustment. First of all, if the company's securities are traded over the counter, the market makers must be factored in, in a dual role as influencers and facilitators. Secondly, the newly public company may find that coverage by analysts on the sell-side is not immediately viable: the company's size or float may be too small to warrant in-depth coverage and attention. This does not mean that the analyst community should be ignored; it merely indicates that a newly public company should recognize that it may take some time to earn the full attention it deserves.

Finally, the newly public company must invest more time and effort to securing the loyalty of its present shareholders than the company that has been operating in the public sector for a longer period of time. Investors in a new issue have less at stake and can afford to be more fickle than those who may have witnessed the company's expertise at managing in a down cycle. This would indicate that a more direct communications approach is called for with present shareholders than might be necessary several years down the road, with a message that clearly emphasizes the competence of management and soundness of the company's strategic plans.

Decision Makers/Institutions. The following chart (Exhibit 7.13) indicates one approach to segmenting and targeting the universe of actual and potential institutional investors in a company's stock. Its intent is to identify the kinds of institutions that might be the target of a

EXHIBIT 7.13 — AUDIENCES

IGNORE	INITIATE	RE-INITIATE	MAINTAIN	INCREASE
• Index Funds	• Institutions with holdings in peer stocks	• Institutions which recently sold out	• Medium institutions	• Medium institutions with rapid asset growth
• Yield Players	• Small institutions		• Large institutions with large holdings	• Large institutions with small holdings
				• Local institutions

hypothetical company's IR marketing program, within the context of the company's ideal institutional shareholder profile.

The primary investment decisions within these institutions are made by portfolio managers and/or management committees, which evaluate research information delivered by internal research departments (buy-side analysts) and other influencers such as sell-side analysts and the financial media.

Institutions with equity holdings in excess of $100 million are required to report their investments on Form 13(F) to the SEC, which is the initial means by which a company can identify the individual institutions holding its stock. A stock surveillance service could be retained to generate even greater positive identification of institutional owners with positions in Street Name. It is a relatively easy matter to then identify the portfolio manager associated with those institutions. Further "audience" research among institutions can determine their general criteria for investment decisions. In many ways, because of the availability of public information about the major investing institutions, it is far easier to segment and target the institutional segment than the more fragmented individual component of the shareholder base.

Portfolio managers should, by all means, be included on a company's informational mailing lists to receive published materials (press releases, Annual Reports, etc.) and invitations to investment community meetings. These mailing lists would include not only current investing institutions, but the broader universe of potential investing institutions as well.

Much can be learned from the quarterly 13(F) reports once a company has obtained them over a period of time. Significant shifts in institutional positions in the company's stock always should be investigated, either through direct contact or a survey conducted by outside IR counsel.

Decision Makers/Individuals. Many companies feel that individual shareholder information needs are satisfied adequately by the Annual Report and Quarterly Reports; the proxy process; the Annual Meeting, and perhaps one or two meetings a year with individuals who have relatively large positions in the stock.

This decision is largely driven by the fragmented nature of the "individual" side of the shareholder profile, as well as by a cost-benefit analysis which reveals that individual shareholder relations programs get less bang-for-the-buck than institutional programs. However, it ultimately can be quite cost-effective to institute an IR program directed to individuals as a way of securing balance in the company's shareholder profile. This is an especially significant consideration given the traditional proclivity of individual investors to be long-term holders and supportive of management's strategies, programs and proposals.

Individual shareholder relations programs tend to be set up to accommodate current shareholding constituencies rather than to explore the potential of untapped segments of retail markets. A notable exception is the company that has not previously encouraged employee ownership and institutes a program toward this end. The typical strategy, however, is to maintain, rather than obtain, individual owners. For the newly public company, an opposite attitude may be more appropriate. The individual segment is an audience which is value-oriented and multifaceted; working through retail brokers to establish an active recruitment program for appropriate individual investor segments will "pay off" if the company desires a diversified, stable and supportive shareholder base.

Facilitators/Brokers. The most practical approach to "recruiting" new individual shareholders is to work through stockbrokers as intermediaries. This indirect approach to reaching individual investors is a viable, cost-effective means of targeting the individual segment.

In considering a program to reach the broker community, segmentation of this large universe according to key criteria is necessary. This might include, for example, brokers in a company's home market; brokers in other selected geographical areas; only those brokers affiliated with firms the company is in the process of courting for analyst coverage; or brokers affiliated with the market-making firms for the company.

A variety of methods may be deployed to reach the selected broker audience. These can include direct mail, and advertising and publicity in professional magazines and investment newsletters.

A retail brokerage program makes a lot of sense for the newly public company if it is coordinated with a market-maker program. "Backyard" or regional brokers with proximity to the company's home office and/or plants or sales offices are a natural starting point.

In positioning a message to brokers the company must acknowledge that brokers are looking for information that will help them sell the company and its stock to clients. Brokers rarely, if ever, deal with securities of exclusively one industry, which means the company must consider itself competing with a cross-industry universe in presenting itself to brokers, rather than with a narrower peer group. And brokers are flooded with information on a daily basis about investment "products," so any information provided by the company must be a "standout" from the pack.

Facilitators/Market Makers. A market maker program is a priority for the newly public company which is listed in the over-the-counter (OTC) market through the NASDAQ (National Association of Securities Dealers Automated Quotations) system. NASDAQ is the market of choice of the majority of IPOs, and its trading operations are quite different than those of the Exchanges. The NASDAQ system is dealer-driven, with competitive trading activity conducted by computer; the Exchanges operate via an open-auction, monopolistic, specialist-driven system.

A dealer, or market maker, represents a securities firm which stands ready to buy or sell a company's stock from inventory. By developing and maintaining relationships with a number of market makers (the average is eight), the company helps ensure that investors will be provided with a liquid market. The market maker provides active capital, accepts a risk position and acts as a salesperson to the investment community on behalf of the company. In exchange, the market maker stands to gain new customers, profit from the trading activity and benefit from arbitrage opportunities.

For OTC companies, identifying, attracting and maintaining market makers involves an understanding of the different types and functions of market making firms. National market makers (e.g., Merrill Lynch or Shearson) have a country-wide presence and can handle substantial numbers of companies—as many as 2,500.. Their sales forces are geographically dispersed. Regional firms may specialize by industry or geography or both. Local market makers tend to be more willing to invest in "small cap" (capitalized) companies with direct ties to their local economy. Wholesalers deal as intermediaries to other broker-dealer firms or those without market making capabilities. Finally, there are the specialty investment banking firms, which provide a market making service to support their underwriting activities.

A newly public company's first and strongest support should come from its investment banker.

For many companies in the first stages of developing an investment community following, it is not realistic to expect immediate and broad analyst coverage. However, a company can "grow" an analyst following over time through its market maker program. The fundamental principles of such a program mimic those of dealing with analysts: research and analysis of the universe of market makers; contacting or arranging for introductions to the market maker; and "selling" the qualities and advantages of dealing the company's stock to them.

A step-by-step approach would include:

1. Identifying local and regional firms,
2. Investigating peer company market makers (NASD has this information),
3. Consulting with and utilizing the resources of the company's investment banker,
4. Cross-checking analyst lists with market making firms, and
5. Investigating market makers by SIC code breakdowns.

Facilitators/Institutional Salespersons. Institutional brokers facilitate investment decisions of institutions, executing buy and sell orders at their instruction. For investing institutions that are too small to have their own research departments in-house, institutional salespersons may go beyond this "facilitator" role to provide research on companies to these investors. It is therefore necessary to consider this group as a possible target for either a broad "familiarization" program, or for personal, targeted relationships with key institutional salespeople.

Information about possible investments is provided by the institutional salesperson's own research department within the brokerage firm. But, like the data base of the portfolio manager, the institutional broker's information may be combined with research from other, outside sources including that provided through media coverage. The institutional salesperson, like the registered representative, is primarily interested in the selling points of a company's stock. For the newly public company that seeks a diverse group of institutional investors, investigating means of developing relationships with institutional salespeople may be one way to achieve this goal.

Influencers/Analysts. Securities analysts come in two varieties: "sell-side" and "buy-side."

Sell-side analysts work for brokerage houses and specialize by industry. A notable exception of importance to the newly public company is the "Special Situations" analyst on the sell-side, an analytical catch-all category for emerging growth, low-price or small cap companies. A company may receive initial coverage as a special situation company, and gradually be "promoted" to industry coverage when it has outgrown the special situation criteria.

Original research is the primary output of the sell-side analyst, in the form of reports which summarize the performance and current situation of the company, provide qualitative analysis of the direction of the company, and offer an investment conclusion. These reports are widely disseminated directly to buy-side analysts and portfolio managers as well as to the institutional sales force of the analyst's firm.

The sell-side analyst community is tight. Because of the expertise developed from intense study of a single industry, analysts tend not to switch industry specialties. When sell-side analysts change jobs, it typically is to accept an analyst position covering the same industry at another brokerage firm.

Buy-side analysts are employed directly by investing institutions, and may cover four to six industries and follow anywhere from 25-40 or more companies at a time (about double the number followed by sell-side analysts). While buy-side analysts do conduct original research, they commonly rely significantly on sell-side research to form a basis for their recommendations.

The power of analysts cannot be underestimated. Indeed, most investor relations programs primarily and directly are targeted to this segment. The following sections on meetings and publications make note of many of the specific activities which a newly public company may undertake to interest analysts. Maintaining relationships with analysts, however, is an ongoing, sometimes daily activity for the investor relations professional, via telephone contact. Reasonable and legitimate inquiries from analysts (or, for that matter, any member of the financial community) should be responded to promptly and accurately. Care should be exercised not to create overly optimistic expectations, for maintaining credibility among members of the analyst community is essential.

Influencers/Financial Press/Media. Third-party, independent endorsement of a company and its activities is one of the key results of a financial media relations program. It is most effective when achieved through favorable press commentary and acclaim.

The extent to which financial publicity and media relations for the newly public company are developed will depend upon previously existing programs, the CEO's attitude toward the press, and the "newsworthiness" of the company's strategic, financial and product information in general.

Properly handled, financial media relations can yield significant benefits to the company in cultivating a positive image, generating new interest, and serving an information distribution function with potentially broader reach than any other vehicle available. An ongoing, targeted and strategic media relations program serves to reinforce in-person financial community presentations and also is an essential aspect of a "crisis communications" plan.

Improperly handled, or ignored altogether, media relations can cause extensive damage to a company's image. "Calls to the company were not returned," or "Company officials refused to comment" statements in newspaper articles send an immediate negative signal to investors.

Financial media relations requires both specialized skills and a dedicated effort in cultivating press contacts. The theme and message that the company wishes to project to the financial media are necessarily coordinated with those it seeks to project to the financial community. Therefore, the individual responsible for IR in the newly public company also should be responsible for the company's contacts with the press. Often the first "assistance" brought in once the investor relations function is established is a media relations professional to help with handling responsibilities in this area. Outside investor relations or Public Relations services often are called upon to support the effort as well.

In the same spirit as the segmenting and targeting approach to reach investors, the financial media relations effort should be focused and directional. The universe of publications in the business, financial and trade press should be identified and efforts made to establish working relationships with the specific editor or reporter responsible for covering the company or its industry. Television programming oriented to the financial markets and the overall business arena is on an upswing; specific programs and interview possibilities can be factored into the plan.

Financial publicity can be bought (as in advertising), or free (as in editorial or reporting coverage). While the latter often is considered the preferred option, "paid" placement of a company's financial results and corporate image advertising should not be overlooked.

The press is of initial and crucial importance to the newly public company as the recipient of disclosure releases. Competition for publication of these, and other "spot news" of a financial nature is intense, and simultaneous delivery of earnings and other releases to the wire services, newspapers, trade publications and other media is advised.

The opportunities for media exposure beyond spot news are open-ended. Speeches by company officials can be submitted to reporters as background information on industry topics; media information kits produced; background briefings arranged between management and selected editors or reporters; interviews arranged and "press conferences" held.

An aggressive media relations program requires development of a press kit with up-to-date materials such as an Annual Report, recent Quarterly Reports, copies or summaries of recent analysts' research reports, a "press backgrounder," or fact sheet developed specifically for this audience, and the most recent press releases issued by the company.

The International Investor Relations Audience. The company seeking a wide geographical dispersion of its securities and additional sources of capital can look beyond the boundaries of the United States markets. Developing an international investor relations program requires communicating to investors with a distinctly different profile than those that characterize the domestic institutional and retail markets. While it may seem impractical for a newly public company to attempt to generate investor attention internationally, there are substantial potential advantages to be considered.

An international investor relations program, under most circumstance, falls in that category of "Future—To Do" activities; unless the initial public offering purposefully attracted a significant number of overseas investors, newly public companies must concentrate their efforts on first establishing a solid IR program at home. However, once the domestic program is up and running and on firm ground, European and Far East markets can be explored.

Overseas programs present opportunities for the company to market itself to investors with different attitudes toward investing. European institutional investors, for example, tend to be longer term holders than their counterparts in the United States. A company may consider an international investor relations program valuable particularly if it has other business or financial goals or prospects in foreign markets. For instance, a company that sells a significant portion of its products outside the United States may find international institutional investors a logical audience for its IR marketing program. Should the company contemplate the possibility of raising additional capital abroad sometime down the road, an in-place IR program may be effective in sensitizing the market to the company's story and establishing productive and beneficial relationships.

Beginning an international IR program requires the same considerable research and planning effort that starting a domestic program needs, and a similar ongoing commitment to maintain that program in the future. Audiences must be investigated, segmented and targeted. Cultural conventions, too, must be researched, adding a new twist to the IR program planning requirements. A thorough program will require regular annual trips plus consistent interim mailings and other communications to provide an even level of contact over time.

Listing a company on a foreign exchange is another option for the company to consider. Additional listings may provide increased visibility and ease of access to international capital markets as well as some potential convenience of trading for local investors. Foreign listings, however, is an expensive process that should be considered for its contribution to an overall profile-raising goal rather than as an end in itself.

Financial Community Meetings

The fundamental difference between the Annual Meeting and the meetings with the financial community discussed in this section is that the Annual Meeting is a legal obligation.

The Annual Meeting is run as a formal meeting, with motions made and "minutes" taken. Although time is allocated at the Annual Meeting to explaining long-term strategic plans and near-term activities that are being conducted or will be implemented, the Annual Meeting usually has a more historical focus. Its purpose is to review the past year and articulate the company's interpretation of financial results rather than present a view of the company as an investment opportunity.

An Analysts Meeting or a Portfolio Managers Luncheon, structured either as a presentation to a group or as a one-on-one (which may, in reality, end up being a five-on-one, or a three-on-two, as explained below) differ from the Annual Meeting both in form and content. Scheduling is under the control of the company. If, when, where and how frequently these meetings will be held are matters to be decided at the company's discretion. The purpose of the meetings, and the information needs of the audiences, are quite different than those of the Annual Meeting.

The overall purpose of these meetings is to acknowledge and meet the diverse information needs of the company's publics, which may include current owners, potential owners or those constituencies which influence these groups. Agendas are not dictated by corporate by-laws, and "approval" of company procedures and activities is not actively sought as in the Annual Meeting. "Approval" is gained far more subtly through the favorable research report, or purchase of stock.

As the newly public company "grows" its investor relations program, time will increasingly be devoted to planning meetings with members of the investment community. In well-established investor relations programs, over one-third of IR professional time may be spent planning executing "meetings." On average, according to responses to a National Investor Relations Institute membership survey, companies held thirty-two one-on-one analyst contact meetings; eight small group meetings (two to ten people); five large group meetings (eleven attendees or more) a year; plus presentations to analyst societies and splinter groups; field trips and tours. This totals close to 50 meetings on an annual basis!

The average number of meetings per year sponsored by companies trading over the counter was 19, compared with an average of 40 for New York Stock Exchange listed companies and 22 for American Stock Exchange listed companies.

The survey also broke out responses by industry type:

Over 40 meetings a year:	Petroleum, Building Materials, Telecommunications
30 to 40 meetings:	Diversified Companies, Food Processors, Chemicals, Aerospace, Computers, Oil Field Drilling, Health Care, Electronics
20 to 30 meetings:	Banks, Electric Utilities, Services, Insurance
Fewer than 20 meetings:	Natural Gas, Retailing, Electrical Equipment, Consumer Products, Financial Services

Thus the number of meetings a newly public company will arrange its first year will depend not only on its internal resources (financial and human) but also on whatever the demand is for holding meetings — as influenced by industry norms.

Using as a base the figure of 20 meetings for the first year, Exhibit 7.14 represents a hypothetical meeting plan. It should be emphasized that this number of meetings is not necessarily a recommended standard, but is presented for illustrative purposes. The number of meetings the company chooses to hold will be a unique function of the individual company's goals and circumstances.

EXHIBIT 7.14 — MEETING PLAN

No.	TYPE	CONSTITUENCY	PURPOSE
4	Analyst Meetings	Analysts, Market Makers, General Investment Community	Present Most Recent Earnings and Maintain Ongoing Open Contact
1	Annual Meeting	Shareholders, Media	Legal Obligation; Press Opportunity
4	Group	Portfolio Managers, Money Presentations (5–20 People)	Initiate, Maintain Managers, Analysts
			Visibility Among Financial Groups
1	Society	Targeted Groups of Presentation	Broad Introductory Financial Analysts
			Exposure
10	One-on-ones	Individuals	In-depth Explorations

General Guidelines For Successful Meetings. These apply to all the presentations outlined in the following pages.

- Thorough research, planning, follow-through and follow-up: have a clear impression of who the audience should be, what should be said, the vehicle for saying it and how aggressive the message should be;
- Strong CEO and management presence;
- Balance audience needs with company's agenda;
- Keep a future focus and demonstrate a big picture perspective: companies complain incessantly about the Street's short-term focus and then cater to it by making last quarter's earnings the focus of the presentation;
- Update key aspects and then build on what the audience

knows; follow a theme but don't be repetitive;
* Know critical issues and vulnerabilities: rehearse, and know the key selling points of the stock and the company; don't gloss over problem areas;
* Make an impression and be impressive — provide speaker training to key members of management;
* Review and critique the performance; learn from experience.

Analyst Meetings.

Variations: Also known As "Investment Community Meeting," "Quarterly Results Meeting," or "Interim Meeting"; these meetings may be held at any time of year, or in conjunction with announcement of quarterly results. The same general format is used if the company has recently made a significant material disclosure (i.e., a major acquisition or divestiture) and feels a group presentation to the general investment community is the most efficient manner in which to explain the strategic implications of the action.

Instigator: Company.

How Long: Two hours max; may be held as a luncheon meeting; ideally, a 30 to 45 minute presentation followed by open-ended Q&A.

Frequency And Timing: Schedule established on a yearly basis. May be held up to four times a year to immediately follow quarterly earnings release or scheduled according to industry cycle — in which case it conceivably might precede release of earnings. The timing is crucial and should be well thought out.

May be held at company headquarters or "on the road" — either consistently at one place with geographical proximity to a key audience concentration or rotated from financial center to financial center. Establishing a yearly schedule and location in advance — and circulating this information — can aid greatly in audience attendance.

Purpose: To establish a habit of providing a consistent flow of relevant information; to present quarterly earnings results; to allow members of the investment community to question management publicly on those results and other issues of importance. Inherently a financial presentation.

Company Participants: CEO, CFO, IR ... Senior Management Team and lieutenants as warranted. If it is held at the home office, make sure the number of internal people attending does not outnumber the invitees! Internal assistance for planning the meeting comes from Finance/Accounting (for help with preparing and double-checking figures); Legal (to confirm that nothing of a material nature is being disclosed or help prepare disclosure release if it is); outside IR counsel may be helpful for guidance and assistance with details and fine-tuning.

Audience: Analysts, buy and sell side; Portfolio Managers; Company's investment banker and primary market makers; interested brokers; significant shareholders. Press is generally not included.

Manner Of Invitation: Broad notice via direct mail (e.g. letter or memo to mailing list) and targeted follow-up.

General Format: Presentation, with Q&A.

Specific Format: CEO presents quarterly and year-to-date figures in a brief review (especially if earnings already have been announced) and presents information in context of company strategy and plans, industry conditions and market viewpoints. A brief topical presentation may be made by a divisional head or a burning issue discussed in depth. Questions are taken from the floor at the end of the presentation, to be answered directly by the CEO or fielded to appropriate members of management team.

Presentation Preparation: Slides are helpful so long as they clarify and don't confound the material. The CEO's commentary should be scripted and rehearsed (and, of course reviewed by legal counsel) and possible questions from the audience anticipated and answers prepared. Handouts might include hard copy of the slides, depending on the information. Input is provided by investor relations in the forms of general review of telephone inquiries and discussions during the quarter, and a pre-meeting briefing to management about the invited constituencies.

Follow-Up: The meeting should be taped, and transcripts made and edited for readability both for the purpose of maintaining permanent records and possible distribution to those who couldn't attend. Immediately after the meeting is a good time to "follow-up" on the effectiveness of the timing, format and content of the meeting. Was the right message communicated? Should the audience be narrowed or broadened?

Tips: Careful consideration should be given to almost all aspects of the first few analyst meetings. Check out the timing of competitors' meetings and other conflicts that might present competition for the audience. Gear the timing (i.e., time of day) to the largest segment's schedule — and likelihood of availability. Mid-morning or mid-afternoon may be good or bad for analysts; stockbrokers as a rule don't like to be out of the office while the market is open which would restrict the hour to either breakfast time, a short luncheon or an after-trading-hours meeting. This presents less of a challenge if the meeting is held in a western time zone. Have a solid and accurate idea of who your audience is, especially on a basis of present vs. potential stockholders and present vs. potential "influencers." Always have a sign-in book, and provide name tags for company representatives as well as attendees.

Group Presentations (5 – 20 Invitees).

Variations: "Road Show," "Press Briefing," "Analyst Luncheon."

Instigator: Company or, less frequently, as requested by an interested party. May be arranged by the Investment Banker or outside IR firm or both.

Frequency And Timing: At the convenience of the company and group. Conventionally arranged around a meal — breakfast, lunch or dinner—with consideration for the specific "lifestyles" of the audience, and regional custom.

Purpose: As a newly public company, the initial purpose may be to establish an orientation to the company and its management; afterwards, the purpose if to further cultivate and keep specific groups of interested parties informed or explore and initiate new relationships within a targeted group.

Company Participants: May vary. The CEO or highest ranking officer is best, but it depends on who the audience is and what the specific purpose of the gathering is in determining who else attends. A high ranking marketing officer, for example, may be brought along to explain marketing strategy if the company is touting a new product or market; the CFO often is appropriate in providing backup and depth to the CEO.

Audience: Usually homogeneous: analysts or portfolio managers or market makers or potential institutional shareholders. Sometimes it can be arranged to gather a group of brokers and institutional salespersons from a single large firm after market close.

Manner Of Invitation: Personal written invitation with RSVP cards or telephone number; follow-up with acknowledgement note and day-before telephone call. Especially necessary if planning a meal! Often the arrangements for these meetings are handled by outside IR counsel, who would assist in establishing the list, format of the invitation, follow-up, and other details.

General Format: Informal discussion before and during meal; opportunity to personally meet and greet attendees; presentation and Q&A.

Specific Format: Socializing over a brief cocktail period prior to lunch or dinner, brief presentation at dessert time with handouts; Q&A.

Presentation Focus: May be general or specific, but always keep in mind the information needs of the audience.

Follow-Up: Thank-you notes to attendees; follow-up on further information requests and inclusion in the next round of meetings.

Tips: Presentations to rating agencies fall in this category, although they are more likely to take place at the company's offices or at the agency rather than at an off-site luncheon; they usually are coordinated by the company's treasurer or CFO.

One-On-Ones.

Variations: Infinite. One (analyst, portfolio manager, individual) visits sequentially for half an hour with the CEO, CFO, a division head (or two); or one (analyst, etc.) visits with a group comprised of members of the above; or two (or more) analysts visit with the CEO (and/or others) and so on.

Instigator: Either by outside request, or at the invitation of the company.

Frequency And Timing: As requested — but keep an eye out for trends and patterns: if several meetings have been arranged for interested parties all covering the same issues, it may be a signal that something more formal should be instigated by the company to deal with the questions or topic. Also, some analysts or portfolio managers may seek a yearly on-site "update" which can, and should, be anticipated.

Purpose: In direct response to whatever the requesting party asks for: an overview or personal exploration of certain topics. It is essential that whatever the reason, it be articulated clearly to those who will be meeting with the individual or group!

Company Participants: As appropriate. A well-versed IR officer should be able to adequately and satisfyingly present a thorough company overview (and put to more efficient use the CEO's time with the individual).

Audience: Buy-side, sell-side analysts, portfolio managers, individual shareholders with significant ownership.

Manner Of Invitation: By company invitation or in response to a request for a meeting. Once a schedule is established it should be documented in a letter detailing where to meet, the agenda (and titles of the people who will be met), transportation arrangements; copies should be distributed to all involved on the company side.

General Format: Casual discussion.

Specific Format: Determined by the purpose. An "orientation" packet or other materials which help explain the topics to be discussed might be appropriate. Certainly good note-taking (by the IR professional or some other participant) is called for, perhaps formally documented in a summary memo routed internally or simply developed as a "memo-to-file."

Presentation Focus: Situational.

Follow-Up: A brief summary/thank you note to the visitor is in good form; feedback (verbal); follow-up to any questions not answered or promises to "get back with that information."

Society Or Group Invitational Meetings.

Variations: NYSSA (New York Society of Security Analysts); Regional Analyst Societies; "Splinter Groups" (by industry specialty); Broker Groups; Investment Clubs (NAIC).

Instigator: The Group or Society, based upon their knowledge of the company and its interest to the group, or by company communication to the Group or Society.

Frequency And Timing: Usually restricted by the Group or Society to once a year or every other year.

Purpose: To showcase the company and management before a group that represents similar interests and is broader than what the company itself typically can gather.

Company Participants: "Command performance" by CEO with backup and support provided by IR.

Audience: Membership of the group. Sometimes press is also invited—find out beforehand!

Manner Of Invitation: The meeting sponsors take care of it. Request an invitation list to cross check, and for future use.

General Format: Presentation accompanied by slide show or video followed by Q&A session.

Specific Format: A straightforward presentation of operations, plans, outlook, with appropriate literature distributed.

Presentation Focus: Tailored to information needs of group.

Follow-Up: Stay in touch with contact person for future scheduling; add attendees to company mailing list; consider developing a printed summary or report of the presentation for distribution to other investment community audiences.

Miscellaneous Meetings.

Variations: Field Trips, Outings, Open Houses, Investor Fairs, Trade Shows ...

Instigator: Company.

Frequency And Timing: Thoughtfully timed, i.e. not too often.

Purpose: To showcase the company and its operations or to provide a relaxed environment for management interaction with members of the investment community. To highlight divisional activities or focus on areas of special interest; to introduce new members of a management team or just to start (or keep up) a tradition.

Company Participants: Many, or at least a wide sample of, members of management usually are invited to mingle with invitees.

Audience: Varies—but again, not fewer than the number of company representatives in attendance.

Manner Of Invitation: Selective and personalized.

General Format: Meaningful combinations of work and social interaction are to be strived for. It really depends on the company, its industry, the industry norms for such activities, and the company's own objectives, desires and creativity in mounting a presentation.

Specific Format: Up to the creative imagination of the organizers.

Presentation Focus: Varies.

Follow-Up: Cost-benefit analysis; post-meeting survey of attendees.

Tips: "Who pays?" is an issue to consider when long-distance travel is required.

CONCLUSION

There is no substitute for experience in IR. Lacking such experience, an IR consultant is the best guide to the business if the company is starting out on to establish its program. There will be areas in which Wall Street investors and analysts want to talk directly to the company, but there are many areas in which the consultant can assist with a candid and unbiased review and analysis of the company's current perceptions on the street. Many companies benefit from an outside perspective on their efforts and incorporate the analyses and recommendations of outside firms. Large capitalization companies will usually take the recommendations and implement most of them themselves. With mid-cap and small-cap companies, investor relations consultants are often asked to serve as the IR department or an important adjunct to the finance area.

RECOMMENDED READINGS

No list of readings can possibly take into account all of the legal decisions, SEC regulations, or stock market requirements, nor can it substitute for years of experience in investor relations. Fortunately, the National Investor Relations Institute (NIRI), published Investor Relations Body of Knowledge, a comprehensive outline, study guide and resource list defining the investor relations profession. This course of study is divided into the capital markets, the investment process, the corporate environment, and the practice of investor relations. NIRI was founded in 1969 as a professional association of corporate officers and investor relations consultants responsible for communications between corporate management, the investing public and the financial community.

Copies of the *Investor Relations Body of Knowledge* are available from National Investor Relations Institute, 8045 Leesburg Pike, Suite 600, Vienna, VA 22182; (703) 506-3570.

In addition, the following list of recommended readings are excellent sources of information on investor relations:

Hogan, J.M., Esq., text editor, Saul, Ewing, Remick, and Saul. 1993 *Annual Report and Proxy Rules of the Securities and Exchange Commission.* Philadelphia: Packard Press, 1992.

Little, Jeffrey B. and Lucien Rhodes. *Understanding Wall Street.* 3rd ed. New York: McGraw-Hill, Liberty Hall Press, 1991.

Mahoney, William F. *Investor Relations: The Professional's Guide to Financial Marketing and Communications.* New York: New York Institute of Finance, 1990.

Rappaport, Alfred. *Creating Shareholder Value.* New York: The Free Press, 1986.

Roalman, A.R., editor. *Investor Relations Handbook.* New York: AMACOM, 1974.

Schneider, Manko, and Kent. *Going Public: Practice, Procedures, and Consequences.* Philadelphia: Packard Press, 1990.

Taggart, Philip W., Roy Alexander, with Robert M. Arnold. *Taking Your Company Public*. New York: AMACOM, 1991.

Waltan, Wesley S. and Charles P. Brissman. *Corporate Communications Handbook: A Guide to Press Releases and Other Informal Disclosure for Public Corporations*. New York: Clark, Boardman Callaghan, 1993.

Wes Truesdell is a full-time senior counselor to The Dilenschneider Group. Following his retirement in 1988 from Doremus & Company, he joined Creamer Dickson Basford as deputy chairman while maintaining a consulting firm in his own name. He came to The Dilenschneider Group in February 1995.

Mr. Truesdell was in charge of Doremus Public Relations for many years as executive vice president and a director of the parent company. Under his lead, Doremus was for a number of years among the top dozen PR firms in the United States, with as many as 10 offices across the country and in London. He has been involved in top-level counseling for public relations and investor relations programs for major corporations, banks and leading Wall Street investment houses, and has specialized in marketing public relations for a wide range of financial services.

In 1978 PRSA presented its highest award, the Silver Anvil, to the City of Niagara Falls, N.Y and Mr. Truesdell for a public relations program which dramatically told how Niagara Falls business groups helped bring the city back from the brink of bankruptcy.

Mr. Truesdell has been accredited by the Public Relations Society of America, and a member of its Counselors Academy. He served in the United States Army Infantry, 1950-1952, in Korea, and graduated in 1956 from St. John's University with a degree in economics. He has been a governor of the Staten Island Institute of Arts and Sciences and for five years was chairman of the nationally recognized environmental education facility, High Rock Park Conservation Center.

CHAPTER 8

THE ANNUAL REPORT

As does no other single document, the well-done annual report speaks with a voice that represents the total "personality" of a corporation. To a substantial degree, an above-average report almost always embodies the views, hopes, goals, and ambitions of the chief executive officer and the board of directors.

Conception, preparation, and production of the better annual report involves the direct efforts of a whole host of people — corporate communications director, head of investor relations, chief financial officer, general counsel, and their staffs; and, from outside the company, the auditing firm and legal counsel, plus public relations and investor relations firms, designers, artists, photographers, and printers. Internally, this list goes on to include heads of operating divisions who are interviewed for information to be included in the report and, in some cases, even regional executives and plant managers. In all, for a large company's report, it is conceivable that scores of persons played some role in its creation and production.

Ultimately, it is the CEO's and the chief administrative officer's job to ensure that the report preparation process moves along smoothly, on a pre-planned schedule, and that its messages about what the company's strengths and business objectives are, and where it is headed, faithfully represent the CEO's views and those close around him. And, while it the responsibility of a company's executive staff to organize and produce the report, it is not uncommon for activist outside members of the board of directors to take an interest and advise the CEO on its approach and content. They may be helpful in establishing the theme and broad outlines for the report.

ANNUAL REPORT TYPES

Annual reports come in several varieties. One is the "official" form 10K annual report (form 20F for foreign companies required to report), which, by statute, must be filed annually with the Securities and Exchange Commission. This is printed in black ink on white paper, and its contents must follow a prescribed format.

More common is the typical corporate pamphlet-type report issued by thousands of companies here and abroad. Most annual reports are organized so that the CEO's message to shareholders and other illustrative and descriptive material is at the front of the "book," and is followed by the more formal required financial statements, much of which is mandated by the SEC, New York Stock Exchange, or National Association of Securities Dealers.

Most annual reports contain anywhere from 32 pages (and covers) to 96 pages; but some may contain more, or fewer. Over recent years as the SEC required more and more financial data to be included in reports that were being printed by expensive four-color process, companies began exploring ways to reduce costs. and the Summary Annual Report was born. In the summary annual report, which must be so labeled, the SEC since 1989 has permitted the upfront portion to be printed separately in color with photos, illustrations, graphs, and the like; and the rear portion — financial statements — to be printed in much less costly black and white. Both portions must be mailed to all shareholders, and a company has the option of including the financial statements in its proxy statement which, like the annual, must be received by shareholders well in advance of the annual meeting.

CONTENTS OF THE REPORT — GENERAL

It is in the report's front section that companies have almost total flexibility in deciding what to include, so long as it is truthful. Typically, an annual report's cover design should help establish the overall "theme" for the book — and the cover of Betz Laboratories' 1995 annual does just that (see Exhibit 8.1). Spherical drawings, some with inset photos, are meant to represent structures of chemical molecules of the types Betz deals with in its worldwide business of the engineered chemical treatment of water, waste-water, and process systems. The "molecular" photo theme is carried into the report on 8 of 18 inside pages and the back cover.

Betz is a technology-based company and it follows good annual report practice in the way it arranges information:

- One-page summary description of the company, plus index to the report's contents;
- Two-page more detailed outline of Betz' four business segments: Water Management, PaperChem, Process Chemicals, and MetChem — and in chart format, details on each of the segments as to its business, applications, customers, services, and recent technological developments;
- One page of income-statement financial highlights, with year-to-year percentage changes and important ratios;
- Three-page "Dear Shareholder" letter, with executive photo — 11-page report of operations and important technological developments, with 11 "molecular" photos on six of those pages.

Skipping past for the moment a report's financial statements, which are covered below, the Betz report, at the rear, contains:

- Two-page, 11-year summary of operating results and key statistics;
- One-page listing of directors, officers, and "boilerplate";
- One page showing worldwide operating locations.

CONTENTS OF THE REPORT — FINANCIAL STATEMENTS

As noted earlier, financial statements in an annual report must meet the basic requirements of the Securities and Exchange Commission, and these, in turn, are governed by the accounting-statement decisions issued from time to time by the independent Financial Accounting Standards Board. As of the end of 1995 there had been approximately 125 such rulings with which all large publicly owned companies must comply. At present, financial statements must include:

- Consolidated Balance Sheets for two consecutive years
- Consolidated Statements of Operations for three years
- Consolidated Statements of Cash Flows
- Consolidated Statements of Common Shareholders' Equity
- Notes to the Consolidated Financial Statements
- Management's Discussion and Analysis of Financial Condition and Results of Operations (MD&A)
- Letter from the company's auditors attesting to the accuracy of the financial statements
- Letter from the company's chief financial officer explaining internal accounting procedures and how the statements were prepared for auditors' inspection and review.

In the Betz annual report there were a total of 12 Notes, and they were quite typical of most companies:

- Summary of significant accounting policies
- Income taxes
- Employee retirement plans
- Segment and geographic information
- Stock option, stock incentive, and shareholder rights plans
- Employee stock ownership (ESOP) and 401(k) plans
- Long-term leases
- Provision for restructuring
- Post-retirement benefits
- Notes payable
- Acquisitions
- Quarterly financial information.

Similarly, the MD&A portion of an annual report, which is prepared by management, often with input from auditors, is divided into sections. The 1995 Betz report had:

- Overview
- Results of operations – 1995 vs. 1994
- Results of operations – 1994 vs. 1993
- Liquidity and sources of capital
- Impact of inflation and changing prices
- Impact of accounting pronouncements.

PLANNING PRODUCTION OF AN ANNUAL REPORT

At some large companies, planning for next year's annual report has begun even before the current year's book has been completed. However, a total of 22-26 weeks will generally be sufficient planning and production time for a report from start-up to delivery:

Weeks 1-3

Develop goals, themes after analysis of prior books. Contact department/division heads for ideas. Circulate probable AR timetable;

Week 4

Rough copy outline, design exploration.

Weeks 5-7

Process continues.

Weeks 8-12

Start photography (remember that most annuals are produced in fall/winter, so good outdoor shots may have to be taken earlier). Develop copy and comprehensive design.

Week 13

Begin production and typesetting.

Weeks 14-15

Final review of comp with photos; copy review.

Week 16

Retouch photos. Develop charts/graphs when financials are available. Semi-final type.

Weeks 17-18

Final typesetting; pre-press production of report on computer disk.

Weeks 19-20

To printer; check blueprints (or dylux proofs).

Weeks 21-22

Printing and binding.

Week 23

Delivery.

Remember to select and deal with your printer early on; he or she will have to schedule adequate press time and order paper.

SELECTING A DESIGNER

Design and printing of annual reports is a big business in the United States, and the selection of a good, experienced designer is critical to the production of a solid report. Remember that designers are more capable of interpreting themes and ideas into graphical expression than they are in developing the underlying themes themselves. That you will have to do for yourself in concert with communications staffs and outside agency people. Designers are useful in selecting appropriate printers, and several printers should be asked to bid on your job. A further caution: towards the end of the production cycle, if you get behind in the timetable, it can be costly.

There are good and not-so-good designers in most large cities of the United States. After you interview them and see samples of their work, make sure you speak to the companies for whom they have designed reports. In the New York City and other large metropolitan regions there are hundreds of design firms, ranging from annual report factories to mid-sized firms and boutiques. At the Dilenschneider Group our usual preference is for the smaller firm, because they are large enough to have back-up in case of accident, yet small enough that we get to work directly with the principals.

Whatever firm you choose, be sure to review dozens of reports from other companies to survey potential ideas for themes, for design concepts and for chart and graph treatments. After you decide how many pages and how much color (and new photography) you'll need, make a firm budget and hold your internal staff and your suppliers to it. The result can be an informative piece that outlines the financial health of your company, details your direction, and presents a positive image of the company to its audiences.

EXHIBIT 8.1

Joseph A. Kopec is a principal with The Dilenschneider Group in Chicago. He began his career in public relations, writing newsletters and internal communications for corporations and business executives. He has advised Fortune *100 (NYSE) companies on many of the largest restructuring communications in recent years. He has created, written, and advised on communications for financial and employee communications issues related to mergers, acquisitions, and divestitures.*

From 1982 to 1991 he was a senior vice president and managing director with Hill and Knowlton in Chicago, where he was head of the communications audit practice. Prior to joining Hill and Knowlton, he was director of communications for the Hay Group, a division of Saatchi & Saatchi. He was an executive vice president with the nation's largest independent public relations firm, and directed public information for the Attorney General of Ohio. He was part of Senator John Glenn's election campaign.

Mr. Kopec is a graduate of Ohio State University where he serves on the President's Advisory Committee. He serves on the board of directors of the National Kidney Foundation, the International House at the University of Chicago, and the Japan America Society.

CHAPTER 9

KEEPING EMPLOYEES INFORMED

Chances are you turned to this chapter because you face a challenge of communicating effectively with employees. Maybe you value the importance of employee communication from your own experiences. Perhaps you've just been assigned to the task of handling employee communication and want to see what the latest thinking is on the subject. Possibly you own a small business and you are reading this book to learn more about improving the way you communicate with your employees. Or perhaps you're a student who is surveying what's available on the subject of employee communication. Whatever your current interest or background, this chapter will give you practical and useful advice based on the experiences of some the leading executives and communicators in the field of employee communication.

You will read about three critical areas of employee communication. The first section discusses the challenges of being a communicator in any organization. The primary focus is on issues you actually face and how to deal with them.

In the second section, you will read about what's called Formal Employee Communication or *downward* communication and the concept of the three concentric circles in the employee communication process. This section includes a detailed review of all the methods used in employee communication, such as printed material, audiovisual tapes, and electronic systems, e-mail, and voice mail. The third section deals with Informal Employee Communication, which is an area that remains largely unexplored. It has tremendous promise for the future and seems most dependent on the grapevine.

THE CHALLENGE OF THE COMMUNICATOR

Let's start with the premise that the speed and amount of change taking place in the workplace are daunting. Research studies conducted by leading opinion research firms show that anxiety, stress, lack of loyalty, and commitment are at the highest levels since such research started after World War II. We are facing nothing short of a revolution in the employer-employee relationship and in our communications practices. We must change not only the way we work, but we must change almost totally the way we communicate.

Much of the advice on employee communication deals with the visible means of communications such as printed newsletters, brochures, videotapes, and, more recently, e-mail and voice mail. There is a growing body of evidence that shows that the widespread availability of modern communicating devices (personal computers, modems, faxes, pagers, cellular phones, etc.) are truly changing the way that all of us communicate. These visible tools attract most of the attention. What is most important is how the process works (D'Aprix 1988) and how it can be improved more effectively by using these tools. We have learned that the increased speed and widespread availability of information from many new sources, including online information services such as CompuServe, America Online, and Prodigy, has reduced the time in which businessmen and women can make decisions. And, therefore, employees are being forced to act quickly on their own without approval from headquarters. The equation is changing from information controlled by a few senior executives to information controlled by employees (Katz 1978).

In other words, the very technology that has made it impossible for authoritarian governments in the former Soviet Union and in the People's Republic of China to control public opinion has now turned on one of the last surviving bureaucratic structures: The corporation.

The changes caused by electronics and computer technology have just started, and their effects are profound. Communications from employees dealing with customers to the center of the corporation will continue to be essential to the survival of the business enterprise. Somehow corporations will be transformed by the communications processes required to manage new enterprises into much less formalized and more free form organizations. Organizational structures look more and more like wheels and circles than boxes. People work in teams with emphasis on support across units rather than in reporting relationships to higher executives.

What is Employee Communication?

Employee communication is the systematic and symmetical process of communicating with and listening to employees to achieve an organization's objectives. It is systematic in that all tools and techniques must be used in order to be highly effective (Grunig, J.E. & Hunt, T. 1984). It is symmetical in the sense that those who communicate seek an interactive relationship. We speak and we listen. We write and we read. It is quite simply a loop.

All of us are *employees*. The archaic Anglo-Saxon word *employee* originally meant an occupation. Even before the Angles and the Saxons, the Romans used a Latin root word *implicare* to suggest involvement or folding in. Today *employee* implies that you do something, typically useful work, and are paid with money in the form of a paycheck. That is unless you work at home as a consultant. Even then you have employers who pay for your services.

Communication is defined as the means of communicating, especially, a system for sending and receiving messages, such as mail, telephone, television, or a network of routes for sending messages. *Communications* is distinctly different from communication. It is the act of communicating or the exchange of thoughts or messages.

James F. Beré, chairman and chief executive officer of Borg-Warner Corporation, was an immensely effective communicator. Reporters, analysts, and employees were surprised when he answered his own phone. One day he described employee communication by saying: "What we have here is highly effective employee communication—in fact, award-winning—that communicates a lot of information. What we do not seem to have is much employee communicating." He answered his own phone to listen to what people had to say. He knew, from these calls, what people were thinking. His attentive listening skills enabled him to quickly diagnose areas that needed additional attention and action.

Dealing with Myths in Employee Communications

Myth Number One: Employees Are Our Most Important Asset.

How many times have you read: "Employees are our most important asset." How can you say that employees are our most important asset and yet not be open and inclusive in the process of obtaining buy-in on critical and basic decisions? Some companies even make it difficult for employees to understand quarterly financial results when those same employees are stockholders. Why is it that if employees are truly so important to the success of most modern enterprises, they are frequently the last audience considered for important announcements and the first audience targeted for cost reductions. It is a dilemma that you will face regularly.

A letter accompanying an invitation to a seminar on change at corporations carried the statement that the biggest lie most companies tell is that "people are our most important asset. This is a total fabrication," the author wrote. "Companies treat people like steel, oil, gas, or other materials. If people are their most important asset, there should be a dramatic increase in investments in people."

The answer quite simply is that it is much easier to measure a return on investment from physical or capital expenditures for bricks and mortar than it is to measure a return on investments in human resources. As a result, managers invest in what they know traditionally produces results.

All of this can be reduced to one word: Credibility. Employees want to know why they should believe what you write or say. In many, but certainly not all, cases with the conflict between what management says and does, how can you be credible? It seems so obvious. Be honest and tell the truth. Not that managers want to dissimulate. It is a question of risk aversion and the unpredictable nature of future events in most organizations. It is essential to effective communications to gather and use specific, factual information.

In other words, be willing to share truly useful information with employees. Do not fear that providing either detailed data, financial results, or negative news will destroy your credibility. Most employees are mature and sophisticated information users. Do not fear overcommunicating or sending too detailed information either. Be willing to send more information and let employees decide how best to use it. A surfeit of information is better than not enough.

Aside from the method and quantity of your communications, get to the heart of credibility by telling the whole story. Use negative information to build credibility. You lost a customer. Say so. You want to tell the employees that you won some big, new customer, too. Fine. Credible communications means factual and balanced. The least believable information involves propagandistic bombast. When State Farm Insurance presents its positions on public issues, the company's backgrounders for the news media always present the pros and cons of an issue. It improves the odds of cutting through the cynicism of a one-side argument.

Despite the difficult circumstances that managers face with employee communication, many other companies have prospered by applying professional techniques to their employee communication. The Whirlpool Corporation is an example of stepping back and addressing what is called a virtual revolution in employee communication.

Corporatespeak Versus Employeespeak: In fact, as Bruce Berger, vice president of corporate affairs at Whirlpool Corporation, said in an illustration (Berger 1996; see *"Revolution at Whirlpool" case history that follows*) for new thinking in employee communication, many managers use "corporatespeak" while employees use "employeespeak."

To better illustrate this situation, a manager at any company might say in a meeting with employees:

Corporatespeak: "The acquisition will assist us in leveraging our strengths, reduce costs, and strengthen our marketing efforts. Unfortunately, some redundancies will occur although we have no precise numbers of positions affected."

Translation into Employeespeak: "A lot of people may not be around in a year or less. With fewer people, if I decide to stay, I will have to work longer hours. I will probably have to do much more with fewer resources. The business area we are adding this acquisition to didn't cut it and that's why we paid a premium to buy an outfit that may or may not get us more market share."

Pay particular attention to "Corporatespeak" in your own communications and try to use plain, direct "Employeespeak" whenever you can. Specifically, you may ask yourself, *"How* do I make myself clearly understood?"

The answer is that you must ask yourself if your writing or speaking, or that of your assistants in the employee communications area, is completely clear. Clear means indisputably easy to understand and without any double meanings. If not, find a way to make it clearer. The best way to do this is for you to turn on a tape recorder and start talking prior to a presentation or sit at the PC and write as the most successful business writers do.

But where to start? With persuasive writing assignments, you should begin by crafting a few *key messages*. A message is nothing more than a simple sentence that contains a number of facts about a situation. As an example, a message in an employee letter might be:

- "I encourage you to make a pre-tax contribution to this 40l(k) plan because *it is the most effective way for you to build your retirement income and shelter your current income.*"

A second message might be:

- *"To encourage you to contribute up to the allowable maximum,* I've asked our chief financial officer, Tim Miller, *to match your contribution with 50 cents for every dollar you invest."*

And finally:

- *"To make it as easy as possible, contributions will be deducted and invested in the funds you have selected with each automatic payroll deduction."*

Establish a conversational style that is less formal. It includes contractions and speaks to the other person in the second person *you*. (Even French presidents now ask their assistant to use the second person in addressing them, *tu* instead of the more formal *vous*.) If you can talk through the subject and explain it clearly with two or three short messages, try it out with your spouse, a friend, or a trusted employee. But work on the points by writing them out before you rehearse the presentation.

Myth Number Two: Tell Employees What They Need To Know

The objective of most employee communication is to inform employees *about what they should know so that they can do their job better.* Notice the phrase is *"what they should know."* We are dealing with the important issue of content. Who is to say what an employee should know or needs to know in order to be productive on the job? In most organizations management decides because management is in charge of making crucial decisions and, therefore, has the information first. That is true because most managerial structures resemble military organizations such as the army. Perhaps large organizations will never get entirely away from information flowing down the organization (Katz 1978). Yet most organizations realize that it is critical to break down work groups and services into smaller units to make them more responsive to customers and users. In creating smaller work groups, a new set of problems emerges which is that critical information is now down in the trenches closer to the battlefield. Now the general has the problem of getting information faster than the troops. The generals typically charge one or more people on their staff with responsibility for employee communication. The job has changed considerably in recent years from distribution of corporate information to one that includes finding out what employees think about issues through the use of research techniques.

People who work in the field of employee communication continue to debate the power and effectiveness of official printed, audio-visual, and electronic communications versus the role of the supervisor to whom the employee reports (Conrad 1985). Common sense and research support the idea that most of us want to get our information from the person who hires, evaluates, promotes, and approves our efforts. And yet there is no question that supervisory communication is much more effective, not alone, but when presented with a variety of repeated messages on a company's values, culture, and attributes. My advice is to train supervisors and arm them with carefully crafted information on all important efforts and projects. But, along with that, build an effective backdrop consisting of arranged support communications. For example, every major announcement affecting employees should include multiple types of communications beginning with a memo, letter, or e-mail to each employee, a copy of the news release distributed to the press, a package for the supervisor containing the same information plus a detailed package of background information and an easy-to-use bulleted series of messages to communicate why the decision was made and a list of questions and answers.

Recent studies on who should introduce change in an organization, reported by the International Association of Business Communicators (IABC) in *Communication World* (IABC 1994, 1995), reveal useful data supporting the role of supervisors in employee communication. Among various findings that support the role of the supervisor in effective communications are the following:

- When asked where they would turn when they have a problem they cannot solve themselves, employees said:
  1. Supervisor
  2. Experienced coworker
  3. Unwritten company policy
  4. Company manual.
  (Source: U. S., U. K., Hong Kong: Mark Peterson)
- Employees say their immediate boss is their most effective communication source. (Europe: International Survey Research)
- 76 percent say communication within their local work area is good. (Source: U. K., Wyatt Work U.K.)
- 83 percent of employees rank their supervisor as their most believed source. (U. S., General Motors)
- 96 percent of frontline employees believe their supervisor is normally or always telling the truth; 45 percent believe the union is normally or always telling the truth. (Source: Australia: Dennis Taylor)

- 71 percent of branch managers describe their relationship with the bank head office as clearly negative, neutral, or they refuse to answer the question. (Sweden: Rita Martenson)
- 64 percent say they often do not believe what management says, according to the U.S. Council on Communication Management and Alexander Consulting Group.
- Only 32 percent of employees believe management decisions are generally good ones.

From this data and other studies, you might deduce that you should:

- Cancel the executive traveling roadshow.
- Stop advising executives to become more visible.
- Give up trying to boost senior management's credibility — there isn't time.
- Don't gather big groups of employees together for a grand announcement.
- Target frontline supervisors as your most important communication priority.
- Spend 80 percent of your time, money, and effort to communicate with supervisors.
- Increase face-to-face contact between senior managers responsible for the change and supervisors.
- Make supervisors feel like privileged senders and receivers of information.

Though there is no question that many studies support the notion that employees want to receive their communications from their supervisor, whom they generally trust far more than the official organization, take some of this with a grain of salt. In truth, a well-managed employee communication effort uses every conceivable communications device that will make the communication clearer and better understood. Supervisors in every organization should be briefed and prepared to communicate. But those same supervisors are going to do a much better job if their communication is presented against a backdrop of highly effective printed, audiovisual, and electronic communications.

Myth Number Three: External vs. Internal Communications "The Chinese Wall Theory"

"The Chinese Wall Theory" of internal and external communications would have you believe that what goes on inside the corporation is rarely or ever known outside the Great Wall of the Organization. A corollary to this is that what is said on the outside of the wall will rarely affect the employees inside the wall. In many organizations these two parallel and ultimately vitally linked efforts are somehow separated and not coordinated, except in the best managed units and organizations.

For example, many employees say that they often read company news first in the newspaper. The oft repeated refrain is: "I never hear about anything unless it's in the media first." A secondary occurrence is for the media to pick up what appears to be an internal document and publish it on the front page or flash it on the news.

In truth there is no wall between internal and external communications. Bill Barnhart, a *Chicago Tribune* columnist who follows the financial markets, said that he can often tell much about the quality of a company by its willingness to send internal publications to him. Well-managed and effective communicators know that their internal publications often become ambassadors for outside audiences. In fact, some publications originally started as employee publications can turn into magazines that have an external appeal. Ford, Allstate, and Monsanto have all had publications that are of such superior quality that outsiders want to read them.

Everyone who has ever worked with employees and the news media knows that many employees can telecopy company memos, newsletters, and other documents to journalists and others. Why do they do this? The motivations vary. Some employees are disgruntled over real or imagined slights. Individuals at pressure-points in the organization come upon what they consider information that they consider unethical. Other employees simply cannot keep information confidential — particularly in the case of reductions of fellow employees — and they spill the beans through an anonymous fax or letter. The best advice has always been to write every item as though it might be reprinted on the front page of *The New York Times*.

The Employee Communication Bill of Rights

You can reduce your own problems in dealing with these myths by adopting an Employee Communication Bill of Rights. Just as our Constitution's framers found that certain issues needed to be emphasized because of their vital importance, employees have the right to expect that communications will take into consideration the following questions that will occur to them immediately.

- As an employee I have the right to know *how this issue will affect me.*
- *... if I will have a job.*
- *... how this issue will affect my paycheck.*
- *... if this decision means more work for less or the same amount of money.*
- *How am I going to handle this additional work with all the work I already have? And with fewer people to help.*

Men and women have always been concerned about their jobs and their organizations. For example, walking around the Acropolis in Athens and looking at the ruin of the Parthenon, it is impossible to ignore the genius that created the wonder of artistic beauty and engineering achievement that is the basis of so much architecture 2,500 years later. But imagine the Athenians who worked on top of the Acropolis in 450 B. C. Pericles decides to build a temple. What do the workers say about his grand strategy to make Athens the top city? Imagine the conversation between the foreman and the architect:

> Calicrates (the architect): Men, we have a few minor changes in the design today and I will need your help to make the new opening date for the festival that's coming up next year. Pericles is counting on all of us to make this happen.

> Foreman: It's all well and good that Pericles wants to build all these buildings to impress everyone with our public works. But how are we going to get all of this done, Calicrates? Look at this schedule. Have you put any of these pediments in place lately. The engineering isn't even proven. How am I ever going to get these men to handle these cranes?

> Calicrates: Look, Xenon, we'll get more volunteers to help build the temple. And as far as the machinery, trust me. I've used it on Delos and it works. I'll be right here with you whenever you need anything. So let's get to it.

Using the Three Circles of Employee Communication

Perhaps a simple thinking framework for being an effective communicator will work for you. Think of employee communication as three concentric circles. The first circle is drawn around you as you plan to communicate and then take the actions necessary to be effective. The second concentric circle contains any sources of information you use and anyone who has to approve the communications you develop. This second circle is vitally important to your credibility and effectiveness. The third, outside concentric circle, is made up of anyone and everyone with whom you are communicating through all the methods at your disposal.

How exactly is effectiveness defined in this context? Define effectiveness quite simply as getting through to whomever you want to communicate. In short, do they understand you? You can think of numerous examples in which you thought you had effectively communicated to someone very specific instructions. For example, with a child about cleaning their room. Did they do it? Many times, they did not. And what's their response when you challenge them? I didn't understand what you said. Most parents respond by repeating the instructions, but enunciating each syllable. Then asking: Have I made myself completely clear?

The first circle of employee communication is drawn around you as you sit down and plan what needs to be communicated and why. If you seek to be effective, you must *write out on paper or on your computer screen what you want to communicate.* How would you react if your supervisor called you in and gave you new information about your job. Put yourself in the place of your reader or listener. Anticipate the questions your employees will have and *write out the detailed answer* to each question.

Advertising and public relations professionals pre-test material. You do not need to conduct focus groups on every item written. If you have trusted advisors who are pragmatic, ask them to read it and react candidly to you by answering the following questions:

1. Is it clear?
2. How would you react to this information?
3. Why?
4. Is there anything that I should add, subtract or improve?
5. Do you believe what I've written? If yes, why? If no, why not?
6. Is the language simple enough and clear enough for practically anyone to understand?

FORMAL COMMUNICATION

Formal communication, what some of us might refer to as *downward* (because it comes down from on high) or *official communication*, comprise a vast panoply of printed, audiovisual, and electronic formats. In most effective employee communication the formal and informal communications perform like instruments in an orchestra. They supplement and reinforce each other, and the repetition of a refrain may take two or three times to register with the employee. You will be introduced to each format and given some examples of how these are used today (Cutlip & Center 1985).

Ten or fifteen years ago, the principal means of communications were then limited to printed materials and slides. A great many letters, brochures, newsletters, and slide shows were written or produced. In addition, an overhead or slide show, along with a tape-recorded audio portion to introduce a new program, would be produced. A script might accompany the presentation so the manager could adapt the presentation to his or her style.

Have things changed! With the advent of the Macintosh computer, we have unleashed a graphics revolution that has changed much *downward communications* with everything from a simple lack of control over logotypes and design quality to underground newsletters that attack management and management decisions. The computer has added a dizzying array of specialized publications and printed pieces.

Print Materials

Just as you must analyze your target audience, the messages you wish to communicate, and pre-test your messages when you write anything for an employee audience, printed materials require that you analyze the answers to such questions as:

- Who will read this information?
- Does this readership share a common bond? What is it?
- Where will they read it? Office? Home?
- How much time will they devote to reading it?
- Will it have secondary readership among spouses and friends?
- Will it be read and discarded or read and saved?
- How can I make it visually easy to read and to navigate graphically?
- Is this a one-time communication or do I intend to produce this periodically? Weekly? Monthly? Quarterly? Annually?
- Who will be responsible for pulling the news together and keeping it on schedule?
- How much money do I have to accomplish the best effort possible?

It pays to prepare a publication business plan that includes all of the details associated with a start-up enterprise. Define the objectives carefully and be realistic. Do some research about the nature of the readership and what they will be interested in. You might use an employee advisory panel or you might conduct your own polling. Discuss the strategy of content and delivery of the information and the *look* of the publication. Then include a one-year editorial calendar of stories or topics you will cover, when the issue will be published, and what is required prior to each distribution to meet deadlines. Part of the deadline will be the approval process. Though approval processes will vary from company to company, the basic system usually requires that the author or editor check the facts and sometimes the precise copy with the corporate source. There may be a final reviewer who is responsible for legal issues or administrative oversight. None of this is necessarily bad unless it causes long delays or onerous processing that squeezes the last drop of sprightliness out of the written or electronic word.

To save time, consider the approval process required to move the draft copy through the chain of command. Remember the second circle concept introduced at the beginning of the discussion of formal communications. This is where it is most useful. What is your policy on approvals? Do you have to have the person who is quoted approve the entire story? Is there one officer who must approve everything that is written? And then, when the final art is complete and ready for printing, do you have to have at least one final review by a lawyer? These are important issues. Be sure to work out the details in advance and expect delays. A rule of thumb: Expect many more delays in the first few editions of a new publication than in an established publication that has been around for a few years and has a well-defined role to play in the communication process.

Let's start with publications that have "periodicity," a word librarians use to mean that you can expect to receive a newsletter, newspaper, magazine or journal a certain number of times each year. If you intend to publish on a regular schedule, you are setting an immediate expectation, that it will arrive at some predetermined date each week or month. And the promise had better be kept if you intend to be credible. In addition, the frequency of the publication should be carefully determined because you or your colleagues will have to produce it. Finding news sounds easy, but it can be hard work when it has to be done every week or every month. The worst thing a communicator can do is start a publication and then fail to publish on a promised schedule. Most of us plan some fixed number of issues per year. Typically, printed periodical materials, in order of increasing cost and complexity, are newsletters, newspapers, and magazines (Lesly 1983).

Newsletters.
Newsletters are the workhorse of formal communications because they are so flexible and efficient. Flexibility in newsletters means that they can be written and printed quickly by someone with limited editorial background. They are efficient because they can cover topics briefly. In addition, newsletters have the great advantage of being relatively inexpensive because artwork is generally limited to a few photographs, simple charts, graphs or cartoons. In terms of content, a newsletter can have a slightly longer shelf life by covering a subject, such as how departments are organized and who does what in each unit, as opposed to simply reporting on news.

Visually, a newsletter is generally, but not always, an 8½ x 11 inch format and may have only four pages or additional pages inserted depending on how much news there is. You can see how flexible this is. If there is not much news, the newsletter can be brief—even just one sheet of paper on both sides. If there is much to communicate, the newsletter expands to a reasonable number of pages. With the availability of computer-assisted design, there is no reason why a newsletter should not be crisp and professional. Just about anyone can design an elegant and well-written newsletter with some lessons and practice. *The challenge is to produce one every time.*

A tip in this area is to think through carefully the staffing requirements for your newsletter. If you intend to follow the axiom, "Keep It Simple Stupid (KISS)," then it should be relatively easy to handle.

Newspapers.
There is a fine line between some newsletters and a newspaper format, but what is it? Newspapers, particularly those published by large corporations, are designed to contain what most of us would consider very perishable news. The newspaper resembles its major daily newspaper cousin in that it is not meant to last either. The front page will generally cover a major breaking story or stories of great impor-

tance. Typically, the news stories will be supported by very good quality black and white photographs, or in some case, color photos. The inside will be devoted to other information dealing with what management and the newspaper editor believe employees need to know. As you can see already, a newspaper is far more complex and demanding than a newsletter. Think of a newspaper as the 747 of printed communications as compared with the newsletter, which is a small single engine plane. (See Exhibit 9.1 for a biweekly newspaper format as published by Tribune Communications Service Center.)

Newspapers are sometimes actually printed on newstock, particularly when huge numbers of copies are required. If handled properly, the format and design give you much more space and flexibility in dealing with a wider array of information than the standard newsletter or magazine.

Delivery of employee newspapers is frequently difficult simply because of the time-sensitive nature of the paper. Many organizations use their internal mail distribution syste. Others have newsstands located throughout the buildings for employees to pick up. Ultimately, many companies decide to mail directly to U. S. employees' homes to be sure the employee gets his or her own copy, can pass it on to family members, and read the information when there is more time.

Newspapers may be designed to accommodate self-mailing with labels. This becomes important when you produce large quantities of the publication. Printing 50,000 to 100,000 copies or more is not that unusual in some large concerns. The cost of mailing is significant and the weight of paper becomes another issue. Timeliness can also become a challenge. Considerable time and thought need to be devoted to the mailing lists used for direct mail distribution. These usually are provided by the human resources department based on the payroll system.

Magazines.

Magazines are the luxury cars of the printed materials world. They cost considerably more to produce and substantial amounts of time to write, edit, gain approvals, and print. Pickup any magazine on the newsstand and you can see why a magazine designed for an employee had better be good. The competition for specialized magazine readership is intense. *Bacon's Magazine Directory* lists thousands of magazines in the U. S. Chances are good that your magazine will be up against *National Geographic*, *Condé Nast Traveler*, or other well-known magazines.

A magazine usually follows a format similar to *Time*, *Newsweek* or *Sports Illustrated*. What differentiates a magazine from a newsletter or newspaper? Among other characteristics:

- Considerable lag time between writing the articles and arriving in the reader's hands.

EXHIBIT 9.1 — NEWSPAPER FORMAT

TRIBUNE
NEWS

New Ideas in Information and Entertainment

News and Highlights

Third Quarter Net Income Per Share Rises 34%

Tribune's third quarter primary net income per share was 5.86, up 34 percent from 5.64 a year ago, excluding a non-recurring loss recorded in 1995. Net income rose 26 percent on the same basis to $60 million, compared with $48 million in 1995.

Madigan Highlights Strategies at Wall Street Conference

Tribune was the only information and entertainment company presenting at the Goldman Sachs Communacopia conference in New York, Oct. 10-11. The annual conference for broker analysts and portfolio managers focuses on the convergence of communications technologies.

President and CEO John Madigan told the audience that at Tribune, "we are digitizing the way we think." The company is asking how customers want information and entertainment and then developing new products and services to be delivered by CD-ROM, online and via the Internet's World Wide Web.

He said Tribune's combination of traditional and emerging businesses is paying off, with upward momentum in operating profit, cash flows that are solid and growing, and earnings that have risen significantly since 1992.

Pull-Out Section: Tribune Values

This special edition of Tribune News includes a report on Tribune's values—integrity, citizenship, customer satisfaction, innovation, employee involvement, teamwork, financial strength and diversity. The report describes the many ways in which employees are translating these values into action.

Not long ago, newspaper journalists rarely provided commentary on television or radio news programs. Today, many of these scribes are finding opportunities to combine the best of both worlds: the immediacy of broadcast and the depth of print media. (continued on page 2)

TRIBUNE
435 North Michigan Avenue
Chicago, Illinois 60611-4041
312-222-9100

‖‖‖‖‖‖‖‖‖‖‖‖‖‖ 5-DIGIT 60602
JOSEPH W. KOPEC
THE DILENSCHNEIDER GROUP
70 W MADISON ST STE 800
CHICAGO IL 60602-4210

BULK RATE
U.S. POSTAGE
PAID
Permit No. 6
FRANKLIN PARK, IL

- In-depth treatment of the subject material in an article that no newsletter or newspaper could ever approach.
- The widespread use of color and the highest quality graphics. It is true that newsletters can also produce excellent color photography and graphics. However, magazines generally provide a broader canvas for photo essays using papers and printing methods far superior to newsletters.
- The possibility of paying well-known freelancers or paid writers who write for publications on a specialized subject.

Brochures.

Brochures are designed to deal with a single subject in some depth. Brochures run the gamut from elaborate technical brochures explaining how to run your videotape recorder to how to purchase Treasuries from the Federal Reserve. In the corporate setting, employee communications brochures often deal with benefits information such as insurance, profit-sharing, and related areas. Another favorite use of the brochure is the executive speech reprint. If you can't be there to hear a speech, the next best thing is to get a copy of the speech in an attractive format to read what was said.

Audiovisual, Video, and Audio Communications

Slides, Overheads, and Presentation Software.

Audio-visual communications used to mean 35mm slides and overhead projectors. Today it involves a wide array of technology that is easy to use and produces excellent quality graphics and impressions. In addition, the widespread use of television production facilities and distribution of video programming through dedicated corporate video-conferencing networks or through video playback units (VCRs) scattered throughout organizations has expanded to practically every organization to help with marketing, training, and, of course, employe communications.

Audiovisual techniques are no different from printed materials in requiring careful planning and design of your messages. If anything, you must be more succinct, because the viewers' expectation is for brevity and speed accompanied by the viewers' ability to scan slide copy much faster than text in newsletters or magazines. Slides are by their very nature highlights. Remember the objective of the communication and keep it simple.

Slides.

Slides have the flexibility of being changeable when an issue changes. There are many formats and designs available in slides that present a highly professional and finished look. But there are disadvantages too. Even though a number of national companies specialize in producing cost-effective slides almost overnight and are available all across the country, delay in production can be a problem. Complex or unusual slides can be expensive.

Software Programs for Presentations.

The advent of new software programs, such as PowerPoint™, has had some impact on slides. It is much easier to click an icon and type your material on a computer screen. You can edit the copy in an airplane or hotel room. It's relatively easy to carry around a computer and several disks rather than slide trays. As an example, CEO presentations can be changed up to the last minute just before delivery. Slides often function as teleprompters for the speakers when they are giving a presentation or speech. An LCD stage has been developed for use with overhead projectors in which you can go directly from your laptop to the LCD and project the material on a screen or wall. Obviously, for large audiences, you need special equipment with enlarged versions. In addition, the crispness of the image may suffer. However the graphics and colors capabilities are really superb. If you take time to learn the program yourself, or identify several people (not one) who work with you to become adept with the software, you will never turn back. The ease and the quality of the product is outstanding. Finally, you can plug your laptop presentation into the videoconferencing network at many organizations and participants at various locations see the same presentation as you give it in the room.

Costs involved with software production is limited to the purchase price of the software and the equipment. Many organizations have PowerPoint™ installed with their software systems and make it available on the organization network to all employees or at least managers as part of the tool kit.

Overhead Slides.

Overhead slides, or acetate sheets with cardboard frames, projected on the screen from the easy-to-use overhead projector are the most flexible, cheapest and easiest to produce. Some presenters use typewritten copy and simply use a copier machine to put this same format on the acetates. You can write on them and use a grease pencil. Some people combine the overhead projector, with the computer formats to make a direct presentation from the laptop or print a hardcopy version that is on acetate for a colorful and professional presentation. Either way the costs are generally modest.

Slides, overheads and software presentation techniques are usually designed to be used with a limited size audiences. Even though slides and software may be used in an audience of hundreds of people, chances are the size of the audiences are still very small compared with television or videotape production.

Television, Videotape, and Audio Production.
Television is a medium that you are comfortable with since most people grew up in front of the television. Television is the medium of choice for many people who are used to getting much of their information from CNN, the local news or buying products from QVC.

However, there is a two-part flip side to this equation. A generation raised on MTV and CNN is used to sophisticated television production. The quality of any organizational offering, and this is not always the case, had better be just as good. The second point is that a viewer gets a superficial overview of a subject and will generally need some written piece, such as a newsletter or brochure, to imprint upon them the key information covered in the visual.

In any case, the tune out and turnoff factor increases geometrically with the length of the program. Unfortunately, too many television productions are *talking heads* or executives who sit in front of the camera and give a speech. These may be accompanied by slides or charts, but they look a lot like the early days of television. Fortunately, a number of companies with video production facilities and outside producers have pushed the edge on television so that offerings are quite good. Television in direct corporate network feed and via computer terminals is clearly the wave of the future. The day may well come when corporate reporters and magazines will vie with network and cable programming to demonstrate in a dramatic and compelling fashion why someone would want to work for a certain company, own their stock, and buy their products. It's being done already. The only question is how long it will take to move the next generation of executives along the curve to a level of ease in dealing with television.

Video productions, though they may have high impact when well done, can be expensive. The cost will depend if you have an in-house production facility or if you must use outside production facilities. A rule of thumb was that it would cost $1,000 per minute of video production. But that is perhaps too simplistic and does not take into account post-production enhancements such as special effects. Nor does it consider the expenses associated with productions crew on location as compared to videotaping everything on a set in a studio. If you have the equipment or a good production house, costs can be minimized by careful planning, production, and distribution. Just keep in mind that you must be brief and you must tell the story visually as well as orally.

Writing for television requires special skills. Just as writing poetry is extremely different from writing an essay, writing for television and video requires a unique writing style. You may be better off working with a professional writer who can advise you how to do it right.

VCR or videocassette recordings, like those you rent from your local video store, are now widely used for a variety of employee communications uses such as training and instruction on everything from computer software to more effective presentation skills. Many are edited versions of corporate television productions or management presentations edited to shorten the length.

Sound, as in that used in radio, is a strong and effective medium. Applications in organizations tend to be limited, but should not be overlooked. The most widespread use of audio follows two formats. One is the ubiquitous 800 number, which must have some audio programming to fill all the time that's available. The other is the audiotape cassette which is useful if you have a captive audience such as employees who work in sales and commute by car or train.

Personal Computers and Computer Networks.

There is no question that the popularity of personal computers in homes and offices has revolutionized the way that we communicate with employees today. Many of us start our day scanning messages from other employees down the hall or around the globe.

Even so, communicating with employees via home systems seems to a way off in the future. You should not be deceived by all the babble about the information highway. While computers are essential to business, a 1995 Times Mirror study (*Times Mirror* 1995) of national home computing habits reported that just 14 percent of the country's households have successfully used modems to get online even once. And most of those go online only to use e-mail and not to take advantage of the many other wonders of the Internet. Based on polling 4,000 people, the study found that the vast bulk of Americans continue to resist taking their homes online in a variety of ways including:

- 55 percent have never had a computer.
- 9 percent had a computer but "gave it up."
- 21 percent had had a computer more than two years.
- 11 percent have had a computer two years or more.
- 4 percent have a computer but never use it.

People still are very much in the exploratory stage with the on-line part of the explosive growth in personal computing and we really don't have enough information to show whether it's going to be a revolution, said Andrew Kohut, director of the Times Mirror Center for the People and the Press.

A 1994 study (*Times Mirror* 1994) found 31 percent of Americans had computers in their homes and the new polling found computers in 36 percent of households. It appears that communicating with employees and their families through home computers is still in the future.

Perhaps the most significant findings was that the "jury is still out" on whether the huge move online anticipated by multimedia proponents will ever come through.

Bearing this data in mind, perhaps the most important consideration for the business communicator to remember is that anything that you have done in print or electronic media can now be done faster, and sometimes better, using these systems and the software that make them possible. However, the audience is limited. Using personal computers and computers connected to networks or local area networks (LANs) requires that you take a new perspective on the medium you are using. You can offer a newsletter format, but you obviously have to take into consideration that the format will be presented in a computer screen and ultimately the reader may or may not print it. So the speed you gain may lose you the attention and concentration that a reader may have taken.

A number of companies have introduced exceptional software products that convert existing newsletters (with very little time and expense) to computer formats. One that is available from Ion Systems is called Designer X (See Exhibits 9.2 – 9.4). They also make a product for e-mail formats.

CD-ROM.

Some systems already are available to send CD-ROM multimedia. CD-ROM personal computers are available on such a limited basis that it will take a few years to use the CD format more extensively. Several companies such as Dow Jones and Microsoft are experimenting with various services that combine copy on the screen, in wire service formats or newsletter layout, along with smaller windows that offer video programming including CNN and other corporate information. Frankly, employee communications is playing catch-up with the financial markets in this area. In technology industries, many companies are already there and the rest of industry and education are not far behind.

e-mail.

Of these systems, e-mail is the most widely available communication used in organizations. All you have to do is type a message, the recipient's name(s), and press a button to speed it on its way. That's the easy part. The difficult part of e-mail is it's so easy to send that many people don't think through what they are sending or how it will be received. Though e-mail is designed to be rapid-fire and easy to use, this does not mean that spelling and punctuation errors are any more acceptable. Despite spell checking tools, which simply do not catch all the spelling errors, you are best served by writing a message and checking it in hardcopy format, particularly if it is vitally important to convince the receiver of the quality of your ideas.

Frankly, too much e-mail is unnecessary and frivolous. One executive said he receives on average more than 300 e-mails per day. He would have to sit at his PC all day to read and respond to messages. Although some CEOs have made it part of their employee communications to welcome such communications and respond, somehow, to all given day crucial documents containing confidential information that is critical to your job will be sprinkled with policies on reserving confer-

EXHIBIT 9.2

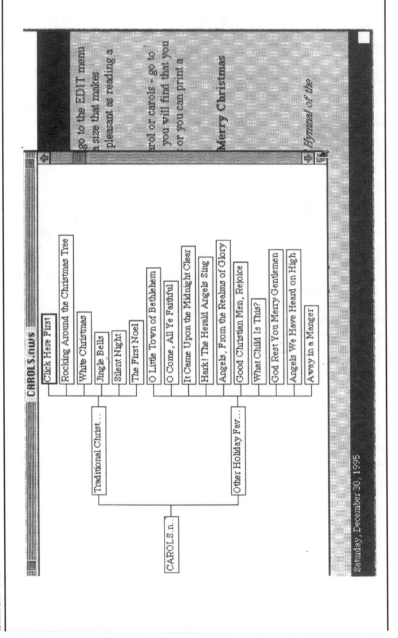

EXHIBIT 9.3

File Edit

© E'News by ION Systems, Inc., 1-314-937-9094

Traditional Christmas Carols ▼

Click Here First

ION Systems would like you to preview how information will appear on the Computer of Christmas Yet To Come. While you are reading in this revolutionary form, imagine trying to read these Christmas Carols in scrolling text or HTML. We are sending you these Christmas Carols for you and your colleagues to use for your Christmas parties. We hope that you all enjoy them as much as we do.

For a list of the carols, click on the Contents Tree icon, which is next to the right-page-turning icon at the top of the screen. Click on any title to immediately move to the song.

Saturday, December 30, 1995

If you find the type too small - go to the EDIT menu and go to Resize Text and find a size that makes reading on the screen almost as pleasant as reading a book.

 oldsan.gif

"I will honor Christmas in my heart,
and try to keep it all the year."
--*Charles Dickens, "A Christmas Carol"*

EXHIBIT 9.4

File   Edit

@ •News by ION Systems, Inc., 1-314-937-0094

Traditional Christmas Carols ▼

Click Her

ION Systems
information
Christmas Y
this revolutio
Christmas C
sending you
colleagues to
hope that you

...and the type too small - go to the EDIT menu
Resize Text and find a size that makes
...n the screen almost as pleasant as reading a

...ould like to print the carol or carols - go to
...menu and go to Print, you will find that you
... print all of the carols or you can print a

Please enter your name for our
readership survey.

| John Smith |

No Response   OK

For a list of the carols, click on the Contents Tree
icon, which is next to the right-page-turning icon at
the top of the screen.   Click on any title to
immediately move to the song

Saturday, December 30, 1995

**ION wishes you all a very Merry Christmas
and a Happy New Year!**

*Words obtained from the 1940 Hymnal of the
Episcopal Church of America*

ence rooms and advice on soft subjects. Clearly, some editorial control is needed. In some companies senior management has asked the communications department handling employee communications to work with the technology and information systems people to harness the effectiveness of e-mail systems so they are more effective. Experiments and trials to improve formats, establish guidelines, and improve the effectiveness of such e-mail systems are widespread and continue to improve e-mail effectiveness.

Finally, use discretion on any e-mail system. Do not write or distribute any message that you would not like to read on a billboard outside your office window. Messages take on a life of their own and can be copied and sent around the e-mail grapevine just as easily as the traditional grapevine. So use good judgement.

Voice Mail.

The blessing of many of our existences is voice-mail. It allows you to organize your day and avoid interruptions when you are working on a task that requires concentration or while you are out at a meeting. In some organizations 70-80 percent of the original calls coming into the organization are received on voice mail after the first few rings. You are advised to keep your introduction really short! Most of us loathe long-winded voice mail messages. If you leave a message, keep it short. Give your name and phone number at the very beginning of the messsage, and again at the end.

On the negative side, voice mail offers the potential to be used as part of a grapevine. Be careful what messages you leave on the system. One experience involved a manager involved in sensitive labor relations with a labor union who categorized the work of a fellow employee in uncomplimentary terms and then found out the next morning, prior to a labor negotiating session, that copies of the message were circulating all over the company.

INFORMAL COMMUNICATION

Informal communication is the *unofficial* communication that takes place in any organization that does not originate with or communicated by the management. These include the grapevine, meetings and any other techniques used by the parties in the organization to move information back and forth, up and down the system. Although e-mail and voicemail are installed by managements to improve the productivity of employees, employees learn quickly that such systems can enhance their ability to speed information to other coworkers. Not all such communication is sanctioned by management. How could it be? So these new systems are sometimes part of the informal communication channels.

Informal refers particularly to the grapevine, or the nerve system of every organization that moves unofficial news or rumors faster than the speed of light. The grapevine takes on a high voltage characteristic as the primary source of information in any organization where the employee communications process is seriously flawed. The grapevine may be swift, but it often lacks accuracy.

Think about a controversial decision that your organization just announced. How did you learn about it? Official memorandum? Newsletter? Grapevine? In many cases, it's the grapevine that delivers the news in a organization.

One CEO stopped to talk with his communications chief on the way back from a particularly tough talk to a rather large group of employees where he threatened to fire any employee whom he found participating in the grapevine or spreading rumors and asked or an evaluation of the meeting. The communicator told him everything went well until he threatened to fire everyone. Then the meeting took on a deadly tone. Like King Canute who sat on the beach and unsuccessfully ordered the ocean to stop washing onto the shore, you are as little likely to stop the grapevine flow of information. Instead, you must make its function less essential by providing detailed, credible communications on important issues very quickly. If an issue gets away from you, it's important to swiftly fill the void with facts to challenge the interpretation of events.

In the past, managers might ignore the grapevine. These days with downsizing and restructuring announcements, you must understand and graft your own line into the grapevine.

The grapevine is a form of communication that provides some of the most valuable information. But you often have to learn on your own how it works.

Rules governing the grapevine are quite different from the formal communication techniques outlined earlier in this chapter. The price of entry is a knack for building relationships and the indispensible currency of the grapevine: Information to trade.

How can a manager become part of a grapevine when a manager may not have extra time to make contacts? Managers must make themselves available, personally visiting other departments and divisions.

As experienced managers have learned, the best time to get information is before or after work. You've probably observed how some people in parts of every company tend to gather a certain times and places. It's the grapevine in action.

When you become part of the grapevine, you have a slightly different role than the average person because you may be asked to respond to information. This is because most information travels the grapevine as headlines: "Jones Gets Canned" or "Jennings Promoted to Heir Apparent." Remember that the headlines will go through an evolving series of changes.

Like the kaleidescope with broken pieces of glass, each person on the grapevine gets only a piece of the whole picture refracted somewhat

differently by how you hold the scope or where you are in the organization. If you are smart, you accept that there's a grapevine in your company, work it to your advantage and provide formal communications to
give more complete and accurate accounts. Still other companies
install 800-numbers just for the purpose of feeding instant information
to the largest number of employees in the shortest amount of time.

What can the employee communicator do to affect the grapevine,
change a story, squelch a rumor?

- Make time for the grapevine. If you are going through change,
  people who work the grapevine have an advantage over those
  who do not.
- Identify and tie into major players. You would be surprised
  how quickly the grapevine can be leveraged by clever managers who include key players in formal communication such
  as editorial advisory boards, messengers, and in all sorts of
  feedback meetings.
- Image is everything when it comes to the grapevine. The tan-
  gled branches of signals, verbal and visual, that people give
  off about themselves are quickly interpreted by the grapevine.
  In the downsized corporation, the grapevine does not miss
  much. Your demeanor, a change in attendance at meetings, a
  lack of enthusiasm, apparent depression or that haggard look,
  are all ripe for the grapevine.

The Rules of Grapevines.

There are three basic rules of grapevines:

1. Grapevines will exist and spread information as long as human
   beings exist.
2. Grapevines operate as pressure valves for people who often
   lack clout or are not involved in decision making as a means to
   ease the stress caused by a lack of information. During periods
   of upheaval, when factual information is scarce, the grapevine
   sprouts longer and stronger tendrils.
3. Use the grapevine, if you can, to plant factual information. Feed
   it and develop a hybrid strain that supplements the official, traditional means of memos, e-mails, newsletters. The grapevine
   is, after all, less reliable but somewhat more efficient.

CONCLUSION

Twin themes of technological enhancements and the speed of change that often accompany them appear throughout this chapter, yet some eternal verities about men and women continue to this day and age. The workmen who carved the Parthenon asked Pericles the same questions that Microsoft employees ask Bill Gates:

1. How does this affect me and my job?
2. How will this affect my paycheck? (Up? Down? Neutral?)
3. And often never stated: Does this make me happy or not?

NOTES AND SUGGESTED READING

Berger, B.K. *Revolution at Whirlpool*. Unpublished presentation, 1995.

Conrad, C. *Strategic Organizational Communication*. New York: Holt, Rinehart & Winston, 1985.

Cutlip, S.M., A.H. Center, and G.M. Broom. *Effective Public Relations*, 6th ed. New Jersey: Prentice Hall, 1985.

D'Aprix, R. Communication as process: The manager's view. In *Handbook of Organizational Communication*, edited by G.M. Goldhaber and G.A. Barnett, 265-272. New Jersey: 1988.

Grunig, J.E., and T. Hunt. *Managing Public Relations*. New York: Holt, Rinehart & Winston, 1984.

Hall, R.H. *The Formal Organization*. New York: Basic, 1972.

International Association of Business Communicators (IABC). *Communication World*. San Francisco: 1994, 1995.

Katz, D., and R.L. Kahn. *The Social Psychology of Organizations*, 2nd ed. New York: Wiley, 1978.

Lesly, P., ed. *Lesly's Public Relations Handbook*, 3rd ed. New Jersey: Prentice Hall, 1983.

Times Mirror Center for the People and the Press. Study on Use of Personal Computers. Los Angeles: 1994, 1995.

REVOLUTION AT WHIRLPOOL

A case history on communication auditing and a
"new approach" to employee communication

By Bruce K. Berger

*(Bruce Berger is corporate vice president, corporate affairs, for Whirlpool
Corporation. He is responsible for employee communications and public and government relations on a global basis. Before joining Whirlpool in 1989 he held
various positions during his 14 years at the Upjohn Company.)*

While many other things had changed dramatically at Whirlpool during the past
five years (e.g., global strategy, new definition of quality, compensation practices, customer focus, etc.), the practice and the understanding of employee communication at
Whirlpool had changed little from the 1970s. Could it really be possible that the rapidly changing world of global business and the dazzling array of new technologies
would leave untouched the complex area of employee communication?

Confronted by these contradictions, Whirlpool launched a major research effort
in early 1992 to uncover barriers to improved communication and to reveal an answer
to the question, "what if?" What if Whirlpool wanted to achieve an outstanding
employee communication program? What changes would have to be made? What
would it take? Was it even possible?

The comprehensive research effort sought to investigate employee communication
from every angle. Elements included a qualitative audit of 26 Whirlpool publications, an
in-depth survey of 32 Whirlpool communicators and communication suppliers worldwide, focus group research at seven plant locations, interviews with more than 100
global managers, research and development of a quality-based communications process
model, review and analysis of employee surveys conducted in 1990-91, and bench-
marking and analysis of more than 15 leading companies with a particular focus on the
communication and continuous improvement processes of Baldrige winners.

The Whirlpool Picture

Analysis of focus group research and of the 1990-91 Whirlpool employee opinion surveys (involving 1,800 people) made it clear that employee trust and management credibility were important issues at Whirlpool, as with most of corporate America,
and that formal employee communication was not meeting company objectives or
employee needs.

For example, the 1990 survey revealed that more than 85 per cent of employees
felt that Whirlpool upper management does not understand employee concerns, and
less than 25 per cent agreed with the statement, when management tells us something,
we believe it.

Employee communication did not fare well in the survey, either. Less than 35 percent of employees felt that "business unit meetings are valuable." Fully 74 percent of
respondents disagreed with the statement, "*Vision* magazine is valuable and believable."

Continued on next page

The 1992 Communicator — Supplier Survey

In March/April 1992, we conducted a worldwide survey of 32 Whirlpool communicators and communication suppliers. The survey was qualitative in nature, asking open-ended questions about topics ranging from quality issues to work processes and practices to communicator supplier relations.

The responses of both groups demonstrated that neither viewed communication as a process tied to business objectives, but rather as a series of projects, programs, events, and fire 'drills.' Accordingly, their process knowledge and skills were relatively undeveloped, although they were highly skilled in dealing with extraordinary time pressures and chronic resource deficits.

While communicators and suppliers were strongly committed to quality, both groups saw themselves as locked in a reactive mode that left little opportunity for planning or the pursuit of strategic long-term objectives. Communicators were almost unanimous in declaring that communication requirements tended to be afterthoughts and add-ons to management initiatives. The ripple effect of this syndrome came through strongly in supplier responses, which indicated that an excessive number of projects started late and without clear direction, resulting in extended review and approval processes, as well as much preventable rework and overtime.

Communicators confirmed and sympathized with supplier views, but were close to unanimous in their belief that the situation could not be rectified, because management basically believed that communication was, indeed, a fire drill or something to be added on after technical or strategic decisions already had been made.

Picture of "Best Practices" and "Best Companies"

Research into communications of leading companies such as Baldrige winners Federal Express, Milliken, Xerox, AT&T, and IBM Rochester, was conducted in the summer of 1992 and revealed eight generally consistent practices including established accountabilities, a process focus that linked communications to business objectives, a culture of face-to-face communications, use of technologies to drive the speed and currency of communication and concrete actions plans to resolve employee opinion survey issues.

One of the many obvious benefits of these "best practices" is the high degree of motivation among company employees. At Xerox, for example, 90 percent of employees say they are "proud to work for the company," despite a decade of intense business pressure in the 1980s that led to significant layoffs. At Federal Express, 94 percent of employees are "proud to work for the company," a recent figure that has remained at this level for several years.

Seven Critical Employee Communication Issues

Analysis of these and other research results made it quite clear in 1992 that the power of communication was largely untapped at Whirlpool. Why? By applying the ideas and practices discovered through the research to the current employee communication situation at Whirlpool, the communicators uncovered seven critical communication issues. Unless these issues were resolved, the power of communication would remain untapped. Whirlpool executives suspect that these barriers apply at other companies, too. The seven issues are:

1. Outdated "Mental Models" of Communication

According to MIT Professor Peter M. Senge, mental modes are: *"deeply held internal images of how the world works ... images that limit us to familiar ways of thinking and acting ... what is most important to grasp is that mental models are active — they shape how we act."*

Thus, if a mental model for something is wrong or outdated, the decisions made and the actions taken will also be wrong or outdated, even with the best of intentions.

Analysis of "best practices," in particular, demonstrated that Whirlpool's "mental model" for employee communication was also certainly outdated — more consistent with a 1950s business model (stability, controlled growth) than a 1990s business model (rapid change, global competition).

Creating a new mental model of communication requires the company-wide repeal of certain key assumptions, including the view of communication as:

- Consisting of discrete activities, events, and programs rather than a long-term process driven by business objectives;

- A low-technology function requiring little more than production technicians to achieve its ends;

- Separate from "real business communications," not as a key part of every one's job; and

- The top-down transmission of "messages" as opposed to the multi-directional flow of information, knowledge, and dialogue about matters of importance to the company.

2. The Continuing Trust Issue

The potential costs of employee distrust are enormous: loss of high-potential employees, defensive reactions to change initiatives, compromised integrity of formal business communication — all of which act as an enormous drag on the corporation's productivity, global strategy and urgent change requirements. Elimination or reduction of employee distrust, however, can be achieved only through a long-term process approach to communication, as well as a highly visible leadership that demonstrates a deep organizational commitment to honesty, whether the news is good or bad.

3. "Companyspeak"

"Companyspeak" is the language of corporations, often passive, and faceless, and designed to promote a kind of endlessly, mindless positivism rather than promote learning or understanding. "Companyspeak" is usually seen by employees to be "disguised" language and it breeds distrust, e.g., the infamous "rightsizing" or "volume-related production adjustment." The solution is to discipline communication. Formal visible employee communications can play a key role in this by:

Continued on next page

- Setting the tone for honest use of language in print;

- Creating more opportunities for direct spoken dialogue between management and employees; and

- Culling out all instances of "Companyspeak."

4. Fuzzy Accountabilities

When accountabilities for communications are fuzzy, then no one is really accountable. For years at Whirlpool the communicator was accountable — sort of. Individual managers and supervisors must be accountable and proficient, while professional communicators need to become expert facilitators, project and process managers, trainers, strategists and counsellors, among others. Establishing such accountabilities is very much a part of creating a new mental model.

5. Communicator Skills and Training Needs

To achieve necessary change in the employee communication function, current deficiencies in skills and knowledge have to remedied. Reasons for these deficiencies at Whirlpool were numerous: there had been little ongoing training of communicators; the project and program orientation of most communicators jobs had prevented their exposure to process thinking; the hiring of communicators had been handled, for the most part, by noncommunicators; communicators had had quite limited involvement in strategic planning; and performance expectations of communicators were related more to budget and deadline than to achieving meaningful long-term goals.

6. Communication Should Reflect WES, our Quality Program

To be consistent with the Whirlpool Excellence System (WES), our quality program, communication needed to be defined as a measurable process tied to business objectives, and it had to seek out the largest value-added role it could play in achieving the company's strategic plans. Extensive consideration of these two criteria led to the following specifications of the role of employee communication at Whirlpool with respect to WES:

- Communication should take a lead in the implementation of WES;

- It should ensure the multi-directional flow of quality related information, requirements, and breakthroughs to parts of the organization;

- It should be a role of the quality culture needed to achieve 10X improvements — by encouraging learning, debate, and employee participation;

- It should help management identify sources of employee fear and distrust that obstruct WES progress.

7. Antiquated Communication Toolbox

Whirlpool's communication toolbox was very antiquated; print communications dominated. Why? Because publication was validation that communication had happened, regardless of whether or not it was received or believed. In the future, analysis of communication problems will be performed with the help of a seven-step process model which requires a systematic and logical approach to communication problems and opportunities. Applying the process model begins with asking functional or business unit management two questions: What are your project or busines objectives? And, what stands in the way of achieving them?

From Research to Practice

In late 1992, senior management approved the new strategic approach and the funding to support it. Here's what's happened since then. Fifteen days of intensive training were conducted with our 35 global employee communicators. Training included: Communication as process, feedback and measurement, strategic planning, process management accountabilities, and the communication toolbox. It has proven to be demanding, highly interactive and effective. An additional benefit has been the increased cultural awareness developed within the group, which represents 12 countries. (Whirlpool now faces a huge managerial training requirement in communication.)

A cross-functional project team completed work on a communications accountabilities model, which is now being established and tested in five locations in Europe and North America prior to company-wide roll-out, probably in 1996. The model defines accountabilities at four levels in the organization and prescribes basic performance requirements. Such accountabilities are slowly being built into managerial objectives.

A seven-step communication process model was developed, tested and then embedded in the global organization (see Exhibit 9.5). Whirlpool used the model to develop specific communication projects, as well as comprehensive regional strategic plans for public relations, government affairs and internal communication. In the minds of management, the model has, for the first time, linked communication to real business objectives, and today we are hard pressed to meet growing demands for facilitating use of the model. Two existing corporate publications were replaced with two new, carefully targeted ones and an electronic newsline. Each of these has achieved credibility ratings of more than 90 percent, a substantial increase from the 50-70 percent ratings of previous communications tools.

Finally, two cross-cultural project teams researched and benchmarked 13 communication technologies in use at 21 leading companies. The teams concluded that six of these technologies, if bundled and applied globally at Whirlpool, could shorten the cycle time for understanding and implementing change and strategic initiatives, as well as enhance training programs and the work processes of global project teams. Senior management has approved funding over the next few years to establish truly global capabilities in business TV, video bulletin board, video and audio conferencing and voice mail. Thus far we have piloted video bulletin board and business TV, and our video conferencing capability is expanding steadily.

Two years after the revolution began to Whirlpool, the company has made steady progress with communication process and quality, with communication training, and with updating the toolbox. Progress has been slower with mental models, trust, and companyspeak. And substantial investments remain to be made in global technologies.

Continued on next page

Conclusion

Whirlpool's top communicator believes the communication problems identified during the research are not unique to Whirlpool. Throughout Corporate North America, employee distrust and other symptoms of weak or failing internal communications are epidemic during this era of rapid and continuous change in the global marketplace. But the fact that the problem is widespread does not excuse anyone from acknowledging it and from making a major effort to alleviate its impact.

That the problem has been created in large part by lack of attention to the communication issues described earlier has been confirmed by senior management's willingness to support new communication initiatives.

Of course, problems that arise from or reach into employee states of mind are not problems that can be fixed with a few well chosen tactics applied over a few months. Some of the issues described here, e.g. mental models and language, are deep-seated cultural issues that will only change with time and continuous attention. Though much work needs to be done and a good deal more must be learned, companies like Whirlpool have made a start and are seeing some early and encouraging results in this important revolution. (See Exhibits 9.6 and 9.7 for examples of Whirlpool communications.)

EXHIBIT 9.5

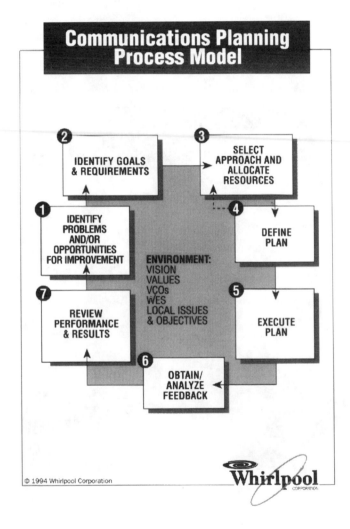

EXHIBIT 9.6

EXHIBIT 9.7

WHIRLPOOL
MANAGEMENT JOURNAL

INTERNAL COMMUNICATIONS

Jonathan Dedmon is a principal with The Dilenschneider Group in Chicago. He has been involved with crises for 22 years both as a journalist and a public relations practitioner.

Mr. Dedmon is a 12-year public relations veteran who has worked on crises in a range of industries, including financial services, manufacturing, transportation, food, health care, and the arts. He also has written crisis plans and other crisis documents and done extensive crisis and media training.

Prior to his public relations career, Mr. Dedmon was a journalist for 10 years for The Denver Post *and* The Rocky Mountain News *in Denver and with the Newhouse Newspapers and States News Service in Washington, D.C., where he covered a variety of issues including government, legal affairs, energy, and politics.*

He attended Stanford University and received a master's degree in journalism from Columbia University.

CHAPTER 10

THINKING THE UNTHINKABLE — CRISIS COMMUNICATIONS

Three Mile Island. Exxon Valdez. Tylenol poisonings. Union Carbide/Bhopal, India. Syringes in Pepsi cans. Flawed Intel Pentium chips. The United Way scandal.

The names and headlines probably have a more-than-familiar ring to them, which is why crisis communications is perhaps the most challenging of all public relations activities. For crisis communications has the ability to not only make your company or organization a household name, but also to affect your image with vast audiences for years and even decades. It literally can make your organization's name a part of the collective public consciousness.

Consider the following. Three Mile Island occurred in 1979. Despite the fact that no one died or was injured and no health problems have been documented other than stress, the incident forever changed the way the industry is regulated and operates and, well into a second decade, significantly affects the debate over nuclear energy policy and safety.

WHAT IS CRISIS COMMUNICATONS?

While the best-known crises and crisis communications have involved major companies, organizations, governments, and individuals, you don't have to be chief executive officer (CEO) of Exxon or head of the nuclear power industry to involved in crisis communications.

In fact, the name itself is something of a misnomer. "Crisis communications," as it has become to be known in the industry, is shorthand for instances in which companies, organizations, or individuals are in the spotlight and require communications beyond the norm.

You can be said to be dealing in crisis communications generally when the following are true:

- The situation or incident is one of major importance or consequence;
- It has major visibility/interest;
- There is elevated risk/stakes for the company or organization.

Having said that, you should be aware that many a crisis has occurred with none of the above being true initially. But then, over time, all three have become true.

Which leads to several other characteristics of most crises:

- They evolve rapidly and in unpredictable ways;
- Events seem to outstrip the ability of organizations to deal with them;
- They require extraordinary levels of communications;

- Each crisis in its own unique and often unpredictable way has the ability to capture some part of the public imagination in a manner that creates strong and lasting impressions and perceptions.

It is this last characteristic that is perhaps the most important. For while the business world is filled with calamities and emergencies every day — fires, explosions, layoffs, strikes, bankruptcies — the importance of crisis communications is in preventing those calamities from forming long-lasting negative impressions about a company, impressions that can take years to overcome.

WHAT CAN BE DONE?

Each crisis is different. There are no hard and fast rules for dealing with them. However, there are two important points to remember:

- There are a number of planning steps that can be taken so that you are at least prepared in the event a crisis occurs.
- But crisis communications planning primarily addresses mechanical issues so that a corporation, organization, or individual communicates *efficiently* as possible when crises occur. Crisis planning, however, cannot replace integrity, judgment, and acting in the public interest when crises occur. The latter is essential if a company or organization is to communicate *effectively* and maintain its reputation.

Was the public relations staff of Exxon incompetent following the Valdez spill? Absolutely not. But what was missing in Exxon's communications was a sense of the *perceived* scope of the disaster and a strategy that demonstrated it not only understood the perceived size of the problem but was acting aggressively as possible to solve it and prevent it from happening again in the future.

PLANNING: THE FIRST STEP — WHAT COULD HAPPEN?

In planning for potential crises, the first step is to assess what types of crises could affect your organization. Ask yourself: Who are our most critical audiences, how do we interact with them, and what could go wrong?

While not a complete list, the following may help you get started in identifying the types of crises that can occur:

- Environmental
  - Spills
  - Toxic waste from manufacturing
  - Emissions from plants
  - Contamination of ground/water table
  - Environmental degradation issues such as logging, offshore drilling.

- Public health/safety
  - Food safety
  - Product safety
  - Plant worker safety/plant accidental deaths.

- Financial/business
  - Layoffs
  - Takeovers/mergers
  - Strikes
  - Succession
  - Shareholder demands.

- Natural disasters
  - Fire
  - Floods
  - Hurricanes/tornadoes
  - Earthquakes
  - Snowstorms.

- Man-made disasters
  - Plane crashes
  - Derailments
  - Chemical explosions/spills
  - Mining accidents.

- Criminal malfeasance by executives/employees
  - Theft/embezzlement
  - Insider trading
  - Price fixing
  - Perjury.

- Civil suits
  - Class action suits
  - Major damage awards
  - Discrimination/harassment
  - Product liability
  - EPA penalties/Superfund citations.

- Governmental
  - Legislation
  - Investigations
  - Regulatory actions
  - Foreign government action.

GETTING READY

Having identified what types of crises can/would be most likely to occur within your organization, the next step is to develop a plan to address the possible scenarios.

Exhibit 10.1 is a table of contents of one organization's crisis plan. It outlines a number of areas that need to be considered in planning for a crisis. We will then talk about each of the chapters in this outline in greater detail.

EXHIBIT 10.1 — CRISIS PLAN TABLE OF CONTENTS

1. Overall Communications Policy
2. What Constitutes a Crisis?
3. The Crisis Communications Team
4. Crisis Team Responsibilities
5. Crisis Procedures
6. Spokesperson
7. Media Guidelines
8. Monitoring
9. Key Audience Lists

THE CRISIS PLAN

Overall Communications Policy

When a crisis occurs is not the time to decide on your company's or organization's overall approach to and policy concerning communications. And in fact, whether you have it written down or not, your company or organization currently has an approach to communications.

Setting your overall policy down in writing and getting signoff in advance is a good way to assure that precious time will not be lost arguing over what the company's policy should be when a crisis occurs.

What should your communications policy contain? Without going into great detail, it should set overall standards and goals with regard to communications.

Exhibit 10.2 offers a communications policy for a health care organization.

EXHIBIT 10.2 —
HEALTH CARE ORGANIZATION COMMUNICATION POLICY

Because we are one of the region's leading health care systems dedicated to providing quality health care to citizens and businesses of our region, our overall policy is to be open, candid and truthful with the public and media at all times.

There may be times when it is not possible to practice full and complete disclosure. These situations could include:

- Overriding concerns and rights of patient privacy
- Competitive business reasons
- Refusal to speculate
- Overriding legal reasons
- The desire to inform employees first.

However, in all such situations where full disclosure cannot be practiced, the reasons for lack of disclosure should be stated. In addition, to avoid misinformation, error, and miscommunications, only designated spokespersons should communicate with the media.

What Constitutes a Crisis?

We have identified a wide variety of potential crises. What kinds are most likely to occur within your organization? They should be identified in your crisis plan so the procedures that are in place are effective with those types of crises.

For instance, a major financial crisis is going to involve very different communications activities and personnel at your company or organization than a plant explosion. Different types of personnel and messages are going to be required for an environmental problem versus labor unrest. And different types of issues and personnel are going to be involved in activities relating to the U.S. Securities and Exchange Commission versus the U.S. Occupational Safety and Health Administration or the U.S. Food and Drug Administration.

The Crisis Communications Team

Your crisis communications plan should identify who will be serving on the crisis communications team. Generally, your crisis communications team should include a senior officer of the company, legal counsel, and the senior communications officer. Appropriate personnel can be added depending on the nature of the crisis, whether operational, financial, environmental, labor-related, and so on.

Crisis Team Responsibilities

What are the responsibilities of the crisis team? These need to be spelled out in advance. Potential responsibilities include:

- Gathering information
- Assessing information
- Establishing communications strategies
- Developing overall messages
- Customer communications
- Employee communications
- Government relations
- Media relations, including:
  - Spokespersons
  - Creation of materials
  - Talking with the media
  - Monitoring
  - Correcting misinformation
  - Logistical media issues such as organizing press conferences
- Identifying parties outside the organization who can support you/your position, referred to as third-party support.

Crisis Procedures

The crisis plan should spell out procedures to be implemented in case of a crisis. These procedures should include:

- Who chairs the meeting?
- Monitoring procedures —
  - How are we going to gather intelligence?
- Switchboard procedures
  - How are customer calls being handled?
  - How are employee calls being handled?
- Media procedures
  - Are all media calls routed to the communications department?
- Spokesperson identification —
  - Who's going to be talking for us?
- Development of core messages —
  - What is going to be our soundbite that people see and hear on TV?
- Review of staffing needs —
  - Are there enough bodies to handle the heightened communications needs?
- Assessment of what's working and what's not.

Spokesperson

Perhaps no issue is more critical to the handling of a crisis than the person who serves as a spokesperson.

In the words of Robert G. Anderson, a veteran producer at "60 Minutes," "The spokesperson is really where the rubber hits the road —

the embodiment and delivery of the company's strategy and action. I find in my work that to the extent the spokesperson is informed and helpful, I'm informed and helpful."

Generally there are several levels of spokespersons who are used in a crisis situation in differing ways. They are:

- The CEO, who needs to make the overall policy statements and umbrella position with regard to the issue. CEO involvement is needed to demonstrate the company's overall commitment to fixing the problem.
- A senior level executive who can function as the CEO surrogate. That person needs to be a senior player perceived as having complete knowledge of the issue and substantial managerial power within the organization, versus a gatekeeper or lower level player. At the White House or a major *Fortune* 500 company, this could very well be the press secretary or senior communications officer. At other companies, the top communications person may not be viewed as senior enough.
- Experts who can discuss technical information in detail concerning the issue.
- Lower level managers, generally in the communications department, who can handle media calls and provide basic information concerning the facts at hand.

The key task, obviously, is to choose the right individual (other than the CEO and to the extent you have that luxury!) and then arming them with the right information and messages to be effective.

What makes a good spokesperson? There are no hard and fast rules, but we would suggest the following are important criteria:

- **Demonstrates knowledge.** People want to know the right actions are being taken by smart people. Any indication that the company doesn't really understand a problem and its ramifications related to the crisis can be disastrous.
- **Shows empathy.** If people can relate to you and feel you have concern for the problem, you are less likely to be a target.
- **Is down-to-earth.** Related to the previous point. Avoids jargon, stuffiness, defensiveness.
- **Has common sense.** Given the need to act and react quickly and to think on your feet, the importance of good judgment and common sense cannot be overstated.
- **Looks good/is comfortable on camera.** You don't have to be Dan Rather, Tom Brokaw, or Peter Jennings. You do have to be comfortable enough with the medium that you can deliver messages effectively. Media training can make you more effective on TV. That is why media training is critical for executives who may find themselves in the limelight.
- **Is comfortable with the media in general.** We find many executives who don't like the media. The media need to be

thought of as a conduit to your important audiences. Sparring with them is not only distracting, but counterproductive. The media play a critical role in shaping the debate and informing your critical audiences. As difficult as it may be or seem, you need to have as positive relations with them as possible during a crisis. This doesn't mean you need to bare your soul or that they won't say anything negative about you or your situation. But at a minimum there needs to be dialogue and ideally mutual respect and credibility.

When it comes to the spokesperson, *perception is reality. It is hard to think of any public relations factor that is more critical to the success of handling a crisis than the effectiveness of the spokesperson.*

Having said that, it also is important to note that aside from their particular skill sets, they need to be able to articulate real facts and actions being taken by the company that demonstrate the situation is being resolved.

Media Guidelines

Media guidelines for a crisis plan are generally of two kinds. One spells out in greater detail your own media policies. For instance:

- What is your policy regarding allowing media/camera crews inside plants/on plant property?
- What sort of clearances are required for press releases/statements?
- A number of organizations have general policies regarding how quickly media calls will be returned. Does this make sense for you?
- Do you have/need a policy for noting and tracking all media calls and the nature of the inquiries?

The second type of media guidelines that you should consider for your crisis plan are some general rules for dealing with the media. Your spokesperson may not be a communicator. For example, if the crisis involves technical issues involving the environment or public health, you probably will need a technically trained person within your organization to address technical aspects of the issue. This spokesperson may have little media experience, and the guidelines can serve as a good quick reference guide to help him or her with the media.

Some general guidelines in your crisis plan can be a useful, handy briefing paper to make sure spokespersons are up to speed. It also can serve as a helpful reference guide for experienced communicators as well.

While general guidelines for dealing with the media can be found in the chapter on media relations, here are some examples from one crisis plan:

- Talk from the viewpoint of your audience. Focus on their self-interests and use information that will arouse self-interest.

- Avoid euphemisms and jargon. Say people died versus "were fatalities." Say "strike" versus "work stoppage." Say "explosion" versus "incident." State that people are being "laid off" versus merely that the corporation is being "downsized." While it may sound harsh, you are more credible when you tell it straight versus what can appear to be dissembling through the use of jargon.
- Keep messages clear and consistent.
- Don't speculate.
- Break through the noise. Make your message concise and memorable.
- Talk in headlines.
- Protect the record:
  - If you make a mistake, correct it.
  - If misquoted, correct the record verbally and in writing.
- If reporters ask questions, they generally are entitled to answers. Answer and then bridge to your message.
- Tell the truth, even if it hurts. Credibility cannot be recaptured once lost. Once Exxon lost its credibility during the Valdez incident, it faced the public relations equivalent of climbing Mount Everest to regain it.
- Don't ever say "no comment." It sounds as if you're stonewalling.
- Don't make "off-the-record" comments. Don't say anything that you wouldn't feel comfortable with on the front page of *The New York Times.*
- Don't repeat negative or inflammatory words used by a reporter. It might end up as part of your quotation.

An important final point: While these points are all made with reference to the media, they also hold true for your communications with other audiences such as customers or employees. For instance, you also shouldn't tell customers or employees anything you don't want to see on the front page of *The New York Times.* It has wound up there more than once in the past!

Monitoring

Your crisis plan should include a monitoring system for media and other important audiences during a crisis.

In addition, your crisis plan should have log forms for both media calls and other important calls during a crisis. You want to be able to track the volume of calls you are receiving, the type of person calling and the nature of their inquiries. This also is a good system to have in place even when there isn't a crisis.

Exhibits 10.3 and 10.4 are two sample log forms.

EXHIBIT 10.3 — MEDIA CONTACT REPORT

Media Outlet _____

Reporter's Name _____

Telephone No. _____

Date of Contact _____ Deadline _____

Interview Content/Issues _____

_____

_____

_____

_____

_____

_____

_____

_____

_____

_____

_____

_____

_____

_____

_____

_____

_____

Signed: _____

Exhibit 10.4 — Caller Log Form

Caller _____

_____

Telephone No. _____ Date of Contact _____

Category (Customer, employee, other _____)

_____

_____

Comments: _____

_____

_____

_____

_____

_____

Action Taken (if any): _____

_____

_____

_____

_____

_____

_____

_____

_____

Signed: _____

Key Audience Lists

In a crisis, you will probably need to communicate rapidly with a number of critical audiences, including customers, employees, media, government officials, and third parties.

Do you have the addresses, telephone numbers, and fax numbers of your critical audiences centralized for quick communications in the event of a crisis? You should. It should be part of your plan.

TRAINING

Having developed a plan, to make it most effective you should undertake some training/simulation of a crisis situation.

Generally the training should include working with the crisis plan through several would-be scenarios, development of corporate statements, and operational steps, and live, recorded media interviews, playback, and critique.

There are a number of firms that offer specialized crisis/media training. You should develop a training program that tests your plan with likely crisis scenarios and also improves the overall media skills of your spokespersons.

The Public Relations Society of America, for instance, an industry trade group based in New York, has a number of crisis communications and media training firms listed in its directory of public relations practitioners. Persons wishing the names of such firms can contact the *Public Relations Journal Register* at:

The Public Relations Society of America
33 Irving Place
New York, NY 10003
(212) 995-2230

WHEN A CRISIS OCCURS

No matter how much preparation is done, one is still never completely prepared for when a crisis occurs and the need for crisis communications arises.

The reasons are inherent in the very nature of crises and communications surrounding them. Among the factors that make crisis communications particularly difficult:

- As the crisis unfolds, generally companies initially have only very limited information to which they must react and communicate intelligently. For instance, an airline may only know that one of its airplanes has crashed, a chemical manufacturer that there has been a large explosion at one of its plants and little else, or a food processor that one of its products *may* be implicated in a salmonella outbreak.
- Companies and organizations are confronted with trying to provide a much larger quantity, a higher quality of informa-

tion and information far more quickly to a much larger audience than they heretofore have had to do.

- Crises take frequent and unforeseen twists and turns that demand adjusting the course, reconsidering strategies, and recalibrating positions and statements.
- Third parties such as special interest groups and/or governmental entities become involved and sources of information. People are going to view anything you say with skepticism and as self-serving. The media in particular are going to turn to outside observers with some knowledge of the situation as more credible for "objective" information. The danger, of course, is that the third parties have their own agendas and points of view, which may be quite different than your own!
- The video age and instantaneous communication mean that no matter where an event occurs, it can quickly become world news, putting a global spotlight on a particular situation even in the most obscure location.
- Company employees unaccustomed to the spotlight are suddenly thrust onto center stage and worldwide perceptions of their performance are used to create instantaneous judgments of right and wrong.
- Just as you are dealing with limited information, the media is dealing with limited information as well, adding to confusion, lack of clarity, and sometimes outright disinformation.

Unfortunately, a good crisis plan is only a good first step in successfully handling a crisis. What are you to do?

WHAT GOOD COMPANIES HAVE DONE

While each crisis is different, there are a number of companies that have dealt successfully with crisis situations. The most often cited are Johnson & Johnson during the Tylenol poisonings and, more recently, the scare over syringes in Diet Pepsi cans. It is possible to point to a number of principles based on successful handling of crises in the past. What are they?

- **Rome wasn't built in a day, and image isn't either.** Have a track record of communications and credibility in place so that when a crisis occurs, you will be seen as a source of credible information. What are you doing right now to demonstrate to your publics and the media that your company is a smart and responsible corporate citizen? Companies already respected are more credible when crises occur.
- **If you are wrong, admit it.** People don't expect you to be perfect. But when problems occur they do expect you to get to the bottom of them and squarely address them. Richard Nixon was forced from office not because of the Watergate break-in, but because of the cover-up that ensued.

- **Get all the bad information out as quickly as possible.**
  Nothing feeds the flames of a crisis situation as much as bad
  news seeping out in small doses. It creates a "tip of the ice-
  berg" impression that things are a lot worse than they really
  are. It also gives the impression that management doesn't
  have a handle on events. Getting the bad information out fast
  also opens the possibility that a bad story will be a one-day or
  one-week story versus one that goes on for months. Also, you
  are much better off providing the bad information on your
  terms than someone else providing it on theirs.
- **Monitor/listen.** Smart companies know what's being said
  about them by their critical audiences, whether the media,
  customers, employees, or government regulators. They are
  able to create communications strategies that correctly and
  directly address audience perceptions and concerns. In addition to monitoring media coverage, consider opinion research
  of employees, customers, etc., to understand what they
  know/understand/feel about the incident.
- **Communicate.** When crisis situations occur, the natural
  instinct of many corporations is to minimize communication
  until they have the problem resolved. However, others will fill
  the vacuum that you create! People realize you may not have
  complete information. Example:

  > United Airlines Flight 232, a DC-10 en route from
  > Denver to Chicago, crashed while attempting an
  > emergency landing at Sioux City, Iowa, at approx-
  > imately 4 p.m. Central Time.

  > The aircraft carried 287 passengers and a crew of
  > 11. There are reports of survivors. Additional infor-
  > mation will be provided as it becomes available.
  > — Business Wire Inc., July 19, 1989

  When the Tylenol poisonings and reports of syringes in
  Pepsi cans occurred, both companies were aggressive communicators with press conferences and interviews with major
  national media. But this communications principle also
  applies not just to the media, but to other audiences as well,
  including customers and employees.
- **Use third parties.** As previously stated, your own statements
  will be viewed as self-serving and suspect during a crisis.
  Third parties can provide needed support. Probably the most
  effective recent use of third parties was by Wal-Mart when it
  came under attack for promoting foreign-made goods as
  American. Major suppliers were recruited to take out newspapers ads supporting Wal-Mart. The ensuing chorus of praise

by some of the best corporate names in America helped bury the criticism.

- **Back it up.** Assemble the strongest body of evidence possible to back up your claims. This can range from scientific studies to job injury data to statements by regulators. The media in particular are not going to be satisfied with you saying something is so. They want to see data and examples that back it up. Look at the following excerpts from a release from Pepsi on the syringes-in-cans controversy as how to provide strong, credible evidence that the consumer had little to fear:

> The spate of complaints about syringes or parts of needles found in Pepsi cans has defied physical evidence and intellectual logic, (Pepsi President Craig) Weatherup said this morning in appearances on ABC's "Good Morning, America," NBC's "Today," and "CBS Morning News." (They're out there communicating!)

> "Our bottlers manufacture more than 20 million cans a day. Each one has a code. Within a 48-hour period, to have needles allegedly show up in cans that were produced in some cases six months apart, in others six weeks apart and in even others six days apart defies intellectual logic and physical probability.

> "Of all consumer products packaging, cans are perhaps the most difficult to tamper with," Weatherup continued. During the high-speed canning process, it is extremely unlikely for any foreign substance to be introduced into a can. In the process, empty cans are inverted upside down, cleaned with air or water and then inverted immediately before they're filled and closed. On the filling line, the cans are open and vulnerable for only 0.9 seconds.

> While the FDA has announced there is not health risk to consumers, they've issued an advisory for consumers to visually inspect the cans before drinking. (Third party endorsement!)
> — PR Newswire, June 16, 1993

- **Aggressively challenge misinformation and rumor.** Part of your monitoring activities during a crisis should be to identify misinformation and aggressively move to correct it. GM's aggressiveness regarding allegations by NBC's "Dateline" concerning exploding gas tanks in its pickup trucks, which turned out to include rigged video footage, turned the tables and did much to dispel concerns.

- **It's a video age.** Use it to your advantage. Television and video, while poor at communicating large quantities of information and data, have strong and convincing emotive power. People believe what they can see. It was the video footage from Vietnam, not the casualty figures, that convinced America we weren't winning the war. No company recently used video in crisis communications as effectively as Pepsi in demonstrating with video from its production lines how it was impossible for syringes to have gotten into Pepsi cans at the company.

- **Related to this, smart companies know that it is increasingly a sound-bite world.** People are exposed to too much information in an overly complicated life. You have to make your message simple and compelling. While not related to a crisis, perhaps one of the strongest messages was Avis' "We try harder." It was simple, reflected reality — the rental car company's number two position — but turned it into a compelling positive.

THE MOST COMMON MISTAKES

Just as there are very good things that companies do in crises, there are also bad things. What follows are a number of common mistakes:

- **Defensiveness/Bunker mentality.** It may be natural when a crisis strikes, particularly where potential litigation is involved (which means virtually anything!), to say as little as possible other than to defend the company or organization as having integrity, being morally upright, etc. This bunker mentality has a number of subthemes:
  - *"The media is out to get me/it's all their fault."* While it may seem like they are out to get you (and occasionally they actually are!), as a rule they aren't. Their job is to report events of public importance and a variety of perspectives on the significance, causes and effects of those events. They know what news is better than you do. While they do make errors and can be overly aggressive, try to understand the situation from their point of view and what their job is versus your own. You will probably be more successful. Twenty-five million people watch "60 Minutes." More than two million people read *The Wall Street Journal* daily. Is it going to be productive to get into a communications firefight with these people?

- *"It's none of the public's or media's business."* See the first point. If you want to judge what's news, become an editor or news director.
- *"This is a great company. I can't believe people are irresponsibly saying these things about us."* Believe it. And do something about it.
- *"If they only had all the facts like I do!"* That's why you have a communications program. See previous point.

- **Corporate Fabianism.** Fabian was the Roman general who popularized dilatory tactics by avoiding battles with the great Carthaginian general Hannibal, eventually defeating him. It is easy to argue for such tactics in a crisis setting. When things go wrong, a natural tendency is to retreat and withhold comment until the facts are in and you have the problem solved. But remember, newspapers come out daily and TV, radio and wire services report constantly. They are going to quote others whether or not you talk. Failure to communicate also means that people are going to wonder: "What do they have to hide?" And these days, your competitors don't have to cross the Alps with elephants.

- **Complicating a complicated story or delivering a garbled message.** There can be simple compelling messages and statements for complicated events, even if you don't have all the answers. Other commentators on the issue are going to have a very simple message, such as to recall the product or shut the plant down.

- **Using the wrong spokesperson.** Is the person a good communicator and senior enough within the organization to have credibility and impact? Perhaps you don't have the perfect spokesperson. It is possible to use tandems of spokespeople. For instance, a senior management official can provide the umbrella communications while a technical expert can address the technical issues. However, make sure those who may be dealing with the media are trained in advance!

- **Misuse of the CEO.** The CEO can have great credibility and impact as head of the company. However, the CEO has to be used judiciously to show that the full resources of the company are behind solving the problem or that the problem is well on its way to solution. CEOs should not be put in situations where they are addressing issues and situations where they are unprepared or have no solutions.

- **Self-serving versus public-serving.** The public doesn't want to hear how great you are, but how you are acting responsibly toward them.

- **Misidentifying the real issue.** What is the real issue of concern? Sure, the financial community is concerned about how the crisis is going to affect your earnings. But minimizing the effect on earnings may be the last thing the media and public want to hear about how you are managing the issue, particularly where public health and safety are involved. While messages obviously need to be tweaked to be most relevant for different audiences — financial, consumer, employees — the underlying set of facts and messages must be consistent.
- **Belittling what is a big problem.** Spilling 260,000 barrels of oil, coming within a whisker of a nuclear meltdown, cyanide poisoning from ingestion of a product are all big problems. Acknowledge them if they are. The best-known recent example of this mistake was Intel's Pentium chip problems. The company said it wasn't a serious problem. Then IBM said it was a serious problem. Whoops, it was a serious problem. Acknowledging the magnitude and seriousness of the problem can help with your credibility and the credibility of your attempts to cope with managing the problem. The Intel example also points to the importance of monitoring customer reaction.
- **No strategy.** Do you really have a strategy to deal with the issue at hand or are you merely reacting? If you have a strategy, is it working? Does it need to be changed? Again looking at Intel, once the company realized it had misread the nature and perception of the Pentium chip problem, it moved rapidly and aggressively to change course and put the problem behind it.

> Dec. 12, 1994 — In response to an IBM press release, Intel reiterated that it has studied the Pentium processor flaw for months and has concluded that the frequency of encountering reduced precision in floating point divide operations is once in every 9 billion random divide operations.
>
> Intel said it regards IBM's decision to halt shipments of its Pentium processor-based systems as unwarranted.
>
> Dec. 21, 1994 — We at Intel wish to sincerely apologize for our handling of the recently publicized Pentium processor flaw.
>
> The Intel inside symbol means that your computer has a microprocessor second to none in quality and performance ... Intel will exchange the current version of the Pentium processor for an

updated version, in which this floating point
divide flaw is corrected, for any owner who
requests it, free of charge, anytime during the life
of their computer.

— Business Wire, Inc.

- **Using jargon/legalese/euphemisms.** People want straight
  talk in terms they can understand. For instance, "remediating
  a site" is the technically correct term for cleaning up a conta-
  minated piece of ground or water. But to the public it sounds
  vague compared to the words "clean up," which people understand. Similarly, legal language designed for court documents
  should be avoided except where specific legal issues are
  involved. Reporters believe (with more than some truth!) that
  corporate lawyers want to minimize the release of information
  to protect the court record and therefore use legalese to minimize the release of negative information versus the truth, the
  whole truth and nothing but the truth. A similar point can be
  made regarding euphemisms. If it's a spill, call it a "spill" versus "accidental discharge." You will be a lot more credible.
- **No demonstration of concern.** Sure, you are embarrassed by
  what has happened on your watch. But your embarrassment is
  not the issue. Protecting the public is.

CONCLUSION

Crisis communications are difficult and the risks high. The reputation of your company can be affected with important audiences for a
very long time. You can and should prepare for them.

However, there is no simple formula or approach to use when
they do occur. They require not only strong and aggressive communications, but also integrity and judgment behind the communications so
that the public understands that the right things are being done and the
problem solved versus spin-doctoring or obfuscation.

Mary Jane Genova is a communications consultant who has researched and written op-eds, articles, and books for corporate executives. She is currently working on three books. One deals with communications, another focuses on the careers of those in Generation X, and a third explains a new approach to weight control.

In addition to ghostwriting, Ms. Genova has been published under her own byline in The Wall Street Journal, The New York Times, Newsday, Public Relations Journal, *and the* Hartford Courant. *Her humor has appeared in greeting cards, articles, and humor publications.*

Chapter 11

WRITING BYLINED OP-EDS, ARTICLES, AND BOOKS

An opinion-editorial (op-ed) in *The Wall Street Journal*, an article in *Harvard Business Review*, or a book on *Business Week*'s best-seller list — all of these are excellent vehicles for communicating messages. In this chapter you will learn strategies to improve your chances of getting you, your company executives, or your client into print.

Although it's been said that we're becoming more of an oral society and that we think visually, there is still a tremendous amount of print material on the market. If you go to a large or super bookstore, you'll see crowds of affluent people shopping for and discussing books, magazines, and newspapers. Walk into an executive's office and you'll still see books proudly displayed. On the coffee table sit journals, magazines, and the daily newspapers. On the commuter train from the "Gold Coast" in Fairfield County, Connecticut, to Manhattan, almost everyone reads.

Print material can still have enormous influence. Here are examples of op-eds, articles, and books that changed how people think:
- Lee Iacocca's op-ed on the level playing field in international trade, which originally appeared in the *Washington Post*;
- Peter Drucker's op-ed on contracting out non-core functions, which first appeared in *The Wall Street Journal*;
- The article by R. Roosevelt Thomas, Jr., on shifting the national mindset from affirmative action to diversity, which first appeared in the *Harvard Business Review*;
- John J. Gobarro's and John P. Kotter's article on "managing" the boss, which first appeared in the *Harvard Business Review*;
- Tom Peters' book *Thriving on Chaos*;
- Stephen R. Covey's book *The 7 Habits of Highly Effective People*.

The authors who exerted this influence knew four things. They knew:
- What ideas were marketable or of interest to certain audiences at a certain point in time;
- How to select just the right evidence to support their assertions;
- How to explain a concept simply and with passion;
- How to convince the gatekeepers — editors, agents, publishers — that their idea would excite other people.

This knowledge helped get them into print. There's nothing mysterious or magical about becoming a published author. What it does require are a marketing mindset and good thinking and writing skills.

READING AND ANALYZING

The best way to learn about how to get published is to read and analyze what's in print. As you read, here are some questions you should ask:

- Why did this idea get into print? Is it provocative, timely, controversial? Or maybe the idea is mundane but the author is well known? Read other pieces by "names." Are they weaker than those by lesser-known people? Often not. Often the big names hire the best ghosts.
- Would this idea have been printed in a different medium? Or was it a perfect fit for *The New York Times* or *Newsweek*? Every publication has its "personality." *The Wall Street Journal* has a different tone than *The New York Times*.
- What evidence did the author use to make a case? What techniques — such as anecdotes and analogies — were used to present the case? Was it easy to read through the presentation of evidence?
- Can the author get more mileage out of this? For example, if the piece gets a lot of attention, the author might consider publishing a book on the topic. In some professions you can't be taken seriously until you produce a book.

EXHIBIT 11.1 — READING AND ANALYZING WHAT'S IN PRINT

- How did this idea get into print?
- Why is this piece a good fit for this medium?
- How does the author present evidence in an interesting way?
- Can a book come out of this?

... What's the publication's "formula"?

If you do this analysis on a regular basis you'll find that certain publications have "formulas" for the pieces they publish. One publication's formula might be: A big idea, no big name. Another publication's formula might be: A centrist position, balanced evidence, recognizable name. It's important that you get to know these formulas. That will increase the chance of getting published.

OPINION-EDITORIALS

Op-eds are relatively short pieces. Depending on the publication, they can range from 500 to 2,000 words. That word count is taken very seriously. If a 1,500-word op-ed is sent to a publication that only prints 800-word op-eds, it may be ignored. Call the publication and ask about the word count. Or monitor the publication and observe this for yourself.

Where to Publish

Op-eds are the quickest and easiest way to get into print. Most newspapers and many magazines take bylined op-eds. Check *Bacon's Publicity Checker*. There is a separate checker for newspapers and for magazines. Copies are available from Bacon's (332 South Michigan Avenue, Chicago, IL 60604; 800-621-0561).

Another source is the *Writer's Market* (Writer's Digest Books, 1507 Dana Avenue, Cincinnati, OH 45207). A new edition is printed each year and is available in large bookstores and libraries.

Don't neglect local media. Editors of daily, weekly, and monthly publications are usually eager to print well done op-eds. In many cases it's the local audience you need to reach and not a national one. Also, once you have the clip from a local publication, you can leverage it to get on local radio and television. From there you can leverage the publicity to go national, if that's useful.

In addition many professional journals and newsletters also print bylined op-eds. For example, the "Speechwriters' Newsletter" has occasional op-eds from speechwriters. In his newsletter "Positioning," executive search recruiter Bill Heyman has guest op-eds. Find out what are the publications with influence in your field.

On a more social level, there may be newsletters from your club or college that print op-eds. Since the audience is usually influential, this avenue shouldn't be overlooked.

What to Write About

There is no standard topic for an op-ed.

In *Newsweek*'s "My Turn" column, topics have covered the unwillingness of a son to forgive his alcoholic father even after the father sobered up; being reasonable about government regulations on pollution; request for an understanding of what it means to be a manic-depressive; and a rejection of the victim role taken on by many overweight people. Many average people's opinions are published in *Newsweek*.

In *The Wall Street Journal* there are occasional light pieces on hating greeting cards or resenting business talk at lunch in the company cafeteria. But mostly the pieces are on serious financial, economic, or social matters. The authors are both known and unknowns. But all have some kind of impressive credentials.

The "Business" section of the Sunday edition of *The New York Times* usually offers provocative op-eds. The authors have an original point of view. In local media, everything from opposition to a new zoning proposal to a plea from a downtown merchant for more parking could be covered.

Should You Do an Op-ed?

If you are thinking of writing an op-ed, here's a checklist:

- What is the purpose of getting published? Will this help the cause? Or would it be more effective to write a letter to a certain senator?
- Has the idea been overdone? Can you add a new perspective? New evidence? New solution?
- Do you have the authority to write on this subject? Often people have a great deal of knowledge about a subject but not the formal credentials. Therefore, their credibility would be questioned if they approached a publication. For example, a person might be a wise investor but not a good candidate to do an op-ed on investing for a financial publication.
- Do you have the time to work on this? It may require several drafts, more research, additional drafts. The editor may ask that it be cut down another 500 words. The challenge is to get your point across in a very limited space. For this, you must be willing to commit time.

Whose Byline?

If you decide to do an op-ed, then your next decision will be under whose byline will it run.

It could be published under your byline. That means you take full responsibility for its content. It also means your credentials are such that using your name is credible.

You also might write an op-ed on child abuse that will appear under the executive director's name of your agency. If it appeared under your name, it might have less credibility or you could find yourself in the unhappy position of "upstaging" a superior.

Consider using a third party. A consumer-products company was concerned about how a proposed increase on a federal excise tax would affect its products. It could have issued an op-ed on this issue. However, it felt it would have more impact if the byline was the president of a retail association, who was able to explain how the tax would hurt his business and his employment levels.

If the publication permits, you might want it to appear anonymously. For example, you might want an anonymous op-ed claiming that sustained emotional counseling should be available to those who are laid off.

Strategies

Consider what strategies to use in approaching the subject. Here are a number of ways to increase the chances of getting into print. You can use one or a combination of them.

- Be a contrarian. If everyone is cheering re-engineering, then write an op-ed on the pitfalls of re-engineering. If everyone is decrying the shutdown of the government due to the budget debate, point out how this period is a good one for taking stock of where we are. Editors are more apt to give space to someone with another point of view.
- Be timely. An op-ed on diversity in the American workplace is more likely to get published around Martin Luther King's birthday. An op-ed on dynasties in American politics is more likely to appear around a Kennedy-related anniversary. If a bill on the environment is in Congress, then that's the time to submit your op-ed on environmental issues.
- Present as much evidence as needed to make the point but don't overburden it with too much information. Use statistics, scientific evidence, the opinion of experts, lessons from history, anecdotes, analogies, personal experience, other people's experience, and data from current events.
- Be willing to be controversial. That doesn't mean to present yourself as a revolutionary. It just means that you are willing to say things others might not. For instance, you might claim too much attention is being showered on abused animals and not enough on abused human beings — ranging from children to the elderly. Whenever you intend to be a little different, though, make sure you have the approval of your superiors, joint venture partners, and any allies.

EXHIBIT 10.2 — STRATEGIES FOR OP-EDS

- Be a contrarian
- Be timely
- Present enough but not too much evidence
    - Statistics
    - Scientific evidence
    - Expert opinion
    - Lessons from history
    - Anecdotes
    - Analogies
    - Personal experience
    - Other's experience
    - Data from current events
- Be willing to be controversial

Placing the Op-ed

The most important question to ask is: Where would this op-ed do the most good? Suppose you want to comment on a state funding issue. It probably would it be more effective to have the op-ed on this in the newspaper that serves the state capital, rather than your local newspaper.

After you decide on the best placement, approach the appropriate editor. Call the publication and find out the name of the editor who handles op-eds. Then either call or write.

If you call, pitch your idea briefly on the phone. Emphasize its importance to the community or to business thinking. Stress any urgency associated with it. Then ask the editors if they are interested in seeing it. If they say yes, get it to the publication immediately. If, in 10 days you haven't heard anything, contact the editor and see if interest still exists.

Send in or deliver the piece. In a one-page cover letter indicate why the publication's readers would be interested in this piece and explain why you're qualified to write on the topic. If you don't hear in about two weeks, call the editor.

What if the piece is rejected? This happens. Editors' tastes are subjective. Perhaps the publication just ran a few pieces of that subject. The best course of action is to review the piece. Is it good? Or can it be strengthened? After revision, try another publication. Keep trying to place it until it finds a "home." Most well-done op-eds will … it is not unusual to be initially rejected at several publications.

ARTICLES

There are many publications interested in receiving bylined articles. Some of them might approach you or your company directly and ask you to submit an article on motivation or the evolving social contract in the workplace. Or you might contact the editor and suggest submitting an article on how a program of incentive based on economic indicators is working out at your company or on your ideas for eliminating the glass ceiling.

Articles Versus Op-eds

There are a number of differences between articles and op-eds. They include:

- Articles are usually longer than op-eds;
- Articles deal with an issue in more depth;
- Articles will use a greater range of ways to present evidence, including interviews;
- Articles can contain several messages whereas op-eds usually have space for only one message.

If you have an idea for an article, contact the editor of the section it will appear in. Briefly describe what the article will cover, why such an article is needed, and why you're the ideal person to write it. Offer to fax an outline. If the editor isn't interested, ask who might be. Try to sell your idea somewhere else.

After the idea is approved, ask the editor to give you a sample of an article that fir their needs. Indicate you want to follow it as a model. It is important here to get the right format. In short, be clear about expectations.

A publication might approach you about doing an article. Here, you must decide if you want to put in the time an article demands. Ask to see a few issues of the publication. Who is the audience? What is the circulation? Is this the forum you want to be associated with?

No matter how the article came to be, negotiate the terms and conditions you'll work under. Do you want to approve all changes? Do you want to approve how the editor describes you? Do you want reprint rights to the article so that you can distribute it?

Distribution

Often op-eds and articles have their greatest influence when they are distributed as reprints after publication. Many authors have "buck slips" made up to send with the reprint. On their mailing or fax list are current clients, prospective clients, government leaders, thought leaders, employees, vendors, and joint-venture partners.

It is usually easy and not very expensive to get reprint rights from the publication. You might want to arrange for this before publication so you can start your distribution quickly.

BOOKS

Senior management from a forest-products company felt the need to do a book on an aspect of the business that had been ignored. However, they never were able to get it off the ground because they were afraid the project would take too much time. That's unfortunate because they had a good idea.

If organized well, producing a book need not overtax an executive. A savvy researcher, a seasoned ghostwriter, an aggressive agent, and, later, an experienced publisher are the ones who carry most of the responsibility. It's rare that doing a book ever burns out the executive.

Why Do a Book

What are some valid reasons — aside from ego — for taking on the responsibility for writing a book?

- Do you have something to say which no one else has focused on?
- Do you have a unique perspective or experience to share with the world?
- Would it enhance the reputation of your organization if you could hand prospective clients a book?
- Do you need a shorthand way to explain your system? If you gave this book to others could they quickly understand what you're trying to do?
- Would your career opportunities improve through a book?
- Do you have a group of people in mind who could help you with the book? The right team can make or break a project.

Testing the Waters

Okay, you have what you think is a good reason for writing a book. Now the next step is to confidentially share this idea with others you trust. Ask for their candid input. Is a book worth doing on this topic?

Another way to test the waters is to do an op-ed or article on the topic. What's the reaction? Did it strike a chord out there? Another advantage of doing an op-ed or an article is that you can take send it along with your proposal.

A third way to find out if there's interest is to approach the media, print or electronic, to do a story on the topic. What kind of reaction are you getting? Incidentally, controversy can be very marketable. If you receive negative reaction, you might be onto something big.

An Agent

The agent is your guide and advocate in the world of books. The trick is to get an agent interested in the project. The best way to find an agent is to ask around. It doesn't matter if the agent isn't in mid-town Manhattan. Many agents are located elsewhere and serve their clients well.

If you get the name of an agent, call them. Briefly describe your project. Usually the agent will ask to see a formal proposal. Getting that proposal together can require a few months.

If you can't get the name of an agent, there are a number of books describing agents and their specialties. One of them is Jeff Herman's *1996-1997 Insider's Guide to Book Editors, Publishers and Literary Agents*. You can find other books in a large bookstore. The library reference desk has guides to literary agents. You may contact multiple agents. When you're sending your proposal, inform each that you're sending multiple inquiries.

When you contact agents they will most likely ask to see "some paper." They want to have in writing a description of the book, your credentials, and a marketing plan.

Once you get an agent interested, that agent will submit your proposal to a number of publishers. In the ideal situation, more than one publisher will be interested and there will be a "bidding war." From that process you should be able to get an advance.

For their services, agents charge a fee. That fee is usually a percentage of what the books earns.

The Book Proposal

Somewhere along the line the agent is going to tell you that you need a formal book proposal. Ask to see a book proposal that was accepted. This could be a model for success. Also, read books on the subject. They include Oscar Collier's *How To Write and Sell Your First Nonfiction Book* and Jeff Herman's and Deborah Adams' *Write the Perfect Book Proposal: 10 Proposals That Sold and Why*.

Different agents want different things. If you've already published a book, your agent may allow you to submit an abbreviated proposal: the idea of the book, who you are, table of contents with brief description of chapters, and a few sample chapters. However, if you're just starting out it will probably be best if you do a full, formal proposal.

Basically a formal nonfiction book proposal is a selling tool. It calls for:

Overview.

Be crystal clear what your subject is, why it's important, and how it differs from what else is on the market. For example, there may have been a lot written about stress. But you intend to discuss stress in an entirely new context. Keep rewriting this section until it captures exactly what you want to say. Your very first paragraph has to attract the reader's attention.

Market Analysis.

Review the major works on the market on the subject. Describe them and show how your book fills a gap. In this section, objectively review the competition in this niche and state why you can stand out.

Review *Books in Print*. Do an online search of books written on the subject. Also, go to a local bookstore and pick up every major book on the subject, read each objectively, and evaluate if each is strong or weak competition. Talk to people in the field and find out if there are any "sleepers" or out-of-print books on the subject.

Approach.

Indicate that your book will be a 75,000- to 85,000-word volume targeted to those whose stress problems haven't been helped by psychotherapy and exercise. Describe how you will present the material diagnosing the problem. Indicate how you'll present the solution. What evidence is there that your system works? Will you have interviews with experts? Will the book be controversial?

The Author.

State your credentials relating to the book. Why are you uniquely suited to be the author of this book? Also here, if using a ghostwriter and making that public, list the credentials of the writer. What are the writer's publication credits? Or you might want to keep the existence of the writer confidential. That's something to negotiate with the writer.

Chapter Outline.

Hammer out what will be in each chapter. This is a map for the agent and publisher to follow. Clearly state the thesis of each chapter, how you will support that thesis, and how it moves the book along. Write the chapter descriptions in an interesting, lively style.

Include mention of any supplementary material. Perhaps you're planning appendices indicating how the reader can set up a support group in the community or online.

Sample Chapters.

Attach two chapters. One is usually from the beginning of the book.

Endorsement.

Include a letter from an appropriate third party supporting your approach.

Marketing Plan.

The agent and publisher want to know if this book is going to make money and how involved you'll be in the marketing. Here you have to have a realistic plan. Don't just say you'll go on all the talk shows. Say, you know you can get on all the major talk shows because your media representative has already booked you on them for another issue. You'll be using the same person for promoting the book.

Will you engage in social activism? For example, will a portion of the proceeds from the book go to research about stress or to help a stressed-out group such as the unemployed?

Will you write op-eds on the topic and be available for print interviews?

Do you know of a publication that might print excerpts from the book?

Who will write blurbs saluting the book?

What contacts do you have with book reviewers?

In short, the publisher expects you to use all the connections you already have. With downsizing, publishing staffs are so lean that they can no longer assume the marketing duties they used to do on behalf of books.

EXHIBIT 10.3 — BOOK PROPOSAL

- Overview
- Market Analysis
  - The Competition
- Approach
- Author
- Outline of Chapters
- Sample Chapters
- Endorsement
- Marketing Plan
  - What You're Going to Do

Your Ghostwriter

Steve Miller, chief executive officer of Morrison-Knudsen, is a fast, facile writer. In an afternoon he can create an excellent piece of work. However, many other executives are too unaccustomed to writing to do it quickly or well. If you or your client is one of them, you might be in the market for a ghostwriter. In the chapter of Speechwriting (Chapter 12) in this book, there is a discussion of how to choose a ghost. Basically, it comes down to three things: Money, chemistry, and writing ability.

Money.

When it comes to books, there are two ways to compensate ghostwriters. One is a flat fee. The other might be both a small flat fee and a percentage of royalties. Have your lawyer put this is writing. It usually is good for the project if the writer shares in the profits. There's greater motivation that way. Your agent can help you work out a compensation package.

Chemistry.

Although it's not generally discussed, chemistry plays a big part in ghosting relations. If the executives are conservative bankers, they probably won't feel comfortable working a flamboyant ghost who once wrote for Lee Iacocca. On the other hand, high flyers in the marketing department of a consumer-products company might be impatient with a buttoned-down writer who works very methodically.

To find the right ghost, interview several. Ask around for names of ghostwriters. Contact executive search firms that specialize in communications. Call the communications departments of companies you work with; the staff may suggest some names. Your agent can help. Also the publisher knows of people with experience writing books. Some executives put an ad in the newspaper or on the Internet to see if anyone is interested in working with them.

Writing Ability.

How do you want the book to sound? Do you want the approach and tone of Dr. Daniel Goleman's *Emotional Intelligence* or the tone of Tip O'Neill's *All Politics Is Local*? Hunt around your book shelves or the book stores and find a book that does what you want to do. Then show this to ghostwriters. Are they comfortable with this approach? Ask to see things they've written similar to that approach. Ask them to write a few pages in that style. Usually they wouldn't expect payment for doing such a "writing test."

Getting Published

Getting published can have enormous influence in how you and your message are perceived. In some circles, print is still the gold standard. From print, you can then move on to audio tapes and video tapes. For most executives, it all begins with print.

SUGGESTED READING

Appelbaum, Judith. *How To Get Happily Published*. New York: Harper & Row, 1988.

Bowker, R.R. *Literary Market Place and International Literary Market Place*. New Providence, New Jersey: Reed Reference Publishing Company, 1996.

Carnegie, Dale. *How To Win Friends and Influence People*. New York: Simon & Schuster, 1936.

Curtis, Richard. *Beyond the Bestseller: A Literary Agent Takes You Inside the Book Business*. New York: NAL, 1989.

Directory of Editorial Resources. Alexandria, VA: 66 Canal Central Plaza, 1996.

Holm, Kirsten. *Guide to Literary Agents*. Cincinnati, Ohio: Writer's Digest Books, 1996.

Kremer, John. *101 Ways to Market Your Books — For Publishers and Authors*. Fairfield, IA: Ad-Lib Publications, 1986.

Parinello, Al. *On the Air: How to Get on Radio and TV Talk Shows and What to Do When You Get There*. Hawthorne, NJ: Career Press, 1991.

Mary Jane Genova is a communications consultant for Fortune 500 executives. *Her specialty is speechwriting. The subject matter of speeches she has written have appeared in* Vital Speeches of the Day, Chief Executive Speeches, The New York Times, Washington Post, Newsweek, Newsday, American Banker, Credit World, Engineering Horizons, *and* Harvard Business Review. *During the 1980s, she wrote for Lee Iacocca, including his opinion-editorial on the level playing field.*

Ms. Genova was a judge for the National Association of Corporate Speaker Activities and is a contributor to "Speechwriters' Newsletter," Executive Speaker, Public Relations Journal, *and* The New York Times.

She earned a master's in English from the University of Michigan and attended Harvard Law School.

Chapter 12

SPEECHWRITING

Being able to write and deliver speeches has become one of the most highly prized skills in organizations. That's because our culture is relying more on the spoken word. What you say on your feet to the board of directors or to the chamber of commerce counts for far more than what you put into a 50-page report. As communications consultant Steve Maloney says in *Talk Your Way to the Top*, "Oral communication is the foundation of business leadership."[1]

But producing speeches, both the writing of them and the delivery, is hard work. If you now write speeches, either for yourself or for clients, then you know that you have to be sensitive to the values, agendas, and interests of many people. Or, to paraphrase Richard Kosmicki and Fred Bona in the general media chapter (Chapter 4) in this book, you serve a number of masters. (Much of the advice in this chapter is directed to those who must prepare and deliver a speech for themselves; however, the information is pertinent for any public relations professional who must guide a colleague or company executive in this endeavor.)

Your Many Masters

One of the most important people you serve is yourself or your client. You or your client must be comfortable with the speech — as comfortable as when wearing a custom-made suit. Another important group you serve are those in the audience. They must sense that "they got something" out of sitting there and listening for 20 or so minutes to a speech.

But in addition to these two groups, there is also a broad variety of others whom you must satisfy. That's what makes the task of writing a speech so demanding. Those other "masters" might include:

The media, print and electronic.

The speech you write should be able to attract the attention of the media. Also you must write the speech in such a way that material from it can't be misquoted by the media. You must scan the speech to see if there are any sound bites that could be lifted out of context and misrepresent your client's meaning.

Your client's organization.

Whether it is GE or the Red Cross, Harvard College, or Greenwich Country Day School, you are responsible for seeing to it that what you write is in keeping with your or your client organization's corporate culture and policy positions. You might say that part of your responsibility is to protect your client from saying things that could put the organization in a bad light.

Your client's "watchers."

Within the organization and in the field, there are those who keep tabs on your client's accomplishments. A successful speech could enhance your client's image. It was Lee Iacocca's iconoclastic speeches that helped him become a folk hero throughout America.

The financial community.

Excerpts from a speech could be brought to the attention of the financial community. On the basis of that, the stock could go up or down. In fact, the occasion of the speech might be used as an opportunity to make a financial announcement — for example, that the company is adding millions of dollars to the research and development program.

The halls of Congress.

Legislators have been known to read portions of speeches on the floors of the House and the Senate. Any part of that could become front-page news.

Stakeholders.

Shareholders, partners in a joint venture, employees, suppliers, and customers all could be interested in the contents of the speech and what it might mean for them. They are likely to "read between the lines." Therefore, in writing the speech you have to anticipate how others with vested interests can interpret what you say.

Others.

For instance, the client's mother may be attending the speech, so you might want some special inserts. The client's chief rival in the business may be there. How does the client want to handle this? A representative of a certain religion may be in attendance, and his beliefs are antithetical to your client's. Does your client want to openly address this difference?

EXHIBIT 12.1 — YOUR MANY MASTERS

- Yourself or your client

- Members of the audience

- The media

- Client's organization

- Client's "watchers"

- Financial community

- Congress

- Stakeholders

- Special guests

SPEECHWRITING, AN ANCIENT PROFESSION

Your challenge is to draft a speech with all these people in mind — and still produce a coherent, stimulating and memorable piece of work. This challenge goes back many centuries.

According to Dr. Jerry Tarver in *Professional Speech Writing*, speechwriting was a recognized profession in ancient Greece by the fifth century B.C. One of the best known speechwriters was Demosthenes, who was also a famous orator. Just as today, the stakes associated with producing a good speech were high. For instance, law in ancient Greece didn't allow representation by a lawyer. Therefore, if you wanted to argue your case eloquently in court you probably would seek help from a speechwriter.[2]

Over the years a body of knowledge has been building about speechwriting. In this chapter you will find out some of the very best thinking on how to write a speech that brings the results you or your clients want.

THE INVITATION

The first major issue in speechwriting is: Should you or your client accept an invitation to give a speech?

Agreeing to deliver a speech involves a significant commitment in time. In addition to the time spent getting to and from the speech site and actually giving the speech, there is the time spent preparing and rehearsing the speech. Even if someone uses a seasoned speechwriter, working with that person still takes precious time.

Another consideration: Do you want to be associated with that particular organization? Perhaps it supports a controversial point of view that you'd rather not be involved with. The organization could stand for beliefs your employer is opposed to. Maybe there's been a financial scandal at the organization.

A third consideration is the kind of results you can anticipate from such a speaking engagement. How much will you be able to influence public opinion? Is this a prestigious forum or would you be appearing at an organization few have heard of. Or, maybe the organization wants you to speak at a Saturday breakfast in August; realistically, you can expect only a small audience. Will media be invited? A primary reason for giving a speech is to get media coverage.

Some large corporations have people who evaluate the invitations which come to members of the organization. But you can do this evaluation yourself. Here are the questions you need to ask:

- What is the mission of the organization? Have any of its beliefs been held as controversial? Controversy in itself is not bad. There are just some controversies you don't want to be associated with. For example, the organization may take a pro-life stance, and your employer has kept a low profile on the issue.
- What kind of people will be in the audience? How many are usually there?
- Ask who has spoken there during the last six months. If possible, ask to see copies of their speeches. Is this a group of speakers you want to be associated with? Ask what kind of reception their speeches received. Is the audience a tough group to please?
- Will the organization handle media relations or allow you to conduct your own? How many media representatives were at the last speech? What kind of TV, radio, and print coverage resulted from the last speech?

Based on the answers you receive, you might decide not to accept the invitation. If you refuse, the conventional way to handle that is to say your calendar is very crowded at that time of year. Some executives leave the situation open and say that they might be available some other time in the future.

However, you might also decide to accept the invitation. Some speakers like starting in the "minor leagues" and testing out the kind of speech they're giving, how they deliver it, and how they handle questions-and-answers and media coverage.

Members of an organization's speakers bureau, for example, might try out their pattern speech at lesser-known organizations. It took a number of such "auditions" for a pattern speech on excise taxes at a consumer-products company to get to its final form. When the speakers initially delivered the remarks they found that the speech contained too much detailed information; the audience lost interest. Based on that audience reaction, the speech was simplified. The new version was then delivered at prestigious forums.

PREPARATION

In *The Quick and Easy Way to Effective Speaking*, Dale Carnegie observes, "There is no such animal, in or out of captivity, as a born public speaker."[3] But the odds of a successful delivery can be greatly increased with careful preparation. The audience can sense when the speaker is well prepared.

For this careful preparation, Roger Ailes, in *You Are the Message*, says there are no cop-outs. Ailes believes there are no valid reasons for not preparing. He advises that if you start to make excuses and procrastinate when you should be preparing, ask yourself: What am I afraid of? Am I fearful of being judged?[4]

Audience Analysis

The first phase of preparation involves an analysis of the audience. Some of this information can be obtained from the organization. For instance, you can ask for the demographics of the audience, their interests, their heartaches, what's happening in their professions, what's most on their minds.

In addition you can do your own research on the audience. If they are middle managers you can do an online search about what is on the minds of middle managers. You can browse through books on the subject. You can try to find out who are the villains and the heroes in the life of middle managers.

Also, you can request the names of a few members of the organization. Ask those members for their candid opinions on what speeches went well and which didn't. Ask them what they would really like to hear from you. You might even send them a preliminary copy of the speech to react to. Their feedback could be very helpful to you.

If you find out that the audience might be hostile to you or to the ideas you represent, one strategy for neutralizing this hostility is to present all sides of the issue in your speech. By being open-minded in this way you can disarm the audience. They may not agree with you but they will probably respect you for your intellectual honesty.

The Event

Often you're invited to give a speech on a day associated with a certain event. Maybe it's Martin Luther King, Jr. Day. Maybe it's the 50th anniversary of your company. Maybe it's the day the organization is dedicating its new building. You must keep that in mind when preparing for the speech. However, it need not dominate the speech.

Skillful speechwriters can use the event as an appropriate launching pad for the real subject of the talk. Sincere comments should be made about the event. If it's the 50th anniversary, there may be some people in the audience who started with the company. Have them stand up. You might cite developments at the company over the 50 years. That can lead right into your subject: The need for continued funding for research and development. The only "ought" here is that the transition ought to be smooth and natural. If it seems a force fit, the audience will become uncomfortable — because you seem uncomfortable.

In *Eloquence in an Electronic Age*, Kathleen Hall Jamieson makes the point that the relaxed air of someone on television has become the new standard by which society judges all speakers. If the speaker seems not at ease, the audience will also become uncomfortable.[5]

The Topic

One of the most difficult parts of preparation is to decide how you're going to approach a topic. The organization may give you as a topic "Communicating with Generation X." As it stands that's a very broad subject. You will have to find your focus.

You can ask the organization questions such as: What aspects of the topic is the audience most interested in? Why does the audience want to communicate with Generation X — to buy products and services? To stay off drugs? To become more a part of the community? To be good employees?

Then you will do your own preliminary research. You can use TV, especially MTV, and radio, scan books about Generation X such as Karen Ritchie's *Marketing to Generation X*, browse through Generation X magazines such as *Details* and have conversations with members of Generation X. From that you will get a feel for who these young people are, what they want, what are their strengths, and what are their accomplishments. That will help you get a handle on the topic you want to talk about. You'll also be able to limit the topic in such a way that it's doable in the time allotted.

Research

Often the quality of the speech is heavily dependent on the quality of the research. There are many forms of research, including interviewing people, formerly or informally.

The first stop when you're doing your research is at the organization that is inviting you. Do they have any material on the topic? For example, suppose Company X wants you to talk about how you re-engineered your human resources department — ask what they've been doing and who they've been talking to about the subject. Perhaps they've called in a consultant you should contact. Also there probably is correspondence tracking how far they've moved along in the process. Ask if you can see that correspondence.

Knowing where the organization actually is regarding re-engineering will help you custom-make your speech for them and avoid any sensitivities. When you have a draft, you might ask someone in that other organization to review it for any hot buttons.

Usually you can get the best up-to-the-minute information from real, live human beings, not books and magazines. You can contact people via the phone, in person, or on the Internet. For instance, if you're doing a speech on the re-engineering of your human resources department, you'd probably want to interview some of the people involved in those changes. Sure, they can hand you a report about it, but you can get a better feel for the subject and good anecdotes if you contact them directly.

In addition to your in-house resources, also contact experts in the field for their input. If appropriate, call trade associations. You might call other human resources companies and find out what they've done in re-engineering and what were the obstacles they faced.

The next stop is your local bookstore. You can usually get insight into the topic by browsing what's on the shelves. Has there been much written about re-engineering? Scan the books to find out what the experts are saying. Is there controversy in the field? For instance, does Expert A say one thing and Expert B say another?

Through online research you can also get a tremendous amount of information. You can search under both the categories "human resources" and "re-engineering."

The point of gathering all this information is to gain perspective on the issue. Also you will have enough insight and factual information to demonstrate to the audience that you know what you're talking about. You will also have examples and anecdotes from other companies, if you need them. When you actually sit down to write the speech, you can feel confident that you've done your homework.

This elaborate preparation also gives you what Carnegie calls "earning the right to speak."[6] In Dale Carnegie seminars students must specify how they've earned the right to speak on a certain subject. If they want to speak on volunteer work, for example, they could assert that they've earned the right to address this topic because they've been a volunteer for 20 years; when a family member was ill they received the services of volunteers; they've directed a group of volunteers for five years; and/or they wrote articles on how to motivate volunteers.

Tone

Before you start you have to decide what tone or tones you'll adopt for the speech. That will depend on your mission or purpose of the speech. Ailes says that the usual goals of a speech are: To entertain, to inform, to inspire, and to persuade.[7] You can do all of this or some of this in your speech.

But you have to be certain that you've adopted the right tone or tones for the topic. For example, if you're addressing a group in a community that has suffered a great deal of hardship, you might want to have a persuasive tone. In the speech you might want to tell them that their situation isn't hopeless — others have dealt with similar problems and have been able to revitalize their communities. However, that might be as far as you want to go. You may not think it's appropriate to be "inspirational." Someone from the community might be able to deliver an inspirational address, but for you as an outsider to attempt that might be seen as insensitive or arrogant.

Using a Ghost

Should you write the speech yourself or use a ghostwriter? Many reasons exist for using a ghostwriter. You might not have the time to dedicate to researching and writing a speech. Writing might not be your strength. Perhaps you need a highly polished speech for the prestigious Detroit Economic Club or the Conference Board. You may be new to writing or delivering speeches and don't feel ready to write your own just yet.

Hiring a ghostwriter for freelance or full-time work doesn't mean you can't write. All it means is that your time is better spent doing other things. After all you might be earning several hundred dollars an hour; a speechwriter earns $75 or $100 per hour. Whose time is more valuable?

If you want to keep the relationship with the speechwriter confidential, explain that in your initial meeting. Refer to what the speechwriter does as "assisting you" or "providing communications coaching."

In *Across the Board*, Bill Breninghouse points out that finding good speechwriters might not be easy because speechwriters are not certified or accredited. He advises those in need of speechwriting assistance to ask their colleagues and friends for names of proven speechwriters.[8]

Another avenue is to contact executive search consultants that handle people with communications credentials. They can supply full-time or freelance help. If you use the services of an executive search firm you may have to pay a fee.

You can also contact a public relations agency that offers speechwriting services. Also you could consult *O'Dwyer's Directory of Public Relations Firms*. It's available from the J.R. O'Dwyer Company (271 Madison Avenue, New York, New York 10016).

Selecting the Right Speechwriter

The best approach is to interview a number of speechwriters. You are looking for a good fit in terms of chemistry and writing style. Mike Morrison might have been a terrific speechwriter for Lee Iacocca, but maybe he wouldn't be a good fit for everyone.

Here is a checklist for screening speechwriters:

Writing samples.

Ask to see three speeches that were well received. If possible, ask the speechwriter to bring along clips or video tapes of the media coverage. Were press releases done for the speeches? It'd be helpful to see them. It might also be useful to show the speechwriter samples of speeches you felt were a good fit for you.

Expertise.

Has the speechwriter done any previous work on the general topic? For example, if the speech is about future applications of telecommunications to the workplace, it would be ideal if the speechwriter has had telecommunications clients. Some subjects are too complex to be handled by speechwriters with no knowledge of the issues.

Writing style.

Good speechwriters are able to write in a variety of styles. However, they have their definite strengths. Some may excel at writing conversational or flamboyant speeches. Others may be great at writing presidential, statesmanlike speeches. You have to make sure that their strengths represent styles you're comfortable with.

You can ask the candidates to each write a few pages of a speech on a certain topic as a way of directly testing their abilities. Such tests are becoming commonplace, and there is usually no charge for them.

References.

Has the speechwriter worked with clients at the proper level of the organization? If the speech is for your chief executive officer, you want someone who has experience operating at that high level. Ask for the names of three references and for permission to contact them. Ask those references if the speechwriter is easy to work with? Does the speechwriter do comprehensive research? Does the writer come up with fresh approaches? Handle criticism in a professional manner? Is the speechwriter discreet about the relationship?

Specialties, such as humor.

The speech you require may be a motivational talk to the sales force. Or perhaps you need some good one-liners. Or maybe you need someone who can put together an inspirational speech that doesn't sound corny. Maybe you have five minutes to tell your whole story to the board of directors — for that you need someone who specializes in tight board presentations.

If there's anything special you need from a speechwriter start your search early. You may find it useful to put a short classified in the Sunday edition of *The New York Times* stating the need for a speechwriter with that particular experience. If it's a telecommunications speech, you might consider calling the public relations professionals or speechwriters at telecommunications companies and find out who they use for freelance speechwriting. You can get the names of contacts in public relations departments from *O'Dwyer's Directory of Corporate Communications*. Executive search firms also might know of specialists.

Compensation.

According to Breninghouse, a 20-minute research-oriented speech costs about $5,000. If the speechwriters bill per diem rather than by the project, they could charge about $750 a day.[9] Ask the speechwriters for their rates.

You might find a wide range of estimates. One speechwriter may charge $2,500 for a 20-minute speech with no slides. For the same service, another might charge $10,000. Often there is no difference in quality between the two. The stated fee is just what the speechwriter feels is a fair price in that region of the country. The price may be higher from a speechwriter in Manhattan than from one in Akron, Ohio. No matter what their average rate is, speechwriters usually are willing to negotiate.

Get in writing the terms and conditions of the contract. Does the fee include two drafts? What is the charge for any further drafts? Does the speech belong to your organization or does it belong to the writer? You might want to discuss this with your attorney. Some speakers want the sole rights to the speech. After the speech is delivered, can the speechwriter use it as a sample to show prospects?

Working conditions.

Usually speechwriters will work with you in any way you prefer. They are accustomed to accommodating busy people. They are used to 10 p.m. calls and meetings in airports. They know that many clients will contact them at the 11th hour and have some fresh input for the speech. Describe how you are most comfortable working and see if that aligns with the speechwriter's.

EXHIBIT 12.2 — CHECKLIST FOR HIRING A GHOSTWRITER

- Writing samples, theirs and yours
- Expertise
- Writing style
- References
- Specialties
- Compensation
- Working conditions

Once you find a speechwriter who can capture your best self, you'll probably be working with that speechwriter for a number of years. Executives will change organizations but will often continue to use the same freelance or full-time speechwriter. The relationship is very important. Often speechwriters become confidants and strategic advisors, in addition to writing speeches.

WRITING THE SPEECH

There is no one right way to write a speech. What counts is that the speech has been carefully tailored for a particular person. You don't want a speech "off the rack." A speech written for GE's Jack Welch would be very different than a speech written for Morrison-Knudsen's Steve Miller. The greatest compliment speechwriters can get is when clients exclaim, "That sounds just like me!"

Guidelines

However, there are some guidelines in writing and delivering speeches:

Unlike a print article, which is for the eye, a speech is for the ear.

Therefore, the sentence construction should be short enough for the ear to take it in. It helpful to read the speech into a tape recorder and then play it back. When you listen to it, is it easy to understand? Every time you hear the words "it," "her," or "him," is it clear what or to whom the pronoun is referring? If you use the initials "MADD," does your audience know that it refers to "Mothers Against Drunk Drivers"?

When the audience is listening to a speech, they can't return to an earlier remark or ponder something that was said. Therefore, in speeches, you have to make everything crystal clear. There can't be any questions or ambiguity. Go through the draft of the speech and look for anything that might not be clear to the audience.

Keep the messages simple.

In the *Fortune* article "What Exactly is Charisma?" Patricia Sellers points out that charismatic leaders distill complex ideas into simple messages. They are able to do this because they know how to use symbols, analogies, metaphors, and stories.[10]

Remember the anecdotes and stories President Ronald Reagan told? Lee Iacocca was the master of analogies. Iacocca's speechwriters would work for hours until they came up with an analogy that Iacocca thought was appropriate. When Steve Miller worked at Chrysler with Iacocca, about one-half of each of his standard speeches was a recount of the Chrysler story — the ups and downs of the early turnaround. Audiences loved it.

Keep the speech short.

It is generally said that 20 minutes is the average time a speaker should talk. After that, it becomes increasingly difficult to hold the attention of the audience. However, there are exceptions to this. When Dick Dauch, manufacturing vice president at Chrysler, gave his standard speech, with numerous visuals, on how manufacturing changed at the auto company, he might talk for nearly an hour. But the subject matter was so fascinating audiences didn't seem to mind sitting there.

The best way to find out if your speech is too long is to deliver it before a group of friends or colleagues. Watch the audience. Is their attention waning? If it is, you might have to rework the speech and shorten it somewhat.

Part of the reason the audience loses interest is that the speech is difficult to follow. Guide the audience through it. Number your points. Tell them what you're going to tell them. Have transition phrases such as "Now we'll move on to looking at another part of this problem."

You're giving a performance.

Most people give speeches to sell themselves and sell an idea, point of view, product, or service. Former Pepsi and Apple executive John Sculley observed that marketing is theater. By that he means that is you're marketing something, you have to engage the audience. What you're doing when you're giving a speech is giving a performance.[11] That doesn't differ much from the performance you give on a job interview or when you're trying to convince your boss to give you more resources for a project. You'll put your whole heart and soul into it, put your best foot forward and present the most persuasive evidence.

Be easily understandable.

If you're talking with medical doctors, you can discuss a medical topic with ease. However, if you're talking at the rotary, you can't assume the audience understands the dynamics of the computer business.

To be easily understandable with general audiences, apply the "bright fifth-grader test." Read out a paragraph and ask if bright fifth graders could understand it. It helps if you translate complex or technical concepts into images laypersons could understand. For example, you can describe feelings, processes, and products in terms of popular movies, athletic contests, the U.S. space program, genetic research, or the search for a cure for AIDS.

Quotes aren't mandatory.

Some speakers never use quotes. Others do. The point about using a quote is that it should be appropriate to the speech. If you're talking to high-school seniors, you probably don't want to quote Winston Churchill. Many young people have never heard of him; even if they have. he doesn't mean a great deal to them.

Another problem with quotes is that some have become clichés.

They don't sound fresh to the audience. For instance, you might quote Churchill's "Overcome" speech; it would be the hundredth time that audience has heard it.

You can find fresh quotes from reading biographies, *People* magazine, and newspapers. While watching television you can jot down what guests on talk shows say. Also it can be very effective to quote someone from fiction or film. But here too you have to watch for clichés. How many times has Alice in Wonderland or Dorothy from the "Wizard of Oz" been quoted?

Involve your audience.

In this day of interactive media, audiences are less apt to be willing to just sit there and not be involved in the speech. There are many ways to have them participate.

For example, you can ask a question of the audience in the beginning or during the speech: How many here feel insecure about your jobs? You can ask someone in the audience to name their favorite brand if your topic is brand names. You can stop your speech at any point and ask if there are any questions or comments. Then you can resume the speech. At the beginning of the speech, you can give out forms for the audience to rate how well you persuaded them that the proposed tax is unfair. Then, after the speech, conduct a question-and-answer session. You can liven up the Q&A period by calling on people in the audience who don't have their hands up.

The Opening

If you've taken a Dale Carnegie or any other good public speaking course, you know that the most important ingredients in a speech are your sincerity and passion. You will have less trouble opening a speech if you forget about writing a "great speech" and focus more on how you can communicate your big ideas to the audience. Keep your focus off yourself and on the message.

There are an infinite number of ways to open a speech. Here are some of the things to think about.

Protocol.

In getting up to the podium, it's traditional to thank the person who introduced you for "that kind introduction." Also you might want to thank the organization for inviting you. Is there a special reason why this is such an honor? For example, you might have attended your first Public Relations Society of America (PRSA) meeting when you were in college. Your dream then was to be speaking at a PRSA meeting some time in the future.

Is there a reason why you're so pleased to be giving this speech in Chicago or San Francisco? Did you grow up there? Was your first job there?

In the introduction you want to establish bonds with the audience. What is it about this audience that you can relate to? One executive speaking at Harvard College built rapport by "confessing" that he had been educated at Harvard's rival MIT.

The next item on the opening agenda is to recognize anyone in the audience who should be singled out. Ask the organization about this. Maybe there is someone there celebrating a major birthday. Maybe the mayor is in the audience.

Cite those people by name and express how terrific it is to have them there. You can briefly mention their accomplishments. Before the speech make sure you have their names and titles right. You might want to check with their office about how a cardinal of the Roman Catholic Church or secretary of state is referred to in public.

Humor.

Some speakers, especially if they are naturally gregarious, like to start with humor. The problem is that their concern about giving a speech frequently makes it hard for them to "think funny." Once they get relaxed, though, their sense of humor usually returns.

For inspiration you can go to the standard joke books. After reading hundreds of bits of humor you may find a joke you could massage. That is, rewrite it until its story line and timing are a good fit for you.

In addition there are a number of books that lead you step-by-step in the writing of humor. Two are Gene Perret's *Comedy Writing Step by Step* and Melvin Helitzer's *Comedy Writing Secrets*.

You can listen to the late night shows and pick up some humor, flip through the cartoons in *The New Yorker* and scan the jokes in the *Reader's Digest*. Then turn that raw material into something that works for you.

Another possibility is to use one or several one-liners to start off with. The easiest way to do this is to have the humor be at your own expense. Audiences love this. If you're known to be a work addict, then you can refer to the time devoted to giving this speech as your vacation, for this year *and* next year. If you were just pushed out of a major corporation, you can have a one liner about being in outplacement or between jobs.

Since what's funny is a subjective thing, it's wise to run this humor by others before you use it. Others may not understand it. They may not think it's funny. They may even find it in bad taste.

Event.

Another way to launch a speech is to reflect on what the particular date or year means. Maybe this is the 10th year since your child's near-fatal accident, and that's why it's so important for you to talk about safety. Or perhaps one year ago on this date, you were out of work and now you're creating jobs for others. The tie-in would be your plea for more tax relief for small businesses.

An anecdote or story.

You might describe how it is to ride the "L" in Chicago and from your window see so many able-bodied people out of work. This would help you launch your speech on the need for more innovative programs for the unemployed. You could also tell a story about one man who got one job — and the difference it made to him, his parents, his wife, his children, and the community. The speech could then go into community programs for the unemployed.

A testimonial.

It's become increasingly popular for people to introduce themselves and their topic by way of personal disclosure. There's the woman who used to be on welfare and weigh more than 300 pounds. Now she's the number-one sales rep for a cosmetics company and gets into a size eight.

Straightforward introduction.

It's often disarming for a speaker to simply jump right into the subject of the speech. This example combines personal disclosure and a straightforward approach:

> Today I want to talk about a problem that has tormented me and my family — and my employer — for 20 years. That problem is mental illness.

Video or slide show.

Sometimes speakers like to begin with a short segment from a video, a scene from a movie, or a collage of slides. They see that as a dramatic way to open their talk. Some have accompanying music.

But whatever way you open your speech, the purpose of the opening is to let the audience know who you are and to build a launching pad for your subject. You might fiddle with a variety of openings. Read them to your friends. Which one gets the best reaction? What you want to avoid is an opening that seems stiff or overly labored.

Keep simplifying your opening until it comes out naturally and smoothly. You can go to the book store or library and pick up books with speeches. Analyze how each speaker opens. Which approaches work and which seem to fall flat? The periodical *Vital Speeches of the Day*, available in many libraries, contains current speeches.

Organization

Your speech can be organized in a variety of ways. One of the most common approaches to organization is to tell them what you're going to tell them, tell them, and then tell them what you told them. This is a useful format because audiences want clear directions about where you're "taking" them.

Another common structure is based on problem–solution. You describe the drug problem in the United States and then suggest a solution.

Another approach is the past, present, and future format. You talk about the history of the issue, how things stand at the present time, and how they can be in the future if the United States takes certain actions.

Or the whole speech can be a string of anecdotes about children who were helped by a certain program.

The speech can be entirely your story. For example, you discuss how working with teams, ranging from the Boy Scouts to a task force in Harlem, kept changing your life.

Again, see how this organization comes across with a real audience. You might find that your own experience with teams can't sustain a whole speech. You might need to bring in material about Babe Ruth's experiences with team work; how a heart surgeon depends on team members; and what your daughter is learning about working with others in the Girl Scouts.

Marshalling Evidence

Many speeches are given to persuade the audience to adopt a certain point of view, buy a certain product, or purchase a certain service. To do that speechwriters have to become skillful presenting a variety of types of evidence. In this, the speechwriter is much like the trial attorney.

It is useful to consider the types of evidence available and how they can be used most effectively:

Statistics.

Statistics can be very persuasive. It might shock an audience to learn that X number of abused children die every year or that X number of men in their early 50s die each day of a heart attack. Because the speech is relatively short, though, you don't want to overwhelm the audience with numbers. Just select those numbers that will bring you the greatest impact. Round off the numbers. If 763 people die of disease Y every day, state that as more than 750. Also, always cite the source of your statistics, be it the Small Business Administration or the program "60 Minutes."

How can you increase the effectiveness of statistics? Introduce new statistics. Maybe a poll or survey was just released. Also, your organization might be funding research on a topic and you can speculate what you anticipate the statistics will be.

You can also make the numbers visual. The amount of jobs a certain program has created would be able to, you say, run three large factories. The amount of money "wasted" by a charitable organization, you say, could house, clothe, and feed five million children for a year. The number of stray cats in a medium-size city like Stamford, Connecticut, could fill, you indicate, the Empire State Building.

Comparisons between statistics usually offer plenty of food for thought. In talking about the information age, a speaker would say there were X number of computers in 1950, so many in 1970. Then in 1990, the numbers jumped to such-and-such. In the year 2000 he predicts the number will be Y. Numbers only mean something in context.

Scientific evidence.

Many groups use scientific evidence to support their claims. The danger with such an approach is that speakers frequently assume the data speaks for itself. That's a dangerous assumption. First of all, scientific findings often have to be translated into layman's language. Secondly, those results usually need to be put into context. If a certain antidepressant can eliminate all depression in 75 percent of the population, then that can be discussed in terms of saved medical expenses, increased productivity at work, and stable relationships.

The experts.

As viewers saw in the O.J. Simpson trial, experts can be used to support just about any line of thinking. The public is becoming aware that what experts say is open to interpretation. That's why it's important to present this type of evidence carefully. If you cite material from an expert, explain why those findings "seem to make sense." Reinforce those findings with information from another source.

Case histories.

People enjoy hearing about other people. Some of the speeches that have had the most impact employed case histories. Usually the histories represent actual people with identities concealed. The material is dense with details. Those details help the audience visualize and get a feel for the individuals beings discussed. The people become presences in the room.

History.

There are those who feel that there is no longer any use for history in society. However, arguments made from history can still be highly persuasive. You would have to do some research on the audience and find out if they respect evidence from history.

Thus, if you want to argue for a public-works program, you can allude to the success of the public-works program during the Great Depression. If you are supporting freedom of sexual choice, you might cite the attitudes towards homosexuality in ancient Greece. Maybe you want to warn the community about being tolerant of people's beliefs. To demonstrate where intolerance could lead, you might discuss the Spanish Inquisition and the Salem Witch Trials.

When using historical evidence, it's very exciting to use visuals from that era. You can contact the graphics department of your organization to get that material. Also the Yellow Pages lists stock photo houses that carry historical material.

Organizational histories.

Organizations are changing so rapidly that there is plenty of material to use to illustrate just about any point. Maybe you want to discuss the danger of success. You can cite three or four successful organizations such as IBM, Westinghouse, and NBC which went into decline. Perhaps you want to discuss how organizations turn themselves around. You can point to Chrysler, Honeywell, and Walt Disney. Your theme might be entrepreneurism in America. You can cite examples from every century.

It is important to make sure your information is correct and that you write it in such a way that it can't be easily misquoted. The press could pick up something you say and Corporation X could react negatively. You might misread a case history and the social-work agency becomes angry. It's wise to run that material by the appropriate people at the organization. Ask them to check it for accuracy and any political sensitivities.

Personal experience.

Many of you have a good story to tell. Then by all means tell it. People respect information from personal experience. However, there are pitfalls.

One problem is that some may assume that their personal experience is as interesting to others as it is to them. And the reality is that others perceive their story as commonplace.

Secondly, a story may not remain compelling. As Chrysler went from being a near-bankrupt company to a more normal corporation, Steve Miller sensed that his standard speech, the "Chrysler Story," should be shortened. He knew that interest was waning in the details of the early turnaround.

Third, the speaker might rely too heavily on this form of evidence and neglect to present other forms such as statistics or scientific evidence.

Anecdotes.

Little stories about others can make a dramatic impact. Frequently the audience remembers these long after the speech. You can get the stories from biographies, articles in magazines, talking with people, surfing the Internet, and watching TV. The power of this evidence can be blunted if the allusion is well known. Speakers who make reference to FDR's triumph over polio or Thomas Edison's struggles might find they're not getting any reaction from the audience. The anecdote has become old and tired.

Visuals.

Showing something rather than talking about it can be very potent evidence. Speakers can bring in video clips, photos, flip charts, overheads, and slides. For example, if the speaker is discussing the problem of abandoned dogs, showing video footage from the Humane Society can make quite a statement.

Visuals can also be used to reinforce a point. For example, if a company's quarterly loss was $800 million, a slide on this can make the point powerfully. If the accident rate among the elderly has climbed during the past four decades, a chart or graph can illustrate this effectively.

The point about visuals is that they should enhance the speech, not overpower it. It's possible that "special effects"-type visual supports can distract the audience from what is being said and fix their attention on the what is being shown.

Several excellent software packages for producing visuals from a laptop computer are available. This is a very cost-effective approach, and it's simpler to make changes than if you're dealing with an outside vendor.

However, effective visuals can be also low-tech. Motivational speakers do an excellent job illustrating and reinforcing points with a flip chart propped up on an easel. As they talk, they jot down key words. The immediacy of the experience frequently creates electricity between the speaker and audience.

Another type of low-tech approach is to bring in props. An executive at a defense company would bring in four exhibits he held up during the talk. They each illustrated a point he was making. They were large enough for everyone in the audience to see.

As you write the body of the speech you'll find that some evidence works better than others. If your personal experience doesn't seem persuasive, for example, you have a number of options. You can make the speech less dependent on this form of evidence. You can shorten the section and rework it. Or you can eliminate the section.

In lining up your evidence, you also want to play devil's advocate. You might mention in the speech that X number of children die from child abuse every year. The devil's advocate in you says, "So what? Just as many children die of disease A or B every year." Think about how to handle that objection. You can, for example, concede that many more children die of diseases every year but the point is that the deaths from child abuse are needless and can be prevented.

Internalize in yourself a "Blue Meany" or the "The Critic" who constantly questions what you do. The official term for that is to become "self-editing."

Also put yourself in the shoes of the audience. If you were sitting where they are sitting, would you be persuaded by this speech? If not, take another look at how you're handling evidence.

EXHIBIT 12.3—FORMS OF EVIDENCE

- Statistics
- Scientific evidence
- The experts
- Case histories
- History
- Organizational histories
- Personal experience
- Anecdotes
- Visuals

More about Visuals

Nobody said that you are required to use visuals. In fact, if you are a chief executive officer, you probably will not use visuals. That can detract from your status.

But if you decide to use visuals, make sure they are of high quality. Yes, you could use your PowerPoint software to make slides. But will they look totally professional? Many speakers still have the visuals done by graphics experts.

When your visuals are ready, ask two people to proofread them. An error on a visual will remain in the audience's memory a long time.

When should you think about using visuals? If the story you're telling is complex, then you may need visuals to help the audience follow along. Another time visuals are useful is when changes are announced. People tend to become uneasy when they're facing change. Therefore, you won't have the audience's full attention. Through visuals, you're more likely to hold more of their attention.

If you're using a lot of numbers, particularly comparisons among numbers, your audience would appreciate graphics. You might pass out copies of the visuals for them to follow as you give your speech.

How can you make sure your visuals are good? Here are some pointers:

Keep the visuals simple.
Too much of anything on the visual might distract the audience.

Limit the amount of information on each visual.
The audience should be listening to you, not reading slides. If need be, use 20 uncluttered slides rather than 10 cluttered ones.

Use graphics that are a good fit with the corporate culture of the organization you're addressing.

If the company is no nonsense, no frills type organization, you probably wouldn't want the style of your visuals to be ornate. If you're making a speech at the White House, your visuals might be elaborate.

Don't rely on the visuals.

The speech should be able to stand on its own, without aids. Machines have been known to break down. Slides have been left in airports. The battery on the laptop needs to be charged.

The Conclusion

When you wrap up the speech, it's time to ask the audience to do something. The conclusion is usually a call to action. Maybe you want them to think about the problem of child abuse as a community problem. Perhaps you want them to do volunteer work to prevent child abuse. Maybe they should make a monetary donation to the cause. Or they should write letters to their state representatives.

How do you make that call to action most effectively?

One strategy is to recap what you said in the speech. Then, given this to be the situation, make it seem logical, natural, or plain common sense that people would want to take a certain course of action. In a sense you've made your case and now, like a trial attorney, you're summing up.

Another strategy is to bring urgency to the cause. You can point out that if nothing is done, child abuse will probably grow at X percent a year. Hammer home that there are real live children in this situation and right this minute they're hoping for a miracle. Mention that the audience can bring about that miracle.

A third strategy is to develop the what-if-nothing-is-done scenario. Has there been a similar situation in which nothing had been done? Here you might introduce a fresh analogy. You might point out what could have happened if, for example, there had been no polio vaccine.

Another approach is to end with a visual collage. You can show photos of young people who were killed by drunk drivers or dogs at the Humane Society.

You also might want to recite something inspirational. Maybe it's a prayer you used when you were just starting out in your profession. Maybe it's part of a poem that has meant a lot to you as you've coped with life's ups and downs.

But however you want to conclude, you don't have to necessarily be theatrical. Some speakers like Iacocca are. And they can arouse powerful emotions in the audience.

But it's more important that you be positive and upbeat. If you've devoted most of speech to describing the problem of child abuse, at the end be optimistic about the solution. If the bulk of the speech is about the problems at the company, you should conclude on a confident note: This situation can and will be turned around. And here are the five reasons why together we can do it ...

Here's a checklist for you to use when it's time to wrap up your remarks:

- Did you say everything in the speech which needed to be said? Would the speech be stronger if you took out one statistic or fact and substituted another? If you were in the audience would you say that the speaker had made a good case? How could the speaker have brought the message home more effectively?
- Have you lead the audience to a point of conclusion? Do they have a sense you are bringing them somewhere?
- As Carnegie would say, have you earned the right to ask the audience to take some action?
- Are you really sincere about this topic? If not, rewrite the speech on some aspect of the subject which you care deeply about.

DELIVERING THE SPEECH

A speech is only as good as its delivery.

Ironically, some organizations invest a great deal of money preparing outstanding speeches for the executives. However, they do not focus enough attention on the delivery.

If you are going to give a speech, practice the delivery. If clients are going to be giving speeches, work with them on the delivery. While practicing the speech, you're bound to pick up on words the clients can't pronounce, arguments which don't sound convincing, a statement that sounds unduly harsh, an analogy which takes too long to explain. That's one big advantage of working together with clients on rehearsal. The speech can be changed right there and then.

Should the speech be read? There are ways to read the speech verbatim that do not look like the speaker is reading. For example, the speaker looks down at the text, takes a snapshot of a cluster of words, looks up says those words, and looks down again. In cases of legal material, testimony, and financial information, your clients might have to read from a text. Let them know it's doable.

If your clients don't have to recite the text verbatim, then there are a variety of ways they can make the delivery easier.

One approach to work from a point outline. That outline will contain major topics, statistics, facts, key phrases, and any quotations. As soon as clients are satisfied with a draft, then a point outline can be written. That outline can be on the back of an envelope or be five pages of bullet points. What's important is the speaker can work comfortably with this tool.

Another approach is to highlight key thoughts, phrases, numbers, and so on in the text. Clients will work from the draft itself, glancing at it every few paragraphs. After practicing like this, clients often want that draft then boiled down to a point outline.

A third approach is to internalize the speech. The speech becomes so much a part of the client that there is no need for the draft or a point outline. The client speaks from the heart. The risk here is that there are those moments when minds go blank. Since there is nothing on the podium to prompt the speaker, there could be an unbearable pause. It's usually wise for clients to bring up an index card with relevant scribbles just in case they lose their train of thought.

There are two ways to practice. One is before a live audience, even if it's just the family. You will see on their faces and in their body languages how you are coming across.

Another way is to have yourself videotaped. Before you're taped making the speech, first be taped in normal conversation with people you're comfortable with. Your goal is come across as relaxed in giving a speech as you are conversing. In essence, delivering a speech is having a conversation with a room full of people.

The Pitfalls

When you're reviewing how you're presenting yourself, what should you be looking for? Here are some common pitfalls:

Self-centeredness.

It's important that your attention be focused on the audience, not on yourself. Some speakers are so terrified of public speaking that they turn inward at the podium. Instead they should be projecting themselves outward to the audience.

One way to reduce stage fright is to plan to rehearse in the room where you will be delivering your speech. That will give you a feeling of control over your surroundings. Use the microphone and if you have visuals go through them a few times. You want to make sure that what you say and what's on the screen are in synch. You might want the person handling the visuals to write down on the speech reminders like "slow down" or "change slide quickly."

If the room isn't available, then find out as much as you can about that particular room. What kind of podium is it? How many does the room seat? Will there be tables? Will anything be on the table? What will you be looking out at? In your city, find a similar room where you can rehearse. Often you can rent it for a few hours at a hotel. Make sure you go through the visuals several times. It's best to have someone take charge of visuals so you can put your full attention on delivering the speech.

A lack of ease.

Speakers who aren't at ease in their surroundings transmit those signals to the audience. It's imperative that you present yourself as relaxed. If need be, get professional coaching from a firm which works with people at your level of the organization. Here it's best to locate the right vendor by asking around for referrals. It's possible to have training just for a specific speech.

Moving too quickly.

Because you probably know the material very well, you might tend to race through it. Remember that the audience has never seen the speech before and has only a vague idea what you're going to say. Speak at the same rate of speed that you would use when discussing a project with a superior.

A lack of commitment.

This goes back to working only with subjects you feel strongly about. When speakers aren't enthusiastic it shows. Demonstrate your commitment by varying your tone of voice to emphasize certain points, speaking directly to members of the audience, allowing emotions to be revealed, and displaying a high energy level.

The famous management consultant Tom Peters demonstrates his commitment by pacing around the stage. He's so keyed up by the issues he can't stand still. You can also step from behind the podium to get closer to the audience. You can step down from the stage and stand right in the audience. However, adopt these tactics only if you will feel 100–percent comfortable doing them.

And you seem to be reading.

That will be the audience's conclusion if you don't maintain eye contact. Suppose you find a page missing from your speech? Continue to make eye contact and ad lib. You won't lose the audience. Some speakers select some friendly faces in the audience to focus on during the entire speech. This is a painless way of maintaining eye contact.

EXHIBIT 12.4 — DELIVERY PITFALLS

- Self-centeredness
- Lack of ease
- Moving too quickly
- Lack of commitment
- Seem to be reading

"Homo Verbus"

As Maloney stresses in his book *Talk Your Way to the Top*, "we are what we say—and how we say it. We are *homo verbus*, creatures of words."[12]

As we move more to an oral culture, your words and the words you write for your clients are going to become more and more important. The board of directors and members of the chamber of commerce are becoming less and less likely to read the report you leave behind. Their interest is in what you say and how you say it.

For examples of speeches, please see Appendix, Exhibits A.1, A.5, and A.8.

NOTES

1. Stephen R. Maloney, *Talk Your Way to the Top* (New Jersey: Prentice Hall, 1992), ix.

2. Jerry Tarver, *Professional Speech Writing* (Richmond, Virginia: The Effective Speech Writing Institute, 1982), 9-11.

3. Dale Carnegie, *The Quick and Easy Way to Effective Speaking* (New York: Dale Carnegie & Associates, 1962), 5.

4. Roger Ailes, *You Are the Message* (New York: Doubleday, 1989), 66.

5. Kathleen Hall Jamieson, *Eloquence in an Electronic Age* (New York: Oxford University Press, 1988), passim.

6. Carnegie, 65-84.

7. Ailes, 67.

8. Bill Breninghouse, "Working with a Ghost," *Across the Board*, September 1991 v28, 48.

9. Breninghouse, 48.

10. Patricia Sellers, "What Exactly is Charisma?" *Fortune*, January 15, 1995, 71.

11. John Sculley, *Odyssey* (New York: Harper & Row, 1987), passim.

12. Maloney, xi.

SUGGESTED READING

Cohen, Allan and David Bradford. *Influence Without Authority*. New York: John Wiley & Sons, 1989.

Dawson, Roger. *Secrets of Power Persuasion*. New Jersey: Prentice Hall, 1992.

Reis, Al and Jack Trout. *Positioning*. New York: Warner Books, 1981.

Phillip P. Fried is a principal of The Dilenschneider Group. His primary responsibility is designing and supervising the firm's media relations programs. Before joining The Dilenschneider Group, he held senior management positions at major public relations firms including executive vice president at Brown Boxenbaum, senior vice president at Fleishman-Hilliard and vice president–director of the media services group at Hill and Knowlton. He was formerly Eastern public relations director for Monsanto Company, manager of press relations for Allied Chemical and public relations manager for Uniroyal, Inc. He has also been a general assignment and business reporter for United Press International and an editor at Ziff-Davis Publishing Company.

He was administrator of a 1,500-bed station hospital while on duty as a U.S. Army medical service officer. Fried holds a degree in Economics from The City College of New York.

CHAPTER 13

PUBLIC RELATIONS
FOR NONPROFIT ORGANIZATIONS

"The Girl Scouts, the Red Cross, the pastoral churches — our nonprofit organizations — are becoming America's management leaders," observes Peter Drucker, father of modern management.[1]

Drucker salutes the nonprofit sector because, he says, it fuses a deep commitment to a mission with use of the best tools in business, including those used by marketers.[2] Consequently, the nonprofit sector can produce outstanding results with limited resources.

One prime example of that is the public relations conducted by nonprofit organizations. Those organizations have shown themselves to be bold, resourceful, and innovative in their use of public relations. They know how to form useful partnerships with both other nonprofits and with corporations. And their volunteers are often some of their best public-relations ambassadors. As a result nonprofit organizations have been able to make a difference across American society. That ranges from changing public perception to helping shape legislation.

The Mothers Against Drunk Driving (MADD), for instance, has been able to change the attitude towards using alcohol before getting behind the wheel. Not too long ago, no one thought too much about drunk driving — and its consequences. Now just about everyone recognizes the seriousness of driving while intoxicated. MADD uses a broad variety of strategies, ranging from the symbolism of red ribbons to full-page ads of photos of persons killed by drunk drivers. MADD is also in the vanguard of fund-raising techniques. It puts its logo on affinity VISA or MasterCard credit cards. When consumers use the card, MADD receives a donation and also gets a chance to deliver its message. In addition, MADD's cards offer the advantage of a lower annual percentage rate on the consumer's balance.[3]

The American Association of Retired Persons (AARP) is another public relations powerhouse. With 30 million members, AARP is the second largest nonprofit group in America. Its specialty is lobbying for legislation favorable to senior citizens. Elected officials and candidates listen to AARP because senior citizens tend to vote.[4] Thanks partly to AARP, senior citizens are one of the most influential groups in America.

LIMITED BUDGETS

Throughout history, nonprofits have had the distinct "advantage" of limited budgets. Limited budgets forced public relations representatives in the nonprofit sector to be more inventive and daring than their colleagues in business. In the early 1990s, Harvard Business professor

Rosabeth Moss Kanter counseled American business to do more with less.[5] That's what nonprofits have been doing all along.

By nature, nonprofits are entrepreneurial. Today, because they're using the tools of business, they're getting even more skillful at doing more with less. In *INC.* magazine, the publication for entrepreneurs, Donna Fenn presents a profile of the Wyman Center, a nonprofit summer camp for troubled children. Its president and chief executive officer, Dave Hilliard, "speaks of customer service, relationship marketing, asset utilization, and 'thinking out of the box' with the zeal of a fast-growth company entrepreneur."[6]

ERA OF NEED

Hilliard has to be 100 percent focused to keep the center going. That's because nonprofits are currently operating in difficult times or what might be called the "Era of Need." Because of his entrepreneurial ways, Hilliard has been able to increase contributions 36 percent and earned revenues 152 percent.[7] For the Wyman Center as for many nonprofits today the situation is binary: Be daring and embrace the tools of business or perish.

At this time, money is hard to get. Many of the traditional funding sources are drying up. Robert Bennett, president of the United Way of Buffalo & Erie County, puts it this way, "We're entering a major new era, with federal cuts, state cuts and (local) economic conditions being what they are." Although the inflation rate grew at almost 18 percent during one particular time period, Bennett's budget increased only 0.2 percent.[8]

Just in terms of federal cutbacks, the Independent Sector, a research group, estimates that donations to charities would have to increase 84 percent by the year 2002 to make up for the reductions. According to *Crain's New York Business*, corporate contributions to nonprofits declined 18 percent from their high in 1987.

At the same time there are cutbacks at every level, the need for services is increasing. Federal and state services and benefits are being slashed as political leaders try to shrink big government. The tasks government used to do are being carried out by nonprofit organizations and individuals.

Meanwhile American business finds itself in the midst of a global economy. All the rules for doing business have changed — and will continue to change. As a result, corporations are re-engineering or restructuring how work is done. The result is ongoing layoffs. Middle-class people who used to be regular contributors to United Way now find themselves in need of its services, ranging from the basics of survival to job-hunting counseling.

There is also the new problem of competition in the nonprofit sector. As Andrew Osterland points out in *Financial World*, "Today competition goes well beyond the genteel struggle of trying to toss a better fund-raiser. Today, nonprofit competition is every bit as strategic in nature as corporate competition."[9]

This is particularly true in health care and higher education. Nonprofit hospitals, once a staid community resource, have to fight like tigers to fill empty beds and make strategic decisions about what facilities to eliminate. Colleges have empty seats; right now demographics aren't in their favor. Their recruiting efforts are intense, and they use just about every technique that Colgate-Palmolive or Ford would use.

Also, health care and higher education are among the services being revolutionized by consumerism. Rather than passive receivers of services, those "purchasing" health care and education want to know what they're getting, why the service is configured as it is, and if there is any "warranty." That increases the need for informational public relations materials and outreach into the community. An increasing number of nonprofits, for example, are providing free lectures for consumers. Colleges are holding open houses off-campus, wherever people are.

Another issue in the nonprofit sector has been scandal. It was disclosed, for instance, that United Way of America president William Aramony was earning about $360,000 a year plus perks. Since United Way is such a high-profile operation, revelation of that salary cast a cloud over many nonprofits. As a result there has been a demand for greater accountability about where dollars are going. The American Red Cross now makes it known that 93 cents of every donated dollar goes towards programs and services. Also, it lets the public know that there are 50 volunteers for every Red Cross paid staff member.

Because of the recent scandals, there has been an erosion of trust. Organizations must now restore their credibility and assure the public that they're trustworthy.

All these problems are obviously serious. Often survival is at stake. That's why nonprofits are searching for more effective yet cost-efficient ways to get their messages out.

In this chapter you will review why you're doing public relations and how you're doing it. This analysis differs from other material in this book in that it's customized for the nonprofit sector. If you want additional information about a specific topic, refer to the appropriate chapter in this book.

ROLE OF PUBLIC RELATIONS

In *Effective Public Relations*, Scott Cutlip, Allen Center, and Glen Broom state that there are five major reasons why public relations is practiced in the nonprofit sector. Those five are:

1. To develop an awareness and acceptance of the organization's mission
2. To create channels of communication with those people the organization serves

3. To establish and nurture an appropriate climate for fundraising
4. To formulate and disseminate public policies that are related to the organization's mission
5. To motivate constituencies ranging from board members and employees to volunteers and relevant officials to work to achieve the organization's mission.[10]

As you see, Cutlip et al. don't separate fund-raising from public relations. Many public relations counselors would agree that the two activities have become intertwined. Indeed, you can ask yourself: When is public relations not fund-raising in the nonprofit sector?

EXHIBIT 13.1 — THOSE YOU SERVE

- Your organization's mission

- The media themselves

- Your constituency

- Those to be influenced

MEDIA — YOUR MASTERS

Let's first look at media. The media are so important to nonprofits because they offer a gold mine of free publicity. The trick is to learn how to deal effectively with representatives of the media. Media relations is an art, not a science. Those who obtain outstanding coverage for their organizations know exactly how to build rapport with the media.

In nonprofit organizations, you serve a variety of masters when dealing with the media. The number-one master is your organization's mission. Before any media activities are undertaken, the question must be asked: Does this help or hurt the mission?

Recently a New York-based public relations firm was asked to help tell a complex medical story. The Nosinger Center at Ohio State University serves clients who are both retarded and emotionally disturbed. Dr. Steven Reiss, the center's director, wanted to educate the public about this condition; inform various legislative bodies of the fact that through proper diagnosis, millions of dollars could be saved while, at the same time, improving care; and request that federal funds not be cut for the special education of physicians involved in treatment.

A number of television networks asked to tape the clients. Had that been done, the media pick-up would probably have been tremendous. But part of the mission of the center was maintaining the dignity of clients. Therefore, after a great deal of soul-searching it was decided not to allow taping.

Environmentalists have also been asking themselves the question: Have our media strategies helped our mission? You can probably recall the time when environmental activism was very theatrical. There were blockades of logging roads and environmentalists boarded boats suspected of polluting.

Andrew Osterland points out in *Financial World*, donations are currently down to organizations which still engage in high drama. On the other hand, the Nature Conservancy, which isn't theatrical, is the hottest environmental group around. Donations keep flowing in. The Conservancy's strategic approach to is buy land that is endangered and then preserve it.[11]

As you can see, what approaches are used with the media must reflect current realities and tastes. As Americans struggle to maintain a middle-class lifestyle in a global economy, their patience for theater has worn thin. It is interesting to note that in the 1960s when the counterculture's "theater in the streets" was popular, the economy was purring.

Other masters you serve include the media themselves. Your job is to make the media's job easier. Therefore, you want to provide them with appropriate story ideas, background information, and access to the right people.

The time to get to know the media is *before* you need them. You must be proactive. Inform local and national media representatives how you, on an ongoing basis, can be an information resource. For example, every time they have a food story, they can get background information and spokespeople from your nutrition think tank. If you learn of useful information which the media would love to know — and you can reveal it — then pass it on. The most successful media representative in New York nurtures his contacts by continuously feeding them useful-to-know information. They remember that when he needs a favor.

But the time for getting acquainted with the media is never around their deadline. Find out from the organization what the deadlines are. Then stay clear of reporters and editors during that period.

The next master is your constituency, ranging from your board of directors and funding sources to your client base and your employees. What you do in public relations shouldn't harm them in any way. That includes revealing their identity if that's not appropriate.

Your next master includes all those whom you need to influence, whether that be Congress or the deli down the street that you want to be a sponsor for your marathon.

When considering a story or a press release, none of these groups can be ignored. For example, suppose one of your funding sources is a petroleum company. In a media release, it would be wise not to have any allusion to or analogy about anything which could reflect badly on the company or its products.

EXHIBIT 13.2 — THE MEDIA — YOUR ADVANTAGES

- The media are service-oriented.
- You're the "underdog."
- You serve the public.
- There's the halo effect.

THE MEDIA — YOUR ADVANTAGES

As a nonprofit you have definite advantages the private sector doesn't have.

Media are service-oriented.

Since you provide an important service at an affordable or no fee, the media usually feel they has a certain obligation to get your story out.

You're the underdog.

Americans root for the organization or person who's struggling. Media try to go the extra mile to help nonprofits get coverage. For example, a president of a small women's college submitted an opinion-editorial (op-ed) to a business publication. The editor went out of her way to help her make the piece publishable.

You can ask for help because you serve the public.

So if you're sponsoring an Adopt-a-Pet Day, you can request the support of media. There was such an event in a Connecticut town and every day for almost two weeks the press release was picked up in local publications. The media showed up to cover the event.

There's the halo effect.

If you're doing good, the media that cover this story can also bask in the good feelings.

EXHIBIT 13.3 — PITFALLS IN MEDIA RELATIONS

- Lack of judgment
- Lack of exclusive packaging
- Doing the homework
- Overpromising

THE MEDIA — THE PITFALLS

Because media are usually very receptive to what nonprofits offer, it's easy for nonprofits to get too comfortable in the relationship. Here are the common pitfalls.

Lack of judgment.

There are marketable stories and there are dogs. Public relations staff have to make a judgment call. If they send releases or pitch story ideas about the dogs too often, they'll lose their credibility with the media. There were some editors who stopped opening envelopes from a certain public relations representative at a university. She sent too many press releases of no interest to the media.

This can be avoided. Target distribution of press releases. A release might be only of interest to the music or the lifestyle editor. Also, put yourself in the shoes of the editors. They have a boss to answer to and readers to keep interested. If you were in their shoes, would you publish this item?

Lack of exclusive packaging.

To attract an editor, you usually need to find an angle on a story you'll give only to that editor. Therefore, if you are approaching four editors, you need four angles.

A Midwest city had two daily newspapers. Both had a drama section on Friday. Unfortunately, the media representative for a drama group gave the same angle to both editors. On Friday, the two stories looked similar and both editors and their bosses were furious. You simply have to be creative about different ways you can position stories.

Doing the homework.

Resources are limited in nonprofits. Therefore some staff might think they can get away with not doing the appropriate background research. That can irritate the media. They are too busy to do your research.

Ideally, the information given to media should be complete but concise. That might mean summarizing a report or describing the matter in laymen's terms. For example, describe the medical procedure in terms of an analogy.

Overpromising.

If you tell the media you will make available the president of your organization, they expect the president. They don't want the assistant vice president. If you project that 1,000 people will attend the free blood-pressure screening at the mall, that's what the media expects. When the reality doesn't measure up to these expectations, your credibility is damaged.

MEDIA — SPECIAL STATUS OF NONPROFITS

Along with a tax exemption, there are other privileges that come with the special status of being a nonprofit. For instance, nonprofits can issue public-service announcements (PSAs). Those could add up to a tremendous amount of free publicity.

Because they are PSAs, they should be designed to serve the public interest. Ask yourself: How will the open house at the college benefit the public? Your PSA should indicate that the education available at your college could help the public become more marketable, change careers, or upgrade current skills.

When creating PSAs, the requirements must be met precisely. A 17-second spot is of no use to the station if it operates in terms of 15-second spots. If the station wants a certain kind of slide, you have to meet those specifications.

Another luxury of being a nonprofit is that your bylined op-eds and articles are more likely to be picked up and published. You have an advantage over the private sector for getting into print. Unfortunately, not enough nonprofits take advantage of this option. (Please refer to the chapter on op-eds.) You may find that an op-ed in your local paper on why pets should be neutered or spayed will have tremendous impact. If you are a national organization, you would put that op-ed in a national newspaper. After the op-ed appears, you could ask the newspaper for reprint rights and distribute the piece.

PUBLIC SPEAKING — IT'S EXPECTED

The community *expects* those from nonprofit organizations to be on the speaking circuit. For example, psychiatrists associated with hospitals go into the community and talk about certain types of mental illness. Hospitals also invite the public in for lectures.

That informational lecture is one type of oral presentation that nonprofits make. There are two other kinds.

One is the public-policy speech. In it, the organization is presenting its position on an issue. For example, a representative from the AARP might argue why a certain tax will hurt senior citizens. The president of a college might discuss why there must be tax deductions for college tuition. A physicians' association might present a talk on how managed care should be reformed.

The third type of presentation nonprofits make is a request for donations. Those donations could be in the form of money or volunteer activities.

Some presentations might cover a number of functions — for example, both provide information and ask for funds.

Unlike business speeches, presentations by those in nonprofit usually don't have to be "entertaining." They may contain a certain polished wit when they are delivered at posh fund-raisers. Or the speaker might enjoy using humor. But in general, a nonprofit speech can be pretty direct and focused on the subject matter. The audience is there because the subject matter is of vital interest to them. Maybe they have a son who is suffering from manic depression or a husband who needs a support group for the unemployed.

Many nonprofit organizations have found it useful to create or revitalize a Speakers' Bureau. One great advantage of a Speakers' Bureau is that it can be operated on a shoestring.

All you need are a script for the speech; visuals, if appropriate; a background paper; volunteers who are willing to speak; and two press releases — one informing the public that speakers are available and one announcing a specific speaking engagement.

The script should be no longer than about 20 minutes. The topic you're discussing is usually a weighty matter, and audiences probably can't handle more than 20 minutes of that kind of material.

The speech must cover all the basic points. For example, a clinical social worker talking on depression should define the term, explain causes, symptoms, and treatments. If the audience is made up of the families of the mentally ill, then it would be useful if the speaker also covers how families are impacted by mental illness. A talk on tax deductions for college tuition must cover why such a deduction doesn't exist today; why one is needed; how such as deduction would be structured; its impact on society in general and what groups might be hurt by the deduction; and what the audience can do to help that deduction become a reality. (Please see the chapter in speechwriting for more detail on preparing for a speech.)

It's useful to "test market" the script. Before you address an audience of 1,000 prominent senior citizens, it'd be wise to try out the script with smaller, less important audiences. Often a script that sounds good when it's being created is too slow-moving and boring when delivered.

Also useful is to have the speech reviewed by your key constituencies. Is there something in the speech that could be misunderstood?

Visuals aren't mandatory. There have been excellent presentations in which no visuals were used. The purpose of visuals is to elucidate and reinforce what's said in the text. The purpose is not to be something the speaker can "hide behind." When that's the case, it's obvious to the audience. If visuals are used they should be of high quality. If you can't afford high quality, then don't have any visuals, or ask someone to donate the funds to have them done professionally.

Having a background paper helps the speaker feel prepared and in control. That paper will contain general information about the topic and questions the audience might ask. The answers should be provided. Again, it would be wise to have this material reviewed by the key constituencies.

Getting employees in your organization and volunteers to speak may not be all that difficult. As Stuart Levine and Michael Crom point out in *The Leader in You*, people want to be feel included in what's going on. Asking them to join will most likely make them feel important.[12] If you position the Speakers' Bureau as an significant outreach activity, people will want to participate. One consumer-products company in New York was under siege because of one of its products. Its employees were eager to join the Speakers' Bureau to explain the company's position on the product and set the record straight. This cause made them feel important. Some organizations provide special recognition for the speakers. There may be a dinner honoring them, awards, mention in the newsletter, and so on.

People will be more willing to join if they feel they are adequately prepared for this task. In addition to the backgrounder, you can suggest guides on public speaking such as Dale Carnegie's *The Quick and Easy Way to Effective Speaking*.[13] If your budget allows, you can provide training in public speaking.

When you do publicity for the Speakers' Bureau that is also an opportunity to deliver your message. The odds are good that your press release will be picked up. That's because the talks are a public service.

PARTNERSHIP

Given the pressures and complexities of the global marketplace, businesses are finding it necessary to join up with partners. Joint ventures, acquisitions, and mergers have become commonplace. From these strategic alliances, business gains access to resources it doesn't have. Partnerships can also save time and money.

Not surprisingly nonprofits are following the example of the business world. They are finding partners among both other nonprofits and among those in the profit sector.

One such partnership is between Colorado's Women's Employment and Education (CWEE) and Dayton Hudson Foundation and U S WEST, the telecommunications company. The organization's mission is to get single parents off welfare and into the work world. The private sector provided funds and actual job openings. So far, 2,000 women have gone to work.

Also open to nonprofits in partnership are all the strategies that for-profits are using in the marketing mix. One of the most effective is special events.

As the marketplace and media become more fragmented, it's getting harder to run mass-market ads that will be seen by all your target groups. In response, companies are taking some of the money they used to put into advertising and are putting it into special events.

The marvel of special events is that they can be custom-made for any target audience. A bank in Jersey City, New Jersey, wants to attract accounts from the residents who have emigrated from India. They can join forces with an Indian clothing store and all the local Indian grocery stores. They jointly put together an Indian festival in the bank's lobby after business hours. There will be sweepstakes and gifts to take home. Key members of the bank can host the event. Their partners in this venture introduce them to the right people.

The human imagination is the only limit on what you can do in special events. As long as there is no conflict in ideology, you can pair up with just about any partners, local or national. You can invite the media—and celebrities.

For example, if your college is scheduling an open house, you can package that as a special event called "2010." Your partners can be computer or athletic-shoe companies. There can be lectures and demonstrations on cyberspace; experts on the future predicting what will happen; and a movie about jobs in 2010.

Partnerships can also be used in lobbying. During the 1970s, the petroleum companies were under siege. They were being accused of everything from manipulating the supply of petroleum to making excessive profits. To tell their story they formed coalitions with those with similar interests. There were third-party endorsements of their positions.

If you're a woman's college in Pennsylvania, your message would probably get more attention if you joined with other women's colleges. If you are involved in animal protection, you'd have more clout in your city and state if you joined forces with other organizations and individuals involved with animal issues.

Of course, working together is often more difficult than working alone. However, there is now a wealth of literature on how to operate in a partnership or joint venture.[14]

Volunteers and Public Relations

Your volunteers are your most powerful public relations tool. That's because, if they feel truly a part of the cause, they will deliver your message in their community by word of mouth. Word of mouth is the best kind of endorsement your mission could get.

To tap into this resource, it's useful to provide public relations training to the volunteers. The volunteers must understand what your message is, what it isn't, and how it can be misunderstood. They must learn how to answer critics.

Volunteers are most useful for outreach into niches, such as the ethnic groups in the neighborhood, those on welfare, the elderly, the young adults, and the political leaders. In "Marketing in an Age of Diversity," Regis McKenna warns that "Managers should wake up every morning uncertain about the marketplace, because it is invariably changing."[15] So should public relations representatives in nonprofit organizations. Both your client and donor base may be changing. Volunteers can brief you on those changes and how to best tailor your message.

Volunteers are also a key resource in networking. They may know the editor of the lifestyle column better than you do. They could introduce you to the chief executive officer of the largest firm in your city. They may be related to the anchor on the six o'clock news.

The best public relations an organization can do is to recognize the accomplishments of the volunteers. Award ceremonies, press releases, newsletter articles are all ways to assure that the volunteers know they've made a difference.

OPPORTUNITY

Nonprofits are ideally positioned for getting their message out — effectively and cost-efficiently. The media are usually in your corner. If you lack resources, you can join with partners who do have what you need. And your volunteers can become your most credible goodwill ambassadors.

NOTES

1. Peter F. Drucker, "What the Nonprofits Are Teaching Business," *Managing the Future* (New York: Truman Talley Books, 1992), 203-216.

2. Drucker, 203-216.

3. Ronaleen Roha, "Charities and Banks Love Affinity Cards," *Kiplinger's Personal Finance Magazine* 45 (November 1991): 102.

4. Eric Schurenberg and Lani Luciano, "The Empire Called AARP," *Money* 17 (October 1988): 128-141.

5. Rosabeth Moss Kanter, *When Giants Learn to Dance* (New York: Simon and Schuster, 1989), 55-226.

6. Donna Fenn, "The New, Dog-Eat-Dog Nonprofit," *INC.* 17 (July 1995): 45-50.

7. Fenn, 45-50.

8. Scott Thomas, "Nonprofits Struggle to Do More with Less," *Business First of Buffalo* 11 (August 28, 1995): 1-2.

9. Andrew Osterland, "War among the Nonprofits," *Financial World* 163 (September 1, 1994): 52-54.

10. Scott Cutlip, Allen Center, and Glen Broom, *Effective Public Relations* (New Jersey: Prentice Hall), 497.

11. Osterland, 52-54.

12. Stuart Levine and Michael Crom, *The Leader in You* (New York: Simon & Schuster, 1993), 45-57.

13. Dale Carnegie, *The Quick and Easy Way to Effective Speaking* (Garden City, New York: Dale Carnegie & Associates, 1962), passim.

14. Kenichi Ohmae, "The Global Logic of Strategic Alliances," *Harvard Business Review* (March-April 1989): 153-154.

15. Regis McKenna, "Marketing in an Age of Diversity," *Harvard Business Review* (September-October 1988): 91.

SUGGESTED READING

Forsyth, Donelson. *Group Dynamics*. Pacific Grove, California: Brooks/Cole Publishing Company, 1990.

Kotler, Philip and Alan Andreasen. *Strategic Marketing for Nonprofit Organizations*. Englewood Cliffs, New Jersey: Prentice Hall, 1987.

Kotler, Philip and Eduardo Roberto. *Social Marketing: Strategies for Changing Public Behavior*. New York: Free Press, 1990.

O'Neill, Tip. *All Politics Is Local*. Holbrook, Massachusetts: Bob Adams, 1994.

Maloney, Stephen. *Talk Tour Way to the Top*. Englewood Cliffs, New Jersey: Prentice Hall, 1992.

Ries, Al and Jack Trout. *Bottom-Up Marketing*. New York: Penguin Group, 1990.

Ries, Al and Jack Trout. *Positioning*. New York: McGraw-Hill, 1981.

Susan L. Hullin is a principal with The Dilenschneider Group. She previously served as executive vice president of Porter/Novelli, which she joined in 1990. In that capacity she supervised client programs in North America and Europe for a leading personal care company and the Ministry of Tourism of a prestigious destination island. Hullin was affiliated with Hill and Knowlton from 1983 to 1990. She has extensive experience in the development and management of public relations/public affairs programs for corporate and association clients, and a variety of consumer marketing programs including new product introductions, product promotions, product recalls, and product repositioning. She has also handled crisis communications for the leading baby food company, a major food service corporation, the Chilean fruit industry, and for the dairy industry during outbreaks of salmonella and listeriosis-related fatalities and heptachlor contamination.

Matthew M. Swetonic is a principal with The Dilenschneider Group. He has more than 25 years of experience in developing and managing environmental, occupational safety and health, and related public relations/public affairs strategies and programs for major American corporations and trade associations. He previously was senior vice president and director of environmental operations for the E. Bruce Harrison Company, where he was directly involved in managing and implementing client programs involving issues such as advertising and First Amendment rights; crisis planning and training; "green" marketing; health hazards of electromagnetic fields; household hazardous waste; indoor air quality; new product packaging; ozone depletion solutions; and product recalls. Swetonic was affiliated with Hill and Knowlton from 1973 to 1991.

James Wieghart serves as a senior consultant to The Dilenschneider Group. Wieghart has had a long and distinguished career in journalism, journalism training, and government service. He is former editor and the Washington bureau chief of the New York Daily News. *In addition to his services with The Dilenschneider Group, Wieghart teaches journalism at Central Michigan University in Mount Pleasant. In 1987, Wieghart was appointed public information officer for the Iran/Contra Independent Counsel, and he continued as a consultant to the investigation. Prior to that, Wieghart was a national political correspondent and a syndicated columnist for Scripps Howard Newspapers and was named staff director for Senator Edward Kennedy in 1986. He was also Pentagon correspondent for the* Daily News *and covered national security affairs, politics, and the Watergate scandal.*

CHAPTER 14

PUBLIC AFFAIRS AND GOVERNMENT RELATIONS: ENVIRONMENTAL AND OCCUPATIONAL HEALTH ISSUES

Over the past 30 years, the government relations and public affairs components of public relations have grown considerably in both size and in scope of activity. The growth began in the 1960s, largely as part of a defensive posture in response to increased pressure for stiffer regulations of business and industry from a wide variety of special interest groups. Much of the pressure concerned environmental protection and occupational health issues.

Spurred by affluence and the virtually unlimited expectations generated by President Johnson's "Great Society" dream, activists of all stripes descended on government with demands to perfect society without regard to cost.

The response of government on all levels, particularly the federal government, was to enlarge and take on new responsibilities for societal well-being. The movement saw its efforts codified in the early 1970s when President Richard Nixon signed into law bills establishing the Environmental Protection Agency (EPA), the Occupational Safety and Health Administration (OSHA), and the Consumer Product Safety Commission (CPSC).

The American business community expanded its government relations and public affairs activities in an effort to stem the tide of regulation, but its initial approach was too defensive, and, as a result, it was generally unsuccessful. Other public policy initiatives followed, and the long legacy of cooperation between business and industry and the government began to erode.

By the mid-1970s, some leading business and industrial leaders began to call for deregulation, contending that the impact of overregulation in terms of cost, legal challenges, additional paperwork, delays in bringing products to market, constructing new facilities, and other impediments to normal business was putting American business and industry at a competitive disadvantage in the increasingly competitive global economy. Business and industry took a more aggressive stance, not only in opposition to further government regulation, but in demanding deregulation.

And, in an important reversal, there was, for the first time, a positive response to these demands from the public at large and, later, from some in the mass media. The public reaction against intrusive government and excessive regulation was generated by the argument that the higher costs and reduced productivity due to overregulation were reflected in stagnant wages, lost jobs, plant closings, and the movement of investment capital and production facilities to cheaper, offshore locations.

By seizing and dramatizing the *issues* related to government overregulation, business and industry were able to begin reversing the trend, first gingerly during the Carter Administration and, later, more aggressively under the Reagan and Bush Administrations.

Indeed, in large measure the public reaction against excessive government regulation in the marketplace was a major factor in the 1994 electoral revolution that saw Republicans, who were running on anti-government issues, win control of both Houses and make impressive gains in state legislatures and governorships across the country.

This dramatic turnaround was essentially *issue based* and, as a result, issues such as environmental standards, product liability, consumer protection, tax policy, and energy resources were placed higher on the national agenda and will from now on play a central role in policy and planning considerations in corporate boardrooms across America. Although the governmental decisions on these issues will continue to be made in Washington and in the 50 state capital cities, the politicians will pay close attention to public opinion before deciding which way to vote.

PUBLIC AFFAIRS AND THE POLICY-MAKING PROCESS

The message of the 1980s and 1990s is quite clear: Those who would change U.S. domestic, economic, trade, or foreign policies should take their cases directly to the people. In this country, the real power on these issues resides with the people, if they are informed and aroused. In order to affect major policy change, the public must be convinced. Without consensus, the president and Congress cannot endorse great change.

Americans as well as foreigners tend to lose sight of the fact that much of American policy simply mirrors public opinion. There is nothing more frustrating to a lobbyist after making a convincing argument on an issue, than to hear a congressman say, "You have all the right arguments, but if I go with you, my constituents will send me home."

The American system of media-fired public opinion and policy-making can be summarized simply: To move our government, get to the people; to get to the people, get to the press. The media moves the message to the people. The people move the government. Then, and only then, the policy shifts. That's when America moves.

The debate and vote over the North American Free Trade Agreement (NAFTA) in 1994 were a case in point. There was powerful opposition to the agreement from organized labor and blue collar workers in the Northeast, Midwest, and Upper Great Lakes regions, who blamed industrial plant closings on unrestricted foreign imports.

They were joined by an unlikely coalition of environmentalists and self-styled populists led by Texas billionaire Ross Perot and agricultural interests in the South, particularly Florida and Texas, who feared an influx of cheaper Mexican produce.

Despite this formidable opposition, which included much of the Democratic congressional leadership, President Bill Clinton was able to win Senate ratification of the agreement. He was able to do so by joining with corporate America, which strongly supported NAFTA, and taking the case to media and to the American public. Not only did Clinton and the business community utilize the traditional news media, but non-traditional media, such as radio and television talk shows, were used as well. The highlight of the bitter fight was a televised debate between Vice President Albert Gore and Perot on the "Larry King Show." Gore won hands down. An important factor in the struggle for ratification was overwhelming editorial support for NAFTA.

In addition to the extensive use of free media, both sides waged extensive (and very expensive) paid media campaigns, as Victor S. Kamber noted in an excellent analysis of the NAFTA battle in the *Public Relations Quarterly* (Winter 1993-94). The advertising budget of USA*NAFTA, the business-backed pro-NAFTA support group, was estimated at from $5 million to $8 million. On the other side, the AFL-CIO spent about $3 million for ads. Perot's advertising buys were estimated at from $1.5 to $2 million for 30-minute infomercials airing in 25 markets across the country.[1]

Kamber, president of the Washington-based Kamber Group, Inc., said that both sides, but especially organized labor, also waged substantial grassroots campaigns as well. The unions mailed hundreds of thousands of pieces of direct mail to their members, established phone banks, and activated their already energized memberships in a way that hadn't happened in years. The union groups also strengthened their ties with others on the anti-NAFTA side — environmental, immigrant, religious, farm, and civil rights groups.[2]

The White House and business groups were unable to match labor's intensive grassroots effort, but the corporate community did make unprecedented efforts at getting their management and non-union employees to weigh in on the pro-NAFTA side.

The message of the NAFTA battle is that the keys to governmental relations that gets results are issue focus and the ability to affect governmental policy by influencing public opinion and public attitudes.

In the decade ahead, the role of public relations will be to advise top management on how corporate decisions will fare in the social and political milieu of the outside world and how such decisions will be accepted by the public and the government. Public relations outside the Washington Beltway will also increasingly reflect this kind of issue-oriented approach.

THE ROLE OF THE MEDIA

It goes without saying that the mass media—broadcast and print—have immense impact on public opinion. As can be seen from the uneven record that editorial endorsements have on election results, the media are clearly not always successful in telling people what to think. But the media are stunningly successful in telling people what to think about, that is, in setting the agenda for what issues are important.

The print media—newspapers, news magazines, and opinion journals—are overshadowed by the reach and power of television in terms of influencing the public. But for a number of reasons, the print media are most important when it comes to setting the public policy agenda. To begin with, the print media can provide more issue-oriented news and can cover issues in much more depth than can the broadcast media. And virtually all of the more than 1,600 daily newspapers and more than 7,400 weeklies carry columns and editorials commenting on and taking positions on the key issues of the day—local, state, national, and international.

The news magazines also carry opinion columns on public policy issues as well and the opinion journals like the *New Republic*, the *National Review*, *Commonwealth*, *The Progressive*, the *Nation*, and others focus almost exclusively on issues.

Three newspapers in particular—*The New York Times, The Wall Street Journal* and the *Washington Post*—are especially important in agenda setting because of their highly respected, thorough coverage of national and international issues and because they are published in the nation's two most important news centers, New York City and Washington. It's no secret that the news judgments of these three newspapers are watched closely by and often influence the editors of other major newspapers across the country. The same is true of the producers and news directors of the three major network television news shows, all headquartered in New York, and CNN, based in Atlanta but with a very large and influential presence in Washington. Two of the three major news magazines, *Time* and *Newsweek*, are also headquartered in New York. *U.S. News & World Report*'s home base is in Washington.

The broadcast media, particularly television, are especially influential in affecting public opinion. Television has become ubiquitous in America. Virtually every American household has at least one TV set, and well over half the households have two or more sets. More than 60 percent of American households have cable and more than 70 percent have VCRs.[3]

When it comes to reaching and moving the American people, nothing can match television. Media critic Jeff Greenfield noted:

> Cutting through geographic, ethnic, class, and cultural diversity, it is the single binding thread of this country, the one experience that touches the young

and old, rich and poor, learned and illiterate. A country too big for homogeneity, filled by people from all
over the globe, without any set of core values,
America never had a central unifying bond. Now we
do. Now it is possible to answer the question, "What
does America do?" We watch television.[4]

Increasingly, while critics may complain that TV news is "sound
bite" journalism, Americans rely on television for their primary source
of news, even though most still continue to read at least one newspaper
and a news magazine for more in-depth coverage.[5] However, the old
fear that the growing reliance of Americans on television news was
placing too much power in the hands of the three major networks —
NBC, CBS, and ABC — has been eased by the growth of cable TV and
the creation of competing networks, beginning with Fox. In addition,
Cable News Network and cable superstations, such as WGN and
WTBS, and pay-for-view cable have combined to fragment viewership
considerably, thus weakening network power. For example, in the early
1970s, more than 90 percent of the national television audience was
tuned into one of the three major networks during evening prime time
hours. By 1993, the combined audience for the three major networks
during prime time had eroded to 60 percent, largely as a result of competition from cable TV, VCRs, and pay-for-view TV.[6]

With its immediacy and its combination of sound and images,
television is clearly the most powerful and influential mass medium.
And despite the fragmentation of audience, network television — NBC,
ABC, CBS, and CNN — can still reach the largest national audiences
with news and public affairs programming and that is likely to continue
for the foreseeable future. This may change dramatically with the mar-
riage of the personal computer to the television, creating interactive
cable television, which will give consumers the ability in their homes
to shop, bank, and even vote and communicate their views directly to
their representatives. Interactive cable will some day soon make it possible for a print-out of tens of thousands of constituent opinions on a
particular issue to be on a lawmaker's desk within a day of a crucial
vote or decision.

Those who wish to influence the American policy-making
process, if they are to be effective, must keep up with the new communications technology and learn to understand it and use it. In the future,
Americans will have the capacity to get the story and get it right from a
wide variety of sources.

THE WASHINGTON NEWS CORPS

The nerve center for this vast national media network is the
Washington news corps, the world's largest and most influential, and
its primary role is to disseminate news and information on the issues

being considered and acted upon by the Congress, the president, and the administration he heads, and the vast federal bureaucracy, the permanent government.

There are relatively few glamour figures among the Washington news corps, but collectively they have unique access to the process of government and its players.

Most Washington news people are experienced, dedicated professionals who have to develop great flexibility to handle the wide variety of stories that come out of Washington each day. They are in Washington by choice and most of them want to finish out their careers there. Washington is a highly competitive arena for news professionals and most welcome pertinent input from public relations people. Whether in initiating a news story with fresh information and ideas or rounding out an in-progress piece, reporters often depend at least partly on public relations persons to help flesh out or update their story. As a result, public relations professionals with reputations for honesty and reliability enjoy relatively easy access to reporters and editors, both print and broadcast.

The exact number of full-time press in Washington is uncertain, but it probably exceeds 7,000. There are 2,100 newspaper reporters accredited to the House and Senate Press Galleries; 1,773 correspondents accredited to the House and Senate Periodical Press Gallery; and 2,500 broadcast newspersons accredited to the Radio and Television Gallery. Some 3,000 electronic and print journalists are also accredited to the White House press corps, but many of them also are accredited to the House and Senate Galleries.

These figures do not include hundreds of freelance writers and reporters who make their living in Washington, nor the continuous influx of foreign press and reporters from all parts of the country who come to Washington to cover a major story that has a special impact on their home audiences.

In addition to this group, there are more than 1,500 reporters, editors, photographers, and others who make up the news and editorial staffs of the two Washington daily newspapers, the *Post* and the *Times*, plus the staffs of other Washington-based publications like *U.S. News, Broadcasting Magazine*, Bureau of National Affairs publications, *Science Service, Congressional Quarterly*, and other research publications, such as *Editorial Research Reports* and the *National Journal*.

Include also the staffs of the local radio and television stations, the ring of suburban papers in Maryland and Virginia and probably several hundreds of reporters, writers, and researchers who work for the many newsletters, business, industry, and special-interest group information services, and the military and governmental research publications that have proliferated in the nation's capital in recent years.

This represents the vast and diversified mix of Washington journalism for the public relations professional to know, cultivate and deal with.

WASHINGTON BUREAUS

The press corps in Washington operate out of news bureaus varying in size from one, representing a newspaper from a medium size city, to more than 100, representing the major American news services, the Associated Press, and United Press International. Foreign News Services, such as Agence France-Presse, Kyodo, Reuters, and Tass, also maintain sizable bureaus. Typical large bureaus maintained by newspaper chains and large out-of-town newspapers include *Chicago Tribune*, Copley News Service, Gannett and its flagship paper *USA Today*, Hearst Newspapers, Knight-Ridder Newspapers, *Los Angeles Times*, Newhouse News Service, *The New York Times*, Scripps Howard Newspapers, States News Service, *The Wall Street Journal*, and scores of others.

Among periodicals, large bureaus are maintained by BNA Publications, FDC Reports, McGraw Hill, *National Journal*, *Newsweek*, *Time*, and *U.S. News & World Report*.

A very large number of newspaper and periodical bureaus are often manned by only one, two, or three persons, some of whom are actual staff members of the news organization, but others are independent contractors acting as special correspondents. These special correspondents frequently represent a specific area of industry interest, such as cotton, tobacco, oil, timber, or textiles. They are often good outlets for public relations practitioners because they are often overworked and like to be helped with information or worthwhile story ideas.

The *Washington Post* and, to a lesser extent, the *Washington Times* are important outlets for political governmental and issues news. They also provide the broadest collection of national columns published in any city in America. Both papers, again, particularly the *Post*, are read closely by Washington insiders, including elected officials and members of the press corps, so exposure in them is highly desirable in terms of gaining significant impact with a most powerful and influential audience.

WORKING WITH WASHINGTON MEDIA

The most important difference between media relations in Washington and elsewhere is that the vast majority of print and electronic journalists in Washington are not local and represent news outlets whose audiences are elsewhere as well. This represents both a great challenge and a great opportunity for public relations practitioners. Since the press focus will necessarily be national and international in scope, rather than local or regional, this means your message generally needs to be tied to a national or international issue to get widespread usage. The upside to this, however, is that if you are seeking a national or international audience, you could not find a better place to operate from.

But even if you are seeking to impact a local or regional audience, you can usually do so in Washington because news outlets from every part of the country — even the world — are present. These local and regional news organizations can also be used from Washington to place news and information in the local and regional outlets in order to get your message to specific members of the House or Senate who represent those areas.

Despite its diversity and relative sophistication, the Washington news corps is generally more accessible to public relations practitioners than press outside the Washington Beltway. In part, that's because journalists in Washington are often responsible for covering such a wide variety of issues that they welcome information, guidance, and story ideas to help fill in gaps in their knowledge. But what reporters are interested in are facts, background, information, and story ideas, not argumentation and ideology. To get your message across to reporters and editors, traditional media relations methods can be used, such as press releases, press conferences, meetings with editorial boards of key newspapers, personal phone calls to media contacts, or breakfast or lunch meetings with influential reporters.

But whether you use these or other methods to get your message across, here is some guidance:

1. One-on-one meetings with press contacts are the most effective way to get a message across and it often helps to go prepared with a brief fact sheet that you can leave behind after the meeting.
2. Providing experts, CEOs, or recognized spokespersons for interviews on a key issue is an excellent means of getting coverage.
3. Press releases, mailed or faxed, while marginally useful, often get thrown aside unread by most reporters who are too busy to read the mountains of such materials they receive each day. If you use the press release, follow it up by a personal phone call to ask if it was received and to offer additional guidance.
4. Press conferences, demonstrations, and formal presentations can be effective, but should be restricted to only the most important and newsworthy announcements or pronouncements. There are literally dozens of press conferences in Washington each day, often covering front-burner issues, and you will be competing with them for attention.

Avoid the excruciating embarrassment of calling a press conference that fails to draw press. When scheduling a press conference, be sure to have it listed on the Associated Press and UPI day book of events.

LOBBYING: ACCESS, PREPARATION, AND HARD WORK

Since actions and decisions of the federal government impact every aspect of our society and, in many cases, the world, it is not surprising that virtually every institution, business, industry, trade and cultural association is represented in Washington to protect their interests. The list is almost endless and includes business, industry, farm organizations, church groups, educators, labor unions, professional associations, trade associations, nonprofit organizations, consumer groups, environmental organizations, state and local governments, foreign governments, and many more.

All of them are there to monitor government and protect and advance the interests of groups they represent — to influence government, to stay abreast, or ahead of proposed legislation or regulation, trends and developments that can threaten the survival or ensure the success of their organizations.

And for good reason. The General Accounting Office estimates that business is regulated by 116 government agencies and programs. Business and industry are especially well represented, with government relations offices for more than 500 U.S. companies and 3,000 trade associations present.

The principal targets of their attention are Congress, the House of Representatives with 435 members, the Senate with 100 members, and the hundreds of key congressional staff members who work for the members or the committees of both houses; the 13 cabinet departments of the federal government; and the dozens of regulatory agencies established by Congress to monitor and police just about every commercial and social activity imaginable, from business and industry, communications and transportation, commerce and trade, occupational health and safety, the environment, and many more.

Both Houses of Congress divide their legislative and oversight workload by committees and often the most important thing you will need to know about a member of Congress is what his or her committee assignments are. The Senate has 16 permanent committees with a total of 69 subcommittees, and four select committees. The House has 19 permanent committees with a total of 86 subcommittees, and one select committee. Together, the two Houses have four joint committees. (See Exhibit 14.1.)

It is in these committees where the most significant work of Congress is done, and the committees cover every aspect of governmental activity, from agriculture to small business and from appropriations and budgeting to foreign affairs, energy, and the environment.

EXHIBIT 14.1—STANDING COMMITTEES OF THE CONGRESS

House Committee	Room[1]
Agriculture	1301
Appropriations	H218
Banking and Financial Services	2129
Budget	309
Commerce	2125
Economic and Educational Opportunities	2128
Government Reform and Oversight	2157
House Oversight	1309
Standards:	
Majority	1307
Minority	1339
International Relations	2170
Judiciary	2138
Publications	B29
National Security	2120
Resources	1324
Judiciary	SD-224
Rules	H312
Minority	234
Science	2320
Small Business	2361
Standards of Official Conduct	HT2
Office of Advice and Education	HT2
Transportation and Infrastructure	2165
Veterans' Affairs	335
Ways and Means	11

Senate Committee	Room[2]
Agriculture, Nutrition, and Forestry	SR-328
Appropriations	S-128
Armed Services	SR-228
Banking, Housing, and Urban Affairs	SD-534
Budget	SD-621
Commerce, Science, and Transportation	SD-508
Energy and Natural Resources	SD-364
Environment and Public Works	SD-458
Finance	SD-217
Foreign Relations	SD-450
Governmental Affairs	SD-340
Judiciary	SD-224
Labor and Human Resources	SD-428
Rules and Administration	SR-305
Small Business	SR-428A
Veterans' Affairs	SR-414

[1] Room numbers with three digits are in the Cannon House Office Building, four digits beginning with 1 are in the Longworth House Office Building, and four digits beginning with 2 are in the Rayburn House Office Building.

[2] Room numbers preceded by S are in the main Capitol building; those preceded by SD are in the Dirksen Office Building; and those preceded by SR are in the Russell Office Building.

No one governmental relations practitioner nor even the largest firms that specialize in governmental relations can hope to be expert on all of the members of Congress, the committees and subcommittees, and their hundreds of key staff members. But there are excellent sources that can help you at least get a start, beginning with the various *Yellow Book* directories, which list all of the members, committee and subcommittees and their members, and key staffers. The *Congressional Directory*, published by the Government Printing Office, and the *Congressional Staff Directory*, are also reliable sources of valuable information.

Because Congress passes the laws and has oversight over their implementation, members of Congress, their staffs, and the committees on which they serve, along with the committee staffs are by far the most frequent objects of lobbying by these various special interest groups. Access to appropriate contacts on Capitol Hill — or to administration departments and regulatory agencies as well — is not the big hurdle it might seem.

The give and take in the legislative and regulatory processes between various conflicting interests and groups require information from all sides of the issues and, at some level, your input will be welcomed.

The key is to approach at the appropriate level. Washington's best consultants know that calls will go unanswered:

- If issues are misdirected to a Cabinet officer or legislator when an assistant secretary or staff aide would have been more appropriate;
- If pleas are not backed by an understanding of the issue and its place on the political or economic agenda;
- If inaccuracies stand uncorrected;
- If competing claims are improperly presented or overstated; or
- If the lobbyist's clients are taken to a busy office just to show they can get access.

Combining expertise with access over the years creates a more credible voice.

Lobbyists cannot just yell "More" or "Now" or "Never" in the ears of influential and accessible friends and hope to succeed. They can, however, provide the best information in a reasoned context, match client needs to public interest, bring experience and expertise to the table. If a lobbyist does all of this, access will evolve slowly into something of real value: credibility. In short, a lobbyist is only as good as the credibility of the last presentation. Before approaching a member of Congress on an issue of vital importance to a client, do the necessary informational groundwork with the appropriate staffer first.

In initially opening that access door to a member of Congress, learn first which staff member is working on the bill or issue you are interested in. This can usually be accomplished with a simple telephone call to the member's office. Here are some tips for how to proceed after that:

- It is always best to make contact with the member or the appropriate staffer through a constituent.
- Learn which member represents the district in which your client's plant or corporation is located. Establish good rapport with the member or staffer.
- It is often easier to see a member of Congress in his or her district. Make plans to invite the member out to the plant or company for lunch with the staff when the member is in town. Or arrange for the plant manager to visit the member when he or she is in the district.
- When the client's company is a member of an association, use the association and its resources in your lobbying efforts. In describing how to best approach to lobbying a member of Congress, Robert Gray, perhaps one of the most successful governmental relations practitioners in recent times, had this advice:

> There is no magic concoction from which a lobbyist is brewed. Likewise, there is no one trait or skill that separates the effective lobbyist from the ineffective one.
>
> A knowledge of the legislative process certainly is essential. The rules under which the House and Senate operate govern the lobbyists' course of action. Plainly and simply, know Capitol Hill, its faces, which are many and always changing, its pace, which can be hectic, and its rules.
>
> A member of Congress survives by keeping one eye on a given issue and the other on the clock, so you have to know the limitations on a Member's time. Prepare your client's case carefully, target your Member, then, when you have been granted an audience, state your case intelligently and crisply. A tip: If it takes less than the time allotted, you will improve your chances for a quick appointment the next time you ask for one.[7]

A most important vehicle for getting your client's message out on a pending matter before Congress is to present testimony at a public hearing before the appropriate committee of Congress. A decision to testify should not be taken lightly. Before doing so, you need to check the various competing interests and work closely with the coalition of interests that support your client's position. Among the considerations are:

- Whether your client's testimony is needed or will it be redundant and unnecessary;
- Will your client's testimony provide important impetus to the issue or position you and your coalition allies are advancing; and finally,
- Will your client's testimony have a positive impact on his or her business and image.

Congressional hearings often provide a high visibility forum for advocating a position. Such hearings are normally well covered by the media and can afford wide public exposure. They also provide an opportunity to the advocate to speak directly to the most important audience of all, the committee that will ultimately decide the issue. If the decision is to testify, refer to the brief checklist (Exhibit 14.2) of things to do before your witness appears.

EXHIBIT 14.2 — BEFORE TESTIFYING

1. Monitor hearings of the committee involved. See which members show up and what kinds of questions are being asked. Identify your friends and your foes.

2. If possible, brief in advance staff members of your friends on the committee so they are prepared to support your presentation. Similarly, point out to the staff deficiencies in the anticipated testimony of those who oppose your position.

3. Prepare as concise an opening statement as you can. If you have detailed back-up material, have that submitted for inclusion to the hearing record.

4. Remember, committee members can interrupt at any time.

5. The person testifying is sitting in front of and below the committee. It is a lonesome place. Have in mind the value of two other representatives, maybe a technical authority and your counsel, as flankers. This is reassuring and often helpful. The witness should introduce these colleagues.

6. The fact that only two or three committee members appear does not indicate a lack of interest. Congress is a place where multiple demands are made of members' time. In any case, the staff members will be on hand, and they are the experts on your issues.

7. Keep in mind that when your witness takes the stand before the committee, there are four immediate audiences:

   - Committee members — those who aren't there will read the transcript.
   - Reporters, sitting at tables to the rear.
   - Committee staff, typically including lawyers, economists, and whatever other specialists the issue requires.
   - The client's associates, interested observers, and opponents.

Following the hearing, you should distribute your witness's statement to the offices of all committee members and other key congressional offices that may have an interest. Also have the copies of the statement placed in the House and Senate Press Galleries.

LEGISLATIVE ANALYSIS AND MONITORING

Skillful legislative monitoring and analysis provide one of the best methods for keeping an organization informed and up-to-date on any congressional actions — bills, hearings, investigations — that will affect its interests, either directly or peripherally.

Some organizations have one overriding interest, such as trade legislation, tax law changes, or environmental and health issues. Others have a number of less dramatic but continuing concerns that must be watched for when Congress is in session.

Those who work in Washington quickly acquire a specialized knowledge of the legislative process, and it is easy to forget that the rest of the nation generally has only a vague memory of high school civics to draw on when trying to understand how Congress works or what makes a bill become a law.

This means it is sometimes easy to impress people in another part of the country by tracking a recently introduced bill to its home in a committee or subcommittee or obtaining the names of additional cosponsors of a bill. This can be accomplished by simply monitoring the *Congressional Record* and the *Daily Digest* printed at the end of each day's copy.

But legislative analysis and monitoring are more complex than simply knowing where a bill is and who its sponsors are or simply attending hearings and reporting back on what took place. However, attending key hearings and knowing which hearings are key is an important part of the job.

Becoming adept in legislative analysis and monitoring means first knowing how the House and Senate function, which committees and subcommittees are concerned with what issues, and understanding the intricate system that causes several different committees to have a voice on the same issue. Committee titles are sometimes misleading, but tracking a bill accurately can be done by simply calling the committee and checking. The daily *Congressional Record* and the *Daily Digest* printed at the end of each issue is the best source for monitoring the daily activities of both houses of Congress and their committees and subcommittees. The *Congressional Record* carries a complete report of action on the floors of both houses, including the speeches, and the *Daily Digest* summarizes the day's action. At the end of the week, the *Daily Digest* carries a schedule for both houses and their committees for the upcoming week. The *Congressional Record* can be ordered from the Government Printing Office where it is published.

It is always useful to understand the concerns of the committee chairmen and committee members and the basics about their constituencies. Do they represent areas of high unemployment? Is acid rain or air pollution a major concern? Does a key member represent a district with aerospace industries so that defense contracts and the defense budget are of vital interest to that member? It is also necessary to establish good contacts with the staffs on the various House and Senate committees you will be working with.

This takes both time and energy, but it is often more important to develop working relationships with these staffers, who do much of the preparation and planning for hearings, than with the members themselves.

Finding and cultivating contacts among staff members can't be done with one phone call and it can't be done at all if the wrong approach is used. They will want to know, particularly if it is a first contact, why you want to know certain information and on who's behalf.

Generally, an open, straightforward answer will satisfy them. It's a mistake to respond with "I can't tell you" or "it's confidential." It's also a mistake to press for information and plans that are confidential or press for answers they're not yet prepared to give.

Once you have established a good working relationship with a staff member, don't become a nuisance by calling for information that can be found easily elsewhere. Capitol Hill staffers have demanding jobs and they work long hours.

Much of the information you will need can be obtained from public sources, such as the *Washington Post, The New York Times*, and the wire services. The *Congressional Quarterly*, the *Congressional Monitor*, or the *National Journal* are filled with very specific information on the status of legislation. The Associated Press and UPI provide daily calendars listing hearings, including witness lists, and scheduled press conferences.

It is also necessary to develop a good knowledge of the 13 cabinet-level departments of the executive branch and of regulatory agencies and how they work. The Cabinet officers and higher ranking executive department officials frequently testify at congressional hearings, providing information and agency positions on various issues. There are more than 50 such agencies, most of them independent, but some tied to various departments in the federal government and their responsibilities range from the stock market to the environment. The *United States Government Manual*, published yearly by the Govern-ment Printing Office, lists the departments and the regulatory agencies, describes their jurisdiction and contains the names of the heads and key personnel. The *Federal Yellow Book* is another excellent source of such information. The *United States Government Manual* is printed each year by the Government Printing Office and can be purchased at the following Government Printing Office Bookstores. (See Exhibit 14.3.)

EXHIBIT 14.3 — BOOKSTORES — GOVERNMENT PRINTING OFFICE

City	Address	Telephone
Washington, D.C. Area:		
Main Bookstore	710 N. Capitol St. NW	(202) 512-0132
McPherson Square	1510 H St. NW	(202) 653-5075
Retail Sales Outlet	8660 Cherry Lane, Laurel, MD	(301) 953-7974
Atlanta, GA	1st Union Plaza, 999 Peachtree St. NE	(404) 347-1900
Birmingham, AL	2021 3rd Ave. N.	(205) 731-1056
Boston, MA	Rm. 169, 10 Causeway St.	(617) 720-4180
Chicago, IL	Rm. 124, 401 S. State St.	(312) 353-5133
Cleveland, OH	Rm. 1653, 1240 E. 9th St.	(216) 522-4922
Columbus, OH	Rm. 207, 200 N. High St.	(614) 469-6956
Dallas, TX	Rm. 1C50, 1100 Commerce St.	(214) 767-0076
Denver, CO	Rm. 117, 1961 Stout St.	(303) 844-3964
Detroit, MI	Suite 160, 477 Michigan Ave.	(313) 226-7816
Houston, TX	801 Travis St.	(713) 228-1187
Jacksonville, FL	Rm. 100, W. Bay St.	(904) 353-0569
Kansas City, MO	120 Bannister Mall, 5600 E. Bannister Rd.	(816) 767-8225
Los Angeles, CA	C-Level, ARCO Plaza, 505 S. Flower St.	(213) 239-9844
Milwaukee, WI	Rm. 150, 310 W. Wisconsin Ave.	(414) 297-1304
New York, NY	Rm. 110, 26 Federal Plaza	(212) 264-3825
Philadelphia, PA	100 N. 17th St.	(215) 636-1900
Pittsburgh, PA	Rm. 118, 1000 Liberty Ave.	(412) 644-2721
Portland, OR	1305 SW 1st Ave.	(503) 221-6217
Pueblo, CO	Norwest Banks Bldg. 201 W. 8th Ave.	(719) 544-3142
San Francisco, CA	Marathon Plz., Rm 141-S, 303 2nd Ave.	(415) 512-2770
Seattle, WA	Rm. 194, 915 2nd Ave.	(206) 553-4271

An example of an independent agency is the Environmental Protection Agency, which was established to allow "coordinated and effective governmental action on behalf of the environment." The EPA's recommendations and actions can impinge on such areas as factories, autos, clean water, asbestos, pesticides, and herbicides, to name just a few. All of these issues have been matters for congressional hearings and concerns.

The Food and Drug Administration is an example of an important regulatory agency that is not independent, but is tied to the executive branch as part of the Department of Health and Human Services. FDA decisions affect such matters as pharmaceuticals, cosmetics, food additives, food labeling, artificial sweeteners, and others, all of which interlock with congressional interests.

The 13 federal departments are: Agriculture, Commerce, Defense, Education, Energy, Health and Human Services, Housing and Urban Development, Interior, Justice, Labor, State, Transportation, and Treasury. Their cabinet officers and high ranking officials often testify before congressional committees on various issues and concerns. In order to produce fully informed analyses, it is necessary to know the functions of these departments and the subsections. Their statutory powers and responsibilities are outlined in the *United States Government Manual*, along with a list of the major officials in each department.

Fortunately, it is generally easier to obtain information from government agencies than it is from Capitol Hill. It often takes several attempts to find the right person in the right department, but that is a by-product of the large staffs and their highly specialized functions. But once you find the right contact, the amount of information that becomes available is truly amazing. In attempting to analyze and track proposed legislation it is vitally important to learn what position the appropriate executive branch department or regulatory agency affected will take on the legislative proposal. Here again, having established contacts with the administrative departments and agencies will be important.

When writing a legislative analysis, it is best to avoid stating flatly that one thing or another will happen, because there will always be too many imponderables cropping up along the way. One should present the views of likely actions of the key players, and should detail any subsurface conflicts or interests that come up. Opinions should be accompanied by buttressing reasons and data as well as an alternative scenario, so as to cover the full range of possibilities. The analysis should also cover possible future courses of action that may be taken as a result of current congressional actions.

The major points for doing legislative analysis and monitoring are:
1. Be thoroughly familiar with the interests of your organization or client and any peripheral issues or actions that may affect them.

2. Know the steps a bill must go through before it can become a law.
3. Know who the chairman and members are for each committee dealing with matters that concern you. Know their constituencies and their interests.
4. Establish good relationships with committee and congressional staff members.
5. Attend all key hearings and news conferences affecting your interests.
6. Know the functions of the federal departments and regulatory agencies. Monitor their actions and positions.
7. Be prepared to write fast and well, against tight deadlines, to keep your organization or client informed.

PUBLIC AFFAIRS AND GOVERNMENT RELATIONS — AT THE STATE LEVEL

The movement to curb the growth the federal regulations since the Reagan–Bush years, has been accompanied by an effort to return power and responsibilities to the states to administer and reshape welfare, health services, and several other programs. This movement, modest though it has been, has been embraced and enlarged by a group of forceful, largely conservative Republican governors across the country.

Although devolution has not really transpired in any major way yet, it is clearly the wave of the future, and it portends a period of state-level activism that will require building government relations programs on a state level.

The move toward devolution has created an upsurge in state governmental activity and has already created a range and complexity of public policy issues. This growth has been fed by the emergence of public-interest advocate groups on the state level, which focus primarily on consumer and environmental issues and measures to restrict business and industry. his movement requires new and more active forms of business participation in the decision-making process. The question is, how does business get more involved before it gets left out?

The answer is that corporations are going to have to treat state government relations with the seriousness and planning devoted to their federal efforts. The "good old boy" network for lobbyists, which involves lunches, banquets, small favors, and remembrances, may never be entirely replaced.

But it needs to be supplemented with modern political techniques, such as state-of-the-art constituent targeting, coalition building, and a grassroots organizing campaign.

As public relations practitioners move to become more active on the state issues, they must consider a few important points:
1. The complexity of issues and the proliferation of individuals

addressing them complicate the job of legislative liaison. Every lobbyist must develop a procedure to gather and process information as well as the ability to use the tools of technology to supplement personal contact and instincts.

2. Planning has assumed a greater importance. The effectiveness of a public affairs campaign is closely associated with the ability of the company or group to gather solid intelligence and set priorities. Success requires preparation, judgment, and the ability to assess and draw on the resources available.

In every public affairs effort, the following should be included:

1. A strategic plan, managed by a central coordinator, but with the approval of senior operating management.
2. A legislative support system that includes a media relations plan and a grassroots organizing plan.
3. Supporting materials — position papers, research documents, third-party documents — and other important information.

A broad-based public relations approach is often the only effective remedy in a crisis growing out of the public's perception that a business or industry has created a serious public problem. Experience shows that it makes little difference in the long run whether the situation grew out of a public interest group's advocacy campaign or arose from a legislative hearing. In such cases, the remedy requires the speedy and effective assembly and distribution of correct information to the public and legislature.

HEALTH, SAFETY, AND ENVIRONMENTAL ISSUES

While there are several dozen issues that are of major concern to business and industry, as well as to government regulators, public-interest groups, and the American public, probably the most difficult and pressing issues concern health, safety, and the environment.

The passage of far-reaching federal and state legislation and of local laws regulating air and water pollution, toxic waste disposal, noise, land use, and hazardous substances has had an enormous impact on the activities of business and industry. Few, if any, major decisions regarding plant operations are made by top management today without serious reflection as to how those decisions might impact the environment. In fact, for major projects, environmental impact studies are now required in most jurisdictions before projects are officially approved.

The issues of public health and safety are also of vital national public interest and in many respects troublesome to business and industry. Regulations by the FDA, the Occupational Safety and Health Administration (OSHA) and other agencies often lay out detailed reporting requirements for the chemical, pharmaceutical, oil and mineral, agricultural, food processing, power, transportation, and many other industries and businesses. Compounding these problems is the proliferation of class-action suits seeking judgments of millions and even billions of dollars.

One need not be an expert in public relations to know the dimensions of the problems in these areas and the enormous stakes involved for business and industry. Environmental problems involving dioxin, asbestos, and lead, and the litigation stemming from them, have made them household words. The same kind of widespread public attention has been focused on whether the regular use of saccharin can cause bladder cancer, or whether radon in basements or mercury in swordfish pose dangers to public health. And the public fallout and immense cost of such disasters as the nuclear accident at Three Mile Island, the release of poisonous gas at Bophal, India, and the Exxon oil spill in Prince George's Sound, Alaska, put all three of these once-obscure places on the map.

Clearly the intense public and governmental interest in these fields has opened great opportunities for rewarding careers in these relatively new public relations specialties. Certainly no governmental relations office can afford to be without specialists in the areas of the environment and health as the issues battles intensify over government regulation in these areas. The fights in Washington and in many states over tort reform to put caps on damage awards and efforts to rein in the regulatory powers of the EPA, FDA, and other federal regulatory agencies and their counterparts in the states are sure to continue and even intensify in the years ahead.

On the governmental relations and public affairs side, the techniques described earlier in waging issue campaigns to affect both public opinion and government policy should prove effective here as well. There are two caveats, however, and both are important for public relations practitioners to understand.

First, it is important to state up front that government regulations to protect the environment and safeguard public health and safety are appropriate activities for government, are in the public interest, and, in general, enjoy widespread public support. The blunt truth is that many of the regulations in existence have a sound reason to be there. Consider this:

- Dioxin is extremely toxic in animal experiments.
- Asbestos caused high levels of disease and death in heavily exposed workers.
- Lead exposure can result in brain damage in children.
- Workers in the PVC industry did develop a rare form of liver cancer.
- The Exxon oil spill in Alaska was an ecological disaster.
- The near-meltdown of the nuclear reactor at Three Mile Island was a matter of great concern.

Thus, responsible public relations practitioners need to stress to clients that the issue should not be focused as to whether government regulations are needed to protect the environment and public health. That battle has already been fought, and the public response has been a resounding yes. Most responsible corporate leaders understand this and are in basic agreement with that decision. Despite the great costs involved, Dow Chemical, DuPont, Bethlehem Steel, and many other major corporations have not only complied with EPA regulations, but have in many cases gone beyond them and have become recognized as environmental "good citizens."

The real focus should be on the issues of bureaucratic overregulation, pressing for regulations in areas where the scientific evidence is insufficient to justify them or where the alleged dangers are so minute and remote that the enormous cost to address them are not justified. These are issues areas in which business and industry can win and which, if they do win, will benefit the American people. For instance, the issue of product liability suits has opened up a public debate as to whether legislative curbs should be enacted, including caps on liability judgments.

The second caveat is the public relations industry must face up to the fact that to be effective in the struggle for the public's mind and heart on these issues, they will simply have to tool up and develop a cadre of specialists in the environmental and health fields, practitioners who are not only skilled in public relations, but are also knowledgeable in science and health. In the earlier days of the environmental movement, practitioners could pick up what science they needed by "learning on the job." As these issues get more and more complex and the outcome over which side is right depends more and more on scientific evidence, the need for advanced courses in chemistry, biology, and even medicine becomes more and more apparent. A successful communicator in this field must not only understand the science involved, but must also be able to translate the complex scientific language into English plain enough for the layperson to understand.

Professionals in the environmental area are likely to be dealing with a number of very different audiences, including:
- Company managers from top executives to first-line supervisors
- Community leaders
- Government officials at the local, state, and national levels
- Scientific and academic groups
- Environmentalists and citizen's groups.

To keep important audiences informed about a company's or an industry's environmental problems and what is being done about them, booklets, newsletters, slide presentations, and videos will become important tools of the trade. Face-to-face meetings and discussions, as opposed to press conferences and presentations, may be more effective in dealing with government officials, scientists, teachers, and environmental groups on complex environmental issues. To win the day in an environmental controversy, it will be necessary to have a message that is of scientific interest. The information must be complete enough to answer the fundamental questions raised. It would also be more effective if you have a scientist to make the key points, an outsider with impressive credentials if possible, but use a company scientist if an objective outsider is not available. Other effective ways to communicate with the scientific community, include:

- Publication of scientific materials in appropriate professional journals
- Advertisements in scientific journals
- Articles in popular science journals
- Direct mail to selected, well-targeted science groups
- Seminars, symposia and other scientific meetings.

A solid science background would also be useful in dealing with the environmental press, which has become increasingly specialized and knowledgeable. In addition to the major metropolitan newspapers and news magazines, which generally have science or environmental specialists, be sure to send your material and cultivate a relationship with the members of the environmental press corps. The Society of Environmental Writers, with more than 1,000 members, can be contacted by writing to P.O. Box 27280, Philadelphia, PA 19118. Other useful media groups interested in science, environmental, and health fields, include:

- The National Association of Science Writers
  P.O. Box 294
  Greenlawn, NY 11740

- The American Medical Writers' Association
  9650 Rockville Pike
  Bethesda, MD 20814-3998

- The International Federation of Scientific Editors Association
  Bioscience Information Service
  2100 Arch Street
  Philadelphia, PA 19103

As with environmental problems, the audiences in dealing with the issues involved in occupational health is specialized and includes:

- Corporate management and supervisors
- Appropriate government agencies and officials at the federal, state, and local levels
- Scientists, including doctors, researchers, and the academic community
- Union officials at the national and local level
- Community leaders in areas where the company has plants

- Science and medical writers, as well as the electronic media.

Working with the media — both print and electronic — on environmental and health issues requires both skill and patience. It is important that the corporation or industry is reacting humanely to environmental or occupational health problems, even if clients are convinced they are blameless. The public generally doesn't want to know how much it is going to cost the company to clean up a problem or how much production is going to be lost. It wants to know how the company or industry feels about the persons harmed and what is going to be done about it. In general, follow these guidelines:

- Tell the truth at all times, even if it hurts. It is far better for the company to disseminate "negative" information than to allow its opponents to be the first to spread the bad news.
- Establish a rapid approval mechanism for clearing responses or new developments. Telling a reporter, "I'll get back to you by tomorrow" when the reporter is on deadline establishes bad will and leaves the field open to comments by your opponents.
- Work to establish the company as the major source of information, both good and bad, on the issue.
- Whenever possible, use scientists as company or industry spokespersons. A reporter is more likely to believe the corporate medical director when he tries to explain the health implications of a chemical spill than he would the head of public relations.
- Whenever possible, have interviews conducted one-on-one with reporters.
- Avoid press conferences as a means of disseminating information, unless you have something positive to report.
- Keep in mind that the media are not your enemy, but can be an effective conduit for getting your side of the issue out.

In the long run, the bedrock of any communications effort on an environmental or health and safety issue will be the science itself. Unfortunately, science seldom provides black and white answers. The situation is never quite as rosy as the company would initially like to believe and never quite as bad as environmentalist and consumer activist groups attempt to paint it, particularly in the media.

Somewhere in between is a position that is the basis for sound public policy. It is a role of the public affairs professional to help his or her company or industry identify that rational, central position, and then to promote it through all available means to achieve a resolution that satisfies both the corporate and public well-being.

NOTES

1. Victor Kamber, "How to Win and Really Lose in Washington," *Public Relations Quarterly* (Winter 1993-94): 5-7.

2. Kamber, 6.

3. Nielsen Media Research, May 1994. Nielsen reports that 94.2 million American households, which is about 98 percent of total U.S. households, have at least one television set. Of these, 99 percent have color, 38 percent have two sets in the home, and 28 percent have three or more sets. Nielsen also reports that 63 percent of American households have basic cable, 28 percent have pay cable, and 79 percent have VCRs.

4. Jeff Greenfield, *Television: The First Fifty Years* (New York: Abrams, 1977).

5. Shirley Biagi, *Media/Impact: An Introduction to Mass Media* (Wadsworth, 1992): 4.

6. Edward Jay Whetmore, *MediaAmerica, MediaWorld*, (Wadsworth, 1993): 187.

7. Fraser P. Seital, *The Practice of Public Relations* (Bell & Howell, 1984): 364.

Robert S. Diamond serves as a senior consultant to The Dilenschneider Group.

Diamond was elected senior vice president-corporate communications of The Dun & Bradstreet Corporation from 1977 and served in that capacity to 1993.

Prior to joining Dun & Bradstreet, Diamond was vice president and director of public relations of The Chase Manhattan Bank, N.A. Previously, he was vice president-corporate affairs of Reliance Group, Inc. He also served as an associate editor of Fortune magazine and a staff writer of The Los Angeles Times and The Arizona Republic.

Diamond received a B.A. degree in Public Affairs from Claremont Men's College in 1961 and an M.S. degree with honors from the Columbia University Graduate School of Journalism.

CHAPTER 15

THE PUBLIC RELATIONS AGENCY

In one form or another, the modern public relations agency has been around for about a century. And it has come a very long way since John D. Rockefeller retained Ivy Lee to get the oil tycoon a public hearing. At its essence, the business is still about getting a hearing for your point of view. But in virtually all other ways, the agency business has transformed and adapted itself as few businesses have.

Once the virtual exclusive province of the newspaperman turned press agent, today's public relations agency is resident to a world of experts, including the fields of science, law, finance—you name it. The agency also is resident to a host of communication and marketing specialists, among them market researchers, speechwriters and speech trainers, lobbyists, graphic artists, and, of course, press agents. This vast change in capabilities and scope, of course, reflects the changes in our society. Breast implants, nicotine, nuclear energy, waste disposal, fossil fuels—these are all the nouns that have become issues, public issues for which many institutions, particularly corporate, require expert help. And that help, in all its many forms, is available in today's public relations agency.

EXAMINING NEEDS

No question about it, the public relations agency can provide enormous, significant assistance to the institution in need. But what need? All too frequently institutions lurch into a search for the P.R. agency without ever seriously examining and defining the need for an agency. Down the line this can lead to a costly mess, especially when the institution's most senior executive or official asks for an informal accounting of "what are we getting for our money." (We should note that this seminal event usually occurs long after the initial need for the agency has been successfully met—and forgotten!)

So why do you need a P.R. agency? This requires some tough self-examination—about you and about the institution you represent. Once you have determined the answers, you will have a better opportunity of selecting the right kind of agency, the right kind of agency account people, and, indeed, the right kind of ground rules and fee schedule. Getting these things right in the beginning improve immeasurably your chances for a productive relationship.

First, let's talk about you and your needs. In examining your requirements for an agency, you need to know yourself, your strengths, your limits. For example, it is not unusual today to find that a line operating executive with virtually no or at least minimal communications experience is appointed to become the company's senior communications officer. (The idea is that having worked intimately with the company's products and services, the executive has a deep knowledge of the company and that he can learn the necessary communications skills from subordinate colleagues in the communications department.) Here is a case where a public relations agency may provide a vital role, virtually tutoring the executive and providing non-threatening arms-length counsel.

More likely is the case of the professional communications executive. And there are a myriad of reasons why this executive may seek an outside P.R. agency. Among them:

- Inadequate inside staff to cover the communication department's stated responsibilities. This may mean a shortage of highly trained, more senior communication personnel or possibly an absence of supporting "back office" staff to produce and distribute the press releases and other work product of the organization's communication department.
- Inadequate resident skills, in areas such as speechwriting, annual report production, press placement, audio/visual, special event planning, opinion research, investor relations, and many others.
- Catastrophic event, scandal, or other one-time event that is beyond the capabilities of even the very best-run and well-staffed institution.
- Corporate policies that limit the size of departmental organizations but leave wide latitude for utilizing outside consultants, including public relations agencies.
- Limited, but highly necessary, requirements for monitoring events, legislation, media that may impact your organization.
- Retention of outside specialists and authorities on special topics (environmental science, economics, labor, etc.) to assist the organization in making a credible case for its products, services, and business practices that may be under attack.

It is also necessary to examine your institution's culture, your Chief Executive Officer's preferences, and the basic controversy quotient of your particular institution. Is your organization multi-product, multi-divisional? Do your responsibilities cover the entire corporation, its flagship operating division, or a new, highly exciting, but relatively unknown unit? How centralized or decentralized? Is the CEO comfortable only with insiders? Is this the tobacco, public utility, or pharmaceutical business? Is this a company that is about to be publicly listed? How well known is the company? Is it one of those just out of the garage high-tech start-ups or a venerable institution that has fallen on hard times?

The answers to these questions and others similar will in the end dictate the kind of public relations agency, the intensity of involvement, and the scope of budget.

SELECTING THE PUBLIC RELATIONS AGENCY

The first thing to recognize in selecting a public relations agency is that agencies can be very different: large and small; all services and specialized; local, regional, and global. This is a research project. The same discipline and skills you would use to determine the best product or service for your particular needs should be utilized here. And one of the best places to start is O'Dwyer's *Directory of Public Relations Firms* (published by J.R. O'Dwyer Co., Inc., 271 Madison Ave., New York, NY 10016). This annual directory provides a core reference tool — not everything you'll need — but certainly an important starting point. The directory, at last count more than 300 pages in length, contains, among other things, profiles of agencies, a list of clients, and a list of the agency's principals. The directory is also indexed for geography and industry specialization and includes rankings of firms by overall billings as well as by areas of specialization, such as health care, entertainment, and high-tech.

As part of your search, seek out those practitioners you respect. Get their opinions based on their experiences. But remember, you must understand your situation. The profile of your institution and of your department may be quite different in terms of size, experience, and needs. Once you have satisfied yourself that you have surveyed the field, start interviewing. This should be, at least initially, an informal one-on-one process. By all means, go to the agencies' offices. You'll get a feel for the activity, their size, even to some extent the seasoning of the staff. Describe your company and the key operational and communication issues as you see them.

As you move through the weeding-out process, you need to keep in mind certain universal principles. Big-time agency or small, East Coast or West, there are certain fundamental issues that you must raise and resolve to your satisfaction. Seemingly obvious, these points too often do not get the detailed attention they deserve. They are:

- Who is going to manage my account? While the total resources of the organization may be at your disposal, ultimately one person is going to connect with you on a daily basis. That someone must have your total confidence, has the seasoning and expertise that fits your needs, and, finally, has sufficient clout within their organization to get you the additional personnel and other resources you need when you need them. Indeed, the agency may have some "stars," and they may be part of the presentation initially made to you. But do not assume they are part of your team. (A word of caution: the billable rate for "stars" obviously is higher. So early on consider what your realistic needs are; you may want to bring "stars" on board occasionally for some special project, but their presence may be unnecessary for most of your projects.)

- What is the background of the proposed account manager? Does the manager's experience give you confidence that he or she can add an important dimension?
- Who are the agency personnel who will support the account manager?
- Realistically, how much time will the account manager devote to your company?
- Are there any accounts within the agency that pose either an outright or potential conflict of interest as a competitor?
- What other accounts are being supervised by the proposed agency manager and should you be concerned as to whether the manager can really handle your account and these others?
- Finally, and most important, does this agency, the account manager and the top executive-level personnel have the experience and the presence to gain the respect of your boss and the top management of your organization? This last point too often is not properly considered and leads to trouble when you can least afford it. Often, agency people are only seen by the top management when crisis comes a'-calling. When that happens — when there is a surprise earnings shortfall, the Justice Department announces an investigation, or a citizens group targets your institution for some perceived outrage, your top management team must feel wholly comfortable with the agency team. They must, starting with the CEO, feel free to share information and confidences. If, for whatever reason, your senior management is uncomfortable with the agency team, you, at the worst possible moment, have compounded your problems.

IS ONE FIRM THE ANSWER?

Our discussion has presupposed the hiring of one public relations agency. But for many institutions this may not be the best alternative. There are few "be-all" solutions in life, and this includes the all-purpose do everything P.R. agency. There are at least two strong reasons why hiring one mega agency isn't for every company.

First, the large agency usually supports a wide and impressive array of collateral communications services, such as annual report and audio-visual production facilities. This obviously implies overhead costs to be covered, and, accordingly, the agency's account managers have a powerful incentive to "sell-in" those services to you. You may need them; then again, maybe not. There is also the issue of whether those same discrete services could be purchased by you independently at lower cost and possibly with, for those particular services, better talent.

Second is the issue of agency effectiveness. Can one agency for one client (particularly a client with less than a mega-size budget) give total focus to multiple ongoing projects simultaneously? That is, can the agency do a top, focused job on an investor relations project at the same time that they are overseeing a product launch? Maybe so, especially since different agency personnel with different expertise are presumably assigned to these different projects. But consider, as an alternative, giving two separate agencies these same two differentiated projects — one agency with a noted expertise in investor relations; the other with a strong team in product launches — even specializing in particular industry areas (high-tech, textiles, toys, hospitals, etc.) Also, by utilizing different agencies for different projects, you can get a much more definitive picture of the precise costs and the results.

We have already noted that to most effectively utilize the services of the outside agency, you must have a thorough understanding of your own organization. Just what are we talking about here? If you're a *Fortune* 500 consumer products organization selling colas with brand identification worldwide, your P.R. needs are quite different than even the same type of company, but one whose brand is known in just one region of the United States. And certainly an industrial company, that by the very nature of its manufacturing process has the potential to pollute, has quite different problems than a software company or a medical center. Is your company well known and, if not, can you benefit from retaining a major firm with a name better recognized with the media, for instance, than your own?

Beyond this is the question of the in-house capabilities of your department. If you are operating with a small staff but have large mailing and distribution requirements to the media, you may want to ascertain that the P.R. agency can remove this burden from your shop. Do you have great bench strength in media contacts so that this resource is not a high priority in retaining an outside firm? Do you have inside expertise to develop comprehensive strategic communication/marketing positioning plans or is this something with which you will need heavy assistance?

DECISION TIME

By now, if you have asked the right questions and done the research, you have probably narrowed your search to one or two agencies. Although it is much the practice in the advertising business (with which unfortunately the P.R. agency business is often linked in a combined business) to have internal committees make the final decision following an elaborate presentation, these exercises are in the opinion of this writer, useless.

You are retaining an agency for any number of reasons, but usually judgment and access to various outside constituencies (media, politicians and policymakers, academics, etc.) is paramount. Having done your due diligence, checked out references, both yours and theirs, now is the time to engage your top management and the more senior executives in your department. Your strategy here is to make certain that:

1. Your top management feels comfortable with the agency, the proposed account manager, and, of course, the agency's top management. If you do not get a convincing sense of affirmation from your top management, proceed with extreme caution! Nothing is worse than when your management distances itself from the agency, makes excuses for not wanting to meet with the agency on highly critical business issues and refers to the agency as "your people." Go to pains to get an honest expression from your management before making the final hiring decision.

2. Equally important, obtain a "buy-in" from the key personnel in your own department. You are not always going to be working directly with the agency. Others will get assigned to projects where the agency is involved, and you must ensure that a comfortable working relationship exists. Translated, this means that your key people regard the agency as important to their own success, too. To accomplish this means that in the later stages of the hiring process, you must introduce the agency to your people. There should be time to meet them both as a group, as well as individually. Seek out their opinions and to the best of your ability diffuse any potential problems now.

NEGOTIATING COSTS

At some point in this process, money will get discussed. Just when is really up to you. If your budget is quite limited, you probably ought to get this on the table early as some agencies may either not be interested or could not provide you with their top talent. This much we can say: There is no scientific formula that can entirely give you a definitive answer to the inevitable question "how much is this going to cost me?"

There are some basic approaches to the cost issue. You can arrange for a monthly retainer. You can arrange for a fee-for-project. You can arrange for hourly billing. And, of course, attached to each of these compensation schedules will be the out-of-pocket costs. Sometimes, you will find these arrangements configured in such a way that you may pay a small monthly retainer for the agency to provide general counsel, monitor news services through its surveillance operation, and then pay additional fees for execution of specific projects. Those special projects, for example, could include handling the opening of your new operations in the Asian market, the launch of a new product, or organizing and providing back-up in a 10-city presentation of your new securities offering.

In the end, what you need to know is this: No matter the fee arrangement, underlying all is the need for the agency to get a certain amount of revenue each hour for each consultant. There are no bargains — or certainly no bargains in the long run. Yes, agencies may indeed offer a "bargain" retainer fee at the beginning. But this usually occurs when the agency perceives that there is a real benefit to the agency in engaging certain new clients. Among the reasons may be the marquee value of a new client, one with an enormously prestigious name that might pull yet other prospective clients. Or a client that represents an entirely new industry not represented in the agency's current portfolio. (As with other kinds of client business services, public relations agencies do face potential conflict-of-interest problems that, accordingly, limit their ability usually to take more than one client in any industry, e.g. airlines, franchise food operations, banks, etc.)

MANAGING THE AGENCY/MEASURING PERFORMANCE

The real savings do not usually come from your skillful negotiation of the initial contract, but from your management of the agency's work on your behalf and through measuring the agency's performance. This is how value is really produced.

Managing the agency means achieving a clear understanding by the agency management and you as to what is to be achieved, in what time frame, and with what results attained. This sounds obvious and simple; in fact it requires you to manage rigorously and, assuming you have a tight budget, to make tough choices.

Initially the agency may suggest doing an overall strategic analysis/audit of your company and its communications. This can be valuable if you have neither the resources nor the experience to take on this essential exercise. If you and your inside team already have produced such a document, share it with the agency as a starting point The important thing is to be clear in your own mind as to what the agency is to undertake. For example, your overall assignment to the agency may be to support one of your operations in the launch of a new consumer product worldwide.

Because of limited inside manpower, you specifically ask the agency to support a marketing plan already written. This may be a product targeted to women, and you may want the agency to help develop the kind of talking points that may make the product worthy of an interview on television shows aimed at woman. You are also requesting the agency to target the so-called women's books — *Cosmopolitan*, *Ladies Home Journal*, and *Glamour*, for special feature treatment. With this kind of approach there should be no confusion about how you wish the agency to utilize their time and resources on your behalf and the result you are seeking, that is creating awareness for the newly launched product.

By contrast, you may be asking the agency to provide "damage control" on an ecologically related accident. Here your purpose in this emotion-charged problem may be to have the agency operate in an arm's-length fashion, critiquing the actions you and your operations people are proposing to take. You may also want the agency to act as a press intermediary, feeding back to you how effective you are in getting your message across to the media. Under these conditions, an agency can do invaluable service in keeping the corporation focused on maintaining its credibility with media, government officials, and, of course, customers.

There are countless permutations regarding the use of skilled agency professionals. The point is to focus the agency on what you regard as their most effective use relative to the particular issue, problem, or project. By taking this tack, you will find it is much easier to defend your utilization of the agency with your company's top management—and much easier to measure results.

In this regard it is usually a good practice to gather the agency and your key communications people together once a quarter to review what has been accomplished and to address new or emerging priorities. However, these meetings, in themselves, can be a costly waste of time. Their purpose should not be to allow the agency to put on a sales promotion. You should control the meeting and keep the focus on moving along your priorities.

As a separate matter, either you or someone you designate—such as a department administrator—should be on a monthly basis monitoring the agency's charges. Do not allow yourself to lose touch with this critical issue. An inside assessment of your management abilities is very much tied to your skill in making your budget. It is a classic mistake to ignore billing against budget until it is too late in the cycle to take remedial action. If you have delayed reviewing the agency billings against budget, you either abruptly have to halt the agency's services for, say, the last three months of the year or seek special dispensation from your boss as well as the senior financial officer. This does nothing for your managerial reputation, and it reduces the agency's effectiveness significantly, given the starts and stops imposed by your poor budget planning and administration. Periodic and consistent budget reviews are an excellent management tool to keep your plan and priorities on course.

Remember that a public relations agency is trained to provide the services you need under the budget and time frame you determine. But the agency is often only as good as the direction given, the goals set, and the performance measured. That is—and will continue—to be your job.

Kenneth G. Trantowski is a principal with The Dilenschneider Group in the firm's Chicago office. He was formerly an executive vice president with Burson-Marsteller where he worked for more than 22 years. His experience includes corporate and marketing counsel for a diverse range of corporations on critical issues affecting their business.

He is well versed in introducing new products, repositioning mature brands, and getting messages across in the overcrowded consumer and professional marketplace. Mr. Trantowski has developed and managed numerous programs in corporate relations and public affairs for major corporations and associations. He developed Sara Lee Corporation's public relations programs for the 1992 and 1996 Olympics and the launch of the Gatorade–Michael Jordan partnership for Quaker Oats. He also established his former agency's health care practice in Chicago with major clients in the health care and medical field.

He is a frequent speaker to communications groups, business organizations, and major colleges and universities across the country. Mr. Trantowski was a Scripps-Howard Foundation Fellow. He holds a bachelor's degree in journalism and marketing and a master's degree in journalism from Northern Illinois University.

CHAPTER 16

POSITIONING PUBLIC RELATIONS
WITH MANAGEMENT

Whether you report directly to the CEO of a *Fortune* 500 company, the executive director of a major association, the president of a hospital, or the owner of an entrepreneurial venture, there is no question
they will each have a very different understanding and quite often an
individual experience perspective on the role of public relations. The
same can be said about everyone else you might encounter within the
organization; from a senior brand manager, to the head of radiology, to
the plant manager, to the director of research and development. Each
brings their own first-hand personal experience and understanding of
the role of public relations, and unfortunately for the most part, it has
only to do with tactics — such as press releases, employee newsletters,
and speeches.

The role of public relation is becoming an even more recognized
and valued part of an organization's policy and decision-making
process. A growing number of business and professional people really
do understand the significance of public relations substance versus
simply the tactics. The higher level of focus for public relations today
includes: issue management and tracking; managing the visibility of
high-profile legal battles among competitors; grassroots or coalition-
building campaigns used to win the public's mind and legislative battles; and the strategic overhaul of employee communications.

A real challenge that public relations professionals have is trying to explain to lay audiences — let alone the management public
relations professionals serve — what is it that we do and how we can
help management address and solve business problems. To begin to
educate management about our role, it is important to have some very
basic understanding of where management is coming from regarding
its priorities.

Without exception, every CEO is focused on delivering maximum value to shareholders. The CEO and management team is seeking
the best ways to leverage the current assets, particularly people, to
profitably grow the business and deliver more value to customers.

Management's highest priorities, however, do include a very
broad range of other options. For some firms, the number-one priority
is fighting off corporate raiders. For many other firms, the priority
is getting certain transition messages out to employees. Still other organizations are seeking an effective way to convince key critical
audiences — including bankers, security analysts, shareholders, and
customers — to have confidence in their ability to compete in the
changing and constantly demanding marketplace.

No matter what the priority, in order to become a valuable and actively involved member of the organization's team, a public relations professional must be able to understand and address senior management's concerns, embrace change, and deal with the public relations ramifications of their decisions. One major—and constantly growing—concern is management's need to justify everything from the organization's existence to its procedures.

CONCERNS ABOUT PUBLIC PERCEPTIONS

Once low on management's long list of priorities, dealing with public perceptions has become an especially important concern. Today, not just business people but the heads of all types of organizations, whether they like it or not, find themselves justifying their organizations' goals, practices, and methods to just about everybody. This can include very diverse audiences: boards of directors, Wall Street, community leaders, industry associations, and the list goes on. Some would say they have to do it just about every day.

This organizational justification extends to an organization's membership, as well as to all ranks of employees, no matter if they are union or non-union, blue, gray, or white collar. In fact, unions are fighting for their life trying to justify their very existence. Unions, such as the Communications Workers of America, United Auto Workers, and Ron Carey and the Teamsters, are among the most media conscious, sophisticated, and proactive in communicating their point of view on issues and justifying their role.

Organizational justification also includes customers, regardless of size or location. Increasingly, one of the major audiences is shareholders, particularly the institutional investment community.

Of course, organizational justification extends to communities and special interest groups, such as conservationists, environmentalists, animal rights, and right-to-life supporters. There is no bottom to the pool of groups targeting organizations. Their leaders are almost as well known as the companies and organizations they are targeting. Jeremy Rifkin and the Center for Science in the Public Interest, Public Voice, and Phil Sokolof and the Physicians Committee on Responsible Medicine have been actively pursuing their own agendas. They have aggressively been targeting companies like McDonald's, as well as associations such as the Beef Industry Council of the National Live Stock and Meat Board, the International Dairy Foods Association (IFDA), and Dairy Management, Inc. (DMI).

There is also no question of the organizational justification required by local, state, and federal legislators and regulators. Justification also is required by well-organized religious groups. Pat Robertson's Christian Coalition has considerable economic and political clout, as do such groups as the World Jewish Restitution Organization and the Concerned Women of America. They are all dealing with public perceptions as a primary concern. Last, but not least, is the organizational justification required by the public at large, manifested through the efforts of the media.

In reality, the public relations function — without a sufficient amount of credit — has shouldered the great burden of this justification process. That, in turn, has accounted for much of the growth in internal public relations staffs and outside public relations consulting firms over the past 25 years. Public relations became the logical organizational function to understand and interpret the questions being put to management and to prepare and deliver the responses. This is true despite the tremendous pressure by every type of company or organization on keeping "head count" at low levels and eliminating unnecessary or marginally important positions.

ACCOUNTABILITY AND RESULTS

As a result, public relations within many organizations has moved from being executors of routine communications programs to participants in the development of corporate strategy itself and has addressed scores of significant business problems along the way. There are great expectations today of the role of public relations in policy-making and strategy in the overall management of the organization or business.

A good example of addressing a significant business problem was the work by Procter & Gamble's public affairs team on the issue regarding misconceptions surrounding disposable diapers (Pampers) and solid waste. In a rather short period of time, Pampers and P&G both became the media symbol for the country's growing solid-waste problem. In reality, disposable diapers represented a minute portion of the actual solid landfill waste. A new dialogue on the issue was needed to put it into its proper perspective. The solid-waste debate clearly needed to be broadened well beyond the disposable diaper symbol. The broadened issue also had to focus on "realistic" solid-waste solutions, such as recycling and composting.

P&G's efforts included third-party endorsements and focused grassroots support for disposable diapers. Since almost every new baby and mom leave the hospital with a package of disposable diapers and supply of coupons, a hospital outreach initiative was an essential part of the effort. In addition, P&G made a strategic and timely announced plan to apply $20 million toward development of municipal solid-waste composting.

This solid-waste debate was clearly a key issue on management's agenda for action. The outcome could have significant bottom-line impact on the company unless the issue was broadened from disposable diapers to the larger matter of solid waste. Within 18 months, P&G's public relations team successfully repositioned the issue without any negative financial impact on the company.

Another example of how public relations took on a new signifi-cance with management is the experience at Wilson Foods. After 15 years as an LTV subsidiary, Wilson Foods, a major meatpacking com-pany, was about to be spun off from its parent company in a public stock offering. Employees were understandably anxious, and Wall Street was skeptical that such a spin-off would succeed, since many of the old-time meatpackers across the country were collapsing under escalating union wage costs, cyclical availability of animals, and increasing competitive threats from non-union firms. Wilson had a strong reputation for innovation and successful belt-tightening. Both of these traits are essential in the meatpacking industry, with its razor-thin profit margins of less than 2 percent. The challenge for Wilson was to generate broad-based understanding of these strengths and to replace employee anxiety with productive optimism. In addition, Wilson had to demonstrate to Wall Street that the new independent Wilson Foods would generate profits despite unionization.

The Wilson public relations team went to work with manage-ment's blessing to reassure employees and generate enthusiasm for its future. They developed an upbeat communications campaign with the unifying theme, "It's a brand new day at Wilson," which was carefully orchestrated in printed materials and face-to-face meetings with union leaders and employees in the company's eight plants across the country.

Within six months of the spin-off, significant improvement in employee attitude and motivation were evident from both research and performance. Wilson emerged from subsequent United Food & Commercial Workers (IUFCW) negotiations with better-than-industry terms, including a 44-month freeze on wage rates. Wilson Foods public relations function clearly emerged with an enhanced reputation. The CEO and the corporation were evaluated on their financial performance and how well they was able to explain themselves to key audiences.

For Procter & Gamble and Wilson Foods, public relations became much more important, much more of consuming of manage-ment's time, and, as a result, much more visible.

Public relations in the well-managed corporation or organization has gained both a role of providing input before and after the decision. Today, public relations must be more accountable to management — prove its value, demonstrate cost effectiveness, and show real results — for the investment in personnel time and financial resources.

Ten to twenty years ago, the management of corporations, asso-ciations, and virtually all types of institutions — inexperienced in the process — accepted on faith much of what the public relations profes-sional recommended. No longer. Management today within every type of organization clearly accepts the need for some form of public rela-tions capability, but they want proof that P.R. is working.

Many CEOs are establishing demanding, measurable performance goals for all their managers and increasing the rewards and punishments associated with success and failure in achieving these goals. This mandate from the top certainly includes the public relations management within the organization. The message is very clear, "Deliver the results or risk being sacrificed and replaced."

You must understand that management is not at all interested in the process of communications itself, but what communications can do for them. They want communications impact. Strategies must lead to actionable tactics, and you don't have forever to get something done and to demonstrate results. (Exhibit 16.1 offers 10 ways to keep management informed about public relations initiatives.)

EXHIBIT 16.1 — KEEPING MANAGEMENT INFORMED

One of the best ways to educate management about the role of public relations and the diverse activities underway is by keeping them regularly informed. There is no single best way to keep them involved and interested in what you are doing. Depending on the organization, there are countless ways of providing regular progress updates and successful results. Here are 10 ways you can keep your management informed, and, in turn, educate them about what you can do for the organization:

1. **Meeting Reports** — After each important meeting on a key project, use a meeting report to summarize the actions or next steps you are going to undertake and the deadlines on which you've agreed. Circulate these reports internally to everyone attending the meeting and to those who have some role in the project, as well. If you have electronic mail, use it. Keep the reports simple and to the point. Avoid too much detail but make sure you provide enough substance to cover the main decisions made at the meeting.

2. **Telephone Conference Reports** — All your meetings won't be face-to-face. At times you will receive important information on the progress of a project by telephone with contacts in distant cities. Use these sessions as another opportunity to report on your work and progress. All too often there is a tendency to underestimate how long it takes to complete portions of an assignment. Reporting progress and highlighting steps underway add credibility. Just make sure you avoid the temptation to report on things that don't require significant attention by anyone but you. Excessive reporting of trips to the printer, photographer or mailing source may generate more questions than it builds awareness for the overall work involved in a project. Once again, you can issue these reports quickly by electronic mail.

3. **Monthly Status/Progress Reports** — You may start this process to keep your supervisor informed. A well-prepared report at the end of every month is often used as a vehicle to communicate with higher management levels, as well as others not currently using your assistance. The reports can demonstrate the scope of activity and depth of involvement you have in your organization.

Continued on next page

4. **Quarterly Status/Progress Updates** — If monthly reports are good, quarterly reports can be an even more effective vehicle. Be sure you avoid too much detail. Don't report on how many calls were made to a single editor or the number of approvals made on a news release. The best reports are short and speak in language that reflects progress toward the agreed-upon objectives. In some organizations, face-to-face meetings are a better way to provide management with some level of progress. Unfortunately, it may take longer to get a meeting scheduled than it actually does to review the quarterly progress.

5. **Annual Stewardship Meetings** — Plan on providing your management with an annual report on your activity for the year. Such a report could summarize progress and results against objectives on all major initiatives conducted throughout the year. It could also highlight the very best media coverage and reflect research findings. It is remarkable how quickly an active year passes and how easy it is to overlook what was done during the first three months when you're immersed in the final weeks. You can also use the annual report meeting as an opportunity to provide recommendations for expanded involvement. If you don't take advantage of this annual session, you are missing the single biggest opportunity to educate management and to indicate your potential to contribute even more. In addition to the meeting, prepare a document to be distributed within the organization.

6. **Annual Plan** — It's hard to imagine that in today's business environment any organization operates without an annual plan and budget. Unfortunately, complacency sets in with some individuals, and they have the mistaken notion that they can succeed or maintain the status quo by doing the same kind of activity year after year. If you're not providing an annual plan with detailed objectives, strategy, an outline of planned tactics, and budgeted expenses, don't wait any longer. Be sure to involve the right members of management in the process, or else you won't need to worry about educating management about your role — you'll be looking for your next position!

7. **Coffee and Conversation** — While there are a host of vehicles to provide information on activities and progress, one of the best is taking advantage of informal face-to-face meetings. You may not always get an audience with the CEO, president, or executive director of your organization, but there are plenty of other opportunities to brief others within the management ranks on your responsibilities. A director–level staff member or manager has the potential to reach the top of the organization, and that is the person you should want to cultivate. There is no secret formula you can use to get the meeting other than ask for it. It's always easiest to meet with people you've already worked with in the past. Tell the person that you want to provide some insight into the kinds of activities underway now and perhaps find out if their needs may require help in the future. Beside being a great way to enhance your visibility in the organization, it's another way to build your

own network of internal feedback and helps keep your ear on the pulse of the organization. You'll find it helps to avoid surprises later.

8. **Broadcast Triumphs Directly** — If you come up with a great idea or solution and it works, don't hide the news. Make sure your management knows about it because they will determine your salary increases, promotions, and, of course, your next opportunity to come up with a big idea. Inform the organization about a success but don't make a big deal of it. Quite simply, your face-to-face comments should be factual, straightforward, and easy to document later if asked. Make sure you report the success in the kind of language your management can't dispute. Quote numbers and percentages that are easy to understand and come from credible third parties inside and outside the organization.

9. **Use the Grapevine** — There is no question that word of mouth is an extremely effective, non-offensive way to increase your visibility and contributions throughout an organization. Not only does it make you look good but it heightens the awareness level of the public relations role in the organization. Provide the most important facts to a few key people at various levels in the organization. Tell them about a specific success or unique effort underway, and they will mention it to other people in the company. A key point to remember is to make sure you're not reporting success on an assignment that needs to be kept confidential.

10. **Interject Achievements in Conversation** — When the opportunity is prime, take advantage of the situation and interject an anecdote that serves to highlight a personal achievement or one by a member of the public relations team. You might want to say, "That reminds me of the problem I was addressing for Mr. Y in the AAA department, and we faced this kind of challenge." This technique permits you to easily underscore your resourcefulness in an acceptable way. It clearly serves to educate a member of management about your experience and problem-solving resourcefulness.

Always remember, when you are trying to educate management on the role of public relations and your contributions to the organization, you are also trying to survive in today's streamlined workplace. Be sure you do it in a dignified, appropriate way. Some well-executed self promotion can be a matter of revealing in an informative and factual way what you in the public relations function have been doing for some time. Just be sure to tailor your approach to the style of the person you are trying to educate. If the person hates or never reads electronic mail, avoid it. On the other hand, a short handwritten note attached to something of interest can go a long way toward winning over a new ally. The benefits of being proactive far outweigh any risks.

TALK IN REAL TERMS

Management doesn't want to talk about employee communications in terms of tactical execution such as employee newsletters, magazines, or company picnics. Management wants to talk about how improved employee communications can make all their employees even more productive and customer focused. If a reengineering effort is going to transform the organization, you must seek new ways to communicate it quickly and effectively. Successful organizations are always changing, and change is inevitable to remain successful. A public relations profession will help management search for new ways to improve its communications and leverage all the resources available. If the decade of the '90s has taught us anything, it is that we must understand that management is prepared to continually reinvent itself in response to the changing demands of the marketplace.

Don't talk to management about the value of annual reports and analyst presentations. They want to know how these time-consuming and costly activities directly impact the value of their stock price report card or the ability to raise capital or identify new sources of investment.

They also don't want to talk to you or anyone else about community relations as only a means to build amorphous goodwill. They want to know how community relations programs will help pass a bond issue, change a truly unfavorable zoning law, or contribute to their recruiting of the very best and most qualified workers.

Don't talk to management about government relations as a process. They want to talk in real terms. For example, talk about ballots in boxes, favorable regulations, legislation that passed, or unfavorable legislation that was amended or defeated.

They also don't want to talk about marketing support for critical new products or services in terms of newspaper clippings or minutes of television interviews. They want to know about their marketshare improvements and products selling off shelves or out of warehouses and services being contracted for extended periods of time at good profit margins.

Management, no matter what kind of organization it represents, wants the right opinion dials to move, the success meter to run, and the money to flow to the bottom line. They want the kind of accountability any demanding business person can understand. Otherwise, they will not give the recognition — nor the funds — to the function of public relations.

By having a strong idea of where your management is coming from, you should be better positioned to begin, or continue, to educate them further on what more public relations can do. Or can you? Chances are very good you'll be able to make some real progress in increasing management's understanding and appreciation for the role of public relations. It is equally important for you to really understand how much management has actually experienced public relations efforts.

LISTEN TO THE QUESTIONS

Over the years there has been a significant "maturation" of public relations and its role within management's decision-making process. This attitude change and new understanding has taken place as a result of the dedicated hard work by some of the most talented public relations professionals in the industry serving some of the most challenging and demanding management in the country. They have helped educate all levels of management about the real role of public relations. They have done it by carefully listening to the questions management ask. After listening to those questions they determined if the management need is to educate, persuade, or motivate a specific target audience or audiences.

While the advice to listen is simple enough, first, you must be sure you really hear and, secondly, understand the questions they ask. By understanding management's need to communicate, a public relations professional can address it with the right action. While the overall directive to the public relations professional has changed, a starting point and entry to our role exist for every member of the management team.

HOW DO I SAY IT?

Role changes by the types of questions we're asked. At first we may be asked, "How do I say it?" by an executive, director, or manager who is encountering a new need. They are looking for someone to help them communicate more clearly and effectively. Sometimes this is regarded as the "editing stage" of a management working relationship. There was a basic need to communicate some decision or organizational action. By doing a good job on this basic request, management will trust you to do even more. This usually works. Quite often this initial good experience is how younger, inexperienced management gets some exposure and involvement in what public relations can do.

WHAT DO I SAY?

A more experienced member of the management team might ask, "What do I say?" which signals a need for far more help than someone who simply has a good grasp of the language. Perhaps as an example your organization is one of 20 national associations asked to contact members of Congress and oppose a bill that would prevent establishing consumer banks and support legislation favorable to consumer banking. The request is clearly a reflection of a need to receive counsel and formulate a response. Management is seeking direction on message content, timing, and style. This type of request signifies more respect for what counsel is offered and shows a level of confidence in the ability of the public relations professional.

WHAT DO I DO?

The most experienced or enlightened members of management (and they may not be the person with the most years of experience or the highest title) will ask, "What do I do?" This question reflects the increasingly supportive and vital role public relations can play in addressing needs. This may be one of the best opportunities you'll have to develop appropriate strategies and positions on emerging public relations issues or serve as an "early warning system" to detect future issues in some group plans. Such efforts will enable your management to pre-empt forthcoming campaigns that could create a negative impact on the company's bottom line. It also clearly signals the public relations professional is no longer merely an executor of routine communications programs. Instead, they have been designated to participate in the development of business or corporate strategy itself.

Again, depending upon the level of management experience with public relations, and the results of that experience, they will regard what a public relations profession can contribute in one of three ways.

1. Solve communications problems;
2. Solve problems with communications; or
3. Solve problems.

So the real work of educating management and positioning public relations in the corporate hierarchy must come by demonstrating credibility, producing exceptional work, and generating results. It does not happen overnight and, realistically, it can require many months and even many years to accomplish.

As all public relations practitioners look toward the future and the next century, there is a very strong drive underway to redefine the profession as one that is truly indispensable to management in the policy-making and decision-making process.

Rather than worry about definition, the focus with management must be with actions and not rhetoric. While once kept in the corporate basement as the alchemy of big business, public relations has made the transition from a "black art" to one of the requisites of a strong and complete management team along such disciplines as finance, marketing, research, and engineering.

The real keys to success with educating management within any organization, large or small, and at any level of experience and responsibility from CEO to assistant director, include exceptional, measurable, results-oriented performance well beyond expectations and doing so with a keen sense of professionalism and integrity. If you perform very well, you can break through some of the incorrect perceptions and misapprehensions the public relations function carries and become a significant decision-making player in what's going on in your organization.

There is likely one more key to educating management and successfully positioning public relations, and that is the importance of a strong working relationship. There is no question regarding the importance of the chemistry between the CEO and the senior public relations executive. The same can be said about the importance of relationship chemistry of a public relations manager or director and any other member of the management team. It goes without saying though that the closer the working relationship at the top, the better it is throughout the organization.

Some observers would say the unique relationship the public relations professional has with the CEO or with senior management is somewhat akin to the "conscience" of the organization. The strength of the relationship permits difficult questions to be asked. Questions like, "Have we considered all the possible options?" or "Are we convinced this isn't simply a legal solution with a resulting public opinion disaster?"

You don't ask those kind of questions of management, let alone CEOs, without earning your dues first. You must have demonstrated that you can exercise sound judgment consistently and you have strong convictions. The dues you pay over time permit a special and unique "chemistry" to develop, which earns you the right to challenge management's thinking. If the chemistry exists, it can serve all parties and the organization well. That's not to say the lack of chemistry with the CEO and senior public relations executive will doom communications efforts. The right public relations judgments can still be made, but it works better when the chemistry exists.

For many organizations, no matter if it's an association, company, or not-for-profit, public relations runs a greater risk of faltering if the chemistry at the highest levels does not exist with the most senior public executive. Special efforts must always be made to create those close working ties and develop the mutual respect for one another. (Exhibit 16.2 offers eight guidelines for Making Management's Team.)

EXHIBIT 16.2—MAKING MANAGEMENT'S TEAM

Within almost every organization there will be opportunities to become integrated as a team player into the problem-solving challenges and issues it faces. Some opportunities will require an invitation, others you can discover on your own. When the management team of your organization does choose to include you in a problem-solving situation, there are several ways you can capitalize on this chance to demonstrate the significant and contributing role you can play.

These eight tips will keep your name and the role you play in the organization prominent.

1. **Ask Questions** — If you're going to be asked to participate in a meeting, be sure you understand what's going to be discussed and who will be attending. If you're unfamiliar with that part of the organization, learn as much as you can, as quickly as you can. Don't be afraid to pick up the phone and ask others attending the session for perspective. Make sure you are familiar with the media coverage the subject or issue has received in the past. You'll be expected to know it, and it can help you assist the group. Try to gauge the nature of the session before you attend. Is it an information-gathering, briefing-type meeting or is it a brainstorming session? Always be sure you are ready to make your very best impression possible.

2. **Be The Best Prepared** — Take advantage of the databanks that are available, and make sure you arrive at the meeting well armed with background on the subject. If the subject involves your competition, gather the most recent media coverage and make a few copies to share. By being prepared you naturally display an enthusiasm for the opportunity that can lead to greater involvement. Try to find out how other organizations addressed the same type of subject you are about to discuss. Search for case history examples in business books and the *Harvard Business Review*. Make yourself an invaluable source from the start by sharing your findings with others.

3. **Look Before You Leap** — The biggest mistake you can make in your early efforts to win management recognition within your organization is to provide answers that you don't yet have. This is particularly true since meetings can provide an environment where every one is looking for a fast diagnosis of the situation and solution. It's always best to avoid making top-of-mind recommendations on approaches without taking the time to think through what needs to be done. If useful, get another opinion to confirm your thinking. If you can't get help internally, look outside to professional associates. These may be former classmates or friends with an outside public relations agency who are *not* affiliated with your organization, but are people whom you trust. Very often a situation may be far more complex than it appears on the surface, and taking the time to study it can provide a very different recommended action. The most thoughtful counsel or recommendation is always better than the fastest recommendation.

4. **Meet Your Deadlines** — Always work toward the deadline you've agreed to, and if it's at all possible — beat it! Don't sacrifice the quality of your response with fast work, but also don't procrastinate with the assignment. You can make a strong impression if you provide your best work promised, and if it's early, all the better.

5. **Create Realistic Expectations** — If you are going to be asked to contribute to the solution, it's imperative that you don't allow others to create expectations for what you can and can't deliver. The best communications solutions to business problems have a realistic expectation level. If you promise more than you can deliver, you have absolutely no chance of living up to your word, and worse, you'll wind up diminishing the real contribution you can make later. Do you need to defeat a proposal on the ballot on an issue affecting your firm which may keep it from expanding the plant? Management may want the item removed from the ballot. Realistically, you know you can't get the item off the ballot, but the odds are good that you can have it rewritten or repositioned in a way that will ultimately lead to its defeat. If your success were measured by taking the item off the ballot you would have fallen short in delivering the desired result. The reality is your results were just as effective as removing the item from the ballot; the issue was defeated.

6. **Ask For A Budget** — If you think some type of funding is going to be required to address the issue or project, ask for it. If there is no budget or an inadequate one available, you'd better know it before you agree to undertake the effort. Unless you are a magician, you can't pull resources out of a hat to get the job done. Management understands the concept of investment spending in communications. There will be times when you have to commit to spending some amount of dollars with no short-term guarantee for the effort to be successful. Unless you spend something now, however, the cost will dramatically increase later and chance of success with the issue in the future will become significantly diminished or even impossible. Addressing needs does cost money, and it must come from some source. You'll be respected for your alertness and, more importantly, you won't have to make excuses later.

7. **Always Be Available** — The workday isn't a 9-5 routine. Problems and organizational needs simply don't follow the time clock. Remember the importance of being available for input at all times and especially the early and end-of-the-day hours. When someone picks up the telephone, sends you an electronic message, or stops by your office, they expect you to respond. Making sure you are around is part of your admission into an organization's innermost activities. Your level of involvement is sure to increase, by demonstrating your willingness to aggressively serve your job.

Continued on next page

8. **Understand Today's Communications Technology** — A certain way
    to impress management is to be well informed about today's newest commu-
    nications technology. You don't have to be a computer wizard to convince
    others of your knowledge. Make sure you are truly positioning yourself as
    the "communications expert" by knowing as much as possible about the lat-
    est technology, and be comfortable conversing freely about today's options
    and future trends. Management most likely will understand the importance
    of demonstrating a knowledge of technology, and it's a role you should
    want to play. The newest and possibly the most effective way of communi-
    cating in the future will involve technology awaiting commercialization.
    Some public relations professionals are already utilizing the company e-mail
    network to reach management at various levels on a regular basis. Others
    are experimenting with the Internet as a tool to reach customers, prospects,
    and employees with interesting new information. Leading your organization
    into these new and creative approaches should be more than a passing
    interest. And understanding of new technology is required. The time you
    invest here will be well spent.

The article, "How Public Relations Fits Into Corporate Strategy,"
by Dena Winokur, Ph.D., and Robert W. Kinkead, in the May 1993
issue of *Public Relations Journal*, is worth noting. The authors highlighted their research on how CEOs assess the importance of public
relations today and how it might in the future. The report reflects that
public relations is increasingly being used as a strategic management
tool. According to this report, the public relations profession has not
yet made as much progress on finding his or her way into a majority of
board rooms with the same footing of law or finance.

So while we may have made a great deal of progress in educating
management in the past, our efforts can never be considered finished,
and they really will never end. Public relations ultimately will achieve
within every organization the same kind of professional respect and
recognition that is accorded MBAs, CPAs, lawyers, and other valued
counselors to management.

By Robert L. Dilenschneider

CONCLUSION

If mankind could predict the future, we'd all be as successful in the stock market as Warren Buffett.

But often we can catch distinct glimmers of trends. Those allow us to speculate about how things could unfold. I've seen some glimmers. And they all bode well for public relations. If I had to sum up those trends in a headline, that headline would read: "P.R. RECOGNIZED FOR ITS POWER (finally)."

One of the things that's already happening is a move back to an oral tradition. If you're old enough, you'll remember those pre-paper, pre-direct-mail days when sales were made eyeball-to-eyeball. For instance, if my mother went into the store to buy a TV or into a bank to open an account, the salesman — and it was usually a man — gave his pitch. There were no glossy brochures "to take home and think about it." And the bank wasn't "more than happy" to give us an annual report we had no intention of reading.

In job hunting, though — just as in my mother's day — it's never been a paper game. As you know, you got the job depending on how you did on your feet during an interview. Paper — that is, a strong cover letter and well-done résumé — could get you in the door for an interview. Then all that mattered was the impression you made.

I remember just one case when a speechwriter blew the first interview and was given a second chance. The executive search firm handling the search was told about his performance and that, if he wanted the job, he should be more outgoing and energetic. He did that and got the job. Most other people aren't as lucky. They're forever perceived as the people they present themselves to be in the first few seconds of the interview.

Today, communications has become a lot more like job hunting and a lot less like writing white papers on the 40th floor of an oil company in Houston. This new need to look the world in the eye and strut your stuff is affecting just about every thing we do in communications.

If you're making a presentation to the board of directors, primarily what it cares about is what you say, not what's in the report you hand out or leave behind. More often than not the board members can't spend time reviewing written materials.

When potential clients contact me about possibly representing them, it's usually by phone and I have about three minutes to give my pitch. Based on that, I'll either get the account or not. No brochure, written testimonials from other clients or annual report about The Dilenschneider Group will any longer push the dial from "maybe" to "yes." The client thinking in this seems to be: We need a public relations firm that is alert and if they can't pick up and give off the right signals on the phone, they're not for us. We need them to hit the ground running.

I also suspect more professional schools, such as Harvard Law School, will require personal or video interviews. How many inappropriate people get into medical school because they're beautiful on paper but disasters interpersonally?

How will all this affect the profession of public relations? We're going to have less written material to prepare and more scripts and point outlines. Our work will increasingly center on coaching clients to perform in person and on video, radio, and TV. We'll also help them draft their remarks.

You might be doing some of this already. What could be new for you, though, is the level of the client you'll be dealing with.

Not too long ago the only people who received coaching in what we used to call "public speaking" were the top tier of the organization. Usually that organization was a corporation. And frequently the training was in connection with a specific event, such as a meeting with security analysts or testimony before Congress. Now, we're going to have ordinary citizens coming to us for assistance for all kinds of reasons, ranging from looking for a mate to performing better at everyday meetings. That is, the world out there is going to recognize that our knowledge can empower them.

Obviously, not presenting yourself well can be a competitive disadvantage in just about every aspect of life. As a result we could see public relations help becoming more or less a "right," much like the right to medical care and representation in a court of law. We could have sliding-scale fees and there could be government funding for the training.

That demand will attract many more talented, earnest people into our profession. They'll want to make a difference.

Some of us will be helping out 10-year-olds who can't relate to their peers. What was once labeled as an emotional problem will more frequently be treated as a lack of social skills. We're already seeing signs of that.

Dr. Daniel Goleman's 1995 book *Emotional Intelligence* has been getting considerable attention. For example, both *Time* and *Fortune* discussed it in depth. In *Emotional Intelligence*, Dr. Goleman contends that learning the social rules of society — empathy, self-knowledge, optimism — can improve people's chances for personal and professional success. Those who don't know those rules or choose to ignore them usually experience problems in every area of their lives.[1]

Some day soon our jobs may include helping our clients to become emotionally intelligent. There will be those of us who specialize in working with the aged. Those specialists, for example, will help the aging to re-learn to present themselves effectively with others. To us might also come mothers wanting to re-enter the work force. We can help them present themselves as confident and ready to work rather than insecure and ambivalent.

This type of coaching will be one of the specialties we can adopt. Although we'll still need a generalist background, the complexity of issues will lead most of us to choose one or a few specialties.

No longer will we be able to go from an account in consumer products to one in mainframe computers. Our clients' organizations will be moving too quickly for us to get up to speed in a new field. Already that is happening. It's much easier to get an account in heavy equipment if you already have a similar account. Clients now need results — quickly. They can't run the risk of turning over the accounts to amateurs. And as the world changes so will our specialties.

Another trend that's surfaced is the emergence of what I call "romanticism." Others call it "post-modern" or "anti enlightenment." Its impact on public relations can be huge.

Just a little background: When romanticism was sweeping Europe and England in the middle of the 18th century and into the 19th century, Americans didn't embrace the movement with open arms. Some such as the writer Edgar Allan Poe were fascinated with romanticism but, by and large, it wasn't for America. America was not ready to follow such romantic notions as: glorification of feelings as opposed to facts, belief that the individual can make a difference, emphasis on the spiritual rather than material, seeking enlightenment from intuition rather than science.

Since the 1960s, we Americans have been willing to experiment with a variety of world views. Just listen to us at a social gathering. More and more of us talk casually about: the higher self, spiritual growth, guardian angel, having a tarot-card reading with a witch in Salem, Massachusetts, and following our bliss. At meetings I attend, it's no longer unusual for someone to turn away from the numbers in a marketing-research report and "talk from the gut." Those interviewing for a job at The Dilenschneider Group ask me: "Can I be really creative here? Can I make a real contribution?"

How is this going to affect you and me in public relations? In many ways.

For example, empowerment has led to the establishment of countless advocacy groups, ranging from Mothers Against Drunk Driving (MADD) to Manic-Depressive Support Group. And they are changing the world.

They are very sophisticated about public relations and want the best public relations counsel. Increasingly they're coming to us, both as pro bono and as paying clients. One colleague, in her pro bono work for a residence for the emotionally disabled, told me that the liaison person in the organization knew exactly what she needed in public relations to set up a special event. She even understood how the organization could turn a profit from it.

In addition, these advocacy groups frequently have other groups as targets. For example, the liquor industry has been significantly affected by MADD as has conventional psychiatry by support groups. As a result, the targets need equally sophisticated public relations to communicate their point of view. For many of them that has meant abandoning their traditional ways of dealing with public opinion.

For example, one industry group used to mostly work on the national level — opinion-editorials in prestigious national papers and a national ad campaign. No more, their public relations has become targeted and local. The group has turned to grass-roots messages. They have assembled third parties, such as retailers, to present their position. They have also worked closely with local media. In addition, they're communicating their message through such vehicles as church bulletins.

In addition to the "watchdog" groups and the "watched," there are the whistle blowers. They feel that it's their mission to stop what they perceive to be a wrong. That is a fairly romantic notion. They're willing to risk all just to do the right thing. Often they seek out the media to tell their side of the story. Archer Daniels Midland whistle blower Mark Whitacre chose *Fortune* as his platform. He understood the power of the business media. Although this whistle blower suffered at the time — he was fired, he attempted suicide — he has gone on to become chief executive officer of another firm. His way of managing his public relations helped him.

In the future, more whistle blowers will seek out public relations advice *before* they go to the appropriate authorities. I sense they're coming to realize that the media can be their best ally.

Also, there are what I call the "educators" or "change agents." They have strong beliefs. They want to discourage domestic animals such as dogs and cats from reproducing because of the explosion in the pet population. There are those who want more research on the connection between physical disease and emotional problems. There are those who believe natural remedies can often substitute for invasive high-tech treatments. To communicate their message they are often turning to professional public relations methods. There is nothing amateurish about their P.R. efforts.

Another development in our romantic view of life is the need for self expression. There's a proliferation of first-person books and documentaries. Average Joes and Janes are joining the lecture circuit to tell about their experience. Those who have a background in film are applying for grants to fund their vision.

All this, of course, means more demand for our expertise. There will have to be more of us to handle the requests. Many of us will develop niches, such as public relations for new-age thinking or public relations for whistle blowers.

We will also see change in politics. Since the American Revolution, our political leaders have been savvy about public relations. However, they will have to become more realistic about what P.R. can accomplish. The public has become very sophisticated about public opinion. An inept candidate will find it increasingly difficult to run and win a campaign solely devoted to P.R. tactics. There's a return to the demand for substance.

That means that there will be much more call for our services during campaigns. We'll have to do a better job communicating the candidate's strengths and getting the public to feel okay about the politician's weaknesses.

As public relations becomes an even more important force in politics, consultants will return to a low profile. We won't be on the "Charlie Rose" or "Larry King Live" show explaining how brilliantly we orchestrated a landslide in Montana. The public relations function was never meant to be high profile. We are a support profession.

But no matter what our specialty in public relations, our firms will have to have an overlay of internationalism. It's not overstating the issue to say that we'll have to have intelligence sources about what's going on in other countries, politically, economically, and socially. Some of us will be more deeply involved in global public relations than others but all must have basic intelligence about what's going on. Kate Connelly in her chapter on global communications discusses the need for up-to-the-minute information in all global environments.

Globalization will directly or indirectly touch all our clients. That's because even a small- or midsize company, which neither exports or imports, can be affected by what goes on in Korea or China. A Korean or Chinese company can introduce a tea that curbs the appetite. That could knock the traditional weight-reduction services in the United States out of business. The global village has become an operating reality.

In my own business, our domestic clients are entering into more and more global alliances, such as mergers and joint ventures. In addition, foreign firms that are acquiring American companies need advice on how to operate in the United States. Public relations will increasingly become a global industry. No firm can remain purely domestic. That would be like declaring yourself a "print only" firm in a post-paper age.

Another change will be a return to the most basic concept of public relations. And that's: forming a strategy. We have to get back to asking: Why are we doing this?

I'm convinced failure in a public relations effort is usually due to skipping the strategic planning phases. Often in meetings, those in the group assume everyone understands the project's mission and goals. Wrong. Strategic planning must be done in a formal way with buy-in from the client and every one on the public-relations team as to the mission and goals. After that, the tactics we use will be more effective. For even clients who come to us on a project basis there must be a strategic plan.

In fact, clients will learn to demand a strategic plan, and a justification for each tactic. That is, for example, how does having an ad simulating the Spanish "running of the bulls" on Wall Street help a new financial-services firm get business? Was this the best tactic to use?

Another change is going to be where we do our work. Way back in 1989, British professor Charles Handy published a manifesto of sorts. Called *The Age of Unreason*, the book found its way onto just about every executive floor of every corporation in the United States.

In *The Age of Unreason*, Handy declared that organizations will break away from the usual hierarchy of numerous chiefs at varying levels and numerous Indians at varying levels. In place of that there would come what Handy calls the "Shamrock" organization. The shamrock would have three leaves.

One leaf, the smallest one, would be high-level experts in their field. They would be based in the corporation and they would act as liaisons to the other two leaves. The second leaf represents part-time workers who come to the corporation and do their work. The third leaf would represent freelance workers who are not affiliated with the corporation.

For example, at one time many corporations had fully staffed public relations departments. Now some such as NYNEX are using their reduced in-house public relations staff to act as liaisons with outside freelancers. The freelancers do an increasing amount of the work and the liaison staff do less of the hands-on projects.[2]

Soon you may not be a full-time employee at a public relations agency or maybe you'll never actually work full-time for any organization. Freelancing will become a recognized mode of work. After you get a graduate degree in communications from Columbia or the University of Michigan, you'll set up shop in your apartment. The "job hunt" as we know it could become an anachronism.

How we add value is also changing. At one time I would congratulate a subordinate for doing a terrific research job for opinion-editorial in *The New York Times*. It was obvious that he was a "digger." Technology, though, has made research more or less a commodity. Now we can go online and key in the search word "romanticism" and within a half an hour we have everything we need. The value added we now bring is the insight we have about the material we've downloaded from CompuServe or Dow Jones. That means we have to go a step further in our work to offer clients value.

The new language of contribution or what we're "bringing to the party" will increasingly be the language of value added. When thinking about hiring Candidate A or Candidate B we'll look less at pedigree and school credentials and more at how they've already demonstrated they have added value. Experience, not an Ivy League education, will be king.

NOTES

1. Daniel Goleman, *Emotional Intelligence: Why It Can Matter More Than IQ* (New York: Bantam Books, 1995), passim.

2. Charles Handy, *The Age of Unreason* (Boston: Harvard Business School Press, 1989), 87-116.

APPENDIX

NEW PRODUCT LAUNCH
A TELECOMMUNICATIONS COMPANY
MARCH 1993

NEW PRODUCT VIDEO
INTRODUCTION BY THE COMPANY'S PRESIDENT

INTRODUCTION

Good morning. As many of you know, I'm Joe Smith, President of our company. Today, I'm here to tell you about Product X.

X is a new generation of products for the private line market. These products are intelligent, fiber-based bandwidth networking services. They're software-controlled. And they provide end-to end private line networking. End-to-end is, of course, a lot different from what we've offered up to now. And up to now we've been offering dedicated lines from one customer location to another customer location.

X's capability lets us do some amazing things — easily and quickly.

By just pointing to a computer screen and clicking a mouse we can wire together all our customer's offices. End-to-end.

With another click we can triple the customer's bandwidth for the next 72 hours. When the 72 hours are over, the capacity "disappears."

Click again and the customer is set up for voice during the day and transmission of bulk data after five.

Click and we've hooked up the customer for a video link for a 3:30 meeting.

Continued on next page

Isn't this incredible!

It's very 21st-centuryish. Seven years early.

We'll be officially launching Product X on April __.

Product X is capable of transmitting data, voice, images and video—over the same wire—and at different speeds. It can facilitate medical imaging, Computer-Aided Design and Computer-Aided Manufacturing—and much more.

But these products are only part of the Product X story.

The other part of Product X's story is just as exciting. And it's about a revolution here at our company.

For our company, Product X represents a 180-degree change—a paradigm shift—a gigantic breakthrough in how we serve our customer.

Before X, we'd create products and then expect customers to buy them. Our attitude was sort of "Build it—and they will come."

Also, our marketing approach was fragmented. Not holistic. We'd develop and sell a service in a vacuum We didn't take into account what were customers' overall strategic needs. By that I mean, we didn't analyze what our customers needed to be successful in their businesses. That meant that we really weren't partners with our customers.

With this product, we brought in a new approach. We overhauled how we do business. Instead of just creating a product alone in our labs, we got the customer involved. In other words, instead of looking inward all the time at ourselves, we looked outward: At the marketplace. At the customer.

For instance, we went to our major customers. We asked them: What do you like and not like about our current services? And what do you really need to be successful?

What we were doing was taking into account their whole business, not just the little piece where we would be installing a service.

This product's focus is the customer's enterprise. That is, their business and its success, short and longer term. Our underlying goal was to help our customers prepare their businesses for the 21st century.

When we went to customers to ask about their businesses, they sure did give us an earful.

_____ (title), will tell you more about that.

Well, we listened. To each and every word.

We had to. This niche is a significant market to us. It's a big revenue producer, with excellent margins.

Another reason the private-line market is important to us is its growth potential. Our latest research shows that this niche is supposed to grow at about six percent annually.

Obviously, here is where the gold is — and will be.

So, one of our key strategic goals for 1993 has been: To position ourselves as a premier provider of this niche product. For us, this is a very ambitious goal. We're really pushing the envelope. See, we've lost market share in this niche. The competition has been eating our lunch.

We realize that there was simply no way we could regain that market share — and grow revenue — by doing more of the same — only a little better.

In other words, we weren't going to get very far just playing catch-up. _____, group vice president, will tell you more about how we changed the competitive field.

Let me just say that this launch will be the most important event in the history of this company. With it, we truly become the new company we claim we are. We have a totally new model for how to conceptualize, design, develop, market, monitor, and maintain private-line service. And if we're smart we'll apply this new model to everything we do.

Continued on next page

Some day, hey, who knows: We could be talking about how things were BP — Before this Product. And how they are now AP — After this product was introduced. I predict there'll be a world of difference between BP and AP.

But, I better stop talking and give _____ a chance to give some details about Product X and how it's going to be marketed.

(Bill Jandovitz)

MARKETING COMMUNICATIONS STRATEGIES FOR A PROFESSIONAL AND PERSONAL DEVELOPMENT FRANCHISE, WOODBRIDGE, CT

SPRING 1994

Submitted to franchise owner

The central challenge is to reposition the organization's brand name locally.

- Conduct focus groups to find out:

  - How people perceive the brand name locally (that information is already available on the national level)

  - What they need/want from the types of courses organization now offers/should offer

  - What they're willing to pay for those types of courses

  - Where they find out about the organization's courses. Friends? Newspapers? Radio? Television?

One focus group must be concerned with professional development issues. Another with personal development issues. There probably should be one of these groups held in a rural area and one in an urbanized location such as Stamford.

After we find out what we need to know then we can correctly position the organization locally and do appropriate marketing communications.

In the interim, before the repositioning, here are some short-term strategies to increase sales:

- Rewrite, shorten, and graphically repackage all the course print materials. The packaging should be youthful-looking.

- Direct mail. Send out a post card with a photo or graphic of a successful-looking man and woman holding wrenches, drills,

Continued on next page

with nails in their mouths. On the other side, words such as:

> Brand name gives you the tools to compete today.
> Tools like ...
> Call 800 for free consultation

• Direct mail. Short letters to CEOs/Training Directors. Focus on how organization concretely helps employees. That is, what the results were.

Perhaps a brochure should be created with short case histories and/or testimonials. Have you kept any type of measurements of results? Give 800 number. Mention free consultation. State you will give one concrete tip for success right on the phone.

• Direct mail. Target small businesses. Emphasize results. Perhaps bro-chure or flyer just for small businesses, with small-business case histories.

New strategy: Guarantee their money back if their business doesn't improve. This will be attractive to small business.

• Direct mail to college students, particularly seniors. Explain how you can help them get that first job. Have testimonials from young people. Enclose a $100-off coupon with no expiration date.

• Direct mail. Target local members of American Association of Retired Citizens (AARP). Discuss how your courses help people with personal and professional development. Enclose a $100- or $50-off coupon which must be redeemed by a certain date.

• Contact singles groups such as the Westport Unitarian Singles and explain how your course can significantly increase interpersonal effectiveness. Give case histories, with identities concealed.

• Bimonthly newsletter. Mailed to graduates, CEOs, training departments and prospects. Will contain short pieces of informational and inspirational nature. In fact, graphics should be that the inspirational pieces can be clipped and pinned up.

- Query the newspapers, cable channels and radio stations — each on an exclusive basis — to see if they're interested in what your organization has to say about topics such as:

  - In this age of television — what you must know about your image

  - How your intelligence can get you fired, divorced, off the network (or stop keep trying to be the smartest in the class)

  - How you're signaling to them: "I'm old," And how to stop it

  - How to be perceived as young and a hard-charger at work

  - How President Clinton got where he did

  - Why we like Hillary, but not Nancy

  - The new office etiquette

  - Helping your child get that first job

  - After a career setback — what not to do

  - What lets them know you're desperate for a job

  - One hundred tips for job interviews

  - All networks aren't created equal

  - Knowing when to compete, when to cooperate

- Opinion-editorials in local newspapers for your byline. The focus can be on such subjects as the pitfalls of networking.

- Inviting a reporter to participate free in one of your new courses to do a story on it (but, of course, not revealing people's real identities). This, of course, carries risk. The reporter could point to what he/she perceives as a negative in the program.

- A joint promotion. Scholarships to your courses for the unemployed. Scholarships will be paid for by participating local

Continued on next page

stores. Winners will be selected in drawings. The unemployed enter by going into one of the participating stores and filling out an entry form. If their name is drawn they have to show proof of unemployment. The sweepstakes can be promoted jointly by you and participating stores through signs on store windows, press releases to newspapers, radio, TV.

• A joint promotion. With a reputable weight-control program like Weight Watchers or a physical-fitness center. For a certain amount of money, person gets 6 weeks of you and Weight Watchers. Price would be less expensive than if taken separately, plus there would be a $100-off coupon.

• Winter Olympics. Press release to all media discussing your in-volvement with Special Olympics. To be sent just before Winter Olympics.

• Special Event. Your instructors and graduate students appear in malls to give free advice to unemployed, those worried about their jobs. This event will be announced with press releases.

• Bumper stickers. These can be placed on instructors' cars and sold in class. A catchy slogan would have to be created. The main purpose would be to position you as a professional tool for the 1990s.

• Start a mentor program. For a year after graduation from one of your courses, people can have access to a mentor in their profession or line of life (such as retiree or housewife). Letters would have to be sent to graduates to ask them to volunteer. *That letter can also be an opportunity to promote new courses.* Studies show a former customer is more apt to buy than a new prospect.

• Franchise paraphernalia. Stuffed animals with inspirational sayings, calenders, boxes of greeting cards, baseball hats, T-shirts and especially things that will be brought in office. Will help to get the brand name around plus bring in revenues. We can even mail catalogues.

After we have the results of the focus groups then we can form other strategies.

MARKETING COMMUNICATIONS IDEAS FOR A DELI IN STAMFORD, CT

SPRING 1994

Submitted to Owner

- **Try a new logo.** A huge pickle. Or some other fun symbol of deli life. Then carry out that motif on all your marketing communications. For example, pickle-green aprons for clerks, pickle-green placemats, a pickle on the window. Put an old-time barrel of pickles in middle of front of stores. Distribute pickle samples or pickle pins or pickle buttons at door or throughout neighborhood. Pass out pickle-green flyers about the new deli.

- **Offer delivery within walking distance.** Hours for this could be 7AM to 8PM. Could impose a 50-cent delivery fee. Can hire senior citizens for this job. Then we can promote the idea that you hire senior citizens. We announce this new service on the window; by someone dressed as a pickle or with a pickle hat giving out pickle samples and flyers about delivery; putting flyers in apartment buildings and office complexes.

- **Invite a local DJ** (there's a radio station right next door) broadcast from the deli. This can be promoted as: A bit of "Seinfeld" in Stamford, CT. DJ can interview customers if they identify with "Seinfeld"; what kinds of things they discuss at the deli; why they come to a deli instead of some other type of eating place. To make sure customers are there, some can be lured to come with a promise of a free lunch.

- **Invite a local cable channel** to come to deli and talk to you, workers and customers about the special place delis are. What's necessary to serve in a deli? How has deli life changed over the years? What do people like about delis? Has the deli been hurt by the recession? There are three other eating places near by. Why do some people come to a deli instead of going to those other places?

Continued on next page

Or else a reporter from the newspaper can be invited for this interview.

- **Start a Friend of (Owner's name) Club.** They get to join the Club when they have sales receipts for purchases adding up to say about $100. This entitles them to:

    - $5 off

    - Their photo is put up on the wall

    - They get to call in reservations for a table and a reservation sign is put on with their name

    This can be a funky idea.

- **Introduce gourmet coffees and add touches in dining area to look like a cafe.** The cafe in neighborhood is doing very well. Announce with sign on window, person dressed as Frenchman with sign about cafe giving out cents-off coupons, flyers, greeter by the door telling people to smell the coffee. Possibly add fancy desserts.

- **Install salad bar/buffet.** Announce it with: Samples given out on street, sign on window, flyers, possible postcards, cents-off coupons, someone dressed as a carrot walking up and down neighborhood with sign about bar/buffet.

- **Partition off sections of back dining area for private meetings.** Announce this in a post card to businesses within walking distances.

- **Install large screen tv.** Show shorts such as cartoons, travels. During slow hours show old movies like "Casablanca." Announce as above. Sell munchies. Announce as above.

- **Keep open through dinner hour.** Position deli as a family neighborhood restaurant. "Cheers" without the drinks and with the kids. For dinner hour buy special placemats for children. Run kids' short movies. Each night or week have a drawing for kids. Winner is announced on window. Prize can be donated by local merchant who would get credit on your window.

- **Have amateur nights.** Anyone, including children and families, can do anything for seven minutes: Do stand-up comedy, play an instrument, play the drums, do impersonations. Then the bell rings. Those performing will bring their friends. Sell snaks. The flyer can say: Do your performance. And bring your own audience. If this works, we can get press coverage, notify Stamford's art leaders.

- **Cut prices.** And announce it.

- **Use some of the dining area to sell high-margin products**, such as take-home gourmet coffees, premium sweets, exotic fruits.

SUGGESTED MARKETING PLAN
FOR ASSISTED-LIVING FACILITY

Submitted to Manager

Mission: To position the assisted-living facility as the First Choice in Assisted Living

Goal: To keep facility filled to capacity

Objective: To enhance the perception by current residents, prospects, their significant others and referral sources that this facility is a wholesome, caring, safe and fun place to be

Cost: Multi-channel marketing, as opposed to reliance on advertising, is cost-efficient

Preliminary Work

Conduct focus groups and/or informal surveys among current residents, possible residents, significant others and referral sources. The objectives would be to find out how people feel about the facility now, what they would like changed and their "wish list" for all such facilities.

Do library research on assisted-care facilities.

Strategies to Increase Awareness of this Facility and Enhance Image

• Personal visits to referral sources and other appropriate agencies. In addition to introducing oneself, the visits serve to get feedback and suggestions.

• Guest presentations at senior-citizen groups, including AARP meetings. The topic would be a general discussion of what this thing called "assisted living" is, who should consider it, how much it costs, etc.

• Who We Are kit. If one doesn't already exist then there should be created an upbeat kit describing life at this facility. The tone should be warm, candid and perky. The materials should be full of pictures, photos and bright colors and contain testimonials from current residents, their significant others and workers at the facility. If the budget permits, it'd be great to also have an audio tape. On it would be comments from executive director, residents, their significant others and workers.

• Media relations. Develop relationships with key editors, print and electronic, in target markets. This means free advertising.

• Op-eds. Write op-eds/articles for directors's byline on various aspects of assisted care. For example, pending federal/state legislation or concept of "ableness." These are to be placed in target markets. Once published, such op-eds/articles can be used in mailings and information kits.

• Newsletter(s). For residents, prospects, prospects' significant others and referral agencies and other professionals. Would include articles by the residents and employees (they could write them or dictate them into a tape recorder and I can brush them up), a column called "Breakthroughs" about residents' achievements, information and research about assisted care, information about what's happening in the facility, humor, articles by or about experts in field of assisted care or related areas and lots of photos.

Residents/employees who contribute to the newsletter would receive a pen, with an appropriate engraving. They could also be recognized in a monthly dinner. Eventually the newsletter could be turned into a profit center by contracting a sales force to sell ads for it.

• Special Events. These could be done either alone or in conjunction with related service or product providers. These events would be both informational and entertainment. They could be held off premises or at the facility. If appropriate, media would be invited. Special events increase awareness of the facility and help it to be perceived as a dynamic leader in assisted care.

Continued on next page

- Open houses, with guest speaker. For prospects, their significant others, referral sources and other interested parties. The guest speaker would be an expert in a topic related to assisted care.

- Ongoing support group for those involved with person in assisted care. Here a credentialed facilitator would have to be hired on a subcontract basis.

- Ongoing support group for those in assisted care. Here a credentialed facilitator would have to be hired on a subcontract basis.

- Computers online. Either get companies to donate or facility buys a few computers, equipped with modems. Those enables residents to communicate with just about anybody electronically.

Training residents to use the computers and electronic bulletin boards could be paid for by the facility, by residents themselves or provided by volunteers. This would greatly enhance residents' horizons. Also it could make a great media story.

- Seminars on assisted care. Public could be informed about these seminars through direct mail, ads in newspapers, community calendars and telemarketing. It would be great if residents from the facility could be there and say a few words.

- Name change for this facility. There could be a contest to rename the facility. The prize could be donated by a service or product provider to the facility. Residents could participate. Judges could provide their time pro bono; they could be professors in a school of communications or professionals in an advertising agency.

- Volunteers. Especially to help residents develop new interests. In the "Volunteer" section of *advocate*, for instance, request volunteers with interesting hobbies to give talks on this at facility.

- Inspirational slogan, to be created. And put on T-shirts, mugs, socks, greeting cards. This would not only promote the facility but could also become a profit center.

- Greeting cards, designed for the facility. This would promote the facility as well as instill pride in it.

- Community outreach. Leasing consultant joins appropriate community groups.

- Possible pet program. Research shows that those with pets are happier and healthier. Residents can be assisted in getting and maintaining pets.

- More activities. Happy, active residents are the best organization's best salespeople. Schools of social work can be approached to provide interns in group activities.

REMARKS BY CHIEF EXECUTIVE OFFICER
OF A MAJOR FINANCIAL-SERVICES FIRM

NEW YORK, 1994

It's great to be here with you, the members of our new diversity network.

If you accomplish all you plan to do, you will be a major force in helping our company become more competitive. That's because this whole diversity issue is, at its core, about gaining a competitive edge through people.

Our competitors can analyze and then imitate our strategies. They can implement similar technologies. They can match our capital position. But what they can't duplicate is you, the employees of this corporation. You're one of our key "significant variables" in competitive success.

But, if we don't do this thing right—that is, manage diversity— this company could become a Has-Been, another one of those companies which couldn't cut in the '90s.

In short, we see diversity as a business imperative, not a Feel-Good social issue.

You've brought a lot of information about diversity to the attention of the company. You've developed a diversity mission statement. All that has helped us make progress on the learning curve. Also, I've recently attended a three-day seminar on diversity.

Because of all this, I've done plenty of thinking, talking and brainstorming about diversity. Today I want to share those thoughts with you. And let me tell you, right up-front, that I don't have all the answers on this one. I'll continue to need your input.

As I see it, diversity is basically about understanding and accepting that people are different from one another.

Continued on next page

We have different backgrounds. We have different talents and strengths. We have different personality styles and lifestyles. We're from different generations; and things are changing so fast that two years could make a generation gap. We have different values. Some people define their lives through work. Some people don't. And often those values keep changing. There are also those differences of gender, race, ethnicity, religion, and sexual orientation.

No, these differences themselves aren't new. What is new is that we're acknowledging that differences exist. At one time, not too long ago, in large organizations there was a tacit assumption that we all must blend in. We even tried to look the same. There used to be a joke that so-and-so was hired or even promoted because he — and it was usually a he — "looked the part." The term "corporate culture" was, in many ways, a code word for rigid "conformity."

But that era of rigid conformity must be behind us. Yes, there will always be core values and rules, written and unwritten. But, hopefully, never again will we all be marching in lockstep to the same drummer. That old type of corporate culture encouraged too much passivity and mindless compliance. It also tended to overlook talent which wasn't "packaged" in what was then the politically correct mode.

To do well in the '90s marketplace we need people who think and take initiative. And people who can produce results have to be recognized and rewarded. That's what diversity is all about. As you can probably see, diversity is part of the many other changes going on at the Bank to make us more competitive.

In managing diversity, we basically have to focus on two things. One is not letting human differences get in the way of all employees achieving their potential. In other words, this is the nurturing of a true meritocracy. Your performance will be what counts, not your "pedigree" — that is, what family, school, neighborhood or specialization you come from.

The second thing we must focus on is getting all these differences to become sources of value in our business. I'm convinced that one reason Bill Clinton's presidential campaign was successful was that he was smart enough to bring together a whole bunch of different people with different backgrounds and different expectations. Every decision during the campaign required them to consider different points of view. Sure enough, what emerged were winning strategies. We can and must have that same type of dynamic environment at our company.

Ironically, those opposed to a more diverse workplace claim that standards will decline. They're way off. If we can access all the talent which is at our company, not only will standards become higher. Performance should dramatically improve. If you look at the so-called Golden Age of organizations such as Apple or CBS, that type of peak performance seemed to have occurred because a diverse group of people were able to pool their talents and skills.

The rewards for us are so great if we can manage diversity. But that will not be easy. For instance, diversity is a tough thing to even talk about in our society. Most of the subjects touched upon in any diversity discussion are emotionally charged and stimulate painful memories for a lot of people.

But even though discussing diversity is going to make many of us uncomfortable, talk about it we must. We have no choice. We must deal with it. Current realities demand that we come to terms with the diversity issue at our company.

For instance, there is the new demographic reality. Of the 26 million new entrants to the U.S. work force between 1987 and 2005, over 85 percent will be from minority groups, women and immigrants. White males entering the work force will become the new "minority."

Also, we're in a global business. We operate in close to 40

Continued on next page

countries. Each country has a distinct culture and, within that, a number of subcultures. That is equivalent to the regional differences in the U.S. marketplace. At one time, some marketing experts believed you could create the same standardized or global products and global promotions for the entire world. That didn't work. Cultures resisted — just as France is now resisting Mickey Mouse.

In addition, many of the countries we do business in are experiencing diversity issues of their own. Immigration, for instance, is becoming widespread in Europe. Germany is struggling to unify two radically different economic systems. And generational differences are emerging in the once-homogeneous Japanese workplace.

Since we operate in so many countries, our customers and clients are diverse. They represent almost every ethnic, national and religious group you can name. Much of what we do in our business is to build long-term relationships with our customers and clients. Well, obviously, we aren't going to be able to do that if we don't understand and show respect for what makes these people "tick," particularly their values and customs.

Another big reason managing diversity is a have-to is that team work is going to become the new business-as-usual. To be more focused, faster and better, our company will be putting together the best people from different specializations and maybe even from different countries to serve customers, launch new products and anticipate trends.

Those artificial walls between job descriptions, departments, organizations and countries will all be coming down. You're probably already working with a broader range of people than you did before.

Also, we'll be seeing more strategic alliances with "outsiders." They'll not only be with other companies. Also in the loop will be our customers and suppliers. What is "inside" and what is "outside" our company will become increasingly blurred.

But you know and I know: These new approaches won't get off the ground unless we can all work together and derive value from those cooperative efforts. The question is: How do we remove the obstacles which stand in the way of our managing diversity?

Well, as I've said, I don't have all the answers on this one. But I do have some hunches about what direction we've got to move in to manage diversity.

But first let me say that the current modus operandi won't change unless all of our executive management is committed to it. That's why I've made managing diversity a priority. And that's why diversity is one of our core values.

What we have to change falls into two categories. One is how we think and act as individuals. The other is how our system works. That is, how we, as an institution, behave with regard to diversity.

Here are some examples of how we can change on an everyday basis.

We need to stop stereotyping. Generalizing about others is a habit, a bad habit. One that's lazy and dumb. What are those generalizations? "All Asians are good in math." "All white Anglo-Saxon men are reserved." "All Hispanics are expressive." "All women are good at details." Let's get rid of the word "all."

But there is the danger of replacing old stereotypes with new stereotypes. A little knowledge, a little reading of *The Wall Street Journal* or *The Harvard Business Review* can be a dangerous thing. Some new stereotypes are: "All women lead through consensus." "All white Anglo Saxon men want to chuck it all and follow the Call of the Wild." "All employees want to be leaders." Again, we've got to get "all" out of our workplace vocabulary.

Continued on next page

From now on, let's put energy into seeing our associates as unique human beings. There's Mary Jones, a person. And that person is a living, breathing entity with plenty of complexity and who's apt to keep changing.

In essence, what stereotyping does is reduce people to one dimension — to almost caricatures of themselves. Just listen to someone talking in stereotype terms about someone else. It sounds comic. That's why bigot Archie Bunker was such a sitcom hit in the early '70s.

Another obstacle to diversity is that very human desire to be "comfortable." To be comfortable, we've tended to restrict our interactions at work to those who look, think and talk like us. Therefore, we may never have gotten to really know those even a little different from us. For instance, with whom do you go to lunch? Also, we've tended to promote those like us. We felt that by promoting clones of ourselves "we knew what we were getting."

At our company, we're going to have to stretch our "comfort zone." If we don't, we're going to wind up a closed system only looking inward. Read the history of business organizations, industries and whole nations. They failed primarily because they became closed systems which lost touch with the outside. That's why businesses which are closed systems frequently underestimate the competitive threat.

A third change we have to make is how we define "success." For as long as I can remember "success" meant climbing the corporate ladder. Organizations tended to pay attention to and develop primarily those going upward.

That kind of attitude is behind the curve, for two reasons. One, our organizations are getting flatter. And hopefully, they'll get a lot flatter. And two, we need everyone's contribution. There are no "minor parts" any more in business. Every person in every job must perform.

The new definition of "success" has to be: Fulfilling your

potential. This isn't Hollywood. I want to see the "star system" die a quick death.

I'm looking to you to make a commitment to change your habits of thinking. In addition, we'll offer formal training to help you identify where you need to stretch your comfort zone. Let's hope much of what I call "old-line" or "pre-diversity" thinking dies with our generation of business persons.

Now let's look at the institutional impediments to managing diversity.

One is what I call "clustering." Women and minorities tend to cluster in certain specializations. There's nothing wrong with that if that's where you want to be and stay. But if you want to become a leader in the organization, you need to gain broader experience. In that way you can move into the feeder pools for leadership positions.

In my experience in business, I haven't seen any born leaders. Leaders are developed, step by step. Sure you have to have some basic talent in dealing with people but you must also have developmental opportunities.

So, in the case of clustering, we've got to rotate you in a variety of jobs. But let me add: Not every one of you is going to emerge from the process a leader. Some of you will fail. Also, some of you will find out that you don't really want to be a leader but probably pursued that path because you thought you "ought to." You might, for instance, find out that a leadership position demands that you radically change your life. Maybe you have to give up most of your free time or hobbies you enjoy.

With diversity comes the new freedom to drop some of the "oughts" about what career path to follow. There's no one ideal career path for everyone. The important thing is that you be able to choose.

Continued on next page

And suppose you opt for a leadership position and fail. Well, now you'll be failing for the right reasons: Your performance. It won't be because of race, gender, ethnicity or sexual orientation.

Another shortcoming in our system is the performance appraisal process. As a tool, it's used too much to document and evaluate and not enough to coach. The performance appraisal system has to evolve into something which can truly help you develop. It should be an ongoing inventory of your knowledge base and skills and what you might need.

Maybe you're not good at getting people to cooperate when you have no formal authority over them. Could something like a Dale Carnegie course help? Are your daily interactions too narrow in scope? What about taking on a responsibility which will get you more into the loop? Or it may be a case that to be taken more seriously you need an academic credential. That might be a degree in accounting or psychology.

Another gap in our system is the flow of information. In organizations information always was a source of power. That's even more true today. So much of what we do is information-based. Many of you aren't getting enough information because you're not part of the "old boys' network." I will see to it you get access to more high-quality information. Also, your network can help bridge any gaps. And that brings me to how I see your network functioning at our company.

I hope that your network will become a model for other diversity groups. We need more networks of people who sense they're not reaching their full potential. That kind of initiative, that kind of self-help thrust is exactly the kind of can-do spirit our company needs. You might say employee networks are a symbol of the new type of organization we're becoming.

As a group, you've already accomplished a lot. You've given us a mission statement. You've gotten your message across — loud and clear — that things are not right. I heard you.

From now on, you will serve as a continuous reality-check. That will help me keep managing diversity on-track. And the momentum going.

Also, you serve in another important capacity. And that's empowering your members. You're teaching, for instance, your members how to be savvy change agents, how to get heard in a large organization. There's that old saying: Give people fish, they eat for a day. But teach them to fish and they eat for a lifetime. You're teaching people to fish — that is, to gain more control over their own professional destiny. If you did nothing else, that in itself would be a profound contribution.

Managing diversity is going to be a continuous process. It'll never be over. That's because human differences will always persist — fortunately. But how will we know that we're making progress on the learning curve?

Well, you'll feel it. You'll feel better about yourself and the job you're doing.

Your expectations are going to change. You'll expect that if you're talented and if you're willing to make the personal sacrifices a leadership position demands, you'll get a chance to try it out. On the other hand, if you choose to continue doing what you like doing, you'll expect to keep developing.

Also, the atmosphere here will be more dynamic. There'll be more give-and-take among different points of view. There'll be more questioning of assumptions. How we do our work will change. There'll be fewer commands and more discussions about assignments. So much of the old system was based on order-giving and order-taking.

And when we say "WE" we'll mean all of us. And "all of us" will include we who are employees of this company. Plus our customers. Plus our suppliers. Plus our joint venture partners. The "THEM" will mean the competition.

Continued on next page

Because we'll be less of a closed system, we'll be more in touch with what's going on outside this company. That'll help us figure out what's going on in our competitors' heads. That means fewer competitive surprises for us.

As a result of all this, our earnings will improve. The bottom line is: If we can access all the talent, energy and enthusiasm that are here, we're going to see our profits soar.

Before I wrap up, let me just say one more thing. If we manage diversity correctly, life at our company isn't going to become like one of those warm-and-fuzzy workplace sitcoms such as "Murphy Brown" or "Love and War." We probably won't love each other or get very involved in each other's personal lives. But we probably will respect one another and the work each one of us does. Also, we will all feel a part of, rather than apart from.

Thanks for your attention.

REMARKS BY ROBERT DILENSCHNEIDER
CHAIRMAN OF THE DILENSCHNEIDER GROUP

DELIVERED TO THE CONFERENCE BOARD
JANUARY 1995
NEW YORK, NEW YORK

FORMING A DISTINCTIVE COMPANY IMAGE

Good afternoon.

And, thank you for that kind introduction.

I'm truly flattered to be here today. Like you, I receive many invitations to speak. But I've never thought that I'd have the opportunity to "pitch" my message to the Conference Board. Gathered in this room are a number of the most influential opinion leaders in the world.

And I'm convinced that you are where you are because you've been able to develop, to project and to sustain strong images. I hope that what I've just said hasn't offended you. I know that to some the word "image" has negative connotations. To them, image may mean anything from an empty suit to manipulation.

Well, they're dead wrong. My talk today will blow out of the water many of those kinds of misconceptions about image. The topic of my speech is "Forming a distinct image for your company." I'll talk a little about image in general: What it is. What it does. Who has it. Who lost it. And who can't seem to get it. Next, I'll discuss what the obstacles are in the 1990s to developing lasting images. Notice I emphasized "lasting." Then I'll propose a five-step program that virtually guarantees you'll be able to create an appropriate image for your organizations.

Okay, what's this thing we call "image"?

Image is something like art. You know it when you see it — and feel it.

Continued on next page

Notre Dame. Warren Buffet. Jack Welch. Jimmy Stewart. Paul Newman. Microsoft. Ben & Jerry's. Lord & Taylor. The Salvation Army. Lassie. Seattle. Bottled water. The Internet.

What all these have in common is substance. Even the water — at least since we've found out that water is good for you and America's new Zeitgeist is health and fitness. Only something with substance can endure. Think about this: Florence, Italy has had an enduring image — and nothing of note has happened there for 400 years. Florence has substance.

Substance is important to us human beings. We see fads come and go. And when they're around we enjoy them. How many here are old enough to remember the hula hoop? — But there's something in us that needs an entity that's bigger than our-selves, that endures no matter what, that has layers of support. Maybe that's why so many support groups today are anchored on the idea of a Higher Power ...

And, incidentally, entities with substance can reinvent them-selves and come back. Keep an eye on Banker's Trust. It's solid. Yes, it's had some rough times but you'll be hearing more from it. I predict California, as a trend leader, will also reinvent itself and come back.

Another quality necessary for image is a sense of pride and a healthy self-love. You see a lot of this in small communities. Maybe it's a school teacher or a banker. They love what they do. They love themselves. And their images in the community are dis-tinct. No, they're not "celebrities." To have a distinctive image you don't have to be a celebrity. Probably most of the men and women in your organizations with the strongest images aren't known outside your company or their profession.

The third quality going into image is peer acceptance. It's important that your colleagues say you're talented. It would also help if *People* magazine and *Business Week* agreed with them.

Isn't a big part of the reason you're in your current positions is that other people recognized your abilities? When they do that things have a way of happening, don't they?

The fourth and probably the most important component of image is emotion. There's Frank Sinatra on the stage. Fat. Voice not too good anymore. And we all know those stories about him. Yet, when he starts crooning ... We can't help but go crazy. The fat disappears. The toupee starts looking better. The voice — heck, nobody's perfect. The stories lose their grime. And we fall in love again with that kid from Hoboken.

And were we willing to pay $3.00 a pint for Ben & Jerry's Cherry Garcia because it tasted better than the $2.00 brand? No way. We paid because we had bonded with everything Ben & Jerry's represented. They're the Peter Pans who didn't have to grow up. They're good guys who contributed to the Rain Forest. They're the employers who treated employees the way we wish we had been treated. It was a stroke of genius that Ben and Jerry put their mugs on every pint of ice cream.

When an image is at its best, we bond. We're more loyal than any dog. That's why our fallen heroes, whether it be a person like O.J. or an institution like IBM, break our hearts. How many times do you hear people say about O.J.: How could he have done this to us?

To sum it all up, I'd say that "image" is a bundle of perceptions and feelings. These all sort of pull together and form one unified concept. For Coca-Cola that concept is Americana. For Pepsi it's youthfulness. For Calvin Klein it's sophisticated. For Weight Watchers it's sensible.

What image does is get you "shelf space" in minds and hearts. That's why it's so potent. And that's what Lee Iacocca did for the Statue of Liberty. New Yorkers who passed the Statue of Liberty every day for years never gave it a thought — or had feelings about it — until Iacocca gave it a distinct image.

Continued on next page

A strong image can lead people to support you, even in bad times. To forgive you. To give you the benefit of the doubt. To take a risk and buy your product or service when others are skeptical.

There are so many examples of this. During the early 1980s, Lee Iacocca, who had been just fired from Ford, went to Chrysler, an almost bankrupt company. Know what Iacocca did? He presented to America the image of both Chrysler and himself as feisty underdogs. He reinforced that image in every way. In TV commercials, in company newsletters, in the frayed carpet in the offices, in the speeches executives gave, in opinion editorials and in letters to consumers.

Know what? Americans bought Chrysler cars even though there was no assurance that Chrysler would be around next year to service those cars. Since then, both Iacocca and Chrysler have had their ups and downs. But the image has survived.

But what happens when an image doesn't work?

I've seen talented, ambitious people, I've seen worthy causes and I've seen well-run companies never reach their potential — and all because they've made an error in how they've created or handled their image.

Who are some of them?

At the top of the list are Bill and Hillary Clinton. Read Elizabeth Drew's book about them — *On The Edge*. Drew's take is: It's image, stupid. Smart, educated, driven people can drop the ball on image as clumsily as anyone else. A few weeks ago on the front page of *The New York Times* was the headline, "Hillary Clinton Seeking to Soften a Harsh Image." That's about the fifth new image Hillary's tried. With image, as with quality, do it right the first time. Otherwise you lose credibility.

Poor Bob Stempel at General Motors. His was the wrong image for the wrong time in the history of General Motors. The times demanded less of a plodder, an old company guy, an incrementalist. But, remember this, nine months after he had been ousted, GM started to turn around. Stempel's plan had worked. Too bad his image hadn't. Otherwise he'd be still at GM, getting the credit for the turnaround. — It's image, stupid.

Bill and Hillary and Stempel aren't alone. More people, more non-profits and more companies fail at creating a distinct image than succeed. I'd wager that Frank Lorenzo, who was perceived as the bad guy, could have achieved his goals had he had some support. Image could have gotten him that support. The same goes for Dick Ferris of Allegis. Whom do you know who's underachieving because they're naive or arrogant about image? How many MBAs have come to your organizations and have gotten sidelined because they assumed credentials put them above image?

Dilenschneider's First Principal of Image is: No one's above image. Just remember: God spent the whole Old Testament developing his image.

There's also another image category. And that's successful images which have gotten tired and stale. What's on the list? Fading icons. "60 Minutes." Mickey Mouse. Japanese management techniques. Ivy league schools. Some computer companies. Some brokerage houses. — Oh, I almost forgot — the liberal Democrats.

Image isn't a new invention. You might say that the first well-organized P.R. firm was probably the Twelve Disciples. Matthew, Mark, Luke, and John wrote all the press releases.

And, international consultant Kenichi Ohmae calls the Roman Catholic Church one of the most successful, long-enduring global organizations. He's right. Thanks to its distinct image, the Church has been able to survive just about anything, including the current scandals and rigid leadership.

There were also: The Pyramids. Julius Caesar. Attila the Hun. Christopher Columbus. Names sound familiar? But what about Greece? Do your kids come running home excited about Aristotle

Continued on next page

and Plato? And, except for the Monopoly Board, when's the last time you've seen the name "Reading Railroad"? The Reading was the oldest company in America. Do you know who invented rubber or the flywheel?

That shows you how once-powerful images can arrive at a new decade DOA. Let me just sum up here. A good image—one that's well made and well cared for—can survive everything, including the test of time. Scandal. Change. Bad earnings.

But creating and preserving an image has never been easy. The Twelve Disciples really had to hustle. And many images have had their ups and down. The solid among them, though, always come back. How many times did FDR and Churchill come back?

During the 1990s, creating and sustaining an image is far harder—and getting harder all the time. You probably already know why that's so.

Basically there are four reasons.

• One of them you know well. And that's clutter. According to the *Harvard Business Review*, we receive over 1800 commercial messages every day.

In Rome during ancient times when the guys were riding around in their chariots there were no outdoor signs about a new cough remedy. No radio pitching pizza. No faxed messages. Nobody calling on the cellular phone with a pitch for getting rugs shampooed.

Do you realize how many messages we end-of-the-century folks get just on the drive to work? What about in the supermarket? Even when we throw something in the garbage there could be a McDonald's logo on a bag to make us think "burger." Some video games now have commercial messages on them.

Wherever there can be a message, there is one.

Added to all that business clutter are the messages from nonprofits and advocacy groups. Look at how the contents of your mailbox has changed over the past few years. I'll bet there's more from Save the Whales and your alma mater's development office than from commercial enterprises. The question you have to ask yourself is: Why in the world would people notice and remember my message as opposed to all the rest of the messages out there? This is the reality test. It's pure narcissism to think your message is automatically entitled to prime shelf space.

• The second reason why it's so difficult to create a distinct image in the 1990s is because there are more entities out there competing for attention. And they're savvy enough to know what a potent tool image is. I sit in my office every day and receive calls from around the world. The callers want image. They want an image which will convince Wall Street that their stock price should go up or a bank should lend them money or the public should buy their cheese. But they don't have a clue what image requires.

And these calls are increasing in frequency. And desperation. That's because of the overpopulating of everything.

Name one profession, one industry, one product line, one franchise, one mail-order business, one area of charity where there isn't a glut. In the mail I got pleas for donations from about a dozen animal advocacy groups. I used to get just one — from the ASPCA.

And in addition to the *Fortune* 1000, you now have a growing number of smaller companies. They've attended Entrepreneurship 101 and are fully aware of the importance of image. They buy some gee-whiz software. And they spend more time producing marketing materials than they do operating the business. Know what? Their priorities are right. And we're getting an avalanche of messages from them. Who isn't sending out a newsletter?

There's also more competition in our economy for resources of all types — for instance, for employees with the right skills. As a

Continued on next page

result, human-resources vice presidents come to my office ready to pay mega bucks for an exhibit and brochure. They want communications which depict their companies as caring and flexible, leading edge and young. And there are more ideologies out there pitching more ideas in more magazines and talk shows and books.

In short, the more competitive the marketplace becomes, the more of a dog fight goes on to transmit a distinct image.

Ask yourself: How am I different from the rest of them?

• The third reason the 1990s makes it tough to form a distinctive image is the scope and pace of change. In Manhattan, the Mom and Pop deli is an institution. But, it could go the way of bicycle messengers when fax came in. Now McDonald's is doing what the deli was famous for: Delivering.

And the life span of innovation gets shorter and shorter. Today you might have a great invention such as a high-tech sneaker. In two days, there's a knock-off of it. And that knock off may be cheaper. And better. So, what happens to your image as an innovator?

No institution is immune from all this change. Colleges, mainline churches, congress, the presidency, hospitals, white-shoe law firms — they've all been chastened by change.

Bennington College has abolished tenure. The president of Harvard has a nervous breakdown during fundraising. And the for-profit college has been invented. In response to all these kinds of upheavals institutions are struggling to find and communicate the right image. It literally means survival.

• The fourth and last factor which makes a distinct image tough to pull off is the degree of negativity in our culture. People have come to love bad news.

Which story do you think people would pay more attention to: The Salvation Army raises a record amount of money. Or the toys purchased with the money raised by the Salvation Army is stolen just before Christmas?

Bad news makes people feel better about their own lives. And in the 1990s people aren't feeling too good about those lives. You might say bad news is the new escapism.

In fact, the power of negativity reminds me of that old E.F. Hutton commercial: When E.F. Hutton talks, people listen. That's exactly what's happening throughout America. When bad news talks, people listen.

What that means is that you have to be more skillful at positioning and packaging your story. A positive news story can be sold to the media. But it requires finesse. And, as I'll explain shortly, media is one of the most important tools for building an image.

So, what do we do about all this? Given all these obstacles how do we generate a distinctive image? I have developed for you a five-step program. It works.

Step Number One: Know where you're going. Did you see the January 16th issue of *Fortune* with Bill Gates on the cover? In it Gates very clearly articulates where Microsoft is and is not going. He knows who he is and who Microsoft is.

Many other companies think they know who they are and where they're going. That's why there's a proliferation of mission statements. In the *Washington Post*, Jay Mathews has a lot of fun with these mission statements. He points out that mission statements are even catching on with community volunteer groups.

What's wrong with most of the mission statements, Mathews says, is that they all sound the same. Also, usually consultants cook them up. As a result, no one in the business understands the mission statement, cares about it or follows it.

What you wind up with is no link between the mission statement and behavior — and therefore with image. Behaviors must support image. Hey, you can't have an image of Taco Bell as sparkling clean if no one ever mops the floor.

Continued on next page

Ford Motor Company, in the 1980s, knew where it wanted to go. It wanted to position itself as a leader in quality. — Its message was and still is: "Quality is Job One." Look where Ford is now.

Ford found a good thing and had the sense to stay with it. The idea was a breakthrough idea, at least for the early 1980s. Ford had to have guts to go for it. It chose to put itself on the line.

Who are you? What's the core competency of your organization? What do you do better than anyone else? And where are you taking all this? Please don't set up a committee to answer these questions. You'll only get group think. And members of that committee usually just put in their time on these kinds of questions and have no passion about them. You and a few of your colleagues have to do this job yourself. — Find the time to get it done.

To recap, Step One says: Take the time to sit down and get a conceptual handle on who you are and where you're going. Write down a few sentences. And don't be afraid to step out onto new terrain.

Step Two is: Target. The mass market is dead. I repeat: The mass market is dead. Politicians know this better than anyone. They no longer go for the whole enchilada. They pick and choose. Pataki did this in New York. He targeted upper state New York and won. Clinton, who was a great campaigner, did his targeting in the electoral college.

Your product or service may be cereal or telecommunications. To get them a distinct image, you simply can't communicate with 280 million Americans. At least not communicate clearly. Your image would get too blurry.

Figure out what niche or niches you must reach. Ford knew not everyone was obsessed with quality. Some consumers cared more about price. Others cared more about styling. But Ford just ignored those non-quality groups. It went after those who valued a defect-free car.

Your niche and your image must have a perfect fit. Anything less is a misfit. Did you see Marlon Brando on "Larry King Live"? He was a terrible fit for that show. He came across as a caricature of Marlon Brando. He was there pitching his autobiography. Know what? The book bombed out. It's on the For-Sale tables.

Step Number Three: Focus on media which works. Print and electronic. National and local. The media is the DNA which is going to program how your image takes shape.

For years I've had executives come into my office and say, "Bob, get me into *The Wall Street Journal*, either an article or on the op-ed page." That's ironic. The people who read *The Wall Street Journal* already agree with them about the environment or government export policies. Whom they really need to reach are people who read *Ladies Home Journal, Parade*, or *Reader's Digest*.

This brings us back to niche. Not every one looks at, listens to or reads everything. You have to target where you want your message to go. And, more often than not, the place it should go isn't *The New York Times Sunday Magazine*.

So, how will you get into your target cable program, radio talk show, ski magazine, or newspaper?

In my years in this profession I've noticed that some do very well with the media. And so do not. I've conducted my own informal analysis as to why this is so.

Those who succeed in getting their stories told in the media have certain characteristics:

• They're humble. They don't tell the media what to think. Instead they present the actions of their companies and let the reporters come to their own conclusions. Never underestimate a reporter.

• They're old-fashioned hard workers. They scurry around

Continued on next page

and put together the background materials that would help the media understand the story. And their attitude isn't, "Hey the media is lazy and I better do all the work for them." No, their attitude is, "How can I help?"

• They have integrity. That means being straight about a story. If they inadvertently mislead, they clear it up.

• They're imaginative. They can weave an event at their company into a trend story for prime time TV.

• They're grateful. They'll call the reporter or interviewer and thank them for fair coverage.

• And they understand how the "favor bank" works. In return for space or time, they'll provide the media with the sources for other stories. For instance, if the media is later doing a story on the new role of CFOs, they'll give the reporter access to their CFO plus provide names of other CFOs who might be a good interview.

There's no mystique about how media works. It's an activity much like football or baseball. That is, it has its rules. And if you follow the rules and are skillful, you can do well for yourself. Step Four is: Repeat. Repeat. Repeat. Keep doing what you're doing. After a decade, Ford is still saying, "Quality is Job One." That seems counterintuitive, doesn't it? — But it works. Have you read *Control Your Destiny or Someone Else Will*? In it, Jack Welch's communication agenda is described. As I see it, Welch has two commandments:

• One, keep your message simple.
• And, two, keep repeating it.

Sure, we all want to be original.

But when it comes to image that can be all wrong.

Consider Christianity. The message has been the same for 2000 years. And it's still working well. Look at some of most durable companies in America — Coca-Cola, Hallmark, *Reader's*

Digest—they all keep reinforcing the same old message. New touches here and there. But it's the same message.

And there's that sad story of the *Harvard Business Review*. During the past seven years there were a number of changes of editor. Each brought a new image to the *Review*. Readers got confused and angry. After a subscription drop, the *Review* is struggling now to get back on its feet. With one image.

Do you know who keeps changing their images? Teenagers — and desperate organizations. Consumers are very sophisticated. They know something is up when companies have a different ad campaign every two minutes.

The innovation part comes in on how you repeat the message. There you have to be creative. Step Five: Be visual. We really are a visual culture. It's the graphics of your brochure that they'll remember, not the words.

Did you hear that the Harvard Press group has formed a new media group to make its products highly visual. CIGNA has a computer-based tutorial on financial services for employees. Guess what? Almost every frame has an interesting, sometimes funny, graphic. And this is happening at a staid insurance company. And Microsoft's Windows is built around visual icons.

You can't get shelf space in the American mind without graphics. And the graphics have to be top-drawer. Believe me, what people will notice about your ad, annual report, video or newsletter is how it looked. On "David Letterman" do you recall what guests say during the program or do you recall their facial expressions, that sparkle in their eyes, their body language?

Soon, if you already haven't, you'll be taking your images to cyberspace. Do you know that IBM already has a very nicely laid out edition of THINK magazine on the Internet? What plans do you have for the "Net"?

Today I said that the 1990s may be the worst of times for

Continued on next page

image-making. Well, now I want to add it may also be the best of times — at least for people with resolve.

If you can slow down enough to figure out where your company's going — if you can take some risks — if you can stay with one image and do whatever it takes to reinforce that image over and over again — then you have a good chance of being seen and heard in the marketplace.

Consumers are hungry — starving — for distinct images. They're just waiting to bond with companies which say loud and clear, "Hey, this is who we are." That's why consumers have embraced Toys R Us, Ben & Jerry's, the Body Shop, Nordstrom, and Snapple.

The question is: Are you ready to say unambiguously who you are? That means you'll also implicitly be saying who you're not. That takes guts since you'll be turning your back on certain niches. Can you stand up to those in your company who say, "we can't do that"? I have been to so many meetings with so many clients whose people have told them, "Joe, we can't do that." And today they're out there, just another company. No distinct image.

If you have courage to create a distinctive image, your business may never be the same. You may, for the first time, bond with your consumers.

Thanks for your attention.

FOR A TELECOMMUNICATIONS COMPANY TRAINING DEPARTMENT

SEPTEMBER 1994

VIDEO INTRODUCING "TEAMING UP FOR THE CUSTOMER" TRAINING

(B-roll or quick succession of slides of the region)

Hello, I'm Joth Smith, (title).

We've had a lot of programs here at Company X. But I don't think there'll ever be one as critical to our survival as Teaming Up for the Customer.

I'd like to tell you why. But, first, consider these three facts.

One, the competition is fierce. And it's going to get worse.

Two, regulation still holds us back.

And, three, technology—whoa—it's moving like a bullet train.

(Pause)

Well, let me tell you something. These three—they're hurdles alright. But—they're not critical.

Why?

The reality is: We could do a terrific job on all three fronts.

We can squash the competition.

We can reform regulation.

And we can become the fastest and cheapest at installing leading-edge technology.

But, none of that matters, *if we don't meet or exceed our customers' expectations.* That's the bottom line: The customer has got

Continued on next page

to choose our company. Otherwise, we're out of business. And out of jobs.

That's the wake-up call here in our region.

And, that's why this training — Teaming Up for the Customer — is the three most important days of our lives. During this training, we've got to get it down cold: The customer and what that customer wants is why we exist.

The training will get into the nuts-and-bolts, the nitty-gritty of:

(BUILD SLIDE)

- What makes this marketplace tick

- What really goes on backstage when we service orders for dial tone and repair. How many hands touch that order? What do they do? What's the flow?

- And, how can we, as individuals and as members of teams, make all that happen in ways that meet and exceed customer expectations. Both our external and our internal customers. — Incidentally, the official term for exceeding customer expectations is "value added." I call it: Smart. (Pause) Hey, come to think of it, maybe a better term for value added is: Survival.

(Pause)

If we get out of this training what we should be getting out of it, then every day on our jobs we're going to do one thing. And that thing is: In every customer contact we're going to treat that contact as if it's our last chance to make a positive impression on the customer. We're going to act as if right after us our competitors are coming in to make their impression on that customer.

Folks, this is no longer a game of singles and doubles. We've got to get those home runs. And we will get them if we Team Up for the Customer.

By Teaming Up for the Customer we're also going to be able to do one other critical thing. And that's make oour company's vision for Long Island come to life.

Right now that vision is just words on paper. And those words on paper say: Here, in this region, we want to maximize profits and provide world-class service.

Sounds nice. But, those words can and will become a living, breathing reality when we, as a team:

(BUILD SLIDE)

- Really know the marketplace
- Care about and trust our fellow employees
- Meet and exceed customer expectations
- Use our resources effectively
- And become the lowest cost provider through new technology and process management.

These are the kinds of behaviors that have to be business-as-usual in this region. It's the only way we can remain big-league players in telecommunications in the 1990.

I hope that it's obvious to you: A lot is riding on this training. And what we do with it afterwards.

(Pause)

So, let me leave you with a little story. You've might have heard of the baseball-team owner Bill Veeck. Veeck was getting philosophical one day and he asked his friends, "Do you know why I love baseball?"

No fools, his friends realized Veeck wanted to sound profound so they shook their heads and said nothing.

"Well," exclaimed Veeck. "Baseball consists of moments of

Continued on next page

utter truth. There's nothing else like it in the world. — For instance if you strike out, that's it. Not even the best lawyer can get ya off."

Well, our contacts with customers have those same moments of utter truth. — We either make a positive impression or we don't.

Hey, have a good three days ... Thanks for listening.

PUBLIC RELATIONS AND ADVERTISING

Thanks, Doug.

We're using a variety of strategies to get the message out.

For instance, we're having a press conference on April ___.

We'll all be speaking at the press conference. Anybody who's anybody in business, telecommunications or New York has been invited. From what I'm hearing, we can expect a good turnout.

We're getting articles and interviews about Product X in all the important trade magazines and newspapers.

We've sent out a bunch of speakers to talk up Product X.

And here's a commercial we've made.

(VIDEO OF COMMERCIAL)

And here are the print ads.

(SHOW PRINT ADS)

But the most important person in getting out the message is you.

It's you who are going to make this product a home run.

We have the five marketing Ps: The Product. The Positioning. The Packaging. The Promotions. And even a Plus — a good ad budget. But if we don't have you 100 percent with us on this one, we're not going to move this baby.

The train is leaving the station. You've got to be aboard.

Thanks for listening to us.

WORKERS' COMPENSATION
AND THE PERFORMANCE GUARANTEE

As a business you're concerned about your workers' compensation costs. We at Company X are just as concerned.

That's why we've created a new claim service Performance Guarantee. It guarantees that we'll perform our services exactly as we promised you. If not, we're financially penalized.

Performance Guarantee is part of our ongoing commitment to manage risk in a cost-effective manner. Through this guarantee you'll have a better handle on containing your costs, improving employee morale and preventing litigation.

American employers spend $70 billion on workers' compensation each year.
                                    —National Council on Compensation Insurance

What's At Stake

To show you we mean business, we put real "teeth" in this guarantee. Everything is measurable. There's no ambiguity about what our performance should be.

• When we exceed mutually established commitments, you pay an incentive compensation that reflects the excellent service you received. But you could still save money. That's because workers' compensation costs are reduced when the overall quality of claims-handling is superior.

• When we meet the commitments, our fees remain the same.

• If we don't measure up, your payment is reduced. That means we pay a penalty to you. Tailor-Made For You Contracts are customized to your specific needs, particularly cost-containment. For example, you might want to apply the guarantee to a specific number of services that are the central aspects of your program.

Continued on next page

The Guarantee

You and an account representative from Company X will meet and decide the criteria by which you'll judge us. For example, by when should our nurse case manager supposed to first contact a disabled employee? How many hours or days constitute satisfactory performance and how many hours or days would make the performance substandard? What time frame would represent superior service? All criteria for Performance Guarantee have to be measurable. And the criteria must be at least as strict as state statutes. Usually they wind up being stricter.

Keeping Score

At regular intervals 5 percent or 50 files—whichever is greater—will be selected for evaluation. You and a Company X representative meet to decide which files will be audited. Each category of service gets a score. Suppose we agree five days is a satisfactory time frame for a particular category. Less than 5 would exceed expectations. More than 5 would be unsatisfactory.

EXAMPLE

Number of Days	Score	Result
Less than 5	1 Exceeds commitment	Incentive Compensation to the HSC
5	3 Satisfactory	No Adjustment
More than 5	5 Unsatisfactory	Penalty Compensation to Client

Suppose your company has selected 9 categories to evaluate. Each file is evaluated for each category. The sums for each category determine whether we've passed or we've failed on our promise.

What You Get from the Guarantee

What You Get from the Guarantee Company X's Performance Guarantee provides:

- Assurance that the claim service will be delivered as promised.

- Greater cost savings that result from effective claim management.

- Opportunities to uncover improvements in your operations.

- Better employee experience with workers' compensation. That could get them back to work faster and prevent costly litigation.

Why We Can Make this Guarantee

We can offer a guarantee on the service which you buy from us because the quality of our service has already been proven. You've been assured through our reputation. Now we're simply making that guarantee formal.

CATEGORIES OF SERVICE

Here are some of the services which may be critical to your workers' compensation process. You could choose to include them in your Performance Guarantee:

- **Nurse Case Management Intervention.** Nurse is assigned and makes contact by an agreed number of hours or days. Coordinating and managing the medical aspects of the case in a timely fashion helps control costs.

Continued on next page

- **Timeliness of Acceptance and Denials.** We will accept or deny the claim within an agreed upon number of days. That means employees aren't left wondering about the status of their claim. If the claim is accepted, then the first payment must be made promptly. If a claim is denied, guaranteed time frames are critical to avoiding automatic acceptance under some state statutes.

- **Initial Claimant Contact.** By an agreed time, a representative of Company X will contact injured employees in person or by phone. This facilitates control of the case and provides a key means of containing costs. Also, because the claimants receive a comprehensive briefing on their benefits, litigation is more easily prevented.

- **Subsequent Claimant Contacts/Diary.** If claimants are receiving benefits, Company X will contact them as often as your guarantee specifies. This signals to claimants that the case is under control. That, in itself, could prevent litigation.

- **Bill Audit and Payment.** You specify the terms and time frames for payment. Each bill is reviewed for charges and utilization. That avoids charges for unnecessary medical procedures, overcharges and billing errors.

- **File Documentation.** Our performance is measured by the comprehensiveness and accuracy of our case management, based on reserve charges, investigations, interviews, phone conversations, diary reviews, files reviews, authority requests, authorizations, report summaries, strategy notes, adjuster impressions, payment changes, delays, denials and any other pertinent material.

- **Data Inteqrits.** This written record demonstrates that the case has been thoroughly managed. Accurate coding avoids costly mistakes and is essential for management of the case. Performance is measured on the basis of accuracy and a availability of up-to-date information.

- **Special Procedure Compliance.** Performance is measured on the degree of compliance with special instructions. Company X representatives managing the case must be alert to compliance issues. If the instructions aren't followed, litigation could result. There may be a number of other categories which affect your Workers' Compensation claim costs. You can discuss your specific needs with a company account representative.

Your next step: To find out more about a Performance Guarantee with Company X, call _____.

Company X is your partner in business.

THE ENTERPRISER

Volume 1, January 1993

Welcome to *The Enterpriser,* a new publication from Company X Enterprises. Quarterly, *The Enterpriser* will provide information about developments at the company; emerging trends in the information industry, particularly how new technologies are being commercially applied; and a variety of business opportunities.

This first issue will primarily focus on our mission, management style, unique investment approach and current investments.

COMPANY X

Company X was established in 1989 as a subsidiary of our parent corporation. Its mission is: To broaden the corporation's reach into new markets. We accomplish this mission by investing in entrepreneurial firms in the information industry. Through those investments it provides Company X with yet one more way the corporation can offer customers innovative information solutions.

We concentrate on entrepreneurial enterprises because it is often the small company which is the source of breakthrough ideas in the information industry. By investing in those small companies, we gain access to leading-edge products or services which enable, facilitate or revolutionize the collection, analysis, distribution, management or use of data. As a result of the investments both the small firms and we benefit. Examples of this synergy will be presented later in the newsletter.

So that it can work well with entrepreneurial cultures, Company X Enterprises is itself entrepreneurial, both in its organizational structure and values. Because Company X is not a passive investor, its approach is fairly unique.

LINKING COMPANY X WITH ENTREPRENEURS

Company X builds bridges between the parent corporation

Continued on next page

and entrepreneurs in three ways:

- By providing venture capital.

- Through assisting, after the Investment, with operations. That ranges from restructuring to developing new marketing strategies.

- And, by investing directly. That is, acquiring companies.

Venture Capital

We carry out the investment part of our mission through a venture capital limited partnership formed as a joint venture between Company X and Company Y. This partnership invests in companies at all stages of development, from start-up to the well established. Typically an investment ranges between $500,000 and $5 million. The percent of equity ownership varies with each deal.

In evaluating a company, we look at: The business concept; management; viability, positioning and growth potential of the product or service; competition; and financial posture. After the Investment Following the investment, we actively monitor the companies' performance; that means they could actually get involved in operations. Through their relationship with us, the entrepreneurial companies gain access to all the expertise, resources and market opportunities of the parent corporation.

Consequently, they can get help in forming product and distribution alliances with the corporation's units and/or outside partners; in making acquisitions; in developing joint products to penetrate new market segments; and in recruiting senior management.

Direct Investments

We also make direct investments and acquisitions. Acquisitions become part of our operating group. Here the management philosophy is: Provide attention and support but do not undermine the companies' entrepreneurial culture.

WORKING IN TANDEM WITH US

Because of its multi-dimensional strategy, we must keep in close contact with the corporation's division management. If we are tuned into what those divisions are doing, we know what kinds of entrepreneurial ventures would be a good fit with what customers need. Also, the corporation's divisions are excellent sources of deal flow for the venture fund. A number of divisions have already formed or are discussing strategic alliances with D&B Enterprises' portfolio and operating companies. In addition, some divisions have become important customers of the portfolio companies.

WHAT HAS BEEN ACCOMPLISHED

During the past four years, we and our joint-venture partner have evaluated over 700 business plans from companies in information-related businesses. They have looked more closely at and performed due diligence on about 50 companies. So far, ten equity investments have been made. They are:

(Information Confidential)

WHAT COMPANY X LOOKS FOR IN VENTURE CANDIDATE COMPANIES

The management of Company X is often asked: "What exactly do you look for in venture candidate companies?" There is no simple answer to that. Each situation is different. However, there are four factors which weigh heavily in any assessment: The business concept; management; viability, positioning and growth potential of the product or service; and financial posture.

The Business Concept

We and our partner have a very specific charter which requires that investment be restricted to companies in the information or information technology industries. That industry definition is broad in that it goes well beyond data content companies; it in-

Continued on next page

cludes such categories as software, communications and information services companies.

Management

Venture capital people often say: There are five criteria for considering a company as an investment and three are management, management, and management. We agree. A strong, resourceful management team is a critical factor in any investment decision.

The types of entrepreneurs we encounter essentially come from one of two paths. On one path are the youthful entrepreneurs. They have little prior management or business experience but are running their small firms on what they believe to be a well- formulated business plan. On the other path are the seasoned executives. They have always wanted to "run their own show" and have put together a new enterprise. Often they join with other seasoned pros.

Both types of situations have benefits. And a combination of the two is highly desirable. However, in all cases, we demand that the company's management have vision, a strong knowledge base and commitment.

The Product and Service

Once the company gets past the initial review, we begin some due diligence work. That entails gathering information about the product or service and its markets. Typical questions are:

- Does the company have a customer base? What do those customers think of the product or service?

- How big is the entire market? How much of that market does it currently own?

- What is the competition like? Does it primarily consist of a number of small players or one or two large, dominant players? How does the company differentiate itself from the competition?

- Is the market new, growing, mature, or is it in decline? If it is growing, how fast is that growth? Is the company's growth keeping pace with the market?

- If it is a new market or product, how are the potential customers meeting this need right now?

Financial History Protections and Capitalization

Protections and Capitalization When we and our partner look at the company's financial posture, the near-term operating income or loss is relatively unimportant. What is important are: Cash use versus cash available; revenue level; revenue growth; sources of funding; resource allocation; expense ratios; and if there has been improvement and growth over time.

In addition, it is expected that the company has made realistic, supportable financial projections for its income statements over a three-to-five-year period. There is also an inquiry into current financing; how the proposed funding will affect capitalization; if other venture capital firms have established interests in the company; and what percent of the company is owned by outsiders.

Also important is finding out how many rounds of financing the company has been through; that helps determine how the entity has been progressing. Lastly, the company and its investors have to decide what is the company's market value.

No Sure Things

Venture investing is a risky business. There are no sure things; no set formulas for success. There are only calculated risks. To lower that risk, we treat each company as a unique case. Market research is done. A variety of financial models are applied. But there are no guarantees; there will always be some successes and some failures.

Continued on next page

READER INPUT

We want to hear from readers about new opportunities and companies. Readers who are aware of appropriate companies needing venture capital or who know of good acquisition candidates should contact:

"Great spirits have always encountered violent opposition from mediocre minds."

— Albert Einstein

Do You Know:

Q: How many EDI transactions take place daily in the world?

A:

EMPLOYEE SURVEY FOR THE EMPLOYEE NEWSLETTER OF AN INDUSTRIAL FIRM

APRIL 1993

If you're wondering what happened as a result of the employee attitude survey you filled out back in August of 1991, the answer is: Lots. You told management how you felt about safety, human resource processes, leadership, reward/recognition, work force diversity, communications and customer focus. And, judging by management's response, obviously they heard you. They took you seriously. And they acted on your input.

And since 65 percent of you participated — the average level of return for mail-in surveys is 50 percent — there was no ambiguity about what you, as the majority of the company's employees, were saying.

The survey was conducted, explains _____, vice president of human resources, because "periodically it's useful to measure the climate of the organization. Not all the responses you get will be favorable. But before you change processes, you must know how people really see the issues."

This survey was part of the overall quality effort. Research shows that there's a direct correlation between employee morale and how well the customer is served. The survey also serves as a benchmark for future surveys which will be conducted every few years.

"After we received the tabulated results," continues _____, "we formed process teams to analyze the issues and then, where appropriate, to take action."

Not all the initiatives going on throughout our company, though, have been a direct effect of the survey. For instance, some projects such as establishing management-development courses were already underway before a team was formed to look into

Continued on next page

leadership. However, the survey results helped confirm that the organization was moving in the right direction and that it should continue what it had been doing.

Also, some issues such as empowerment and the perception that promotions depended on "who you know" came up in several categories. Employees, for example, were concerned about empowerment both in terms of how the company's leadership was interpreting it and in terms of being rewarded/recognized for taking on greater responsibility.

It'd be impossible to cover all aspects of the survey and what they mean for you, for the organization, and for the customer. So, this newsletter will highlight seven themes which were most on people's minds and briefly explain what's being done about them.

• **Safety.** The term "safety" covers everything from employee well-being to environmental impacts. This issue was particularly important in the survey because a growing body of research shows that there's a link between safety performance and employee morale. If employee morale is high, then safety is probably a priority in the organization. Interestingly, this was confirmed by the survey. Almost a third of employees thought that accidents were primarily the result of bad morale.

The good news is that employees gave our safety processes high grades. Seventy-four percent felt that the company, including top management, was sincere in its concern for employees, the community, and the environmental impacts of processes and products.

However, our philosophy is continuous improvement. So, there have been three actions taken in the safety area.

Operations Surveys. After the initial survey, explains _____, International Manager of Safety and Environmental Services, "we conducted a more in-depth 'climate' survey. That asks questions about the practices, conditions and perceived attitudes in actual operations. According to experts, the climate survey will turn up any negatives in the work environment.

Local Actions. Based on the results of the two surveys, managers at sites are formulating their own action plans. The goal is prevention.

Best Practices. The advantage of being part of a larger organization is the access to knowledge about what's working well in other parts of the company. Currently, (title) is visiting sites and sharing that kind of information with operations managers.

* **Human Resources Management.** The major areas of concern for employees were career advancement and professional development. Sixty-seven percent perceived internal politics/"who you know" as the reason for advancement. Sixty-two percent were dissatisfied with how the performance appraisal process covered career development; this was especially significant since 89 percent felt that help with career planning was the key factor in attracting and retaining employees.

In examining these concerns, a process team found that the promotion and career development processes were a big mystery to most employees. In the absence of concrete information, myths and half truths took root about why some people got ahead and others didn't. As a result, here are things which are helping correct matters.

Career Planning Pilot Project. Eighty exempt employees with at least three years with the company have been given candid, detailed information, including mentoring, on what's needed to progress in the company. That might mean getting more training. It might mean job rotations to broaden experience. It might mean switching from a certain specialization to another which has more upward potential. The original project lasted a year. The results are being studied. And the pilot has been expanded to non-exempt employees.

Continued on next page

Performance Appraisal as Career Development Tool. Unfortunately, the performance appraisal process had been used primarily as a report card. That's changing. Managers are being encouraged to focus on this review as a means of career development. This should be supplemented with regular, less formal chats about career goals and how to reach them.

Job Communication System. All openings up to Grade 12 are now posted. That helps demystify what the opportunities are and what experience and skills are necessary to compete for them. This kind of knowledge allows employees to plan to get the experience, academic credentials and job-related training they need to enhance their career potential.

• **Leadership.** The core issues centered on senior management. More than 50 percent of employees thought that senior management wasn't visible enough, wasn't providing adequate information about the company's strategic direction and paid only lip service to empowerment. Here's what's happening as a result.

Management by Walking Around. Members of senior management are out of their offices more, visiting employee locations. Mechanisms like Forum — which is a type of "town meeting" — allow management to explain what's going on in the company and answer employee questions.

The Vision Thing. The lack of communication about the strategic direction of the company happened partly because this company was just becoming a separate entity. After it had split off from the parent company, it didn't have its own vision. So, our president spent a lot of time working on that. Essentially that vision is: We are to be the best performing industrial gas producer in the world. Now it's possible to inform employees, in detail, about what strategies are being used to make that vision a reality.

Management Development Curriculum. About 30 courses are currently available to help managers make the shift to a corporate culture based on empowerment. That means a change in mind set from a paternalistic culture — do it my way — to one in which the person actually doing the job takes responsibility for deciding how it should be done. That represents a major cultural change. The adjustment isn't easy — for either managers or some employees.

- **Reward/Recognition.** The chief complaint was that there was too much criticism of performance and not enough reward/recognition. Only 41 percent said that their managers recognized them for a job well done. Interestingly, what was most important to 95 percent of employees wasn't an award per se. What they wanted more was to see that their recommendations influence decisions. In short, they wanted to be truly empowered. Here are some of the action plans generated by those findings.

Determination of Core Values. When the team started working on this issue they saw that first they needed to be clear on what kind of performance should be rewarded/recognized. With the transition from being a division of a large corporation to being an independent company came the question: What are the core values going to be for us? From those core values would come the criteria on which to base the reward/recognition process. So, the team then shifted its focus from reward/recognition per se to a discussion of values. It's just finishing up. Stay tuned for more news about this.

Shift from Negative to Positive. The team found that there was in-place a broad range of mechanisms available to reward and recognize performance. They ran the gamut from the Chairman's Award to letters of commendation to just a simple oral thank-you. The problem here, states, is "that many in the organization just aren't using these mechanisms." Managers tended to be in the bad habit of remarking on performance when it was below standard but ignoring it if it was superior. One way we are trying to get managers to break this habit is by making them more aware of their attitudes and behaviors.

Continued on next page

Special Recognition Award. Employees can now nominate other employees for outstanding contributions to the organization. To reinforce the importance of these awards, the winners are given star billing.

• **Work Force Diversity.** Diversity is, of course, a huge issue. It covers every type of difference between workers, ranging from different personalities and professional backgrounds to different sexes, races, religions, and sexual orientations.

However, in the survey, employees had basically two concerns. Sixty-eight percent of women and 80 percent of blacks indicated the company needed to do more to advance work force diversity. And 72 percent of women said that more flexibility will help them work more effectively.

From the company's point of view, states _____, assistant director of human resources, learning to manage diversity is critical because "it's the right thing to do and it's key to our global competitiveness." Because the issue is significant and so broad, a lot is going on in managing diversity. Here's just a sampling.

Top Management Support. For any diversity initiative to take hold in the organization, top management must send the message that diversity is a priority. Corporate officers have met with their direct reports to analyze all the implications of a diverse work force. The subordinates, in turn, then are bringing the discussion to their staff. "Cascading" the message in this way highlights its seriousness and ensures that everyone in the organization will hear it.

Policy Making. Almost every human-resource issue is somehow linked to diversity. That issue could be flexible scheduling, leaves of absences, special leaves, recruitment of women and minorities, equal opportunity for women and minorities, sexual harassment, accommodating the disabled, or "cafeteria" benefit plans. And just about every one of these requires a new policy decision. To help with those decisions there's now a cross-functional Steering Committee made up of women, minorities, and white males.

Training and Communications. Since diversity is such a dynamic issue, there's continual training and communications about what's going on. That includes both formal briefings, memos and brochures and informal sharing of experiences among managers.

The informal sharing is becoming very useful because managers have to now make more decisions for which there are no policies or precedents. For example, a full-timer might request part-time work. Knowing what other managers have done helps.

- **Communications.** Employees had three basic complaints: There wasn't enough information. It wasn't timely. And it wasn't highly credible. Sixty-five percent said that the company told them what it wanted employees to know rather than what they needed to know. Only 37 percent felt information was up-to-date. And 47 percent found that they questioned the truthfulness of information. It was obvious, states _____ , director of corporate communication, "that we had to change a lot about employee communications. And now that we have it's one of the most exciting areas in the company." Here are some of those changes.

Reorganization. Previously employee communications had been a part-time effort with no senior person in charge. Now it has a full time staff. Just like external communication it has senior leadership. And there is a strategic planning process for how messages are to be communicated; therefore, if there's a major change in the organization, there could be an integrated, well-thought-out communications effort.

Wider Distribution. It used to be that a small number of people received the bulk of communications. Now a greater number of people are in the information loop, ranging from memos to seeing videos. Timeliness. The quarterly magazine has been changed to a monthly. There is an employee bulletin board. And through electronic mail employees learn about events as they're happening.

Continued on next page

Credibility. In preparing articles, explains _____, "we now interview the so-called 'average' employee instead of just senior people. That gives us and the audience a greater understanding of how an event is perceived by employees and how it affects them."

Accessibility. To attract and hold employees' attention, communications are now "packaged" in ways that are easy to understand. For instance, the writing of this newsletter is more direct and conversational; the graphics are as eye-catching and sophisticated as one would find in *USA Today*. We know, stresses _____, that we have to "break through the clutter" and compete for employees' interest and time just like all the other media in their lives.

Messages. Both the look and the content of communications vehicles help communicate the unique corporate culture and global range of our company.

• **Customer Focus.** Those closest to the customer — merchant and on-site sales — felt the most negative about senior management's commitment to customer focus. Thirty-five percent of the sales force perceives the top layer of the organization as lacking in a passion for customer service. Obviously, this was a finding that had to be acted on quickly. "We reviewed all our systems," _____, explains, senior market research analyst. "What we needed to find out was how the customer really saw us."

Additional Research: The traditional modus operandi was a survey every two year. Now there are more frequent and more in-depth customer research. They include calls from this company, calls from independent research firms, focus groups, and questionnaires.

The major three areas of concern are, explains _____, associate director of merchant sales, are delivery, billing, and overall account maintenance. "When we get the results," states _____, "we not only let our employees know what they are but we also share them with the customer." That type of sharing lets customers see that our company is serious about continuous improvement.

Being Proactive. When asked what "responsiveness" meant to them, many customers answered that they perceive our company as appropriately responsive when it is proactive. Instead of waiting to hear from them, we should be able to anticipate what customers need and want. Also they want us to be more of a partner who would help them solve their business problems.

Communications. In the spirit of being proactive, we now regularly provide customers information about emerging technologies, processes and products that might be useful to them. To keep lines of communication open customers are on the mailing list for company publications.

Executive Visits. Senior management is now on the road more, personally calling on customers. _____ (title) is championing the customer satisfaction process. As you can see from these many action plans, you did the company a great service in giving your opinion in the 1991 survey. That information proved to be a powerful tool in helping the organization become the best performing industrial producer in the world.

According to _____ , the next employee survey will probably be conducted during the first quarter of 1994. We look forward to hearing from you then.

TESTIMONY OF A CHIEF FINANCIAL OFFICER OF A HIGH-TECH COMPANY

DELIVERED BEFORE THE CONGRESSIONAL COMPETITIVENESS CAUCUS

WASHINGTON, DC, 1990

INTELLECTUAL PROPERTY RIGHTS AND U.S. GLOBAL COMPETITIVENESS

Thank you, (naming those at main table), I want to thank you and everyone else here for your interest in protecting America's intellectual property.

Perhaps because of all the legal baggage it carries, intellectual property has not attracted much attention until recently.

The Congressional Economic Leadership Institute's superb new study on intellectual property is just one sign of the growing concern about this issue. Finally, we are recognizing that protecting the rights to our innovations is right up there with all the other big global competitive issues.

I know this from first-hand experience. My company is a high-technology global company. About a third of our $6.1 billion in sales of controls technology comes from international markets. We spend over $280 million a year in research and development, or R&D. And we are international market leaders in what we do.

But, all that high-tech R&D and marketing savvy are not enough. To remain leaders in the global marketplace, we need standardized international rules for protecting our rights to our intellectual property, particularly our patents.

Right now those rules do not exist. Because they do not, Honeywell is losing hundreds of millions of dollars every year to those who steal our patent rights. And our company's story is

Continued on next page

being replayed throughout high-tech corporate America. The International Trade Commission — or ITC — reports that piracy of U.S. business' intellectual property adds up to between $43 and $61 billion a year. That represents 30 to 50 percent of our trade deficit.

You can help us protect our patent rights and therefore keep alive our incentive to invest in high-tech research.

The General Agreement on Tariffs and Trade — or GATT — is conducting negotiations in Geneva, called the Uruguay Round. One of the 15 issues under discussion — at America's insistence — is intellectual property. On October 15th, all of GATT's 100 or so member nations will submit their final requests. This is your last chance to let the Administration know what is at stake.

And what's at stake is America's core competency. Every nation has its industrial strengths. Technical innovation is ours. If they asked America: What business are you in? We could and should answer: We are in the business of innovation.

And the raw material for that business is R&D. Last year U.S. industrial R&D totaled about $65 billion. This year it will probably reach about $74 billion. And according to the Congressional Economic Leadership Institute, about 23 percent of our exports have a high content of intellectual property — versus seven percent in 1950. That reflects the globalization of high tech.

But the incentive to keep investing money, brains and creativity into high-tech research if being undercut by the disarray of intellectual property laws around the world.

That disarray is manifesting itself in outright theft of patent rights as well as market-access barriers created by differences in nations' laws governing intellectual property.

In addition to the piracy, American's technical investment is also being shortchanged by trade barriers created by differences in intellectual property laws around the world.

One kind of barrier comes from what I call "sins of omission." Many developing countries have no or weak protection for intellectual property. That, in effect, closes off whole countries to us. Why go in with expensive, gee-whiz technology where it is perfectly legal to copy it?

Another type of trade barrier exists because of vast disparities in the developed nations' patent systems.

For example, in Japan, the patent system is based on the First-to-File versus the America's First-to-Find. The Japanese system does not require a search to be made of existing proprietary technology in the field; the U.S. system does.

Eighteen months after the patent filing, detailed information about the technology is made public in Japan. And that is done even before the Japanese patent office decides if it will issue a patent. Therefore, we could lose out on both counts — information about the technology and eventual patent protection. In the U.S., patent information regarding a technology is confidential.

The upshot is: Frequently American companies find they have little practical choice but to license their inventories in Japan rather than manufacturing or selling them themselves.

That can significantly limit potential revenue. It can also undercut the incentive to keep investing in R&D.

In addition — and this is important — the shape of intellectual property laws in Japan and other countries — what they cover or do not cover — is also shaping American companies' decisions about what technical research to pursue. As a result, America could wind up losing its leadership position in whole areas of technology where we have plenty of runway left; for instance, bio-engineering, information resources and optoelectronics.

To stop piracy and harmonize patent laws, a GATT agreement must have four components:

Continued on next page

- One, there have to be common standards for protection of all types of intellectual property—patents, copyrights, trademarks, and trade secrets.

- Two, there has to be a common international patent system. This will require, of course, some legislative changes in our system.

- Three, timely resolution of disputes.

- And, four, and most important, is the enforcement piece. Infringing goods should be seized at the border. The enforcement part is key because, here, as in most trade sanctions, it can act as a deterrent.

Obviously, any GATT agreement will have to be phased in. During the interim, we need to hold onto whatever protection we are getting from U.S. trade laws.

Those trade laws recognize that international patent infringement is not a commercial matter; it is a matter that has to be settled between governments.

One especially powerful trade law is the Amended Section 337 of the Tariff Act of 1930. As amended in 1988, Section 337 allows U.S. companies to seek redress with the ITC if they have made a substantial investment in developing patented technology or have made a significant effort to license it. That means that companies do not have to actually manufacture the product to have standing under U.S. trade laws.

Why is this important? R&D can take many paths and not all of them have to go the whole nine yards to actual product development. In itself, the technology can become the marketable commodity. The amended Section 337 addresses this growing trend in America's high-tech sector. We considered using 337 in the our suit but we decided to continue the litigation route.

Under Section 337, a company can petition the ITC to review

a suspected patent infringement. A ruling is made in 12 to 14 months—versus the years involved in going through the U.S. courts. For instance, the Minolta suit is now in its fourth year. If infringement is proved by the ITC, the product will not be imported into the U.S. During the horse-trading at GATT, it is imperative that 337 not be traded away prematurely. Right now, the ability to stop infringing goods at our border is the best thing we have to not only halt the piracy but also to give other nations the message: "Hey, guys, don't even think about it!"

When GATT comes up with an agreement, you in Congress have to pass legislation implementing. If that agreement does not offer strong protection for intellectual property, then forget it. A bad agreement is worse than no agreement. And that is because, with any agreement, there will be pressure for us to give up Section 337.

At GATT, the stakes for America's high-tech section are high. And so are the opportunities. For instance, the intellectual-property content of both goods and services will continue to soar. That will allow us to get away from trying to reduce imports and go on the offensive and concentrate on boosting up exports.

The business of America and our company is innovation. Depending on what happens at the GATT, that business will get better. Or get worse. With your help it can get a whole lot better.

We ask you to communicate to the Administration what we need to protect our intellectual property. This may be the last time in this century that there is a chance to have a multilateral agreements.

Contact: John Jones   **FOR IMMEDIATE RELEASE**
(803) 834-4111

SAFETY EQUIPMENT ELECTS EDWARD SMITH

EXECUTIVE VICE PRESIDENT – FINANCE AND CHIEF FINANCIAL OFFICER

MADISON, CT, September 20—The board of directors of The Safety Equipment Corporation today elected Edward Smith, 48, executive vice president – finance and chief financial officer. In this planned, orderly transition of the CFO, Mr. Smith succeeds Michael York, Jr., who retires following a successful 40-year career.

"Strategic financial management is critical to SE's future," said Robert F. Haas, chairman and chief executive officer. "Ed Smith brings a rare combination of financial, strategic and operations experience to the company. He is an aggressive innovator with a proven ability to execute complex strategies, such as completing the $6.5 billion merger with Conrail and negotiating the $1.2 billion sale of Watts while CFO at ABE."

Mr. Smith previously served as executive vice president – strategic planning and group president at ABE Corporation, with revenue of $20 billion in 1994. Responsible for ABE's long-range strategic planning, he also managed the Telecommunications Products and Services Group, including ABE Mobilnet, ABE Information Services, ABE Government Systems Corporation and ABE Airfone. He was a member of ABE's board of directors, and the office of the chairman.

"Ed Smith's initial objectives at SE will be to implement a long-term strategic financial plan and to accelerate the transition of our finance function to a true business partnership with the operating divisions," said Mr. Haas.

Continued on next page

Mr. Smith joined ABE in 1988 as corporate vice president and controller and was elected senior vice president–finance and CFO in 1989. He was named executive vice president–strategic planning and group president in 1993. He began his career with Arthur Wyatt & Co. in 1968, became a partner in 1979 and was appointed managing partner of the Westport, Conn., office in 1986.

Mr. Smith holds a degree in accounting from St. Gregory College in Brooklyn, N.Y. He is a member of the American Institute of Certified Public Accountants and the New York, Connecticut, and Louisiana Societies of Certified Public Accountants. He is a director of Johntown, Inc., Southern Energy Systems, Woodvale Mutual Insurance, Junior Achievement and St. Joan's Medical Center, as well as a trustee of Eureka College in Wellesley, Mass.

The Safety Equipment Corporation is the world's largest marketer Safety Equipment, with worldwide revenue of $4.9 billion in 1994.

* * *

September 20, 1995

FOR IMMEDIATE RELEASE Contact: Joel Pomerantz
The Dilenschneider Group
(212) 922-0900

TOMA CORPORATION REPORTS
SECOND-QUARTER RESULTS

WESTPORT, CT, August 10, 1995 — Toma Corporation (NYSE: TOM) announced that net sales for the second quarter of 1995 were $269 million — a 36% increase over the $198 million of sales reported in the second quarter of last year. Excluding the revenue associated with TOM Washers, a worldwide Washers business that was acquired on May 9th, the increase, quarter over quarter, was 17%. For the first half of the year, sales (excluding TOM Washers) represent a 22% increase over the first half of last year.

Operating profit for the second quarter ending June 30, 1995 was a positive $1.0 million. This includes TOM Washers. Excluding TOM Washers, operating profit was $2.7 million and this compares to an operating profit of $2.8 million for the second quarter of last year.

TOMA CONSOLIDATED RESULTS

| | Second Quarter | | First Half | |
	'95 (A)	'94	'95 (A)	'94
• Sales	269.4	198.2	483.5	366.2
• Operating Profit (B)	1.0	2.8	7.0	(4.5)
• Net Income	(23.9)	(10.0)	(25.8)	(0.8)

(A) Includes TOM Washers acquired on May 9, 1995.

(B) Excludes two one-time charges in 1995 and 1994 related to severance and facility closures.

Continued on next page

Net income for the second quarter of 1995 was a negative $24 million, reflecting $14 million of one-time charges, of which $7.5 was associated with the May refinancing of the company's debt. This refinancing enabled the company to secure better terms on new senior notes due 2002 as well as increase its working capital credit facility.

Commenting on the second quarter, Toma's Chief Executive Officer, George M. Wallace, said: "There was much positive activity at our Company during the second quarter. We acquired TOM Washers in May and refinanced all of our debt at the same time — adding financial liquidity to the Company which continues to improve. We are now implementing initiatives to address the performance issue of our Washer business where supplier cost increases combined with marketplace pricing pressure affected performance. The performance of Toma will improve with these initiatives."

The Company has established a separate segment for its Washers business, combining TOM Washers with its pre-existing division. As a result, the Company will now consist of, and report on, three segments — Toma Washers, Washer and Heavy Washer.

TOMA WASHERS' COST REDUCTIONS AHEAD OF SCHEDULE

Toma Washers had sales of $65 million in the second quarter of 1995, compared to sales of $25 million in the second quarter of last year. Excluding the revenues associated with TOM Washers, the sales increase, quarter over quarter, was 12%. Operating profit in the second quarter of 1995 was $1.2 million, compared to $2.1 million of operating profit in the second quarter of last year. Excluding TOM Washers, operating profit was $3.3 million in the second quarter of 1995, representing a 57% increase over the $2.1 million last year.

With respect to our Washers business, Mr. Wallace said: "This strategy associated with the acquisition of TOM Washers was to make our Washers business a force in the marketplace and to enhance the profitability of our existing division. With a powerful combined distribution network of over 300 independent dealers across the world, and some of the best brand names in the industry, we now have the critical mass needed to be a profitable major factor in the industry.

"Our division continues to show significant progress — with first-half revenues up 14% and first half operating profit up 55% over last year. For the first half of the year, gross profit margins are up and operating expenses, as a percent of sales, were down when compared to last year. Consequently, operating profit, as a percent of sales, improved — going from 7.4 percent last year to slightly over 10 percent for the first half of this year. One of the major strategies for the acquisition is to implement the programs at TOM that have proven so effective at."

Backlog at the Toma Washers business remains solid overall with backlog at the end of June 1995 of $60 million. This compares to a backlog, including TOM, at prior year-end of $53 million.

MATERIAL HANDLING GROUP REVENUES IMPROVE BUT MARGINS BELOW TARGET

In the Washer business, second quarter sales were $136 million, representing an increase of 17% over the $117 million in sales reported in the second quarter of last year. The business had an operating loss of $1.9 million in the second quarter of 1995 compared to an operating loss of $2.7 million for the same period last year. For the first half, this business had an operating loss of $1.2 million compared to an operating loss of $11.7 million for the comparable period of 1994.

"We have already taken actions to further reduce costs through headcount reductions and closure of certain of our administrative and warehouse facilities in order to put the profitability picture back on track for the remainder of the year. These actions

Continued on next page

are traceable to the one-time charges that are reflected in the net income line for the second quarter. In addition, we have implemented price increases in our parts offerings in North America, and effectively raised selling prices on certain of our product offerings — including our new Genesis line. We are also working closely with our principal suppliers with respect to improving production schedules."

Toma Corporation is comprised of three key operating groups: Washer Company, Toma Washers and the Heavy Washer Group. The Washer subsidiary, based in Lexington, Kentucky, is a leading manufacturer of Washers serving a diverse worldwide base of industrial customers.

Toma Washers, based in Conway, South Carolina, is the second largest manufacturer of Washers and related Washer Equipment in North America. The Group, based in Tulsa, Oklahoma, designs and manufactures a wide range of heavy-duty, laundry washers.

TOMA CORPORATION
SUMMARY OF OPERATING RESULTS
SIX MONTHS ENDED JUNE 30, 1995
(In Thousands, Except Per Share Data)

	Three Months Ended June 30,		Six Months Ended June 30,	
	1995	1994	1995	1994
Net Sales	$269,409	$198,249	$483,485	$366,287
Income (loss) from operations before severance and exit costs	1,044	2,788	7,046	(4,482)
Severance and exit costs	(3,478)	(4,549)	(3,478)	(4,549)
Income (loss) from operations	(2,434)	(1,761)	3,568	(9,031)
Income (loss) before extraordinary items	(16,416)	10,254	(18,301)	(570)
Extraordinary loss on retirement of debt	(7,452)	(233)	(7,452)	(233)
Net Income (Loss)	**(23,868)**	**10,021**	**(25,753)**	**(803)**
Less preferred stock accretion	(1,789)	(1,444)	(3,518)	(2,824)
Income (loss) applicable to common stock	(25,657)	8,577	(29,271)	(3,627)
Earnings per share:				
Primary				
Before extraordinary items	(1.76)	0.64	(2.12)	(0.33)
Extraordinary items	(0.72)	(0.02)	(0.72)	(0.02)
Net income (loss)	(2.48)	0.62	(2.84)	(0.35)
Fully Diluted				
Before extraordinary items	(1.76)	0.60	(2.12)	(0.33)
Extraordinary items	(0.72)	(0.01)	(0.72)	(0.02)
Net income (loss)	(2.48)	0.59	(2.84)	(0.35)
Weighted average number of shares outstanding (1)				
Primary	10,322	13,839	10,316	10,303
Fully Diluted	10,322	16,961	10,316	10,303

(1) As determined under GAAP rules for purposes of EPS calculations only. Conversion of preferred stock and warrants is not assumed if such conversion would increase the earnings per share or decrease the loss per share.

November ___, 1995

Mr. Peter Smith
217 Oak Street
Conemaugh, PA 10003

Dear Mr. Smith:

In your recent letter to our chairman you requested information about our global activities in environmental protection and energy conservation and development. You stated that this information might prove useful in helping your community improve the environment.

Our Company shares your concern about both these issues. In order to be a good corporate citizen both in the United States and around the world, we have always made environmental protection and energy conservation high priorities in our business activities worldwide.

In terms of protecting the global environment and the health and safety of our employees and the communities in which we do business, our approach has been proactive.

That means that in addition to complying with current national and local regulations worldwide, we attempt to anticipate what substances, technologies, processes and procedures may have adverse effects on the environment, human health and safety. To that end we make substantial investments in environmentally-oriented research and development, programs, procedures, education and training.

For example, we are conducting basic research on state-of-the art systems and techniques to prevent and solve environmental problems, including restoring conditions to their original state.

Continued on next page

One of our businesses, Environmental Services, Inc., supplies air-pollution control equipment.

Throughout our global operations, we have a network of professionals and outside consultants whose sole function is to guide our environmental programs, education and training, Industrial hygiene experts monitor all indoor facilities, ranging from plants to office, for substances which could affect employee health and safety; that intensive effort has substantially reduced employee exposure to known and potential risks. We also take advantage of all opportunities to recycle materials, including those used in our chemical and metal-fabrication operations. That not only reduces environmental waste but makes us more cost-efficient.

To ensure that employees and others who work at our facilities understand and comply with all environmental directives, we have developed and continually update detailed internal guidelines and manuals. Some of those are available for external distribution. If you judge that they might be helpful to you or your community, you can obtain copies by contacting _____.

To remain a low-cost producer, we constantly evaluate our operations for ways to conserve energy. Our Powers Systems business produces the most advanced energy-efficient generation and distribution equipment. Our Motors business is conducting research on energy-efficient motors.

To adequately describe all that we have been doing to address environmental and energy issues would, of course, require many, many pages. For your information, I have enclosed some materials that you might find interesting — and useful.

Thank you for taking the time to contact Company X. And best of luck with your community efforts to improve the environment.

Best regards,

_____

Attachments

FOR IMMEDIATE RELEASE   Contact: John Jones
(803) 834-4111

TELEMARKETING WORKSHOPS HELP
LOCAL BUSINESS COMPETE

Telemarketing workshops, sponsored by Company X, offer
New York companies training in how to become more competitive
through use of the telephone. Conducted by senior consultants
from Company X's Telemarketing Group, the one and two-
day workshops are available from _____ (month) through
_____ (month) at the _____ (name of hotel) and, by
special request, on-site at companies.

Appropriate for businesses of all sizes, the workshops help
companies assess their telemarketing needs in marketing, sales,
customer relations and accounts payable and set up cost-effective
telemarketing programs. The instructors have broad-based experience in marketing, sales and customer relations as well as specializations in telemarketing.

"The telephone is business' most underutilized — and misunderstood — tool," states _____ (name), senior telemarketing consultant who has been teaching workshops since 19___.
"If used appropriately, the telephone can offer the 'total solution'
to routine as well as unanticipated problems in every aspect of
business."

The newest workshop "Stress Survival," examines both common and individual sources of stress among telemarketers and
provides practical techniques for coping (date).

The "Managers Workshop" provides step-by-step training for
establishing and running cost-effective telemarketing programs as
well as background information on the industry, including statistics
for success (date).

Continued on next page

The "Selling Skills Workshop," designed for sales staff and managers and account executives, covers planning, customizing and conducting sales calls as well as proven techniques for closing the sale (date).

The "Customer Service Workshop," designed to turn cost centers into profit centers, covers how to make customer relations also perform marketing functions, including research (date).

The "Professional Telephone Techniques Workshops," appropriate for all employees whose work involves the telephone, focuses on professionalism including screening, time management and dealing with difficult callers (date).

The "Telecollections Workshop," designed for those in accounts payable, presents proven techniques for improving the rate of collections while preserving good customer relations (date).

Workshops are also customized for the specific need of any organization.

Information on registration and fees for Company's X Tele-marketing Workshops is available by calling 1-800-000-0000.

# # #

Contacts: Joseph Smith
Acme Records
(000) 000-0000:

Joel Pomerantz
The Dilenschneider Group
(212) 922-0900

ACME RECORDS WINS CONTRACT FROM ROUND RECORDS TO DIE-CAST ALL ESCALATOR STAIRS FOR L.A. TRANSIT AUTHORITY SYSTEM

TOLEDO, OH, June 29 — Acme Records, Inc. announced today it has been awarded a contract by Round Records, Inc. to die-cast the aluminum components of all CD Players installed at passenger stations operated by the Los Angeles Transit Authority in the Southern California metropolis.

James Jones, Acme Records Director of Marketing, Asia/ Pacific, said the contract reflected accelerated efforts to further expand the company's customer base beyond the recording sector.

Until now, Round Records had been importing CD players from Japan, but rapidly-increasing import costs and the Los Angeles Transit Authority's status as a quasi-governmental agency influenced the decision to source the program to a U.S. manufacturer.

Based in Cleveland, Ohio, Round Records, Inc. is a technological leader in the design, manufacture, installation and service CD record equipment. It is part of the worldwide Round Record Group, internationally headquartered in Toyko, Japan.

A company spokesperson said Acme Records, Inc. was selected for the program because of the its recognized expertise and long experience supplying record players. CD record players is the preferred manufacturing procedure for music systems which require exceptional accuracy in sizing and shaping and superior

Continued on next page

product reliability to meet safety standards. The Columbus-based firm will produce about 5,000 CD units annually for Acme Records. Machining and final assembly will be completed at the Round Records plant in Columbus, Ohio.

Founded in 1907, Acme Records, Inc. is the largest independent manufacturer of CD players in North America with production facilities in Columbus, Ohio; Nashville, Tennessee; and Johnstown, Pennsylvania.

# # #

INDEX

A

B

C

D

N

O

for newly public company, 133–134
registration process and, 124
standard, 83
video, function of, 73
Print journalists, *vs.* television reporters, 60
Print materials, for employee communication, 180–182
Print media
speechwriting for, 241
vs. electronic media, 61
vs. television, on public opinion, 286–287
Problems, public relations, research relevant to, 43–44
Proctor & Gamble, 321, 322
Producer, reviewing work of, 68
Products, pretesting, 51–52
Professionalism, standards, in trade publications, 79–80
Professional publications, 77
Professional Speech Writing, 243
Profile survey, 48–49
example of, 55–56
Projects/programs, special, 23
Promotions, joint, 13–14
Proofreading, visuals, 260
Prospectus, preliminary, 121
Proxy solicitation
planning schedule, sample, 140–143
process of, 136
PSAs (Public Service Announcements), 276
Public affairs
lobbying for, 291–297
NAFTA and, 285
policy-making process and, 284–285
state level, government relations and, 301–302
Washington new corps and, 287–288
Publications
analysis of, 228–229

T